Constructing Image, Identity, and Place

Constructing Image, Identity, and Place

Perspectives in Vernacular Architecture

Edited by Alison K. Hoagland and Kenneth A. Breisch

IX

The University of Tennessee Press

Knoxville

Library of Congress Cataloging in Publication Data

(Revised for volume 9)

Constructing Image, Identity, and Place/edited by Alison K. Hoagland
and Kenneth A. Breisch.—1st ed.
   p.   cm.—(Perspectives in vernacular architecture; 9)
Includes bibliographical references and index.
ISBN 1-57233-219-0 (pbk.: alk. paper)
   1. Vernacular architecture—United States.
   2. Architecture and society—United States.
   I. Hoagland, Alison K. II. Breisch, Kenneth A.
  III. Series: Perspectives in vernacular architecture (Knoxville, Tenn.); 9.

CONTENTS

Part III. Place

ILLUSTRATIONS

Figures

Maps

INTRODUCTION

Constructing Image, Identity, and Place is volume IX of *Perspectives in Vernacular Architecture,* a biannual publication of papers drawn from annual conferences of the Vernacular Architecture Forum. Founded in 1980, the heart of this organization has always been its annual meetings. Comprised of two days of field tours and one of papers, these gatherings draw together a disparate group of practitioners and scholars who share an interest in the study of "common" buildings and places. This volume's essays are from meetings held in Annapolis, Maryland, in 1998 and Columbus, Georgia, the following year. Since papers dealing with local topics are encouraged at each meeting, there is some concentration evident in this volume on the mid-Atlantic and the Deep South regions of the country. Other contributions represent the broad range of topics and methodologies current in the field of vernacular studies. Consistent with the series' previous volumes, this work reveals vernacular scholarship to be defined less by what is being examined than by the method through which the built world is being investigated.[1]

In contrast to a focus on the taxonomy of style, students of the vernacular tend to be more interested in how things are made, in the design process, in patterns of use as reflected in plan and spatial relationships, and in the more subtle, often cloaked, meanings that buildings and places convey through form. As witnessed by this volume, intensive fieldwork often lies at the heart of the investigation. Although the field of vernacular studies has expanded beyond its core fascination with "common" buildings and places and how they were put together, its atten-

tion remains fixed on the social function of building. The chapters in this volume address a broad range of topics and time periods, yet common themes emerge across centuries.

The buildings and landscapes we create reflect our struggle to negotiate the world around us, and the way in which we construct them reveals how we desire to present ourselves to this world. This construction of image is nowhere more evident than in the houses of the elite, where, during the eighteenth century, the impact of Renaissance ideals on British colonial architecture demanded the dominance of social form over utilitarian function. Camille Wells, in her essay, "Dower Play/Power Play: Menokin and the Ordeal of Elite House Building in Colonial Virginia," explores how the suppression or enhancement of classical Georgian ornament was employed by Virginia landowners to signify hierarchies of status and dependence. She demonstrates this through a careful analysis of the plantation house at Menokin, which was constructed by John Tayloe II for his son-in-law, Francis Lightfoot Lee, on land neighboring his own home at Mount Airy. Wells contends that the relatively subdued decorative treatment of Menokin can be read as evidence of a strained economic and social relationship that resulted from Lee's marriage into the Tayloe family, a union that his father-in-law only reluctantly accepted.

In his essay "Anglican Church Design in the Chesapeake: English Inheritances and Regional Interpretations," Carl Lounsbury likewise looks at the function of ornament as signifier of status, but even more so at the way in which plans and spatial relationships might be employed as a means of delineating different Chesapeake ecclesiastical traditions. Like the homes of its colonists, these now appear to have comprised many more subregional variations than historians have previously identified. Based upon a close examination of more than two dozen surviving churches, and all of the existing, late seventeenth- and eighteenth-century vestry books in Maryland, Lounsbury's study reveals a varied and vigorous religious architecture that by the middle of the eighteenth century had begun to distance itself from the more restrained conventions of the late colonial Virginia tradition examined by Dell Upton in his book *Holy Things and Profane: Anglican Parish Churches in Virginia*.[2]

The centrality of the church in American spiritual, as well as civic, life is the topic of Maurie McInnis's study of the rebuilding of St. Philip's in Charleston, South Carolina, after it had been destroyed by fire in 1835. As in the colonial homes of Virginia and churches of Maryland, architecture was viewed by the congregation as a physical embodiment of established social order. Their carefully considered and documented debate over the form that the reconstruction of this Episcopal monument should take reflected a strong desire to reaffirm their longstanding hegemony in Charleston society. As an early instance of the recreation of past architectural form for its historical associations, this episode offers unexpected insight into the origins of the preservation movement in the United States. That it took place in Charleston is all the more provocative and revealing.

Following independence from Britain, Americans also began to turn their attention more strongly to the symbolic nature of public architecture. In "A Public House for a New Republic: The Architecture of Accommodation and the American State, 1789–1809," Andrew K. Sandoval-Strausz demonstrates how the demand to accommodate increasing numbers of travelers coincided with civic boosterism, an impulse toward gentility, and postrevolutionary nationalism to encourage the creation of the first American hotels. Combining the amenities of the inn and tavern within the more urbane and monumental envelope of European civic design, Americans established this institution as a new arena for public discourse that

would significantly impact the subsequent development of the republican city.

By the early twentieth century, responsibility for the construction of image was often handed over to the professional, especially in the competitive world of commerce. "The Production of Goodwill: The Origins and Development of the Factory Tour in America," by William Littmann, looks at the creation of commercial imagery through the development of the factory tour. Employing maps and written descriptions of factory tours, he focuses on the increasingly sophisticated methods by which American corporations exhibited their workplace in order to develop brand loyalty, while attempting as well to assuage growing concern over the rise of mechanization and its impact on the structure of society. In reaction to increasingly scathing critiques of American industry by the Progressive reform movement, Littmann argues that manufacturers increasingly sanitized their tours through the exclusion of many of the more unpleasant realities of the workplace.

Questions of image in architecture may also be examined in the way in which public and private spaces are consciously utilized. Jessica Sewell's examination of the political appropriation of the sidewalk and storefront by suffragists in San Francisco in 1911 redefines the image of a department store as one which is no longer a strictly private enterprise. In her chapter, "Sidewalks and Store Windows as Political Landscapes," Sewell argues that the dual nature of these intermediary spaces, associated with the feminized realm of consumption but also with the masculine world of work and trade, made it an ideal landscape for confrontation and interchange between genders.

While the distinction between image and identity can blur, the latter often takes the forefront in the struggle of minority or oppressed groups to exert their position in society, whether they construct this identity themselves or appropriate the place in which they find themselves, manipulating its forms and meanings to their own ends. Steven H. Moffson's essay, "Identity and Assimilation in Synagogue Architecture in Georgia, 1870–1920," investigates the dichotomy that developed among southern Jews between the maintenance of a Jewish identity and cultural assimilation as embodied in the form and style of their religious monuments. Based upon an examination of some thirty-five synagogues in Georgia, Moffson has concluded that the adoption of neoclassical modes of design in Georgian synagogues after the turn of the last century can be associated with the rise of Reform Judaism, as well as the desire on the part of older, primarily German, congregations to disassociate themselves from more recently arrived Russian Jews.

The reinforcement of identity through the overt display of social and economic hierarchy in architecture is equally evident in the construction of accommodations for the less powerful. When it came to the creation of tenant and mill housing, for example, the nature of American production demanded a hierarchical and clearly ordered landscape designed to put and keep one in one's proper place. Employing extensive archival research and fieldwork, oral histories, and a close reading of the landscapes themselves, both Mark Reinberger and Robert W. Blythe have adapted methods pioneered in the field of social history to their studies of the built worlds of agricultural laborers and mill families. Reinberger, in "The Architecture of Sharecropping: Extended Farms of the Georgia Piedmont," examines the world of southern tenant farmers, delineating in graphic detail the reality of rural poverty in the antebellum South. Yet he reminds us of the dignity with which many of these farmers carried out their lives and the pride they took in their homeplaces. Blythe, likewise, looks at everyday life in five factory towns operated by the West Point Manufacturing Company in Chambers County, Alabama. Focusing on the families of mill workers—as opposed to the owners and town planners—he analyzes the manner in which these people occupied and, at times, exerted their own individuality in environments otherwise controlled by the mill companies and their managers.

The necessity people often feel to create distinct private domains in the landscape also forms the theme of Martin C. Perdue's essay, "Hiding Behind Trees and Building Shelter without Walls: Stick and Foliate Structures in the Civil War Landscape." In the arbors and monuments erected by American soldiers in military campgrounds, Perdue has rediscovered the sentimental impulses of the soldier at war yearning for the visual and physical reassurance of home and church, for a secure place in the midst of conflict. Delineating private space, decorating bleak surroundings, or building honorific monuments that were neither monumental nor permanent, these activities served an important function in the life of the camp. Relying heavily upon photographic evidence, which had only recently become available as a means of documentation, Perdue has been able to reconstruct a tradition of building that, because of its ephemeral nature, has heretofore been overlooked by historians of the built landscape. In this essay, Perdue continues an examination of impermanent constructions of the Civil War begun by Dean Nelson in the first *Perspectives in Vernacular Architecture.*[3]

In "Roomful of Blues: Jukejoints and the Cultural Landscape of the Mississippi Delta," Jennifer Nardone likewise sheds new light on a similarly complex response to a hierarchical world, one now shaped by intense racial segregation. Through oral histories and personal observations, Nardone closely examines the coded messages conveyed by the anonymous facades of these semiprivate establishments and contrasts this with the familiar nature of their interiors, helping to further expand our understanding of social relationships in the South. The identities of the jukejoints are deliberately obscured to ensure that only known customers will frequent these places, providing a familiar setting in a segregated society.

While indications of image and identity are found in prominent or public parts of buildings, such as exteriors, ornament, plans, or arrangement on the landscape, a building's relationship to its place can also be found in deliberately hidden parts of a building, such as its structure. Two papers in this volume concern wooden structures that were concealed in order to give the buildings a different exterior appearance. The buildings' structures, once revealed, relate the buildings undeniably to their place, despite external efforts to link them to British society. In his essay on preindustrial framing in the Chesapeake region, Willie Graham reveals how the use of earthfast, or "impermanent," construction during the early years of British settlement forced significant changes in structural systems on this side of the At-lantic, leading to a reduction in the size of the framing members. During the eighteenth century, moreover, a growing desire to display personal wealth and status led to the concealment of primary structural elements be-hind Georgian finishes and detail. Expanding upon the groundbreaking study of impermanent building published by Cary Carson and his colleagues in 1981, Graham's work forms an appropriate complement to the archaeological investigations of Moser, Luckenbach, Marsh, and Ware in Anne Arundel County, Maryland.[4] Like them, he uncovers systems of construction far more diverse and dynamic than previous studies have led us to believe. The discovery by Moser et al. of deco-rative fireplace tiles and sophisticated finishes at four sites in the now-vanished town of Providence likewise belies the notion that earthfast houses were intended merely as temporary shelter. Their extensive archaeo-logical fieldwork, supplemented with archival research, also points to the early emergence of distinct sub-regional traditions of building adapted to the new cir-cumstances encountered by early settlers in the Chesa-peake region.

While the automobile is one of the technologies that has been credited with homogenizing place and di-minishing regionalism in America, the essays included here discuss automobile landscapes whose forms are influenced by their respective places. Shannon Bell's essay, "From Ticket Booth to Screen Tower: An Archi-tectural Study of Drive-in Theaters in the Baltimore–Washington, D.C.–Richmond Corridor," examines theaters in the mid-Atlantic region. By analyzing di-mensions of class and race as displayed in the landscape of the outdoor theater, Bell relates these new institu-tions to their particular place in the region, finding, for example, segregated facilities in Baltimore and white-only establishments farther south.

The ascension of the automobile in American so-ciety is a topic that both Timothy Davis and Kathleen LaFrank also treat in their studies of the intrusion of early parkways into this country's rural landscapes. Intended to provide a pleasant, "country-road" ex-perience to travelers, parkways were carefully de-signed, often sanitized landscapes. Drawing on years of research, Davis takes a broad look at parkway de-velopment in the United States from the late nine-teenth century to the present day. In "'A Pleasant Illusion of Unspoiled Countryside': The American Parkway and the Problematics of an Institutionalized Vernacular," he examines the tensions that developed between the official and the vernacular in parkway de-sign, discovering a complex relationship rather than a simple "top-down" narrative. In "Real and Ideal Land-scapes along the Taconic State Parkway," LaFrank fo-cuses her attention on a single parkway, examining the traveler's perception of the landscape in contrast to that of the local populace. LaFrank evokes the experi-ential quality of a transportation system rather than the static appearance of a road on a map and portrays the landscape architect's efforts to control interaction between tourist and resident.

Yet another outgrowth of the popularity of the au-tomobile was the rise of the regional shopping mall, the subject of Stephanie Dyer's chapter, "Designing 'Community' in the Cherry Hill Mall: The Social Pro-duction of a Consumer Space." Dyer traces the histo-ry of a specific New Jersey mall developed by James Rouse and designed by Victor Gruen in an effort to provide a public focus for a sprawling and suburban-izing region of the East Coast. Comparing patrons' opinions to the stated goals and theories of manage-ment, she concludes that while this mall may have been initially successful, it was rapidly superceded by others and the "community" it was intended to create turned out to be ephemeral.

This collection of essays, then, represents not only a vibrant and diverse inquiry into the field of vernac-ular studies but also the unselfish contributions of many members of the Vernacular Architecture Forum who selected the papers that formed the basis for this collection, organized the annual meetings at which they were presented, and vetted the final selection. We would like to thank all of these individuals for their generous help. As VAF enters its third decade, it is clear that it continues to serve as a vital and collegial forum for the study of the built world. It has been our pleasure to participate in this inquiry into what our buildings and landscapes reveal about us and our past.

Notes

1. Previous editors of *Perspectives in Vernacular Architecture* have wrestled with the definition of our field. See Thomas Carter and Bernard L. Herman, "Introduction: Toward a New Architectural History," *Perspectives in Vernacular Architecture,* IV (Columbia: University of Missouri Press, 1991), 106, and Camille Wells, "Old Claims and New Demands: Vernacular Architecture Studies Today," *Perspectives in Vernacular Architecture,* II (Columbia: University of Missouri Press, 1986), 1–10.

2. Cambridge: MIT Press for the Architectural History Foundation, 1986.

3. Dean E. Nelson, "'Right Nice Little House[s]': Impermanent Camp Architecture of the American Civil War," *Perspectives in Vernacular Architecture,* I (Annapolis, Md.: privately printed, 1982), 79–93.

4. Cary Carson, Norman F. Barka, William M. Kelso, Garry Wheeler Stone, and Dell Upton, "Impermanent Architecture in the Southern American Colonies," *Winterthur Portfolio* 16, nos. 2/3 (Summer/Autumn 1981): 135–196.

PART I

IMAGE

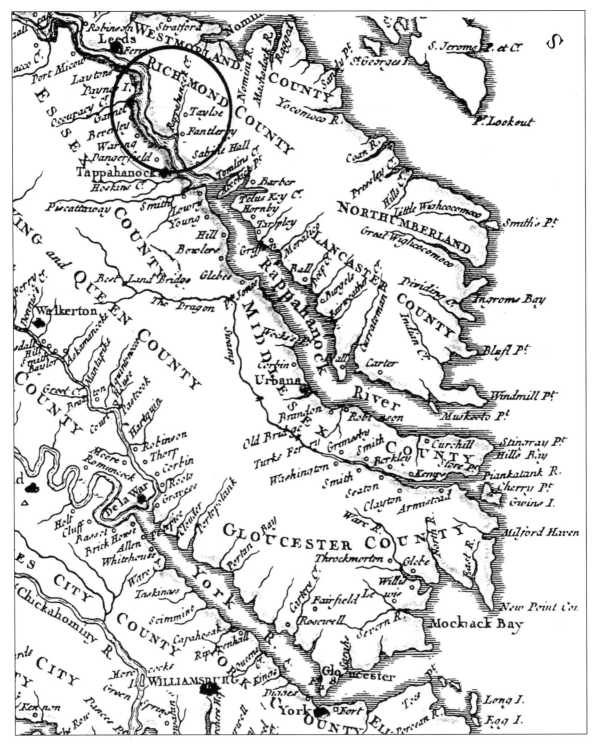

Map 1.1. Detail of the 1751 Fry-Jefferson map of Virginia highlighting Rappahannock Creek. Courtesy of the Library of Congress.

1

DOWER PLAY/POWER PLAY

MENOKIN AND THE ORDEAL OF ELITE HOUSE
BUILDING IN COLONIAL VIRGINIA

CAMILLE WELLS

In many places today, thick swaths of woodland obscure the contours of its terrain, just as dense layers of
silt blur the shorelines of its watercourses, but remnants of the colonial past linger still in the landscape
of Tidewater Virginia. Back then, Richmond County's
shallow, marshy, meandering Cat Point Creek was
known by a different name. Deep, wide, and comfort-
ably navigable for several miles inland from the Rappahannock River, "Rappahannock Creek" was also
shapely with protected coves where the flowing water
became calm and gentle beaches welcomed the construction of docks or landings (map 1.1). Such a
remarkable avenue of travel and trade made the surrounding land susceptible to early patents and partitions. At first the tracts around Rappahannock Creek
were settled mostly as quarters or leaseholds. Overseers, tenants, indentured servants, and slaves shoul-
dered aside the resident Algonquian Indians to raise
tobacco, corn, beef, and pork for the profit of landowners who lived farther downriver or on one of the
lower Tidewater peninsulas.[1] In time, however, the
sons and grandsons of the original landowners began
to seat the shores of Rappahannock Creek. By the
third quarter of the eighteenth century, the broad
flood plain on either side of the creek, as well as the
brow of an escarpment that rears above it, were studded with the genteel seats of elite families whose
names everyone knew: Fauntleroy, Belfield, Carter,
Brockenbrough, Beale, Tayloe, and Lee (map 1.2).

Like most of Virginia's colonial gentry, the wealthy
families whose lands surrounded Rappahannock
Creek were concerned with their "vistas" and "prospects," were concerned with their capacity to see and
be seen.[2] So they kept the land between the water and
their dwelling sites cleared not only to facilitate agriculture and other productive activities but also to

open lines of sight to their houses—to make their presence known.[3] For the same reasons, these elite planters thought carefully about the sorts of impressions their houses and related service buildings conveyed to passersby. Some, like the Beale family, communicated their early arrival and sustained regional prominence through a clearly venerable though architecturally modest house located on an elevated site.[4] Others, like Moore Fauntleroy, chose a shoreline location where the varied and useful-looking outbuildings clustered around his house could indicate the diversity and success of his affairs, and where the entire assemblage, noted on contemporary maps as "Fauntleroys," became a landmark for every sailor who wanted to gauge his progress along the Rappahannock River.[5] Still other planters, like Landon

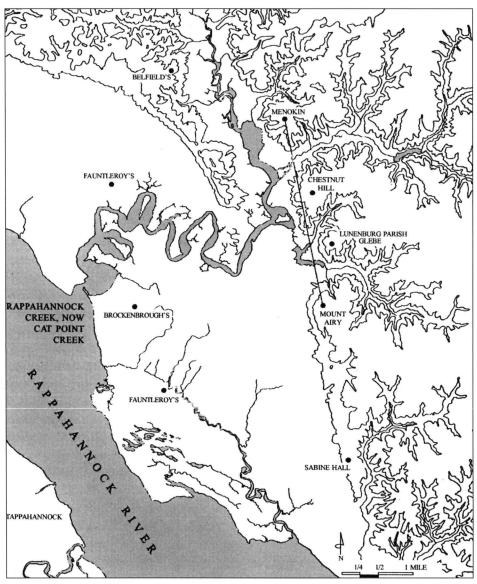

Map 1.2. Virginia's Rappahannock Creek neighborhood in about 1770 delineating fifty-foot and one-hundred-foot contour intervals and noting house sites of the most prominent eighteenth-century planters. Drawing by the author, with Whitney Morrill.

Carter and John Tayloe II, decided to cut more dramatic figures in the landscape through the building of houses which showcased their exceptional sophistication and taste. Carter sharpened the points he wished to make about his two-story brick mansion, with its bright checkered brick walls and its carved stone dressings, when he gave it the classically inspired name Sabine Hall.[6] With similar flourish, Tayloe built his house on the highest eminence overlooking Rappahannock Creek. He also enhanced the visual power of his Mount Airy by closely basing its design on an image in an English pattern book and by choosing to build and embellish his house entirely of brown and white stone (fig. 1.1).

Fig. 1.1. North elevation of Mount Airy, Richmond County, Virginia.

By 1775, a new house with its complement of outbuildings had been raised near the edge of the bluff overlooking Rappahannock Creek. Built for Francis Lightfoot Lee, this gentleman's seat was called Menokin from an Algonquian place name with currency in the locality since time out of mind. Though located nearly two and a half miles from Tayloe's house and separated from it by the dwelling sites of several other prominent planters, Menokin was situated on an eminence only a few feet below Mount Airy's, so each house almost certainly served as a distant focal point in the sweep of the other's prospect.[7] This mattered, for the most arresting characteristic of the house at Menokin was the way it set up a call-and-response relationship with Mount Airy through remarkable

similarities as well as equally intriguing differences in materials, scale, and composition (fig. 1.2). Both similarities and differences manifestly were calculated to convey a nuanced relationship between the two houses that extended beyond matters architectural. Even if colonial observers did not know enough about the individuals and relationships involved to grasp the substance behind the signs, few could have overlooked the architectural cues Menokin thrust into the landscape. Few modern scholars of early Virginia can resist the invitation to unravel Menokin's tale. Indeed, the story of how Menokin was designed and built offers an opportunity to observe the elite Virginia housemaking enterprise as a series of strategic maneuvers behind which lurk quite compelling human experiences: promises half kept, legacies provisionally bestowed, patriarchal authority aggressively enforced, and filial resistance materially encoded. Above all, the planning, design, and construction of Menokin stand at the center of a sustained and obliquely articulated debate in colonial Virginia concerning the prerogatives inherent in individual ownership and the obligations associated with intergenerational fortunes.

In the beginning "Menokin" was the name of a thousand-acre tract, first delineated and designated in 1658. John Tayloe II (1721–1779) added Menokin to his substantial Richmond County landholdings through purchase nearly a century later.[8] The profits

Fig. 1.2. North and west elevations of Menokin, Richmond County, Virginia, in about 1930. Courtesy of the Library of Virginia.

from Menokin and Tayloe's other outlying plantations constituted a significant portion of his wealth, but he also prospered from shipbuilding, grist-milling, and iron-foundrying enterprises as well as from shrewd involvement with the transatlantic trade in staples and luxuries.[9] All of his property and its carefully managed capacity to generate income made Tayloe one of the very richest Virginians of his day. This, along with the social connections which his family had been cultivating over the course of four generations in Virginia, won for John Tayloe II appointment to key political offices, the most prestigious of which was a seat on Virginia's Council of State. He also made, in 1747, an exceedingly advantageous marriage to Rebecca Plater, daughter of George Plater II, Maryland's secretary of state and deputy governor.[10]

John Tayloe II worked hard to increase his wealth, but he also worked hard to enjoy it. By 1765 he had completed on the highest plateau of his Richmond County land a "daring scheme of a mansion" surrounded with every structure and planting agreeable to genteel living and lavish entertaining.[11] Tayloe also indulged himself in the construction at Mount Airy of a mile-long race track. He imported a blooded stallion and several mares, bred a stable full of fleet colts and fillies, and joined with alacrity in the games of public showmanship and chance which preoccupied many of the Virginia elite by the middle of the eighteenth century.[12] Fecundity enlivened matters within the Mount Airy mansion as well as among the stables, pastures, gardens, and crop lands surrounding it. Starting in 1750, Rebecca Plater Tayloe bore healthy infants at intervals that suggest her happy capacity to bring live births to term.

In 1765, at the mature but still vigorous age of forty-four, John Tayloe II had everything a Virginia gentleman could want; everything except a son. Frolicking about him and his wife in their fine new mansion house were seven daughters at various stages of growth and development.[13] Tayloe loved his girls, gave them pet names, and sent affectionate messages to them when he was away from Mount Airy.[14] Still, no Virginia gentleman could take lightly the lack of a male heir to whom he could proudly pass on the bulk of his estate—a lifetime of successful work indelibly imprinted with the family's noted and enviable name. Tayloe's concern was poorly concealed by the light tone he adopted in writing his friend William Byrd III: "I have neither prospect nor hopes of a son therefore will indeavor to make [of my daughters] good wives for your boys."[15]

Whether he thought so or not, there was still reason for optimism in his wife's continuing pregnancies. Nevertheless, in 1767, the many-daughtered John Tayloe II found himself forced to think about the disposition of his wealth, the survival of his family name, and the impact on his prestigious position of legacies to the next generation. The issue emerged when Tayloe's oldest girl Elizabeth received an offer of marriage from Edward Lloyd IV of Talbot County, Maryland. Young Lloyd was heartwarmingly rich and well connected with a bright political future, so Tayloe agreed to the marriage and promised to enhance the union with a handsome dowry of two thousand pounds sterling.[16]

In bestowing cash on the Lloyds, Tayloe was embracing a time-honored strategy among the Virginia elite: generous dower gifts of money to daughters confirmed the well-lined pockets of the bride's father, solidified ties between families, and helped ensure the prosperity of next generation; settlements of land and slaves on sons preserved the association of a particular family name with the indispensable building blocks of colonial Virginia wealth and status.[17] Landed estates also helped sons attract brides from respected families with the capacity to bestow hefty cash dowries, the sustaining value of which often was acknowledged by calling a first or second son by his mother's original surname.[18]

In the end, these strategies for preserving colonial Virginia fortunes worked for John Tayloe II of Mount Airy, for in 1771 Rebecca Plater Tayloe at last presented her husband with a baby boy.[19] Two year later, though he was still "in good health & perfect memory," John Tayloe drew up a will in which he promised each of his daughters a settlement of two thousand pounds, while his little son—predictably christened John Tayloe III—received most of Tayloe's slaves and personal property along with all of his land and business interests.[20]

The exception to this tidy arrangement was Rebecca (1752–1797), second of the numerous Tayloe daughters. In his will of 1773 John Tayloe II stated that "the Menokin Estate [was] to be reckoned in full for her fortune of two thousand pounds."[21] Young Rebecca Tayloe was singled out in this way because she had decided to marry in 1769, during that uneasy period after John Tayloe II had begun to face the challenges of estate distribution and before the birth of his legacy-solving son. Furthermore, while Rebecca had chosen in Francis Lightfoot Lee (1734–1797) a husband from an eminent Virginia family, one with whom the Tayloes acknowledged distant ties of kinship and close ties of rank, their match posed several problems—or perhaps they were opportunities.

The prospective bridegroom was the son of Thomas Lee, the rich and powerful master of Stratford, an elegant seat located in contiguous Westmoreland County. In terms of birth order, however, Frank Lee stood at a relative disadvantage: he was one of eight children and the fourth of six sons.[22] When

Thomas Lee died in 1750, he left his dwelling plantation and the lion's share of his Tidewater landholdings to his eldest son. This allocation had to do with neither differentiated fatherly affections nor the English system of primogeniture. Thomas Lee simply was securing the continued viability of his ancestral Tidewater stronghold. Believing that Virginia's eastern elite were poised to establish primacy farther inland as well, he bestowed on his younger sons thousands of acres located in the Piedmont region and on toward the base of the Blue Ridge Mountains. Although Lee had begun patenting this land decades before, it was poorly developed and inaccessible, with a value calculable largely in its potential.[23]

Frank Lee's share of his father's estate included over thirty-eight hundred acres in Fairfax and Loudoun Counties and a labor force of thirty slaves. His brothers received bequests of similar quality. By the standards of wealth known to most colonial Virginians, these were fabulous legacies, but Thomas Lee's five younger sons were accustomed to life at the pinnacle of social and

Map 1.3. Colonial Virginia. Drawing by Whitney Morrill.

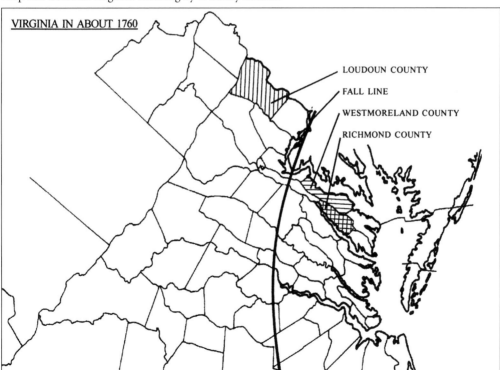

economic privilege, and they were not impressed. One referred to his inheritance as a "small pittance," while another characterized himself mournfully as "not having been born to a fortune."[24] Two of Frank Lee's brothers found ways to continue living in Tidewater Virginia, and two others decided to try their luck in England.[25] Notable by contrast—and apparently to the sustained amusement of all his brothers and sisters—Frank Lee struck out in 1756 at the age of twenty-two to live and work on his backcountry land (map 1.3).[26]

The young man prospered. He arrived to discover that he was the tenth largest landholder in Loudoun County and the only one of this number who had any intention of residing on his land.[27] This position won him, despite his youth and status as a newcomer, nearly instant primacy in local political affairs. In 1758 he served as a trustee for the founding of Loudoun County's courthouse town—named, not incidentally, Leesburg. That same year he was elected to represent Loudoun County in the Virginia House of Burgesses. In due course he was commissioned at the rank of colonel of the county militia and appointed to serve as senior magistrate in the county court.[28] Lee also proved his merit as a planter. He did not augment his inherited land with any new purchases, but he obviously was clearing enough on the sale of crops, timber, and livestock to do so. He chose instead to invest in labor. Between 1756 and 1768 he more than doubled his slave population from the original thirty to at least sixty-three.[29] Drawn though he still may have felt to the Tidewater region and the haunts of his boyhood, Frank Lee had probably settled on a life in Piedmont Virginia by 1765, when, at the age of thirty-one, he purchased an undeveloped lot in Alexandria.[30] This suggests his intention to establish a presence in the burgeoning port town which owed much of its vitality to the reception of harvests from Loudoun County and its backcountry neighbors.[31] Lee's circumstances, however, were about to change.

A seat in the House of Burgesses required of Frank Lee several protracted stays in Williamsburg each year, and it may have been during the flurry of social activity which attended "public times" in the colonial capital that he became acquainted with the second daughter of the eminent councillor John Tayloe II.

Certainly their betrothal, when it became known in Williamsburg, was considered a notable community event. William Nelson, then president of the council, wrote to William Lee in London, "No doubt you have heard of the happiness of your brother Frank and Miss Becky."[32]

Lee's engagement to the seventeen-year-old Rebecca was resolved by the early weeks of 1769, when their connection became the subject of comment among the Virginia gentry. Matters could not have proceeded so far, of course, without formal conversations between the hopeful suitor and the man he was asking to become his father-in-law. These negotiations presented John Tayloe II of Mount Airy with a notable dilemma: here was an offer of marriage from a mature and accomplished member of the Virginia gentry who was acceptable in every respect—except that his estate in life paled beside those of Tayloe himself, Thomas Lee, and Edward Lloyd.[33] Furthermore, his plantation seat lay beyond the limits of Tidewater navigation and beyond the advance of genteel society. It was all very well for Tayloe to send his daughter Elizabeth off to married life on the extensive and well-appointed Lloyd estates in Tidewater Maryland, but a newly wedded Rebecca would confront in Loudoun County something close to a social and material desert. Even if Frank Lee could promise to make commodious accommodations for his intended bride, all of her neighbors would be tenants, overseers, and small planters living in small, roughly made houses with few of the accouterments basic to domestic comfort.[34] Tayloe knew this well, for he himself owned nearly nine thousand acres of Loudoun County land.[35]

Other considerations also may have affected Tayloe's deliberations. Contemporaries often remarked on Frank Lee's gentle disposition, thoughtful behavior, and probative statements.[36] Perhaps this younger man might prove a tractable son-in-waiting and, if Madam Tayloe's pregnancies continued to result in girls, ultimately a responsible new master for Mount Airy. In any case, the documentary record is clear. John Tayloe intended to keep Frank Lee close at hand, and the two men struck a singular bargain. Lee could marry his young Becky if he agreed to turn his Loudoun County plantations over to tenants and abandon his social and political primacy there.[37] In return, Tayloe would use his wealth and influence to compensate his son-in-law with similar assets in Richmond County.

During elections for the House of Burgesses in November 1768, Frank Lee did not stand for re-election in Loudoun County. The following spring, Landon Carter of Sabine Hall observed that through "Colo[nel] Tayloe's asserted interest . . . his son in law, F. Lee was elected" to represent Richmond County in the House of Burgesses. Lee's status as a colonial legislator barely suffered a pause. Appointments to Richmond County's militia and magistracy followed within a year.[38]

Tayloe also made good on his promise to supply his daughter and son-in-law with resources suitable for elite Tidewater status. At about the time of their marriage in May 1769, he composed a deed of gift for Menokin's thousand acres and its population of twenty slaves. Beginning in the following year, Tayloe's plantation daybook began noting payments and provisions for workmen "at Menokin." Later, in his will of 1773, Tayloe not only mentioned Rebecca Tayloe Lee's legacy in terms of "the deed I have made" for Menokin but also specified: "the buildings to be finished at the expence of my estate." Thus he confirmed that the genteel house and attendant buildings under construction at Menokin were significant components of Rebecca Tayloe's dowry.[39]

All of this seems agreeable and straightforward. Lurking beneath the surface, however, were indications of conflict. Dissatisfaction and distrust probably remained unexpressed, except in indirect or encoded exchanges, but eventually they attained eloquent representation in the design and construction of the house at Menokin.

The first clue that all was not harmony and contentment is in the construction of Tayloe's deed of gift for Menokin. The document emphasizes that the terms of the deed were to be effective from May 24, 1769—the eve of Frank Lee and Rebecca Tayloe's wedding day—and that the conveyance was to Rebecca and her heirs alone. The document also contains several passages restricting Frank Lee's interest in the property to a life estate.[40] At first, this appears to be a fatherly maneuver to protect his daughter's legacy

from any financial misfortune or miscalculation that might befall Frank Lee, but both Tayloe and Lee were sufficiently well versed in colonial Virginia law to know that from the moment of her marriage, Rebecca Tayloe Lee's property became her husband's to own and to treat however he liked.[41] So Tayloe took a second precaution. He enacted the agreement—that is, he gave the newlyweds possession of their plantation and involvement with its new buildings—but he kept the documentary proof of its conveyance among his own papers.

Not until October 1778, six months before his death, did Tayloe have his deed of gift entered into the records of the county court. Even then, Tayloe permitted the presentation of the deed only on condition that the Lees relinquish their right ever to sell Menokin by instantly conveying their property in trust to a third party.[42] Tayloe correctly surmised that after nine years of marriage, Frank and Rebecca Lee were not going to have any children to whom Menokin might descend. Apparently, then, he was gambling that the terms of his deed of gift would hold—during the revolutionary era, after all, Virginia property laws were changing—and Menokin would pass at Rebecca Lee's death to her Tayloe siblings, nieces, and nephews.

A bland assessment of the documents concerning Menokin and its disposition would emphasize John Tayloe's deft use of prevailing techniques for shrewd estate preservation and descent. Also discernible, however, are the high-handed, competitive, and prideful impulses which dominated the darker side of colonial Virginia's patriarchal elite.[43] John Tayloe II, acknowledged master of Mount Airy and much else besides, could not, where young Frank Lee was concerned, resist his moments of manipulation. That this is a significant, even a primary, part of Menokin's origins and its meaning as a gentry mansion is best articulated not in the documentary but in the architectural record.

When Tayloe devoted the extraordinary quantities of time, money, and craftsmanship necessary to build his own Mount Airy, one of the messages he conveyed was that he, like most members of the Virginia elite, believed in the efficacy of appearances. Exceptional and possibly unique in its faithfulness to an English pattern book source, Mount Airy stood for John Tayloe's

English education, his coastwise and transatlantic business concerns, his understanding of Anglo-American trends in fashion and learning.[44] Figuring in a Tidewater countryside dominated by jury-built wooden houses, most of which were small or, if they achieved any spaciousness at all, did so through many episodes of accretion, Mount Airy's symmetrical composition of masonry elements announced that it was built all in one carefully planned and seamlessly executed campaign.[45] In this respect, it stood for Tayloe's access to skilled workmen and expensive materials as well as his sustained control over a labor force and his capacity to glide financially above seasonal fluctuations in potential profits. Because Mount Airy was built to say so much about its owner, John Tayloe had solicited for his house the finest of builders, but he himself had remained involved in the making and finishing of the grand new dwelling.[46] For the same reasons, Tayloe's involvement with the making of Menokin extended beyond paying for its construction to encompass attention to its appearance as well.

Fig. 1.3. Presentation drawing marked "Monokin House & Offices" found among eighteenth-century Tayloe Family Papers. Courtesy of the Virginia Historical Society.

The substance of Menokin, the iron-infused Choptank sandstone from which Mount Airy itself largely was built, came from a vein of this native stone on Tayloe's Richmond County land. Furthermore, the design of the house appears to have been Tayloe's own selection: the unique presentation drawing labeled "Monokin House & Offices" survives among Tayloe's personal papers (fig. 1.3). The architectural messages that Tayloe's design decisions conveyed were several. First, there was the insisted-upon association of Menokin with Mount Airy through the use of identical stonework in a region where most important buildings, including Thomas Lee's Stratford, were made of brick. Then there was the juxtaposition at both houses of brown-and-white color schemes. At Mount Airy, creamy pale Aquia freestone quoins and architraves set off the richness of the dark sandstone walls that, in turn, frame the Aquia stone entrance pavilions centered on both the land and river facades.[47] For Menokin, Tayloe approved a design involving a house and corresponding pair of offices that were white with dark accents. From a distance, the chocolate-brown architraves and quoins accenting Menokin's creamy light walls would appear precisely and wittily to reverse Mount Airy's palette. Upon closer acquaintance, however, the economy of the scheme would become obvious: Menokin's pale presentation was to be achieved not with Aquia stone, which had been laboriously quarried in and transported downriver from Stafford County, but from coats of comparatively inexpensive stucco and whitewash neatly applied to walls built from the locally available, and thus thrifty, brown sandstone.

The subtle expression of Menokin's architectural fealty to Mount Airy was to extend still further—beyond the matters of color schemes and facade arrangements to include matters of dimension and scale. Menokin is too distant and too imposingly sited for any visitor to have mistaken it for an actual outbuilding in the Mount Airy complex. Yet the nearly identical ground dimensions of Mount Airy's formal offices and Menokin's principal dwelling speak forcefully in an architectural language almost any colonial Virginian could grasp of patriarchal primacy and filial deference (figs. 1.4 and 1.5).

Eighteenth-century lines of sight only served to reinforce the point. Mount Airy is less than ten feet higher in elevation than Menokin, but in changing light, the dark brown edifice with its soft ivory accents would have continuously emerged from and vanished into the surrounding vegetation. In Menokin's vista, then, John Tayloe's house was a distant presence, but

Fig. 1.4. Mount Airy's northwest dependency.

Fig. 1.5. Comparative plans of Mount Airy and Menokin. Adapted by Whitney Morrill from drawings by Thomas Tileston Waterman.

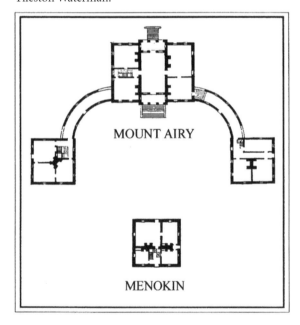

one not fully attained or delineated. From Mount Airy, by contrast, Menokin's white elevations would have stood out, crisp in form and clear in view amid the greens and browns of its plantation setting. Perhaps even at such a remove, it would have appeared in the gaze of viewers at Mount Airy as a kind of architectural outpost of the larger mansion's domain.[48]

In these ways, the designs for Mount Airy and Menokin articulated familial bonds and intergenerational obligations as firmly and obviously as stone and

mortar ever could. Menokin gave John Tayloe II the satisfaction of knowing that the agreeable situation in which he had placed the Lees was manifest and comprehensible to his friends and competitors, for whom Menokin must have looked like the ultimate in conspicuous dowering. While Elizabeth Tayloe's marriage to Edward Lloyd IV told Tayloe's many genteel associates that he was quite wealthy enough to attract the most privileged of mates for his many daughters, Menokin was meant to say—loud and clear—that Tayloe was in no way obliged to fret over the matter. Indeed, he was so financially secure that he could receive a worthy young man of substantial but lesser means and, literally, make his Tidewater fortune. Furthermore, Tayloe could reap all the benefits of his apparently unconditional generosity to Rebecca and Frank Lee, but by withholding the deed of gift from the official record, he indefinitely kept these members of the next generation in a form of social and economic thrall.

This was the same ostensibly favored but emotionally demeaning dependence in which Landon Carter kept his oldest son. As the presumed heir to nearby Sabine Hall, Robert Wormeley Carter, who was exactly Frank Lee's age, watched as his two younger brothers received outlying tracts of their father's land on which they became masters of their own households and heads of their own families.[49] By contrast, Robert was "compelled to live," despite his marriage and five children, in a kind of perpetual adolescence under his father's elegant roof in Richmond County.[50] He rebelled, of course. Landon Carter's diary is filled with outraged denouncements of his son's bad judgment, irresponsible behavior, and defiant attitude.[51]

The arrangement that John Tayloe II and Frank Lee made was far more respectful and significantly less restrictive. Moreover, Lee was too circumspect and deft a participant in his own culture ever to speak, or at least to write, about such things. Clearly, however, he chafed under Tayloe's presumptions and found relatively harmless though architecturally resonant ways to subvert the full realization of his father-in-law's half-gracious offerings with their entangling strings attached. He did this in his role as general supervisor of Menokin's construction.

On April 11, 1770, Landon Carter made a visit to Mount Airy, where Frank Lee was then staying with his bride. In the course of their conversation, Lee told Carter that he had "intirely laid aside all thoughts of a crop of tobacco" at Menokin that year, for he was "building and intend[ing] to make use of his hands to assist his building."[52] Lee and his workmen—hired, indentured, and enslaved—were about the work of transforming Menokin from the quarter plantation it had been into the gentleman's dwelling plantation Tayloe had promised.

Construction at Menokin involved much more than the erecting of the great house, more than the construction of the flanking office which the eighteenth-century drawing of Menokin proposed. Making a quarter plantation over into a gentleman's "seat" required a dairy, smokehouse, and stable as well as one or more domestic slave dwellings that were in some measure superior in quality to those the field hands had been occupying. There also might be the addition of such conveniences as a plantation store, coach house, lumber house, or spinning house. Lee probably also rebuilt or improved Menokin's agricultural buildings. Better or more numerous tobacco houses and corn houses may have been part of his scheme; relocated or expanded quarters for the field slaves probably also found a place in his agenda. Lee's expertise with grain production in Loudoun County motivated him to erect a capacious barn. There was, moreover, the ditching and fencing of more numerous and orderly fields, the enclosing of gardens and the planting of orchards.[53] Frank Lee's decade of experience transforming his unimproved Loudoun County land into profitable plantations had taught him the wisdom of preparing his land and agricultural buildings for production before turning his attention and resources to an expensive dwelling. Yet there is at least a hint, in Lee's decision to postpone the construction of a genteel house which so clearly manifested his father-in-law's preference, of defiance—of insisting on the significance of his own priorities.

Sixteen months after Landon Carter confirmed that Lee and his laborers were busy with their formidable tasks, Frank Lee wrote to his brother William, "In three or four weeks I shall be under my own vine & shall remember to drink health & every blessing to my dear connections [William Lee and his wife] in London."[54] Indications are that Frank and Rebecca Lee did move to Menokin that summer, but their abode was a modest secondary dwelling, for the main house at Menokin was may not yet have been undertaken. It certainly was not complete, for the trees from which the roof was framed were not cut until 1772.[55] Indeed, there remained substantial work to be done at the site in May 1773, when John Tayloe's will provided for the funds to finish Menokin's buildings, and Tayloe's daybook notations concerning workmen and provisions for Menokin continued for at least two years more.

Confronting a design he did not necessarily approve, accepting building materials he did not necessarily prefer, supervising craftsmen he did not necessarily choose, Lee proved a desultory construction manager of the Menokin house. Once it was complete, moreover, it displayed many signs of inconstancy in design intention and workmanship. Idiosyncratic juxtapositions of elaborate and plain, polished and rough elements indicate that the initial shaping of stones as they came from the quarry drew on a much more elaborate, academic vision for the house than that ultimately executed. The sophisticated double architraves and quoins enframing two of the second-story windows almost certainly were meant to enhance all of the openings—at least all of those on the north facade. The carved keystone and bracketed cornice over the north doorway represent some of the most intricately carved stonework known to have been produced in colonial Virginia, yet this crowning component of the entrance also manifests the presence of two, and possibly three, stonecarvers of differing skills or sensibilities. Instead of the assertive classical profiles that distinguish the carved window architraves and the cornice above the centered entrance, the keystone is embellished with delicate, fancifully trailing, flowered vines. This shallow relief carving is juxtaposed with a deeply carved, three-dimensional rosette centered on the keystone's reveal. Adding to the idiosyncrasy is the flanking of this remarkable entrance with windows outlined with heavy, starkly unmolded architraves (fig. 1.6).

Fig. 1.6. Door and window details of Menokin's facade showing their varied embellishments. Adapted by Whitney Morrill from drawings by the Historic American Buildings Survey.

Clearly, at some moment in Menokin's construction, an authoritative voice and hand—those of Francis Lightfoot Lee—halted the remarkably elaborate carving of stonework for the house and ordered instead a rapid completion. To be sure, Lee and his builders thriftily and ingeniously incorporated the sophisticated carved components where they would fit, and this explains the classical architrave-and-quoin schemes which distinguish the facade's second-story windows. Lee and his builders undoubtedly knew that such a composition would communicate to Virginia's architecturally literate elite that Menokin enclosed—although it never did—an important public room on its second story, but they also knew that the prevailing taste for regularity lent some efficacy to their decision. Furthermore, the expertly finished quoins and finely molded double architraves deserved visible placement. So did the massive arched doorway with its embracing components of a classical entablature.

Nevertheless, the final result was notable more for its inconsistencies than for its refinements. The walls of the house are composed of ashlar only on the north side—the rest is coursed rubble construction steadied at the corners by beveled quoins. Excepting the north entrance and the three second-story windows, all of the doors and windows are framed with unembellished rectangular slabs of sandstone. Finally, the rare and complicated double-hipped roof structure bears down aggressively on the lintels of the second-story windows, leaving room for nothing but the most slender and plainest of cornices.

The interior detailing of Menokin suggests perhaps an even more significant rift between the original conception of the house and its eventual execution. The surviving paneled jambs of the windows involve bold three-dimensional moldings characteristic of the third quarter of the eighteenth century, the period of Menokin's construction, while the rest of the interior detailing, including that of the staircase and chimney breasts, incorporates more delicate, shallow shapes (fig. 1.7). These light molding profiles and their combinations are nearly identical to those at Grove Mount, another house of the Rappahannock Creek neighborhood built between 1782 and 1787.[56] No fire or post-revolutionary remodeling can account for the disparity at Menokin between a 1770–75 period of construction and a 1780–90 period of interior finish, for the surfaces to which the late-century craftsmen affixed their plaster and wainscotting had received no previous treatment.

There is little doubt that after Frank and Rebecca Tayloe Lee moved to Menokin in 1771, they lived amid a sequence of cacophonous building activities—both at the main house site and about the plantation which surrounded them. Moreover, from 1771 until sometime during the 1780s, they identified themselves with a gentry seat dominated by a house that manifestly was not finished. This is perhaps the most significant aspect of the Lees' material circumstances, for it challenged, almost stone for stone, John Tayloe's intention that his architectural dowry boldly express his own patriarchal primacy. There was no more resonant facet of

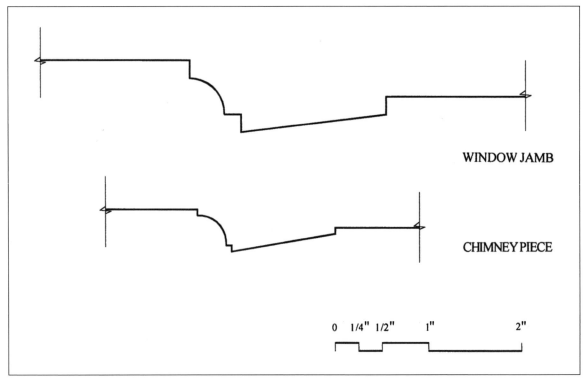

WINDOW JAMB

CHIMNEY PIECE

0   1/4" 1/2"   1"   2"

Fig. 1.7. Molding profile of the panels for Menokin's window reveals, set into the openings at the time of construction, compared with a profile consistently employed for the later interior woodwork.

this challenge than Lee's studied neglect of what was to have been Menokin's most remarkable characteristic. Lee never had his house stuccoed or whitewashed.[57] There it stood, stolid in form and earthen in color. Whether or not such an edifice was perceptible in the distance from Mount Airy was a matter of little concern to Francis Lightfoot Lee.

Just as Menokin embodied the clear signs of Tayloe's prideful intentions in its codes of siting, proportions, materials, and composition, so in its erratic execution, its inconsistent levels of workmanship, and its ultimate departure from several conventions of elite colonial house design, Menokin embodied Frank Lee's silent but eloquent defiance of those intentions. With his bargain, his marriage, and his fortune made, Lee had scant opportunity to protest or reject. He could, however, turn to his own purposes the architectural gestures employed by the man to whom he had obliged himself. At Menokin, he could use the medium of architecture to suggest diffidence—even, to the keen observer, defiance—toward the relationship John Tayloe II meant so deftly to articulate. He did this by managing the process of genteel house building with coolness and dispatch rather than with the obsessive concern for classically correct elegance and consistent polish manifest in so many other elite construction campaigns. The result was a dwelling that clearly belonged among the genteel "great houses" of the Virginia countryside, but one with slightly askew, disheveled qualities, a vigorous toughness around the edges: the suggestion, perhaps, of a rebellious son.

Francis Lightfoot Lee's most famous historical act was to sign the Declaration of Independence. He also represented Virginia, serving with characteristically calm efficiency, in the Continental Congress from 1775 to 1779.[58] Certainly the tale of Menokin's origins offers a new vantage from which to observe and interpret revolutionary-era denouncements of tyrannical and unjust subjugation as well as the growing insistence on inherent rights of self-determination. Indeed, the Revolution began as protests over high-handed acts of England's Parliament and ended with a full-scale revolt of American "sons" against their English "father" King George.

The correspondences, however, are hardly so simple. After Frank Lee departed Virginia to take his seat in the Continental Congress, he exchanged cordial letters with his father-in-law, who was as determined for the American cause of independence as any Virginian.[59] Still, what Menokin may be saying is that the Revolution obscured or overran a crisis in patriarchy about to emerge in Virginia. Its volatile components included the increased longevity of fathers, the survival of numerous children, the resulting difficulty of shepherding a cohesive family fortune through time, and the gentry's uncertainty about replicating its material moorings beyond the Fall Line. In any case, the architectural messages embedded in Menokin, its substantial connections to and contrasts with Mount Airy, and its associated documentary record which sometimes clarifies, sometimes merely hints at the intentions of the house makers themselves, all demonstrate the power of old buildings to bring the past and its dilemmas compellingly back to life. In so doing, houses like Menokin draw those who closely observe them toward the insight that the configuration of architecture and the management of families are, in various and sometimes unsuspected ways, all of a piece with momentous—even radical—shifts in the course of human events.

Notes

I am most grateful to Nat Alcock, Turk McCleskey, and Fraser Neiman, who thoughtfully commented on drafts of this chapter. Hal Sharp was an extraordinary research assistant. Allan Brown, Ray Cannetti, Edward Chappell, and Jeffrey Plank contributed to this piece in the form of agreeable and perceptive on-site conversations about the construction and orientation of Menokin. Research fellowships at the Virginia Historical Society and the Virginia Foundation for the Humanities provided critical and generous support.

1. Stephen R. Potter, *Commoners, Tribute, and Chiefs: The Development of Algonquian Culture in the Potomac Valley* (Charlottesville: Univ. Press of Virginia, 1993), 14–20, 27–42; Helen C. Rountree, *The Powhatan Indians of Virginia: Their Traditional Culture* (Norman: Univ. of Oklahoma Press, 1989), 32–78.

2. Camille Wells, "The Planter's Prospect: Houses, Outbuildings, and Rural Landscapes in Eighteenth-Century Virginia," *Winterthur Portfolio* 28 (1993): 28.

3. In 1774 Philip Fithian visited John Tayloe's Mount Airy, where he remarked, "From this house there is a good prospect of the River Rapahannock [*sic*]," which is about three miles away. "We can also from the chambers easily see the town Hobbes-Hole [*sic*] & the ships which lie there." Hobbs Hole, now known as Tappahannock, is four and a half miles from Mount Airy. Today, mature trees completely obscure this vista. Hunter Dickinson Farish, ed., *Journal and Letters of Philip Vickers Fithian, 1773–1774: A Plantation Tutor of the Old Dominion* (Williamsburg: Colonial Williamsburg, 1965), 95.

4. Thomas Beale II, whose father was a member of the colony's council of state, patented 929 acres of land "on Rappahannock Creek near the head" on May 28, 1673, and named it Chestnut Hill. Virginia Land Office Patent Book 6:24, Public Records Division, Library of Virginia, Richmond, Va.; William Waller Hening, ed., *The Statutes at Large: Being a Collection of All the Laws of Virginia . . .* (Richmond, 1819–23; reprint, Charlottesville: Univ. Press of Virginia, 1969), 2:320; Old Rappahannock County Record Book 1686–92, Public Records Division, Library of Virginia, Richmond, Va.; Aug. 7, 1689, p. 126. The plantation remained in the hands of Beale's male descendants through the first quarter of the nineteenth century. A room-by-room inventory of the house, which stood at Chestnut Hill in 1822, indicates that it had a two-room plan with an enclosed porch or "portico" instead of a first-floor passage. Inventory of George Beale, taken Nov. 4, 1822, proved Dec. 2, 1822, Richmond County Will Book 10:11–14, Richmond County Clerk's Office, Warsaw, Va. This reference to a lobby entrance, combined with the very early style of woodwork and hardware salvaged from the house before it was demolished, suggests that it was built no later than 1725. Thus the wealthy Beale family apparently remained content with—perhaps even proud of—their relatively small and old-fashioned house throughout the eighteenth century. Notes from site visits by the author to the house at Chestnut Hill built in about 1842 and incorporating components of the colonial house, May 10, 1989, June 29, 1989, and June 26, 1990.

5. "Fauntleroy's" dwelling plantation is marked as located at the confluence of Rappahannock Creek and Rappahannock River on Joshua Fry and Peter Jefferson, *A Map of the Most Inhabited Part of Virginia . . .* (London, 1751), Library of Congress. The diversity of agricultural and commercial buildings at Fauntleroy's site is suggested in Inventory of Moore Fauntleroy, recorded Apr. 7, 1740, Richmond County Will Book 5:356–61, and Inventory of Moore Fauntleroy, completed Feb. 7, 1791, Richmond County Will Book 8:116–24.

6. William M. S. Rasmussen, "Sabine Hall: A Classical Villa in Virginia," *Journal of the Society of Architectural Historians* 39 (1980): 286–96.

7. Edward Chappell, "Menokin: Prospect, Orientation, and Outside Finish," *Menokin Afield* 2 (1999): 1–3.

8. John Stephens first patented a thousand acres on "Manakin Creek" on March 13, 1658. Virginia Land Office Patent Book 4:303, Public Records Division, Library of Virginia, Richmond, Va. The tract passed undiminished, and apparently always known as "Menokin," through several owners until 1751, when John Tayloe II purchased it from the Ludwells. This deed, recorded in and subsequently lost among the papers of the Virginia General Court, is referenced in a subsequent transaction. Tayloe to Lee Deed of Gift, Richmond County Deed Book 14:501–2.

9. "A List of Lands belonging to the Hon'ble. John Tayloe in the Northern Neck," Tayloe Family Papers, Virginia Historical Society, Richmond (hereafter cited as Tayloe Family Papers). The management of Menokin as a Tayloe quarter from 1751 until 1769 is clear from notations made in the Daybook of John Tayloe II, which was kept on blank pages of the Accounts and Letter Book of Stephen Loyde, Tayloe Family Papers. As a plantation lying near the periphery of Tayloe's domain, Menokin's woods and waters also welcomed gentlemanly recreation. In 1766, Robert Wormeley Carter wrote that he "went to hunting at Manokin with Coll. Tayloe & Mr. Ball." Entry for Jan. 31, 1766, Robert Wormeley Carter Diary, Swem Library, College of William and Mary (hereafter cited as Carter Diary).

10. For a thorough account of John Tayloe's wealth-generating enterprises, see Laura Croghan Kamoie, "Three Generations of Planter-Businessmen: The Tayloes in Virginia, 1710–1830" (Ph.D. diss., College of William and Mary, 1999), 50–142. The rise of the Tayloe family is also treated in "Resignation of John Tayloe from the Council," *Virginia Magazine of History and Biography* 17 (1909): 369–75, and in Richard S. Dunn, "A Tale of Two Plantations: Slave Life at Mesopotamia in Jamaica and Mount Airy in

Virginia, 1799–1828," *William and Mary Quarterly*, 3d ser., 34 (1977): 33.

11. The characterization of Tayloe's house-building plans as "daring" is in Edmund Jenings to John Tayloe II, June 9, 1754, Edmund Jenings Letter Book, Virginia Historical Society. Notations among Tayloe's accounts make it clear that the actual building began in October 1760 and continued through late 1764. Thus Mount Airy was almost certainly complete by 1765. Daybook of John Tayloe II.

12. Fairfax Harrison, "The Equine F.F.V.s: A Study of the Evidence for the English Horses Imported into Virginia before the Revolution," *Virginia Magazine of History and Biography* 35 (1927): 345–46; T. H. Breen, "Horses and Gentlemen: The Cultural Significance of Gambling among the Gentry of Virginia," *William and Mary Quarterly*, 3d ser., 34 (1977): 239–57.

13. "John Tayloe II and His Children," *Virginia Magazine of History and Biography* 25 (1917): 191–92.

14. In Williamsburg for the October session of the General Court, John Tayloe II wrote to Landon Carter of Sabine Hall, requesting that his neighbor tend to some plantation matters at Mount Airy. He closed by asking Carter to give "my love to my dear girls." Tayloe to Carter, Oct. 16, 1762, Carter Family Papers, Albert H. Small Special Collections Library, Univ. of Virginia, Charlottesville, Va. Ten years later Tayloe wrote a letter to Ralph Wormeley of Rosegill in which referred to his daughter Anne as "Nannie" and noted the tenderness he felt for his daughters. Tayloe to Wormeley, Aug. 4, 1772, cited in Winslow Marston, ed., *In Memoriam: Benjamin Ogle Tayloe* (Washington, D.C., 1872), 346–47.

15. Rebecca Plater Tayloe was then ill after the birth of their daughter Sarah, and Tayloe obviously feared she would bear no more children. Letter of John Tayloe II to William Byrd III, Apr. 4, 1758, William Byrd Papers, Virginia Historical Society.

16. Jean B. Russo, "A Model Planter: Edward Lloyd IV of Maryland, 1770–1796," *William and Mary Quarterly*, 3d ser., 49 (1992): 62–88.

17. Kathleen M. Brown, *Good Wives, Nasty Wenches, and Anxious Patriarchs; Gender, Race, and Power in Colonial Virginia* (Chapel Hill: Univ. of North Carolina Press, 1996), 247–60; Barbara Burlison Mooney, "'True Worth Is Highly Shown in Liveing Well': Architectural Patronage in Eighteenth-Century Virginia" (Ph.D. diss., Univ. of Illinois at Urbana-Champaign, 1991), 158–66.

18. To cite but three of many colonial Virginia examples, the union of William Randolph and Mary Isham produced, among ten children, a son named Isham Randolph (1687–1742). Nathaniel Burwell honored his wife Elizabeth Carter the dowry she brought from her father Robert Carter by naming his second son Carter Burwell (1716–1755). Matthew Page and Mary Mann christened their first-born son Mann Page (1691–1730). Gerald S. Cowden, "The Randolphs of Turkey Island: A Prosopography of the First Three Generations, 1650–1806" (Ph.D. diss., College of William and Mary, 1977), 50, 353; Florence Tyler Carlton, *A Genealogy of the Known Descendants of Robert Carter of Corotoman* (Irvington, Va.: Foundation for Historic Christ Church, 1982), 128; Rachel Most, ed., *Discovering Rosewell: An Historical, Architectural, and Archaeological Overview* (Gloucester, Va.: Rosewell Foundation, 1994), 1–3.

19. John Tayloe III and a twin brother were born on September 2, 1771. Only John survived the first few days. Jane Tayloe followed three years later. This last babe brought to nine the total number of children whom John Tayloe II and Rebecca Plater Tayloe raised to maturity. "John Tayloe II and His Children," 191–92. A. G. Grinnan, "Marriage Records from Ralph Wormeley's Bible," *William and Mary Quarterly*, 1st ser., 6 (1898): 153–55.

20. Will of John Tayloe II, written May 22, 1773, proved July 5, 1779, Richmond County Will Book 7:354–58.

21. Will of John Tayloe II, 354–58.

22. For particulars of the Lee family of Stratford, see Paul C. Nagel, *Lees of Virginia: Seven Generations of an American Family* (New York and London: Oxford Univ. Press, 1990).

23. Will of Thomas Lee, written Feb. 22, 1750, proved July 30, 1751, Westmoreland County Deed and Will Book 11:311–15, Westmoreland County Clerk's Office, Montross, Va. Thomas Lee was a founder of the Ohio Company, the most important attempt by colonial Virginians to press their governance beyond the Allegheny Mountains and into the Ohio Valley. Alfred P. James, *The Ohio Company: Its Inner History* (Pittsburgh: Univ. of Pittsburgh Press, 1959); Marc Egnal, *A Mighty Empire: The Origins of the American Revolution* (Ithaca: Cornell Univ. Press, 1988), 215–26.

24. William Lee complained of "the small pittance which my father left me" in a letter to his eldest brother Philip Ludwell Lee dated October 31, 1770. Edmund Jennings Lee Papers, Virginia Historical Society. Arthur Lee exclaimed, "Good God what trouble does the not having been born to

a fortune, give me" in a letter written on October 20, 1770, to his elder brother Richard Henry Lee. Lee Family Papers, Virginia Historical Society.

25. Thomas Ludwell Lee settled on the easternmost edge of his inherited land in Stafford County. In order to stay in the neighborhood of his birth, Richard Henry Lee settled tenants on all of his back country lands in Fauquier County. For a dwelling plantation, he leased five hundred acres in Westmoreland County from his eldest brother Philip Ludwell Lee, the fortunate eldest son who had inherited Stratford. The two youngest sons, William and Arthur Lee, both left for England, where they remained until after the Revolution. Nagel, *Lees of Virginia*, 65–97.

26. Lee family letters often call or refer to Francis Lightfoot Lee as "Loudoun Lee," even after he had moved back to the Tidewater region. For numerous examples, see Worthington C. Ford, ed., *Letters of William Lee . . . 1766–1783* (Brooklyn: 1891).

27. In 1765 there were 872 heads of household in Loudoun County, out of whom 267, or 30.6 percent, owned land. Of this group, 164, or 61.4 percent, owned less than four hundred acres. Francis Lightfoot Lee was not only the tenth largest landholder in Loudoun County, he also figured among the wealthiest 4.5 percent of the landholding population. Furthermore, he was better off, in terms of land and labor, than about 99 percent of all resident heads of household. These figures are calculated from information in Marty Hyatt and Craig Robert Scott, *Loudoun County, Virginia Tithables* (Athens, Ga.: privately printed, 1995), 1:125–66.

28. Lee's role as a trustee for Leesburg is recorded in Hening, *Statutes at Large* 7:284–86. Lee's first election to the House of Burgesses in 1758 is confirmed in a letter of John Kirkpatrick in Alexandria to George Washington, July 21, 1758, cited in W. W. Abbot, ed., *The Papers of George Washington Colonial Series* (Charlottesville: Univ. Press of Virginia, 1988), 5:315. Lee's appointment as county magistrate on October 23, 1764, is recorded in "Justices of the Peace in Colonial Virginia, 1757–1786," *Bulletin of the Virginia State Library* 14 (1921): 57. Lee's membership and rank in the Loudoun County militia was confirmed in 1764 when Landon Carter referred to him as "Colo. FLL." Jack P. Greene, ed., *The Diary of Colonel Landon Carter of Sabine Hall, 1752–1778* (Richmond: Virginia Historical Society, 1965), 1:255.

29. Sixty-three slaves is a minimum number; they represent those listed in two of the leases Lee later made for his Loudoun County land. Other slaves may have been hired out without written notation. Still others—probably including the most skilled individuals—likely traveled east with Lee to settle at Menokin. Lease of Lee to Cleveland, Dec. 1, 1772, Loudoun County Deed Book 1:183–89; Lease of Lee to Humphries, Dec. 3, 1772, Loudoun County Deed Book 1:189–94, Loudoun County Clerk's Office, Leesburg, Va.

30. This 1765 purchase of a newly surveyed lot bounded by Wolf and Pitt Streets in Alexandria is confirmed in Lee's 1795 conveyance of the lot to Bushrod Washington. Richmond County Deed Book 17:127.

31. An English farmer intent on settling in Virginia noted the importance of Alexandria's role as a point of distribution for "backcountry" wheat and flour when he visited there in 1774. Nicholas Cresswell, *The Journal of Nicholas Cresswell 1774–1777* (New York: Dial Press, 1924), 27.

32. Cited in Alonzo Thomas Dill, *Francis Lightfoot Lee: The Incomparable Signer* (Williamsburg: Virginia Independence Bicentennial Commission, 1977), 15.

33. It is significant that the other seven Tayloe daughters married eldest or only sons who had inherited or expected to inherit notable Tidewater estates. "Resignation of John Tayloe," 374–74.

34. An analysis of all inventories recorded in Loudoun County between 1766 and 1771 indicates that householders had little time and few funds to devote to domestic comforts. Of seventy-two decedents, total wealth in personal property ranged from a low of 10 shillings to a high of £1,431; the median estate value was about £86, and 80.6 percent of all personal estates were worth less than £200. That none of the inventories mention room names implies the appraisers were doing their work in houses with only one room or with poor differentiation of rooms by function. A comparison of numbers of beds (a rough indicator of household population), listed in these inventories with the occurrence of hearth tools, conveys something of the materially improvisational quality of life in the Loudoun County at this time. Twenty-seven (37.5 percent) of the decedents owned only one bed; the rest owned more—up to eleven in one case. Yet forty-eight of the inventories (66.7 percent) list no hearth tools of any sort. This suggests that any fireplaces available to the residents of two-thirds of Loudoun County's houses had to be tended with implements, such as hoes,

flesh forks, or cooking spoons, intended for other purposes. Among the remaining twenty-four inventoried house holds, nine had only one hearth tool—usually a set of tongs. Nine others had two implements—most frequently a shovel and tongs. Four households had three—a poker, a set of andirons, a second shovel or set of tongs. There remained only two households with four or more tools for tending a fire. Of all seventy-two inventories, only three, or 4.2 percent, included "andirons, shovel, and tongs," the complement of fireplace equipage which was standard among most inventoried households in the Tidewater region by the middle of the eighteenth century.

35. John Tayloe II was taxed for 8,942 acres of land in Loudoun County in 1765. Hyatt and Scott, *Loudoun County, Virginia Tithables* 1:166. The Tidewater gentry's distaste for the perceived or imagined roughness of life in Piedmont Virginia persisted well beyond John Tayloe's day. In 1802 John James Maund of Westmoreland County wrote to his brother-in-law George Carter of Loudoun County that his reason for visiting was "from affection," otherwise he would have "nothing to do with the stumps, the sticks, stones and blocks of your county." "Letters of John James Maund," *William and Mary Quarterly,* 1st ser., 20 (1912): 280. In that same year, Henry St. George Tucker acknowledged to John Hartwell Cocke that Virginia lands west of the Fall Line "surpass in fertility the low, level, dry lands" of the Tidewater region, but living so far inland cost him "the pleasures of society." Tucker to Cocke, Aug. 12, 1802, Cocke Family Papers, Albert H. Small Special Collections Library, Univ. of Virginia.

36. Remarks on Frank Lee's sensible, mild, and responsible character appear in Dill, *Francis Lightfoot Lee,* 1, 5, 18, 22.

37. Between 1771 and 1774, Francis Lightfoot Lee leased most of his Loudoun County land to tenants. Loudoun County Deed Book H:182–90; Deed Book I:183–94; Deed Book K:311–20, 366–70; Deed Book L:30–35, 108–13; Deed Book M:21–26.

38. John Pendleton Kennedy, ed., *Journals of the House of Burgesses of Virginia, 1766–1769* (Richmond, 1906), 135, 228–29; *Diary of Colonel Landon Carter* 2:1008–9; Francis Lightfoot Lee became a magistrate of Richmond County and a member of its quorum on May 11, 1770. "Justices of the Peace in Colonial Virginia," 100.

39. The existence as early as 1769 of this deed of gift for Menokin is inferred from the reference Tayloe made to it in his will of 1773. Tayloe wrote the deed of gift that was at last recorded on October 5, 1778, but twelve days earlier. Tayloe to Lee, Richmond County Deed Book 14:501–2; Will of John Tayloe II, 354–58; Daybook of John Tayloe II, Tayloe Family Papers.

40. Tayloe to Lee Deed of Gift, Richmond County Deed Book 14:501–2.

41. Marylynn E. Salmon, *Women and the Law of Property in Early America* (Chapel Hill: Univ. of North Carolina Press, 1986), 55; Linda E. Speth, "More than Her 'Thirds': Wives and Widows in Colonial Virginia," *Women and History* 4 (1982): 5–41.

42. Lee to Lee Deed of Trust, Oct. 5, 1778, Richmond County Deed Book 14:502.

43. The most perceptive treatments of the sort of patriarchy peculiar to colonial Virginia include Rhys Isaac, *The Transformation of Virginia, 1740–1790* (Chapel Hill: Univ. of North Carolina Press, 1982), 322–57; Rhys Isaac, "Communication and Control: Authority Metaphors and Power Contests on Colonel Landon Carter's Virginia Plantation, 1752–1778," in *Rites of Power: Symbolism, Ritual, and Politics since the Middle Ages,* ed. Sean Wilentz (Philadelphia: Univ. of Pennsylvania Press, 1985), 275–302; Dell Upton, *Holy Things and Profane: Anglican Parish Churches in Colonial Virginia* (New York: Architectural History Foundation and MIT Press, 1986), 101–96; Brown, *Good Wives, Nasty Wenches, and Anxious Patriarchs,* 137–86, 247–83.

44. The most recent of many architectural histories which identify the source for Mount Airy as plate 58 in James Gibbs's *Book of Architecture,* published in London in 1828, is Charles E. Brownell, Calder Loth, William M. S. Rasmussen, and Richard Guy Wilson, *The Making of Virginia Architecture* (Richmond: Virginia Museum of Fine Arts, 1992), 25.

45. For the continued prevalence of small houses built entirely of wood in eighteenth-century Tidewater Virginia, see Wells, "Planter's Prospect," 5–12.

46. To supervise the masonry construction and rough carpentry at Mount Airy, John Tayloe II hired William Waite, who came down from Alexandria for the duration of the project. For the finer carpentry and joinery, he hired William Buckland, who in accepting the job, moved from Fairfax County and stayed in Richmond County until 1771. Daybook of John Tayloe II. Rosamond Randall Beirne, and John H. Scarff, *William Buckland, 1734–1774: Architect of Virginia and Maryland* (Annapolis, Md.: Gunston Hall

Board of Regents and Hammond-Harwood House Association, 1958), 34–48.

47. Though some architectural historians entertain the possibility that John Tayloe II originally intended to stucco Mount Airy, the precision of the brown sandstone ashlar and the quality of its mortar joints testify to his intention that the house retain its strong polychromy. Chisel stippling on the equally precise sandstone ashlar of the two formal offices do not suggest an anticipated coating of stucco for these secondary buildings: the pattern of stippling is so precise and controlled that it is clear the mason involved was creating a "pecked" finish intended to distinguish the appearance—and status—of the flankers from those of the main house. For Aquia stone, see "Freestone from Aquia," *Virginia Cavalcade* 9 (Summer 1959): 35–40.

48. Dell Upton has described how the eighteenth-century land approach to Mount Airy meanders in a way which gave visitors a sequence of momentary and anticipatory glimpses of the house from different perspectives before the full impact of arrival could occur. Upton, "White and Black Landscapes in Eighteenth-Century Virginia," *Places: A Quarterly Journal of Environmental Design* 2 (1985): 59–72.

49. Landon Carter the younger settled at Bull Hall on Bull Run Creek in Fairfax County. John Carter settled at Sudley in Prince William County. *Diary of Colonel Landon Carter* 1:130–32.

50. Entry for Aug. 25, 1766, Carter Diary. Young Carter married Winifred Travers Beale of Chestnut Hill. Their children—Landon, George, Elizabeth, Frances, and Ann Beale Carter—apparently were all born and complicating domestic affairs at Sabine Hall by 1769. Louis Morton, "Robert Wormeley Carter of Sabine Hall: Notes on the Life of a Virginia Planter," *Journal of Southern History* 12 (1946): 345–65; Carlton, *Genealogy,* 372–80.

51. Landon Carter's diary contains accounts of fifty-four quarrels with his son Robert Wormeley Carter between 1764 and 1778. Most had to do with the younger man's drinking, gambling, insolence, or ostensible idleness. Far more numerous than these narratives are the complaints about his son which the elder Carter scribbled in his diary. *Diary of Colonel Landon Carter,* vols. 1–2, numerous entries; Daniel Blake Smith, *Inside the Great House: Planter Family Life in Eighteenth-Century Chesapeake Society* (Ithaca: Cornell Univ. Press, 1980), 192–94.

52. *Diary of Colonel Landon Carter,* 1:386–87.

53. The only outbuilding which survived at Menokin long enough to attract the attention of a photographer was the stone office located to the northeast of the main house. Archaeological testing has turned up signs of numerous other buildings close the house, and remnants of the excavated terraces are still visible. William F. Rust, III, "A National Register Assessment of Menokin," unpublished report prepared for the National Park Service, 1985. That Lee had a barn at Menokin is confirmed by a 1780 entry Rebecca Plater Tayloe's Account Book: Lee gave her nearly three thousand nails "in leu of those he had for his barn." Tayloe Family Papers. The range of service and agricultural buildings which Lee built at Menokin is based on conclusions in Wells, "Planter's Prospect," 1–31.

54. Francis Lightfoot Lee to William Lee, June 7, 1771, Robert E. Lee Papers, Perkins Library Special Collections, Duke Univ., Durham, N.C. Lee's use of the phrase "under my own vine" is drawn from the Old Testament. Under the reign of Solomon, "Judah and Israel dwelt safely, every man under his vine and under his fig tree" (I Kings 4:25). The reference was popular in eighteenth-century Virginia. Among others, both William Byrd II and George Washington employed it. William Byrd II to Charles, Earl of Orrey, July 5, 1726, in Marion Tinling ed., *The Correspondence of the Three William Byrds of Westover, Virginia 1684–1776* (Charlottesville: Univ. Press of Virginia), 1:355–56; George Washington to George Mason, Mar. 27, 1779, in Robert A. Rutland, ed., *The Papers of George Mason, 1725–1792* (Chapel Hill: Univ. of North Carolina Press, 1970), 2:493.

55. Evidence concerning the cutting date of Menokin's structural wood is not conclusive, for the material has suffered the insults of long exposure to the weather. Undeteriorated bark edge survives on one sheltered roof strut, and dendrochronological analysis of that member determined that its last year of growth was 1772. Dendrochronological sampling and provisional dating of Menokin was completed between January and March 2001 by William J. Callahan Jr. and Edward R. Cook as part of a project, still underway, to dendrochronologically date a set of eighteenth-century Virginia houses. This project has been sheltered by the University of Virginia School of Architecture and supported by a grant from the Jessie Ball duPont Religious, Charitable, and Educational Fund.

56. The remarkable similarities between the woodwork at Grove Mount and Menokin were first observed by Grove

Mount's current owner. Martin Kirwan King, interview with author, July 13, 1988, Grove Mount, Richmond County, Va.

57. In the middle of the nineteenth century Menokin's north entrance received the shelter of a roughly built porch. The outline of this porch is still imprinted on the facade where plaster was never applied. Thus the north side of the house, at least, was not stuccoed until some half-century after the Lees had died. Camille Wells, "A Tale of Two Houses: Menokin and Mount Airy," *Menokin Afield* (Spring 2000): 1–4. Analysis of the plaster on all four elevations of the house confirm a consistency of composition in base, intermediate, and final coats of plaster for which only a single campaign of application can reasonably account. David S. Lane, "Examination of Menokin Exterior Plasters" (Charlottesville: Virginia Transportation Research Council, 2000), 1–2.

58. In 1775 Frank Lee took Rebecca Tayloe Lee with him to Philadelphia, and the couple remained entirely absent from Menokin, except for a five-month leave from Continental Congress, which extended from June to October 1778. Dill, *Francis Lightfoot Lee,* 45, 47–49. It was during this visit back to Virginia that Tayloe permitted the deed of gift for Menokin to become a matter of public record in Richmond County court. Francis Lightfoot Lee's contributions to the revolutionary cause in Continental Congress were valued and valuable. The Philadelphia patriot Benjamin Rush wrote that he had an "acute and correct mind. He often opposed his brother [Richard Henry Lee] in a vote, but never spoke in Congress. I never knew him wrong eventually upon any question." George W. Corner, ed., *The Autobiography of Benjamin Rush* (Philadelphia: American Philosophical Society, 1948), 158.

59. In February 1776, Landon Carter noted that Frank Lee, then in Philadelphia, had written John Tayloe II on the matter of getting arms and powder from Europe. *Diary of Colonel Landon Carter* 2:989. Lee subsequently sent his father-in-law a "parcel" of copies of Tom Paine's *Common Sense* to be distributed among their Northern Neck friends. Letter of Francis Lightfoot Lee to Landon Carter, Mar. 18, 1776, cited in John Hazelton, *The Declaration of Independence: Its History* (New York, 1906), 93–94.

2

ANGLICAN CHURCH DESIGN IN THE CHESAPEAKE

ENGLISH INHERITANCES AND REGIONAL INTERPRETATIONS

CARL LOUNSBURY

Traditional architectural historiography has lumped Maryland and Virginia together as "the Chesapeake," a region where any provincial variations were overshadowed by the commonality of plan types, construction methods, and decorative details. The evidence from the ecclesiastical landscape, however, belies this assumption. The thirty surviving colonial churches in Maryland and the slightly larger number in Virginia share many of the same architectural features ranging from materials to joinery methods that are common to the region. Yet they differ significantly in terms of plan and decorative brickwork. In Maryland, attached vestry rooms, porches, and articulated chancels, and the penchant for selective glazing and bonding patterns, combined to create a building form set apart from its Virginia counterpart and more closely resembling Anglican churches in other colonies. Built to serve similar functions, the parish churches of Virginia and Maryland varied due to the influence of

local building practices and the dynamics of Anglican church planning in the seventeenth and early eighteenth centuries.

Their differences underscore the fact that Chesapeake builders were constantly adapting metropolitan ideas. However, the integration of novel forms in one part of the region did not necessarily mean the wholesale rejection of older ones elsewhere, especially if they seemed to satisfy certain social and cultural expectations. From first settlement through the end of the colonial period, Virginia vestrymen favored an Anglican church form that had developed in England by the first decades of the seventeenth century. When the Anglican Church was established in Maryland nearly a century later in the 1690s, the vestries there chose a modern form made popular in England in the last quarter of the seventeenth century, ignoring the traditional plan embraced by Virginians. Virginians, in turn, adjusted the decorative treatment of their parish

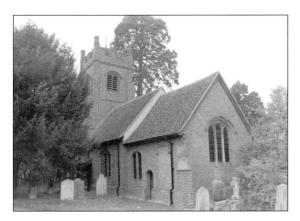

Fig. 2.1. St. Nicholas, Chignal Smealey, Essex, c. 1530. A brick church built just prior to the English Reformation. Typical of late medieval churches, it features a deep chancel, at the east end of which the priest said mass before the altar. The east end has a large window lighting the altar inside and a chancel door on the south wall. The division between the chancel and the wider and taller nave was demarcated by a rood screen separating the laity from the priest.

churches in the eighteenth century but made few alterations to a plan that suited their spatial proclivities and spiritual needs. The power of local tradition counterbalanced the appeal of novelty.

Virginia's Anglican heritage grew out of an earlier period when the Church of England's architectural and liturgical ideas were shaped by an attempt to reconcile Protestant theology with buildings erected for pre-Reformed worship (see fig. 2.1). Most English churches of the late sixteenth and early seventeenth centuries were divided into two distinct spaces, a nave where most of the service, including the sermon, took place, and a deep chancel that contained the altar. However, the relationship of these two spaces—one for preaching and one for the sacraments—was a constant source of friction between the extreme wings of the Anglican Church. At one end, the Puritans, who wished to rid the church of all vestiges of its pre-Reformed past not grounded in biblical precedent, desired one central space with a prominently positioned pulpit and a movable and inconspicuous communion table. At the other end, conservative high churchmen wanted to retain those ceremonial aspects that emphasized

the "beauty of holiness," the sacramental importance of the Holy Eucharist, which required an appropriate setting for this rite. Amid the wide variations in forms of worship, high churchmen in the 1630s, under the leadership of Archbishop William Laud, attempted to impose greater liturgical uniformity and a more decorous style of worship. To underscore the visual and sacramental aspects of prayer book worship, the church hierarchy ordered the replacement of wooden communion tables with stone altars placed against the east wall of the chancel, the construction of a balustrade around the altar to protect it from profane use, and the erection of a wooden screen between the chancel and nave if none existed.[1]

Many of the architectural manifestations of the high church principles of Archbishop Laud were abolished with the triumph of Calvinist theology wrought by swords of Cromwell's Puritan armies in the 1640s. Puritans destroyed stone altars, tore down balustraded railings surrounding the altars, and covered over or destroyed images that may have survived the earlier iconoclasm of Edward VI's reign. However, the Puritan moment was short lived. Despite the rupture of the Civil War, the Restoration in 1660 returned the Episcopal hierarchy and reestablished many of the Laudian ideals, though they now were tempered by a more tolerant approach to diversity in liturgical matters.

A number of new churches built in the years after the Restoration conformed to many of the traditional internal arrangements advocated by Laud, especially those built in rural parishes. For example, St. Ninian, Brougham, Cumbria (1660), St. Saviour, Foremark, Derbyshire (1662), and St. Mary, Monington on Wye, Herefordshire (1679) retained the long narrow proportions of what church historian Nigel Yates has called the traditional Anglican plan. Foremost was the clear division between the area reserved for the sacrament and that used for the main service and preaching. The traditional plan still conceived of the church as two distinct rooms or spaces. While this is articulated on the outside by a separate nave and chancel at Monington on Wye, there is no structural division between the two at Brougham and Foremark, each of which is enclosed under a single roof. In all three churches, the division between the body of the church

Fig. 2.2. St. Saviour, Foremark, Derbyshire, 1662. Interior view toward the east end with the pulpit on the south wall near the chancel screen, which separates the altar from the nave.

and the altar is demarcated by a chancel screen, epitomizing the duality of the Anglican liturgy (fig. 2.2). A central, east-west aisle divided the seating in the nave, most of which faced eastward toward the pulpit and reading desk that were located near the chancel screen at the east end of the nave (fig. 2.3). A railed balustrade enclosed the altar at the east end of the church. Few of Laud's stone altars were reused; instead, most churchwardens erected wooden communion tables. In some instances, the chancel contained an open space or seats where communicants could gather or be seated before taking communion at the altar rail.[2]

The plan suited small, rural parishes, especially ones that served a manor or village. The remote location and diminutive size of these traditional Anglican churches hardly brought them architectural acclaim beyond their immediate region. Yet the inherent conservatism of the arrangement appealed to many and the plan continued to be used across England in the eighteenth century in such places as All Saints, Trusley, Derbyshire (1713), St. Leonard, Bradley in the Moors, Staffordshire (1750), and the estate church of St. Mary, Avington, Hampshire (1768). However, for many larger congregations, this arrangement was inconvenient because distance and visual impediments between the pulpit and the east end of the chancel blocked a clear view of the liturgical activities. As a result, in growing towns and in the metropolis of London, churchmen experimented with radical new liturgical forms that would have a profound impact on church

Fig. 2.3. Plan, St. Saviour, Foremark, Derbyshire, 1662. The elongated proportion of the traditional Anglican plan is evident in the plan of this rural estate church. The pulpit, reading desk, and clerk's desk are located on the south wall near the chancel screen. Benches inside the chancel provide a place for worshiper to sit before taking communion at the three-sided altar rail.

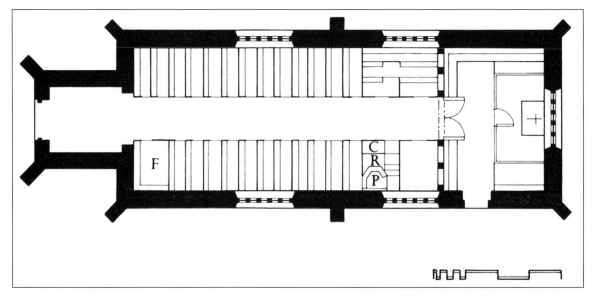

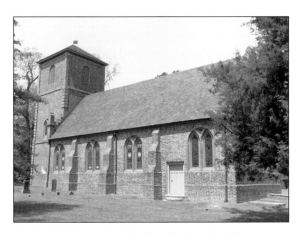

Fig. 2.4. Newport Parish Church, Isle of Wight County, Virginia, c. 1682. The traditional Anglican church plan is evident in the earliest surviving church in Virginia with its axial center aisle, chancel screen separating the body of the church from the altar, and a chancel door on the south wall near the east end. The west tower is an exceptional extravagance that seldom appeared in later rural parish churches.

building in Maryland and other newly established Anglican colonies.

No matter how tenuous its roots or how poorly it served Virginia during its first century, the Church of England had been an integral part of the colony since its founding. The transplanted church was conservative in doctrine though not doctrinaire.[3] Long after Laud had been executed and Cromwell's Commonwealth had been made a reality, Virginia correspondents observed that "wee serve god after the old way as was once in England" and that the Book of Common Prayer was used throughout the colony except in two or three churches of Puritan persuasion. There may have been as many as forty churches by 1650, most if not all of which were "built of wood, [and] very handsome for such work."[4] These churches, and the ones built in the second half of the seventeenth century, probably reflected the traditional Anglican arrangement. There is little information about the first generation of church building in Virginia. The documents and buildings that survive from the 1660s onward indicate that vestries designed buildings of elongated proportions with a central, east-west aisle. The pulpit stood in front of the chancel screen, which was locat-

ed ten to fifteen feet west of the altar at the east end of the church.[5] Virginia churches never displayed a distinct architectural division between body and chancel as many English ones, but the internal arrangement with the chancel screen and chancel door at the southeast end of the south wall followed the traditional configuration, evident, for example, in the design of the Newport Parish Church, Isle of Wight County (c. 1682), and in the 1708 plan for a church in Chowan County, North Carolina (fig. 2.4).

As Dell Upton has argued, Virginians reshaped some aspects of the traditional church plan, such as moving the main entrance from the south wall to the west facade and ceasing to erect chancel screens by the 1720s. These trends were not exclusively colonial but mirrored similar English revisions of the early eighteenth century. However, in all major respects, the internal arrangements and proportions of late-seventeenth- and early-eighteenth-century Virginia parish churches were similar to traditional English forms. Once established in Virginia by the 1660s, the plan remained unchanged for the next century, although there were some variations and experimentation, especially along the margins of the Anglican Tidewater heartland, such as the Potomac and newly settled regions to the west (fig. 2.5).[6]

The Anglican Church was a latecomer to Maryland. Established by act of assembly in 1692, there was literally little to build on from the first sixty years of settlement. Before its elevation to a state-supported institution, the record of the Church of England in the colony was episodic and piecemeal. There were few early Anglican ministers working in the colony, and "if they remained in one place their support was derived not from a church or congregation which they had served, but rather from the plantations which they farmed. . . . There was no official body such as vestry which could legally hold property. Such churches as were founded were in fact congregational or private chapels, and the only fact which made them Anglican was their ministers were in Anglican Orders and that the Anglican forms of service were used."[7] Not that Anglicans were alone in their plight. For a colony owned by a Catholic proprietor, who by necessity professed a toleration of all Christian denominations, seventeenth-century Maryland was a particularly

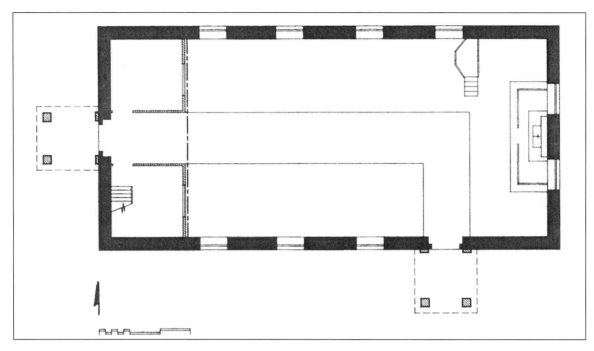

Fig. 2.5. Plan, Fork Church, Hanover County, Virginia, c. 1737. With its west entrance, chancel door on the south wall, and central aisle, the plan is typical of rural parish churches erected in Virginia in the eighteenth century. The pulpit was originally located between the first and second window to the east on the north wall, one bay westward of its present location. The porches and vestibule walls date from the nineteenth century.

ungodly place. An itinerant Anglican cleric lamented in 1676 that "noe care is taken or Provision made for the building up [of] Christians in the Protestant Religion by means whereof not only many Daly fall away either to Popery, Quakerism or Phanaaticisme but alsoe the lords day is prophaned, Religion despised, & all notorious vices committed soe that it is become a Sodom of uncleaness & a Pest house of iniquity."[8] Conditions were no better twenty years later. A churchman wrote to the bishop of London after establishment that "there were but 3 Clergymen in Episcopal Orders, besides 5 or 6 popish priests, who had perverted divers idle people from the Protestant Religion. There was also a sort of wandering pretenders to preaching that came from New England and other places; which deluded not only the Protestant Dissenters from our Church but many of the Churchmen themselves, by their extemporary prayers and preachments."[9] As Jon Butler has observed, "The collusion of geography, shifting immigration and settlement patterns, and

government inaction left most settlers without the simplest rudiments of public Christian practice between 1630 and 1690."[10]

The weakness of organized religion in seventeenth-century Maryland is evident in the few structures built in the colony. Anglicans had very little to show for their efforts, perhaps a few frame chapels at best.[11] Chapels and meetinghouses built by Catholics, Quakers, and Presbyterians were modest in size as well, rarely as large or as well finished as the Quaker Third Haven Meetinghouse built in the early 1680s in Talbot County.[12] A 1698 survey of newly denominated dissenting places of worship revealed a few wooden Catholic chapels in the southern counties and on the lower Eastern Shore, and Quaker meetinghouses on both sides of the bay, but nearly all of these were no more than twenty by thirty feet and were described as "plain country buildings" or "clapboard houses" built "after the manner of a tobacco house."[13] The one exception was a brick Catholic chapel built in St. Mary's

City in the 1660s with a cruciform plan with side chapels in narrow transepts. That building was short lived, however, as it was systematically dismantled in the first decade of the eighteenth century when Protestant prohibitions put paid to public popery.[14]

With access to public money, an institutional structure, and the patronage of the Society for the Propagation of the Gospel in Foreign Parts (SPG), the Anglican Church in Maryland developed its own identity in the period between 1692 and the third decade of the eighteenth century. Thirty parishes were immediately created, vestries were organized and began to exercise their social and moral duties, taxes to support ministers and build churches became an accepted obligation among all residents, and SPG mis-

sionaries filled the pulpits of dozens of new churches.[15] Within a generation of the act of establishment, a landscape so devoid of sacred spaces was beginning to show signs of sacerdotal success. Each parish built a mother church, replaced its early wooden building with a brick one, and added chapels of ease. Nothing substantial appeared until the late 1690s, when, through the "indefatigable Industry and Zeal" of Governor Francis Nicholson "to promote the Interest of Protestant Religion," the first parish churches began to be erected.[16] Many were small timber-framed structures such as the twenty- by forty-foot St. James Church, erected in Anne Arundel County in 1695.[17] Others were more substantial and ambitious. The first St. Anne's in Annapolis was designed in 1698–99 as a

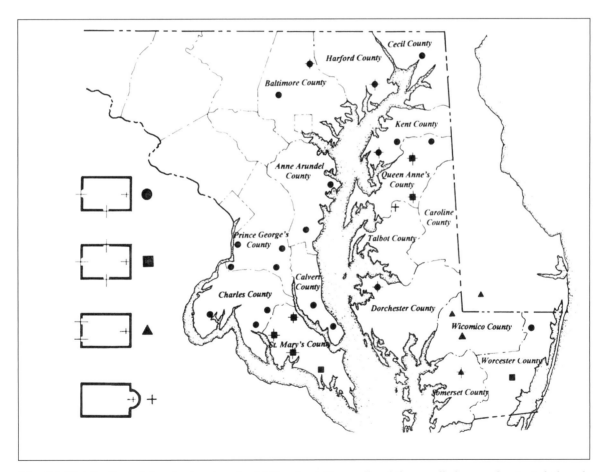

Map 2.1. Distribution of church plans in colonial Maryland. Two-wall and three-wall plans predominated, though there were some local variants, particularly on the lower Eastern Shore, where double-west-door plans appeared. Churches with chancels could be found throughout the colony on many of the principal parish churches.

brick church whose internal dimensions measured thirty by sixty-five feet, with a fifteen-foot square south porch and similar-sized north vestry room attached to the center of the building.[18] Church building was an uneven process, well supported in a few places but still thinly developed elsewhere. Or as one minister observed, "Religion among us seems to wear the face of the Country, part moderately cultivated, the greater part wild & savage."[19]

Of the nearly fifty known Anglican church plans, the overwhelming majority fit into two principal plan types (map 2.1). The most common consisted of a central doorway on one of the longer side walls with a second entrance in the center of the west gable end.[20] The altar stood against the east wall opposite the west entrance. A central aisle ran from the west door to the low altar rail surrounding the communion table in the east. From the central door in the long wall, another cross aisle ran northward to meet the east-west aisle and was generally terminated by a tall, two- or three-tiered pulpit against the north wall.

A variation in this plan developed when a small, centrally located vestry room was built perpendicular to the north wall of the church. At Middleham Chapel, Calvert County (1748), the cross axis extends from the south doorway, which is enclosed by a porch, across the main aisle to an opening into the vestry room of similar dimensions as the porch (fig. 2.6). With such a plan, the pulpit was displaced from its usual position in the center of the north wall to an

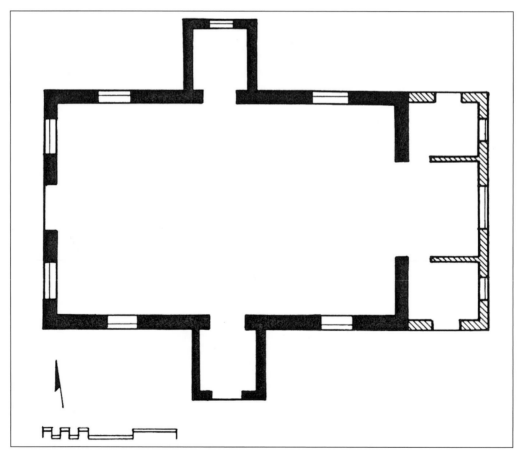

Fig. 2.6. Plan, Middleham Chapel, Calvert County, Maryland, 1748. The south entrance porch is matched by a small vestry room on the north side. The pulpit originally stood just east of the doorway to the vestry room. The church was extended eastward in 1893 to provide room for the new altar, vestry room, and sacristy.

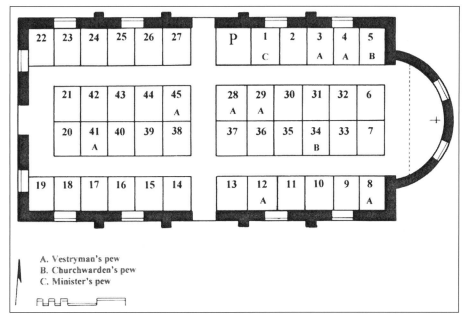

Fig. 2.7. Pew plan, St. Luke's, Church Hill, Queen Anne's County, Maryland, 1731. Narrower than most three-door churches in Maryland, St. Luke's does not have internal columns to support the arched roof span. As the pew plan indicates, the pulpit stood against the north wall just east of the central cross aisle. The communion table stood against the east wall of the apse, which was raised a step above the body of the church.

area farther eastward, as was the case at St. Paul, Baden (1733), and St. Thomas, Croom (1745), in Prince George's County.[21]

A second plan contained an additional entrance so that there were central doorways on the two long walls as well as another on the west gable end. Because of this third doorway, the pulpit was located farther east rather than in the middle of the north wall as was the case at Middleham Chapel. The plan could be found in a few narrower churches. St. Luke's, Queen Anne's County (1731), is slightly less than thirty-four feet wide (fig. 2.7). The three-door plan became standard form for those that measured more than forty feet in breadth. At Christ Church, Chaptico, St. Mary's County (1736), and neighboring All Faith, built some thirty years later (1767), a row of columns on each side, running in an east-west direction, supports the span of the roof (fig. 2.8). The ceiling in the central part of these churches was arched while the shorter span on both sides between the outer walls and columns contained a

Fig. 2.8. Christ Church, Chaptico, St. Mary's County, Maryland, 1736. The church is the earliest of a group of southern Maryland churches that had internal columns to support a broad roof span. The location of the pulpit originally would have been just to the east of the now-missing central cross aisle. In the early nineteenth century, the long-wall doorways were converted to windows, the cross aisle filled in with pews, and the pulpit moved to the east end to create a longitudinal plan.

flat ceiling. While the pulpit was generally located against the north or south wall, the disadvantage of the plan was the presence of columns at regular intervals, which could interrupt visual contact with the pulpit among some worshiper.

A subregional variant found mainly on the lower Eastern Shore had two entrances on the west gable end only. These doorways led into a double-aisled interior with pews ranged along the walls and a double set of pews in the center range. Green Hill Church (1733) in Stepney Parish, Wicomico County, is the earliest example of this form, followed by two framed chapels of ease erected in the early 1770s, Spring Hill and Christ Church. Now in Delaware, Christ Church retains its original unpainted fittings, including a generously proportioned pulpit standing in the center of the long north wall and a communion table enclosed by a balustrade on a raised platform against the east wall.[22]

A small but significant number of Maryland churches were built with articulated chancels, a few rectangular, but most commonly apsidal, in form as at St. Luke's, Queen Anne's County (fig. 2.9). The only known Virginia church to have had such an

Fig. 2.9. St. Luke's Church, Church Hill, Queen Anne's County, Maryland, 1731. The shallow apse at the east end appeared on a number of parish churches in Maryland in the eighteenth century, where it accentuated the ecclesiastical orientation of the building and provided a dramatic setting for the Eucharist. Maryland builders selectively used glazed headers to emphasize primary facades such as the south entrance wall and apse of St. Luke's. The north pulpit wall has no glazing.

appendage was Pungoteague Church in St. George's Parish, built in Accomack County, which borders Maryland's lower Eastern Shore. If rare in Virginia, the shallow chancel form probably derived from English precedents, most notably in the designs of Christopher Wren, James Gibbs, and others. Marylanders used the articulated chancel sparingly, generally on the most prominent parish churches, where it accentuated the ecclesiastical orientation and provided a dramatic setting for the Eucharist. The form appears elsewhere in the American colonies; St. Paul's Church in Edenton, North Carolina, has an apsidal arrangement with all-header bond, while Pompion Hill, outside of Charleston, is rectangular and illuminated by a Venetian window.

One of the most significant differences between Virginia and Maryland churches is their proportion: Maryland churches are boxier than the elongated footprint of Virginia churches (fig. 2.10). Except for a small pocket of buildings bordering the Potomac River whose form, plan, and proportion are more closely akin to Maryland buildings, Virginia parish churches were usually twice as long as they were wide. This ratio remained constant for a century, from late-seventeenth-century structures through those erected on the eve of the Revolution. Newport Parish Church in Isle of Wight County measures twenty-eight by sixty-four feet. Built seventy years later, the now-ruinous Lower Church of Southwark Parish in Surry County follows the same pattern, ranging from thirty-four feet in width compared to seventy-four feet in length, making its length more than twice its width. Maryland parish churches, by contrast, are between one and a third and one and two-thirds as long as they are deep. A church of similar square footage as Southwark Parish Church is St. James, Anne Arundel County (1762). The west facade is forty feet wide, while the main facade on the south side, accentuated by a small porch with compass-headed openings, extends sixty feet, creating a 1 to 1.5 ratio of width to length (fig. 2.11).

A few Maryland churches were built with the elongated proportions of Virginia buildings, but most were of the scale of St. James or even squarer.[23] Two churches

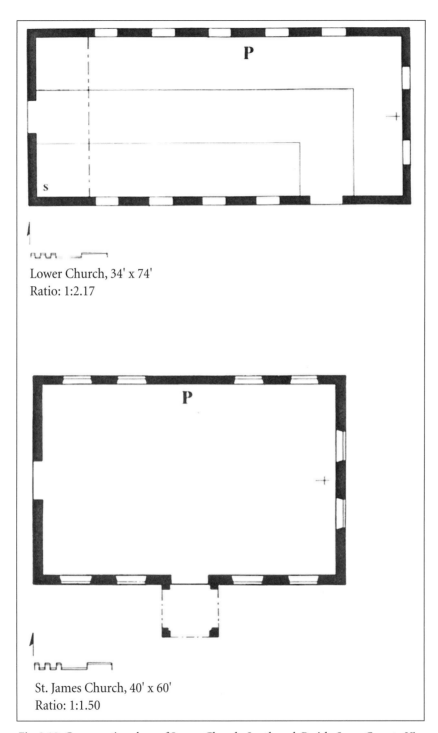

Lower Church, 34' x 74'
Ratio: 1:2.17

St. James Church, 40' x 60'
Ratio: 1:1.50

Fig. 2.10. Comparative plans of Lower Church, Southwark Parish, Surry County, Virginia, c. 1751, and St. James Church, Anne Arundel County, Maryland, 1762. On the whole, Virginia churches were twice as long as they were wide. By contrast Maryland churches were squarer, their length seldom surpassing one and a half times their width.

Fig. 2.11. St. James Church, Anne Arundel County, Maryland, 1762. The primacy of the central entrance on the long south wall is acknowledged by the porch and the use of header bond. The secondary entrance on the west facade is also laid in header bond, but there is no porch. The two back walls on the north and east sides are laid in English bond.

erected at the end of the colonial era are little more than big preaching boxes. St. Barnabas is two stories and measures forty-six by sixty feet, while All Saints is fifty by sixty feet, proportions that match the shape of many New England Congregational meetinghouses. This willingness to enclose large spaces under one roof marks yet another distinction between Maryland and Virginia. Virginia churches rarely spanned thirty-five feet. In planning large parish churches, Virginians seldom increased the width to accommodate additional space but stretched the length or added wings to form T-shaped or cruciform plans. A few Maryland churches received later wings, but none were planned at the outset and no cruciform churches appeared in the colony. To get the appropriate square footage, Maryland churches were expanded in width in order to match the capacity of Virginia's winged churches.

The source of inspiration for these boxlike buildings was not New England or the mid-Atlantic colonies with their dissenting meetinghouse plans. Maryland Anglicans need not have looked outside their denomination for their inspiration. Rather, since the end of the seventeenth century, Anglican churches throughout the American colonies, with the exception of Virginia, were planned along similar lines. Whether in large cities, such as King's Chapel in Boston (1689),

small towns, such as St. Paul's, Edenton, North Carolina (1736), or small rural parishes, such as Trinity near Philadelphia (1712), they were built with central doorways, cross aisles, and liturgical arrangements that replicated standard Maryland practices.[24]

Maryland's Anglican experience matched in many ways that of South Carolina, a staple-producing colony whose gentry identified with the cultural and religious attitudes of the Church of England after it was established by legislative fiat. As the church grew under the patronage of rice and indigo planters, buildings such as St. Stephen's Parish Church, Berkeley County (1767), with centralized plans and boxy proportions, were erected in the rural parishes surrounding Charleston. The now-ruinous Sheldon Church, Prince William Parish, Beaufort County (1753), measures forty-five by sixty-five feet, with three doorways, in the middle of the north, south, and west walls. Others had shallow chancels and Venetian windows in the east end, repeating features found in Maryland designs. In terms of size and plan, these South Carolina parish churches match the larger ones built in the wealthier parishes of colonial Maryland. Erected between 1748 and 1756 in the Eastern Shore Parish of Snow Hill, Worcester County, All Hallows is the same size as Sheldon and originally had a large entrance in the middle of each of its two long walls and another on the shorter west wall.

These proportions and plans took their inspiration from a form known as the "auditory" or "room" church. Evolving in the early seventeenth century and elevated to prominence by Christopher Wren in his designs for London's parish churches following the fire of 1666, the auditory plan was a single rectangular room with little or no spatial or visual division between the body or nave and chancel or altar place. The chief characteristics of these room churches were the absence of the traditional screen subdividing the chancel from the nave and their broad proportions.[25] In keeping with the emphasis on the auditory nature of the service, of hearing the word clearly spoken from a pulpit prominently placed in a central location, Wren stressed that a church should be organized in a way so that all who attended could both hear and see the preacher. Based on the limit a preacher's voice

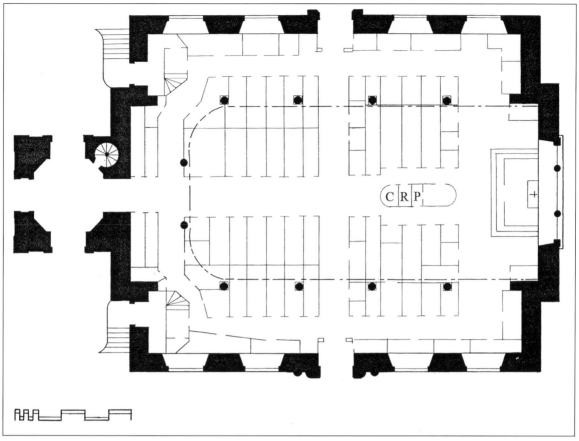

Fig. 2.12. Early-eighteenth-century pew plan, St. James, Piccadilly, London, Christopher Wren, architect, 1676–84.

could be heard distinctly by his congregation, Wren calculated that a new "church should be at least 60 Feet broad, and 90 Feet long, besides a Chancel at one End, and a Belfry and Portico at the other."[26] The proportions of such a church were far squarer than traditional long, narrow churches of the medieval and Reformation eras, roughly two thirds the length, or 1 to 1.5, the same as many Maryland buildings.

Wren cited his St. James, Piccadilly as "the most capacious, with these Qualifications" in that it was very broad with pews arranged around a tall pulpit placed in the center of the church (fig. 2.12). The interior of this very broad church contained a single open room unencumbered by internal walls. The roof rested upon "Pillars, as do also the Galleries," which Wren believed to be "beautiful and convenient" in

that they provided a relatively unobstructed view of the pulpit and "the cheapest of any Form I could invent" to support the span.[27] Entrance into St. James was through three doorways, one in west through the bell tower, and the others in the center of the two longer walls, which produced a north-south cross aisle. A broad, but shallow chancel, lit by a Venetian window, contained the communion table at the east end.[28] Wren's cross-axial plan of St. James was further elaborated by his assistant, Nicholas Hawksmoor at St. Alfege, Greenwich (1712), and Christ Church, Spitalfields (1723), where long wall entrances were balanced by a monumental west entry.[29] Inside, two narrow aisles demarcated by sets of columns running in an east-west direction supported galleries.[30] If the scale and decorative elaboration were far beyond the colonial grasp, the proportions, plans, and liturgical arrangements of these buildings and others like them in London served as the conceptual models employed by Maryland vestrymen and rectors in their parish designs.

This type appealed to Anglicans in Maryland because it was up to date, widely known, and had no local precedent to retard its reception. London served as the architectural clearinghouse for design ideas in America. The Wren city churches and those that followed under an act for "Building . . . Fifty New Churches" (1711) were novel and easily accessible to a large segment of the population of American visitors and English emigrants. Institutionally, the American colonies were part of the Bishop of London's diocese and many of the Anglican clergymen who were licensed to officiate in American pulpits passed through the SPG offices in London. Jacob Henderson, minister to St. Barnabas Parish in Prince George's County was obviously familiar with the metropolis since he reckoned his church to be "as decent as any church in London that I have seen & I have been in most great churches."[31] Images and descriptions of Wren's and Gibbs's churches eventually appeared in architectural books and other publications, making them further accessible to those vestrymen, clergymen, and craftsmen responsible for the design of new parish churches and chapels.[32] Novelty and popularity served to heighten the appeal of those forms in colonies where the Church of England was first gaining a state-supported foothold. By contrast, coming as late as it did in the context of Virginia's ecclesiastical development, the auditory plan made little headway in England's oldest American colony.

The singularity of Virginia's traditional Anglican plan in colonial America was further accentuated by the distinctive manner in which its parish churches were embellished. In the first quarter of the eighteenth century, the architectural expression of this conservative plan crystallized as Virginia vestries developed the forms and degrees of elaboration consonant with the status and ambitions of it chief parishioners.[33] Brick became the material of choice and the manipulation of a standard repertoire of decorative features provided visual guideposts to the relative importance of various elements of the building. The fanciful late-

seventeenth-century artisan mannerist use of shaped gables, decorative projections, pilasters, buttresses, and molded mullions disappeared, replaced by a more restrained decorative wall treatment. Large-scale compass-headed apertures, rubbed and gauged frontispieces, molded watertables, and glazed header walls were combined in such ways as to create a public architecture that was at once distinct and similar to domestic forms. The enlarged apertures provided churches with a public monumentality absent in domestic architecture. The better Anglican parish churches had finely molded brick frontispieces, a feature often found in the grander gentry houses of Virginia. Their appearance in an ecclesiastical setting provided a costly but highly symbolic architectural device to signal the transition from secular to sacred space (fig. 2.13).

Fig. 2.13. West frontispiece, Christ Church, Lancaster County, Virginia, c. 1732. By the early 1720s, gauged, rubbed, and molded frontispieces often decorated the entrances to the best Virginia parish churches. Such ornamental brick frontispieces never appeared in Maryland Anglican churches.

Whereas late colonial Virginia churches displayed a certain restraint evident in specifications calling for "neat and plain" features, Marylanders employed decorative brickwork in slightly different ways to emphasize the orientation and significance of their buildings. The molded frontispiece never made it north of the Potomac. Instead, builders chose to use a variety of techniques to distinguish principal facades. Until the second quarter of the eighteenth century, Virginians occasionally used all glazed header patterns to accentuate the west and south entrance facades, while the two back walls were randomly glazed. After that time, if glazed headers were part of the decorative scheme, they were used on all four walls. In contrast, Marylanders followed the older scheme of selective glazing through the colonial period. The south entrance wall and apse are glazed at St. Luke's, Queen Anne's County, while the west and north walls are unglazed. The west facade of St. Luke's in Talbot County (1717) contains the only entrance into the building and is glazed while the other walls are not. Other glazing patterns could also be used to accentuate a facade. St. James in Baltimore County (1750) has glazed diamond patterns only on its south and west entrance walls. Even bonding patterns varied to provide visual orientation. The west and south entrance walls of St. James, Anne Arundel County, are laid in header bond, while the rear or subsidiary walls are in English bond. The three entrance walls of the Chester Parish chapel of ease, Chestertown, Kent County (1768), are similarly finished in the distinctive all-header bond.

In addition to decorative glazing and bonding patterns, other elements were treated in a similar hierarchical fashion. For example, the apertures on the entrance facades of St. John's, Broad Creek, Prince George's County (c. 1766), are capped with segmental jack arches, while the north side windows have no arches at all. Impost blocks and keystone bricks in compass-headed apertures might be accentuated by being raised beyond the wall surface, or rubbed, glazed, or molded according to their location. Generally, south and west entrances were the most elaborately treated while back walls were simpler, as at St. Mary Anne, North East, Cecil County (1743) (fig. 2.14). The south entrance facade is finished with glazed headers, a string course, and raised keystone

Fig. 2.14. St. Mary Anne's Church, North East, Cecil County, Maryland, 1743. View from the southeast showing the use of glazed headers on the south entrance but not on the east wall. The string course and raised keystone bricks appear on both these facades but not on the back north wall. The south porch tower is a 1904 addition.

bricks over the apex of the compass-headed windows. The string course carries around the west entrance facade and east end and the apertures on these walls are crowned by raised keystone bricks. However, there is no decorative glazing on them. The back or north pulpit wall is plainly treated by comparison, bereft of glazed headers, string, and raised keystones. The hierarchical pattern was often subtle as is evident at All Hallows in Worcester County. The two, long-wall doorways have raised impost blocks and linenfold keystone bricks and soar to near the height of the eaves. The shorter west wall doorway has linenfold keystone bricks but lacks the raised impost blocks. At St. Martin's, Worcester County (1756), the flat arch of the south and west doorways are gauged and rubbed and have a carved ogee pattern on their lower face. However, the south entrance contains a transom light below this arch and the west doorway does not.

By the second quarter of the eighteenth century, the form of the Maryland parish church had taken shape. There was little divergence from the two or three distinctive plans, only elaboration of details in parishes with deeper pockets. There were subregional variations in plans—the double-west entry churches of the lower Eastern Shore, for example—or choices as to whether to add an apse or vestry room to the basic form, but vestrymen now thought in customary terms about plan, scale, and level of finishes. When Virginia builder John Ariss ventured across the Potomac to undertake the construction of Trinity Church, Newport in Charles County in 1752, he merely executed the designs laid out by the parish vestry.[34] The plan and proportions were Maryland ones. So too was the detailing of the brickwork down to the characteristic stepped watertable. When Ariss returned to Virginia to work on public buildings, including a few Anglican churches, he executed them in the architectural language familiar to his clients.[35]

The intersection between design ideas and the architectural execution of forms occurred in the first third of the eighteenth century. Changes continued to occur—the introduction of header bond for principal facades, for example—but the basic plan and elaboration of the Anglican parish church in Maryland was established by this date. Its auditory plan set it apart from it neighbor to the south and its modulated brick detailing varied from the neat and plain of Virginia. Within the Chesapeake, there were pronounced parochial particularities that derived from an Anglican inheritance that had changed over time. Maryland and the rest of America found inspiration in forms that were novel in 1700. By contrast, Virginians had so absorbed an earlier Anglican tradition that even as the style of building changed in the early eighteenth century, vestries saw no need to embrace the auditory form, but followed an older Anglican plan that was by now thoroughly ingrained in a provincial building vocabulary.

Notes

1. Darren Oldridge, *Religion and Society in Early Stuart England* (Aldershot: Ashgate, 1998), 37–59.

2. Nigel Yates, *Buildings, Faith, and Worship: The Liturgical Arrangements of Anglican Churches, 1600–1840* (Oxford: Clarendon Press, 1991), 68–70.

3. Constantly plagued by a shortage of ministers and poorly organized parishes, the Church of England in Virginia struggled to maintain a presence in many parts of the colony. Church historian Edward L. Bond has argued that this weak presence allowed wide latitude toward theology and devotional practices. A de facto "confederal system" developed "over several widely dispersed and divergent local groups, leaving plenty of room in the colony for the beauty of holiness and the plain style of the Puritans." Edward L. Bond, *Damned Souls in a Tobacco Colony: Religion in Seventeenth-Century Virginia* (Macon, Ga.: Mercer Univ. Press, 200), 134.

4. "Michalle Upchurch his Answares to divers queeres sent to him 1649 And Answed 1650," Document 1182; "Richard Collett's Answers" [1647], Document 1121; both in Ferrar Papers 1590–1790, Magdalene College, Cambridge, England. For the strength of Puritan churches in the Southside in Norfolk, Nansemond, and Princess Anne Counties, see Bond, *Damned Souls,* 147–55.

5. See, for example, Petsworth Parish [Gloucester County, Va.] Vestry Book 1677–1793, 3, Oct. 8, 1677, and Christ Church Parish [Middlesex County, Va.] Vestry Book 1663–1767, 57–58, Oct. 3, 1687, Library of Virginia, Richmond, Va.

6. Dell Upton, *Holy Things and Profane: Anglican Parish Churches in Colonial Virginia* (Cambridge: MIT Press, 1986), 47–98. See especially figure 117.

7. Nelson Rightmyer, *Maryland's Established Church* (Baltimore: Church Historical Society, 1956), 19.

8. Rev. John Yeo to the Archbishop of Canterbury, May 25, 1676, *Archives of Maryland,* 72 vols. to date (Baltimore, 1883–), 1887, 5:131.

9. "The Maryland Clergy to the Lord Bishop of London," May 18, 1696, in *Historical Collections Relating to the American Colonial Church,* vol. 4, *Maryland,* ed. William Perry (Hartford, Conn., 1879; reprint, New York: AMS Press, 1969), 8–9.

10. Jon Butler, *Awash in a Sea of Faith: Christianizing the American People* (Cambridge: Harvard Univ. Press, 1990), 51.

11. Claims have been made for a seventeenth-century date for a few Anglican churches, such as the ruinous parish church of St. Peter's, White Marsh, in Talbot County and the heavily restored Trinity Church in Dorchester County. None can be documented as early. The form and detailing of these brick buildings are closely akin to those buildings erected in the first half of the eighteenth century.

12. See Orlando Ridout V, "An Architectural History of Third Haven Meetinghouse," in *Three Hundred Years and More of Third Haven Quakerism,* ed. Kenneth L. Carroll (Easton, Md.: Queen Anne Press, 1984), 67–87.

13. "Return of Romish Priest and Lay Brothers Resident in the Province of Maryland, Together with Returns of Quakers and other Dissenters," May 24, 1698, in Perry, *American Colonial Church* 4:20–23.

14. On the St. Mary's Chapel, see Carl Lounsbury, Willie Graham, and Jonathan Prown, "The Architecture of Seventeenth-Century English Catholicism: The Chapel at St. Mary's City, Maryland," unpublished report for Historic St. Mary's City, Sept. 1993.

15. Patricia Bonomi notes that "owing to the lateness of Maryland's establishment, its vestries never gained the power that Virginia's had achieved in the more fluid climate of the seventeenth century. . . . County courts, rather than vestries, provided for the poor; vestries, however, policed moral infractions committed within their parishes. . . . Most important was the governor's power both to appoint and to induct rectors." Patricia Bonomi, *Under the Cope of Heaven: Religion, Society, and Politics in Colonial America* (New York: Oxford Univ. Press, 1986), 46. In addition, Maryland vestries, like those in South Carolina, had to apply to the general assembly for funding of major building projects.

16. "The Present State of the Protestant Religion in Maryland, 1700," in Perry, *American Colonial Church* 4:33.

17. St. James Parish Vestry Book, 1694–1793, Apr. 29, 1695, Maryland State Archives, Annapolis, Md.

18. Design and construction of St. Anne's were a fitful process overseen in its early stages by Governor Nicholson. Among the exterior features mentioned in early specifications were a series of wooden figures or *terms* "representing Banisters round the eves of the Roof." *Archives of Maryland* 23, Mar. 16, 1698, 396; *Archives of Maryland* 22, 1699, 580–82.

19. Rev. Thomas Bacon to the Secretary, Society for the Propagation of the Gospel, Aug. 4, 1750, in Perry, *American Colonial Church* 4:324.

20. Following ancient Jewish precedent, a number of Protestant denominations in the seventeenth and eighteenth centuries seated men separate from women. At the new Bruton Parish Church in Williamsburg, for example, the vestry in 1716 ordered that "men sit on the North side of the Church and the women" on the south. This segregation sometimes manifested itself architecturally by the presence of separate doors for men and women, a practice clearly seen in Quaker meetinghouses erected after the 1750s. However, this practice was not universal in the southern colonies, and whether specific doors in Anglican parish churches in Maryland were reserved solely for one sex or the other is unknown. W. A. R. Goodwin ed., *The Record of Bruton Parish Church* (Richmond: Dietz Press, 1941), 137.

21. St. Paul's Vestry Book 1733–1819, Oct. 19, 1733, Oct. 27, 1742.

22. The land in Broad Creek Hundred on which the church was built was claimed by both Maryland and Delaware until the mid 1770s. Henry Hutchinson, "Christ Church, Broad Creek and Her Neighbors," *Archaeolog* 23 (Summer 1971): 4–5.

23. Erected in 1732, Durham Parish Church in Charles County measures approximately twenty-nine feet by sixty-three and a half feet, making its ratio 1:2.18.

24. Donald Friary, "The Architecture of the Anglican Church in the Northern American Colonies: A Study of Religious, Social, and Cultural Expression" (Ph.D. diss., Univ. of Pennsylvania, 1971), 325–32, 458, 815.

25. Some conservative congregations insisted on having a chancel screen. Wren was obliged to erect one at St. Peter's, Cornhill (1675–81), for example.

26. Quoted in G. W. O. Addleshaw and Frederick Etchells, *The Architectural Setting of Anglican Worship: An Inquiry into the Arrangements for Public Worship in the Church of England from the Reformation to the Present Day* (London: Faber and Faber, 1948), 249–50.

27. Ibid., 249.

28. Paul Jeffrey, *The City Churches of Sir Christopher Wren* (London: Hambledon Press, 1996), 250–52. See also Kerry Downes, *The Architecture of Wren* (New York: Universe Books, 1982), 55–67.

29. At Christ Church, the side entrances were removed later in the eighteenth century.

30. Kerry Downes, *Hawksmoor* (Cambridge: MIT Press, 1980), 156–83.

31. Jacob Henderson, Rector of St. Barnabas, Queen Anne Parish, Prince George's County, "Answer to Query, 1724," in Perry, *American Colonial Church* 4:209.

32. From the early eighteenth century onward, the iconography of London churches was readily accessible to colonial Americans through the mass printing of individual engravings and bound volumes illustrating the public buildings of London such as R. West and W. H. Toms, *Perspective Views of All the Ancient Churches and Other Buildings in the Cities of London and Westminster* (London, 1736–39), and through architectural treatises such as James Gibbs, *A Book of Architecture,* first published in 1728, which had wide currency in America.

33. Upton, *Holy Things and Profane,* 158–62.

34. Trinity Parish Vestry Book 1750–1795, Oct. 14, 1752, Maryland State Archives, Annapolis, Md.

35. The career of John Ariss has never been fully explored for the lack of adequate documentation. Because of an advertisement in the *Maryland Gazette* in 1751, which noted that he was lately from Great Britain armed with the ability to execute any work in the most up-to-date style of James Gibbs, many historians have been led to believe that Ariss was an English architect. He was actually from a Westmoreland County, Virginia, family and may have spent a year at most in England before placing his advertisement in the Maryland newspaper. After his work for Trinity Parish, Charles County, Ariss worked on other Anglican churches in Virginia. He supplied the designs for a church for Truro Parish, Fairfax County, in 1766 and for Frederick Parish, Frederick County, in 1773. For a fanciful recreation of Ariss's career, see Thomas Waterman, *The Mansions of Virginia 1706–1776* (Chapel Hill: Univ. of North Carolina Press, 1946), 243–48, 407–8. A less-inflated assessment appears in Carl Lounsbury, "John Ariss," in *Dictionary of Virginia Biography,* ed. John Kneebone, Jefferson Looney, Brent Tartar, and Sandra Treadway (Richmond: Library of Virginia, 1998), 1:199–201. For the Virginia churches, see Truro Parish Vestry Book 1723–1785, 94–95, Feb. 4, 1766; Frederick Parish Vestry Book 1764–1780, 53, May 31, 1773, Library of Virginia, Richmond, Va.

3

CONFLATING PAST AND PRESENT IN THE RECONSTRUCTION OF CHARLESTON'S ST. PHILIP'S CHURCH

MAURIE D. MCINNIS

The early antebellum period was a time of transition for Charleston, South Carolina, from the fluid, cosmopolitan society of the late eighteenth century to the fortressed city-state that ultimately led the call for secession in 1860. Marking that transition were important historical moments—the most important being the 1822 Denmark Vesey intended slave insurrection, the Nullification Crisis, and the rise of abolitionism— that helped shape the collective consciousness and that found material expression in the cityscape. At the outset of the antebellum period, power in Charleston was firmly controlled by the city's upper class. As the period progressed, however, their ascendancy was assailed on many fronts.[1]

As external pressures and internals threats rose, upper-class Charlestonians increasingly felt their way of life was in jeopardy. They compared their own political, social, and economic circumstances to Charleston's past. Most painfully, Charlestonians felt their economy was in decline—and in relative terms it was. In 1774, the South Carolina Low Country was by far the wealthiest area in British North America. Economic historians have estimated that in the Charleston district, per free capita wealth was more than ten times greater than that of New England. By 1860, the Low Country still compared favorably to other regions, with a per free capita wealth still more than three times greater than most northern cities. But it was this relative decline that gave rise to the perception of a previous golden age, leaving many nineteenth-century Charlestonians dissatisfied. In trying to recreate the economic miracle of colonial South Carolina, they identified slavery and agriculture as the keys to prosperity. The past gained a mythological importance, and it guided them in shaping their society as they believed it had been, not as it truly was.[2]

This mythology of the golden age of colonial Charleston loomed over the city throughout the antebellum period and significantly affected the decisions made by Charleston's ruling class. Central to their mythology was the planter and a plantation aristocracy. Drawn from English notions of a landed gentry, Charlestonians emphasized their inheritance of an aristocratic order. Despite an eighteenth-century reality in which local merchants were both extremely wealthy and socially prominent, by the nineteenth century, status was most closely linked with landed wealth. Thus mercantile pursuits fell out of favor and the leisured and cultured life of the planter was the goal sought by many. In celebration of their stratified society one Charlestonian wrote, "The possession of an inferior population, and of various castes, makes us, to a certain extent, an aristocracy. Our manners are decidedly those of an aristocracy . . . [and] we would not wish them to be, otherwise."[3] This statement was a revealing comment on how Charlestonians perceived themselves and how they wished to be portrayed. The social and economic pressures of the antebellum period, though, were producing change— slow but inexorable change. The perception of the changing complexion of society, of a sense of loss, of control slipping away, in part accounts for the overly anxious devotion to maintaining the distinctions of class, caste and race in antebellum Charleston.

Unlike other American cities where building booms were generated by both private and public interests serving a variety of constituencies, most of the architectural projects in the 1820s and 1830s serviced only the upper class in Charleston; whether it was elite churches, domestic structures, or social clubs, most of Charleston's architectural energy was generated by private, or at the least only semipublic, endeavors. The few public buildings that were erected served to support and solidify Charleston's social and racial hierarchy, most particularly in projects to control the slave population, such as the Arsenal/Citadel (James Gadsden and Edward Brickell White, 1825–30, 1849), the Guard House (Charles Reichardt, 1838–39), and the Work House (Edward Jones, 1851). Even benevolent organizations, such as the Charleston Orphan House (Thomas Bennett, 1792–94, and enlarged by Jones and Lee, 1853–55), benefited from the political realities of the perceived threat to Charleston's slaveholding society. As historian Barbara Bellows explains, support of the white nonslaveholding population increased whenever threats were perceived. Thus, children at the Orphan House not only had their basic needs met but also "learned [their] place in the urban community and their role in a biracial society."[4]

For the most part, these buildings were written in the grammar of Charleston's eighteenth-century architectural past and overlaid with a new vocabulary of bold, monumental classical ornament, thus conflating past with present. This combined architectural vocabulary communicated a unity of shared heritage and goals. For Charleston's aristocracy, the classical vocabulary represented their shared classical education, world travel, allegiance to an aristocratic society, and their commitment to preserving those privileges. The consistency in building grammar and vocabulary communicated their class unity.[5]

Of all of the buildings erected in antebellum Charleston, none more clearly proclaimed Charleston's conflation of past and present, and Charleston's commitment to the inherited social hierarchy than the reconstruction of St. Philip's Episcopal Church. When a fire broke out in a brothel in the middle of February 1835, heavy winds spread the fire rapidly. Most of the area in danger consisted of wooden houses, "of small value, and occupied by persons in moderate circumstances, and many of them by persons of colour," and wooden commercial buildings such as those of the fruiterers on Market Street and the Livery Stables on Church Street. Both St. Philip's Church and the Circular Congregational Church were surrounded by large burial grounds and considered relatively safe from fire. As a precaution, however, a slave was lowered by a rope onto the roof of the Congregational Church to extinguish any flames that might erupt. No such precaution was taken at St. Philip's. Before long a spark landed on its dome and soon "wreathed the steeple—constituting a magnificent though melancholy spectacle, and forming literally a pillar of fire." Another witness spoke of watching the dome burn slowly downward and then fall with a crash—the flames from the tower resembling the eruptions of a volcano. At last, the entire body of the church was engulfed with flames and left a smoldering ruin.[6]

Immediately the mourning process began; newspapers bemoaned the loss of the "Old Church." It was Charleston's oldest church (c. 1711–23); it was also one of America's most lavish colonial Anglican churches. An undated drawing of the church (fig. 3.1) illustrates its most distinguishing characteristics: the three Tuscan porticoes at the entrance of the church and the octagon domed tower. Visitors to the city commented on the building's fine architectural design and its emotional impact. As Edmund Burke wrote in 1777, St. Philip's "is spacious, and executed in a very handsome taste, exceeding everything of that kind which we have in America." Architect Robert Mills, not generally generous when describing South Carolina's architectural heritage, designated it as having "more of design in its arrangement than any other of our ancient buildings erected here." He also remarked on its emotional power, noting that "the effect produced upon the mind in viewing this edifice is that of solemnity and awe, from its massy character: when you enter under its roof, the lofty arches, porticoes, arcades, and pillars which support it, cast a sombre shade over the whole interior, and induce the mind to serious contemplation, and religious reverence."[7]

This building was revered as much more than a religious structure. For most Charlestonians, this building served as an evocative symbol of the city's past; for others it served as a symbol of their own social position within the city. The day after the fire, the writer in the *Courier* lamented the loss of the "Old Church." To him, the building served as a "hallowed link between the *past* and the present—with its monumental memorials of the beloved and honored dead, and its splendid new organ." The writer for the *Mercury* was equally struck by the evocative power of the past: "Its antique walls and arches were richly crowded with monuments that carried the mind far back into our revolutionary and colonial history. Every one felt in its fall, that a link was harshly sundered in the chain of cherished associations." The connection between

Fig. 3.1. St. Philip's Church, Charleston, South Carolina, ink on silk drawing, date unknown. Private collection. Courtesy of the Museum of Early Southern Decorative Arts.

St. Philip's and Charleston's past in the minds of Charlestonians was due to much more than its position as the oldest religious structure in town. A circular addressed to the community at large, printed only two days after the fire, called for city wide support:

Because the Church . . . is identified with the colonial, revolutionary, and ecclesiastical history of the whole country. We appeal to the inhabitants to South Carolina, because it is more particularly *their* history and biography, of which this Church was the memorial. We appeal to the citizens of Charleston, because this Church was an honorable monument of the taste, and the public spirit, and piety of its founders—it was the ornament most attractive to the stranger, which every eye greeted, and the imagination and the heart must miss, whenever the vicinity is approached—a great moral monument . . . which all would be delighted and benefited by beholding risen from its ashes. . . . We appeal most especially to the members of the Protestant Episcopal Church, because this edifice decisively marked . . . the high intellectual character of their fathers in the faith, by whom it was built, and of their immediate ancestors, by whom it was preserved and improved from time to time, and because its restoration will be an evidence of their solicitude, that the principles and institutions of the Church, in which they were educated . . . may be transmitted unimpaired to posterity.[8]

In citing the arguments for broad support in the rebuilding of St. Philip's, the authors outlined the many levels of association which the structure had for all Charlestonians, not just parishioners. It served as a symbol of the history of the colony and the Revolutionary War; it served as a reminder of the religious commitment of the colony's founders and the primacy of the Episcopal Church; it served as the temporal connection between Charlestonians and their ancestors for it was in that building where many worshiped, married and were buried. The symbolic affiliation between past and present was reinforced by the memorialization of past individuals in the monuments which adorned the pillars of the old church.

This collection of memorials led one writer to elevate St. Philip's to an elite rank among the world's churches. He suggested that while the names of St. Peter's, Notre Dame, Westminster Abbey and St. Paul's were well known, and "deeply engraven on the mind of every pensive admirer of antiquity," for those who have been unable to visit them, "St. Philip's may well be substituted." Because it was here, under the roof of St. Philip's, that one had the opportunity to ponder the actions of the illustrious dead; because it was here, "amidst the mausolea of heroes," that the latent spark of patriotism might be kindled. The article illustrated the tendency in the 1820s to idolize and mythologize the heroes of the Revolutionary War, as it recounted the many memorials to Revolutionary War heroes contained in the church, including that to Gen. William Moultrie, that "old Roman," only recently erected and others that extolled their classical virtues of patriotism and sacrifice. It was the combination of the building's antiquity in the city's history, judged the "greatest ornament of our city," by one writer, and the many monuments and memorials to the city's heroes, and the many associations held by Charlestonians of

St. Philip's as the place of worship for many of those illustrious dead, that made the building so important in the minds of many Charlestonians.[9]

Just as St. Philip's was a symbol of the past history of the city and the state, it was also an evocative physical embodiment of the power of the Episcopal Church and of Episcopalians in Charleston. Only a quarter of the city's wealthy worshiped at the city's Presbyterian and Congregational Churches while more than half worshiped at the Episcopalian churches. Even more significantly, of the city's individuals with modest to high status, more than two-thirds were Episcopalian. Thus when St. Philip's burned, many felt that what was lost was much more than a building. For many, the building was a powerful symbol of their personal status in the city. This was true for both members and nonmembers of the congregation. For members, the reasons are obvious. For nonmembers, however, the church held similar evocative potential. With Charleston's society so dedicated to preserving rigid stratification and maintaining an aristocratic order, St. Philip's Church served as a looming symbol of that English derived social order. Built with English revenues when South Carolina was still a royal colony, the church thus served as a powerful reminder of the city's English past. As the place of worship for so many individuals with upper-class status and economic power, the church symbolized the continuance of that tradition in contemporary Charleston.[10]

The symbolism of St. Philip's was so powerful, that when the vestry met the day after the fire the following resolution was offered by Nathaniel Russell Middleton: "Resolved that in the opinion of the vestry, a new Church should be built upon the same plan and on the same foundation as the old with the addition of a Chancel." It was unanimously approved two days later, and the following week it was offered to the congregation. If there was any disagreement on this proposal, none was recorded, and the building committee moved forward with those plans. In voting to rebuild the church exactly as it was, the members of St. Philip's parish confirmed the power of family history. A comment made by the Reverend Paul Trapier, the rector of St. Michael's Episcopal Church, could just as easily have been made about St. Philip's: "I had taken charge of a congregation made up on large part of old families, priding themselves upon ancestry and attached to the church rather because their fathers had been there than from enlightened acquaintance with its principles, and consequently bent upon going on as those before them had gone, whether there was reason for so doing or not." Similarly, the parishioners of St. Philip's were "bent upon going on as those before them" by reconstructing their venerable edifice.[11]

In voting to rebuild the church as it was, Charlestonians also followed English precedent. An editorial written shortly after the fire supported the reconstruction of St. Philip's according the original plan. The writer argued that even if the "most magnificent church which has ever been," were constructed, that Charlestonians would still weep when they thought of the original St. Philip's. Thus it was important to try to "revive" some of the feelings and meanings associated with the old St. Philip's by building the new one in the same style. To support his argument, he turned to English precedent, reminding readers that a "like attempt" had recently been made at York-Minster "with the most gratifying success." While this assertion lent support to their plan, the situation was not truly comparable. The fire that damaged York-Minster only destroyed the woodwork in the choir and a section of the roof; the entirety of St. Philip's lay in ruins. With this editorial though, the reconstruction of St. Philip's acquired the authority of English precedent, a connection historically celebrated by the city's elite.[12]

Before construction began, a letter to the editor in the *Charleston Mercury* criticized the plan of reconstructing the old church. The pseudonymous "Citizen" urged the Charleston City Council to take this opportunity to straighten Church Street. The controversy arose from the fact that the old St. Philip's projected into Church Street and forced that street to bend around it (map 3.1). It was suggested that this was a deliberate decision made when constructing the church. In the early eighteenth century, St. Philip's stood at the northern edge of the city. By placing the church across Church Street, "Citizen" argued, the building acted as both a visual termination to the street and as a barrier of defense against Indian incursions. Whether there is any truth in this story or whether it is purely apocryphal is not known. Nevertheless, as the city expanded northward, Church Street was extended around the projecting portico of the church and was narrower at that point than elsewhere on the street. Thus after the destruction of St. Philip's it was suggested by some that Church Street be not only widened but also straightened. The first public call for this action rather exaggerated the potential difficulties posed by the old church:

> To the City Council of Charleston—GENTLEMEN,—The destruction of St Philip's Church by fire, puts it into your power to prevent the contemplated re-building of that Church in its former situation. It is demanded of you by the concurrent voice of the whole community (some of the Church members excepted.) When you remember, gentlemen, the number of lives that have been lost by persons thrown from horseback and their brains dashed out against the pillars of that Church, humanity calls upon you to arrest that mad project; and as guardians of the public welfare, it is a duty which you owe to your fellow citizens. There could not a better opportunity than the present for straitening that street. Let the Church be remunerated for the loss of ground, and they could not have any reason to object to the improvement. A CITIZEN.

Even the writer's inflated claims of bodily injury did not diminish the many objections raised by St. Philip's parishioners to the straightening of Church Street, and the resulting discussion over this issue was contentiously debated in Charleston. Only a few days later a member of St. Philip's congregation responded to "A Citizen." While he ridiculed the other writer's implication of danger and death, he offered no reasons why the church should not be moved: "Messrs. Editors, inquire of 'A Citizen,' . . . whether it might not be an improvement to have our brick walls . . . well padded, stuffed and cushioned? . . . If this cannot be done, I would have you apply to our humane city council . . . to raze our city, and rebuild another on a new and improved plan. If not, at least . . . stretch all out in a straight line, then a man, especially when sober, may drive in perfect safety of brain, limb, or cranium." It soon became apparent, however, that the anonymous writer of the first article was not alone in his desire to have Church Street straightened and widened; the debate continued.[13]

What emerged was a contest between different factions of the Charleston community. City council decided to "enquire into the expediency" of widening Church Street at the site of St. Philip's; shortly thereafter they met with the vestry of St. Philip's. The vestry's answer was defiant. They responded that since the decision to build the church on the same site and on the same foundations as the old one was one agreed to by the congregation and since money had been raised according to that plan, that they did not have the power to make any changes. The council was not, however, moved by the vestry's argument and thus voted eleven to one that it was desirable to widen Church Street. The eleven votes in favor of the changes came from individuals who, not surprisingly, were not members of the St. Philip's congregation. The only dissenting vote was placed by Thomas Middleton, who himself was probably a member of St. Philip's, and whose brother, Arthur, was on the building committee at St.

Philip's. The council then instructed the city surveyor to submit a plan for the widening of Church Street so that the church would be thrown back to the eastern line of the street, and that the plans be sent to the standing state-appointed Commission for Opening and Widening Streets, Lanes, and Alleys for their approval. Instead of approving the wishes of city council, however, the commissioners contradicted their findings and submitted a report detailing their objections. After examining the site of the church, the ground to its rear, and the graves that would be disturbed in order to accommodate the straightening of Church Street, the commissioners rejected the forty-eight feet suggested by city council. In explaining their decision they cited that what public benefit would accrue did not compensate "for the great injury" that the congregation would face. The forty-eight feet recommended by the council would not only necessitate the building of a substantially new foundation but also push the church over the graves "which are consecrated by feelings the dearest to the human heart" and place the new building near a narrow alley, thus placing it once again in danger of being destroyed by fire. In response to the charges of the public convenience, they answered that they knew of no accidents due to the winding path of the street. In

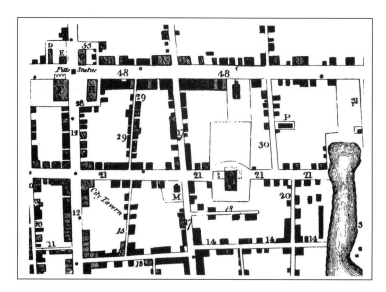

Map 3.1. Detail from "Ichnography of Charleston, South Carolina," 1788, showing how Church St. (21) curved around the portico of St. Philip's Church (North is at the right). Courtesy of the Library of Congress.

response to the charge that it would improve the appearance of the street, they retorted that the classic portico of the church must surely be more attractive than an ordinary private house. As a compromise, they suggested moving the church building back twenty-two feet, which would place the columns of the west portico over the eastern sidewalk of Church Street as they formerly were and bring the North and South porticoes nearly in line with the east line of the street. By moving it back twenty-two feet, it would be possible to widen the street to its normal width of fifty feet but not to straighten it. Since this move would involve a heavy expense in the laying of new foundations for the church, the commissioners suggested that the congregation be compensated by the city.[14]

The intervention of the commissioners in what should have been a local matter is especially significant when one considers the composition of the members of that body. These commissioners were appointed not by local officials, but by the state legislature; the two groups came from widely different social and economic classes. Charleston City Council in the middle of the 1830s was dominated by middling merchant interests; there were few professionals and planters involved with city politics. The commissioners appointed by the state legislature, however, were drawn mostly from the city's upper class. Even more significantly, many were Episcopalians, several were members of St. Philip's congregation, and a few were vestrymen. When it was decided to investigate the decision made by the council concerning the straightening of Church Street, commissioner and chairman of the St. Philip's vestry, William Mason Smith, was present, along with commissioners and vestrymen Joseph Manigault and Joseph W. Toomer. The influence of these individuals was angrily noted by an editorial writer: "A serious public nuisance, we are informed, must not be abated, because the feelings of a small portion of the community are in the way. . . . It is time they [the public] should know that it is not the representatives of the public, but of St. Philip's Church, who address them through this report."[15]

At the heart of this debate was not whether Church Street was to be widened, but who possessed the power to enact their will in the city of Charleston

and to control the construction of space in the city. A compromise was reached, but the members of St. Philip's congregation were the symbolic victors. True, they had to move their church back twenty-two feet, but the portico of the church still projected over the side walk and the road was still forced to curve around the building. Thus, the only thing gained spatially by the city was a wider street while St. Philip's Church was able to use the majority of the previous foundation, disturb little of its burial grounds, and physically rebuild a structure that maintained its previous relationship with the city, serving as a visual terminus to Church Street.

The debate over this issue did not disappear quietly. Many other articles appeared, for the most part evenly split between adopting the compromise of twenty-two feet or pushing for the full forty-eight. After evaluating the claims made by the commissioners in favor of the twenty-two foot compromise, the pseudonymous "A.B.C." warned, "It is obvious that the deformity and nuisance of having a Church in the midst of one of our streets must be barred at once, or it will take its station there forever. The members of the Church say it shall stand. Will the citizens countenance such selfishness?" Another writer suggested they move the church back but make it wider in order to accommodate all the congregation. Several letters were published arguing that the church will serve as an ornament, not a detriment, to the prospect of Church Street and that the congregation had already sacrificed enough. Ultimately, the interests of the church prevailed, and the new St. Philip's was built with its portico projecting over the public sidewalk on Church Street. For the right-of-way to foot passengers, the city paid the church twenty-five hundred dollars.[16]

While the debate continued about where the building was to be placed, the building committee moved forward with plans to reconstruct their venerable edifice. They first contracted with Frederick Wesner, a local builder and architect, to make plans and drawings of the old St. Philip's, "for the purpose of erecting another as much like it as possible." Upon discovering that Wesner had made little progress, however, the building committee contacted Robert

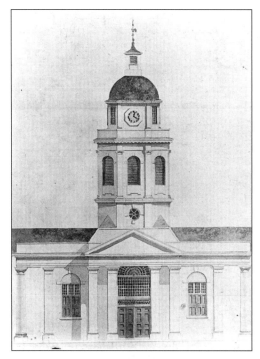

Fig. 3.2. St. Philip's Church, elevation by an unknown draftsman, perhaps made soon after the building was destroyed in 1835. Courtesy of The Charleston Museum, Charleston, South Carolina.

Mills, "who promptly came on from Washington and supplied the designs herewith submitted." Despite having been absent from Charleston for more than five years, Mills, like Wesner, was extremely familiar with the old St. Philip's, because both had been engaged to work on the building in the past. At the request of the building committee of St. Philip's Church, Mills made a series of plans and drawings of the old St. Philip's. These were discussed by a subcommittee and then submitted to the congregation for approval: "[They] are now submitted to the Congregation with a recommendation that they be adopted as some slight deviations and additions have been made."[17]

An unsigned drawing (fig. 3.2) may be one of those executed by Mills after the destruction of the church. If this drawing was intended to guide the reconstruction of the church, it differs in one respect from the church as it was eventually rebuilt. The outer columns of the western portico were originally attached to the building with an arch. In this drawing, the shadow of the arch is visible to the left of the portico. As the church was built after the fire, the arches were not reconstructed. This may have been viewed as better suited to its role as the public sidewalk on the eastern edge of Church Street.

Only a month after receiving plans and drawings from Mills, amateur artist and lawyer John Blake White offered the following resolution opposed to rebuilding the interior exactly as it was: "Whereas much inconvenience has been long felt by many of the Worshiper in the late St. Philip's Church before its destruction in consequence of the heavy pillars which intercepted their sight and hearing . . . be it therefore Resolved, that the massy pillars and pilasters which formerly supported the Arch and ceiling be dispensed with, and that a more light or modern interior, be substituted for the same." White's comments unleashed a vigorous debate that was waged in the newspapers and periodicals, at church meetings and in drawing rooms. White's particular complaint was that the large piers in the body of the church obscured the vision of many worshipers.[18]

The best surviving image of the interior of the church is one painted, ironically, by White. Shortly after the fire, White painted an interior scene of the church (fig. 3.3) that he offered to the vestry for exhibition, allowing them to keep the proceeds for the rebuilding of the church. Several editorials praised both White's painting and his motives. The view shown placed the spectator entering the church under the

Fig. 3.3. John Blake White, *Interior of St. Philip's*, 1835. Courtesy of St. Philip's Church, Charleston, South Carolina.

organ loft, with the congregation seated and the Reverend Dr. Gadsden in the pulpit. Newspaper editorials commented on the accuracy of the image both in capturing the somber tone of the interior and the individual monuments that decorated the piers. The painting also corresponds with a description written in 1820 by Frederick Dalcho capturing the salient decorative and structural features of the interior:

> The roof is arched except over the galleries; two rows of Tuscan pillars support five arches on each side. . . . The Pillars are ornamented on the inside, with fluted Corinthian pilasters, whose capitals are as high as the cherubim in relief, over the centre of each arch. . . . Each pillar is now ornamented with a piece of monumental sculpture . . . finely executed by some of the first artists in England. These add greatly to the beauty and solemnity of the edifice. There is no chancel; the communion table stands within the body of the church. The east end is a paneled wainscot, ornamented with Corinthian pilasters supporting the cornice of a fan-light.[19]

Even though White urged a change to the interior, his accurately rendered and evocative painting was seen by at least one commentator as a valuable tool in the debate to rebuild the interior of St. Philip's as it was: "The friends of the Church owe Mr. W. a debt of gratitude . . . for awakening and keeping alive pleasing and salutary reminiscences, and in particular for developing the appropriate magnificence of the lost building, and thus justifying the general desire and determination that the new building shall be a copy, not an original, or in other words as much like Mr. White's noble picture as possible."[20]

After White's resolution was offered, the congregation decided to adjourn and discuss the matter at the following meeting. The subject of discussion was advertised in the newspapers, and the result was an unusually large number of attendees. The style of the interior of the church obviously elicited great interest and strong feelings—so much so that no agreement was reached at the next meeting either. Finally, at a meeting of the congregation held at the end of August, the chairman of the vestry, William Mason Smith, responded to the numerous calls for an alteration to the interior. He acknowledged that many had called for a removal of the "massive piers," but since

"the internal appearance of the Church will be changed, and the value of different pews effected thereby it is proper and right that the matter be referred to all who are members." He then established a committee of twelve persons, six in favor of altering the interior and six opposed, to canvass the members of St. Philip's. Only a vote of three-fifths would result in a change to the interior.[21]

The debate about the interior centered on the piers. One of the complaints frequently encountered was that they kept some parishioners from seeing the minister in the pulpit; another was that the piers disrupted many pews. Supporters of the piers responded that only during the sermon is the sightline a problem because you should have your head bowed in prayer at other times. Not all who sat behind the piers were dissatisfied: "Now my pew happened to have a large pillar in it; I like that pillar; I turned my face towards it during the prayers, and sat behind it when the lessons and sermon were read, and thus my attention was not liable to be distracted by passing occurrences, and I was exempt from being gazed at by my neighbours." Another proponent of maintaining the interior of the old St. Philip's rejected the notion that modern architecture was superior to ancient. To buttress his argument, he offered the following comparison: "Let the old large private dwellings in Charleston be compared with those more recently built, and I am very much mistaken, if the general, as well as the scientific, and the tasteful eye will not give the former the preference. The comparison holds good in favour of the old public buildings also, and more particularly of the Churches." Additionally, he rejected the argument that modern architecture eschewed the massy pillars which distinguished St. Philip's interior because they had only been recently implemented in Benjamin Latrobe's Roman Cathedral in Baltimore (1804–18). About this church, the writer attributed its "solemn and sublime effect" to the "sweeping arches and massy, well-proportioned pillars, on which they rest." Many also felt that the beauty and solemnity of St. Philip's was due to the pillars and arches.[22]

When the cornerstone was laid on November 12, 1835, plans were to rebuild St. Philip's along the old plan, twenty-two feet back from its original site. Apparently, when the committee appointed to secure votes visited the members of the church, the majority were in favor of retaining the original interior plan. The capstone was inscribed with a history of the buildings:

ST. PHILIP'S CHURCH
THE FIRST EDIFICE, BUILT OF WOOD 1681, ON THE
SITE NOW OCCUPIED BY ST.
MICHAEL'S CHURCH, WAS TAKEN DOWN 1727.
THE SECOND, BUILT OF BRICK, WAS COMMENCED 1710–11;
FINISHED 1723, AND BURNT FEBRUARY 15,
1835. THIS THIRD, COVERING THE GREATER PART
OF THE SITE, WILL BE OF THE DIMENSIONS AND
ORDER OF ARCHITECTURE,
AND AFTER THE PLAN OF THE
SECOND, WITH THE ADDITION OF A CHANCEL.

Some parishioners were not willing to let the matter rest. In May 1836 the issue was once again raised in the Charleston press. The pseudonymous "Charity" advocated altering the interior of the church, urging readers to reconsider the issue now that emotions had subsided. The points enumerated by "Charity" in favor of changing the interior included (1) a "more simple, chaste and beautiful [interior], more suitable to our climate, and in better conformity with our taste and habits"; (2) an interior cheaper to build; (3) an interior more quickly built; (4) an interior which saves space; and (5) an interior which allows a third of the congregation to see and better hear the minister. A few weeks later "Charity" offered additional arguments in favor of altering the interior: "Let no one flatter himself or others with the belief, that they will ever 'see again the interior, the solemn, awe-inspiring St. Philip's,' as it was," for a number of changes have already been planned. These included raising the body of the church three feet, lowering the pews, and, most significant, adding a chancel.[23]

There were those who still clung tightly to the plan of rebuilding St. Philip's as it was. One supporter, who believed that it was the pillars and arches that gave the church its "grandeur and solemnity," did not care if it cost five thousand dollars more and took six months longer. In direct response to "Charity," he revealed the importance of recreating an interior that was reminiscent of the original church, if not an exact replica:

Dispense with the arches and pillars, and make it as "simple, chaste and beautiful" as you please, it will not

be St. Philip's—the solemn, awe-inspiring St. Philip's: and I should be as well satisfied to worship God in the humble building in which we now meet for that purpose, as in one, which however it might approve itself to the eye of modern taste, yet bearing no similitude to the former venerable temple, would present nothing when I entered its doors to aid in awakening through the sense of sight, the thoughts and feeling appropriate to the sanctuary, or to make me feel in some degree at least, that I was again in the Church of my fathers.[24]

To this writer, and likely many others, the question of the interior architecture of the church was not one of convenience, or modernity, or cost, or time, or acoustics and vision; no, the question of the interior architecture of the church was one which centered on their collective past. As the oldest church in Charleston, as the first seat of Episcopalian power in the city, and as a symbol of familial lineage and the city's history, prosperity, and taste, the burning of St. Philip's had severed an important link in the chain of past associations. The debate over the interior was really a debate over the symbolic importance of architecture.

The resolution of this debate between those who wished to resurrect the symbol of St. Philip's almost as if the fire had never occurred, and those who called for a change was finally achieved when the congregation was offered specific choices. Instead of the vague discussion about change, the supervising architect, Joseph Hyde, drafted a series of three designs and a letter from "Charity" urged members to view them:

Mr. Hyde, that Architect, employed to superintend the building, has politely executed a drawing of the interior of the Church, according to the proposed plan of improvement, with corinthian columns, instead of the doric pillars. He has also prepared a draft, with columns and arches, according to the plan of one of the most beautiful Churches in England, *St. Martin's in the Fields,* and according to which it was originally the design to have built St. Philip's Church; but from certain causes (now unknown,) that plan was departed from. . . . [He has also prepared one in] which the pillars are retained.[25]

Now members of the congregation had three designs from which to choose. Apparently, this concrete representation of another alternative was sufficient to

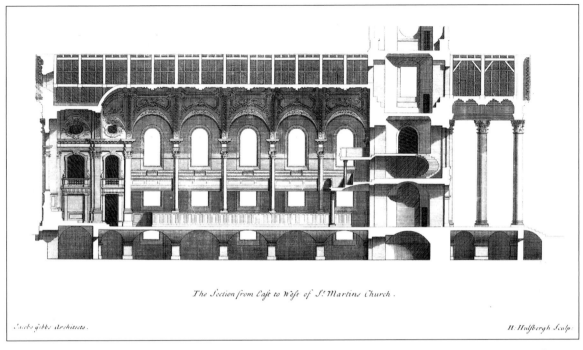

The Section from East to West of St Martins Church.

Iacob: Gibbs: Architecto.   H: Hulsbergh Sculp:

Fig. 3.4. James Gibbs, *A Book of Architecture* (1723), plate 5, "A Section from East to West of St. Martin's Church." Courtesy of the Albert H. Small Special Collections Library, University of Virginia Library.

convince enough parishioners to compromise and vote for a change on the interior.

After a community-wide debate over architectural styles on a scale not previously known in Charleston, and not common in America, it is important to consider why the congregation might have finally decided to change the interior of the new St. Philip's.

Before them were three plans: the first a modern design with Corinthian columns, probably Greek revival in design; the second after James Gibbs's St. Martin's-in-the-Fields (fig. 3.4); the third based on the old interior. The interior plan adopted (fig. 3.5) was, significantly, not the most modern one but the one "according to the plan of . . . *St. Martin's in the Fields.*" One of the compelling reasons may have been the belief that the second St. Philip's was originally intended to have been based on this church. Thus, while having the advantage of removing the pillars and silencing the critics, one could rationalize that the decision to change may not be rebuilding St. Philip's as it was, but it was at least rebuilding St. Philip's as it was meant to be. At the very least, St. Martin's in-the-Fields could be viewed as

a reasonable alternative because the second St. Philip's was a contemporary of St. Martin's. It allowed for the retention of many elements of the original interior of the church, including the arches, the cherubim at the head of the arches, and the barrel-vaulted ceiling. More important, however, the congregation of St. Philip's

Fig. 3.5. Interior of St. Philip's before the chancel addition in 1920. Photograph by George S. Cook. Courtesy of the Valentine Museum, Richmond, Virginia.

Fig. 3.6. Church Street, Charleston, looking north to St. Philip's Church (Joseph Hyde, 1835–38; steeple by Edward Brickell White, 1847–50). In the right foreground is the Huguenot Church (Edward Brickell White, 1844–45). Photograph by George W. Johnson. Courtesy of Gibbes Museum of Art/Carolina Art Association.

affirmed their allegiance with the past by selecting St. Martin's, the most influential ecclesiastical building in the English-speaking world in the eighteenth century.

The construction of the third St. Philip's (fig. 3.6) is an extraordinary example of community self-definition. While there were changes made to the interior of the structure, it is important to note that no one called for a change to the exterior. Consider, for a moment, consider how remarkable it is that when given the opportunity in 1835 to construct an entirely new church, when given the opportunity to work with Charleston native Robert Mills, one of the nation's leading architects, or with German architect Charles Reichardt, who came to the city in 1836, the congregation of St. Philip's chose to rebuild the former structure, not to build a modern church. Contemporary church architecture, mostly in temple form without a spire, was already well-represented in Charleston.

Robert Mills first introduced this form to the city in his First Baptist Church (fig. 3.7). Other churches followed this model, including one new evangelical Episcopalian parish, St. Peter's, completed in 1834. Its Greek revival interior, noted for its "Christian simplicity," was lauded, by one opponent to the St. Philip's

pillars, as an appropriate model for St. Philip's. To most of the St. Philip's vestry, however, St. Peter's was not an appropriate symbolic precedent.[26]

When the largely aristocratic parish of St. Philip's chose to rebuild their church as it had been they defined the present through the lens of the past and asserted their position within the city's hierarchical structure. When they chose to base their interior on that of St. Martin's-in-the-Fields, they confirmed their cultural identity with England and their stylistic preference for eighteenth-century English classicism. Although St. Philip's reconstruction participates in a broader practice among the city's elite, no single construction project in Charleston better illustrates the struggle of Charleston's aristocracy to maintain their social and cultural hegemony in the city. With the resurrection of its ancient edifice, St. Philip's Church was able to maintain its physical dominion over the prospect of Church Street and to assert its figurative dominion over the city.

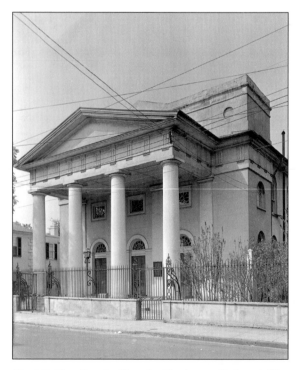

Fig. 3.7. First Baptist Church, Charleston (Robert Mills, 1818–22). Photograph by Carl Julien. Courtesy of Gibbes Museum of Art/Carolina Art Association.

Notes

This chapter is drawn from my dissertation, "The Politics of Taste: Classicism in Charleston, South Carolina, 1815–1840" (Ph.D. diss. Yale Univ., 1996). For guidance and suggestions on that, I owe special thanks to Edward S. Cooke and Bernard L. Herman. For comments on this manuscript, I would like to thank Louis P. Nelson and the anonymous readers.

1. For a general history, see Walter Edgar, *South Carolina: A History* (Columbia: Univ. of South Carolina Press, 1998) and George C. Rogers Jr., *Charleston in the Age of the Pinckneys* (Columbia: Univ. of South Carolina Press, 1980). For recent work on the Denmark Vesey insurrection, see Michael P. Johnson, "Denmark Vesey and His Co-Conspirators," *William and Mary Quarterly* 58 (4) (Oct. 2001): 915–76, and Edward A. Pearson, *Designs Against Charleston: The Trail Record of the Denmark Vesey Slave Conspiracy of 1822* (Chapel Hill: Univ. of North Carolina Press, 1999). For the Nullification Crisis, see Richard E. Ellis, *The Union at Risk: Jacksonian Democracy, States' Rights, and the Nullification Crisis* (New York: Oxford Univ. Press, 1987), and William W. Freehling, *Prelude to Civil War: The Nullification Controversy in South Carolina, 1816–1836* (New York: Harper & Row, 1966).

2. For more on the economic history of South Carolina, see Peter A. Coclanis, *The Shadow of a Dream: Economic Life and Death in the South Carolina Low Country, 1670–1920* (New York: Oxford Univ. Press, 1989). The statistics quoted here are taken from 125, 116, 128. In 1860, Charleston's per free capita wealth was more than $2,200, per capita nearly $800, while in Massachusetts per capita wealth was just over $625 and New York's under $600.

3. "Domestic Improvement," *Southern Literary Journal*, n.s., 3, no. 1 (Jan. 1838): 2–3.

4. See McInnis, "Politics of Taste," 139–68, 177–205, and Barbara L. Bellows, *Benevolence Among Slaveholders: Assisting the Poor in Charleston, 1670–1860* (Baton Rouge: Louisiana State Univ. Press, 1993), 120–23, quotation on 122.

5. On the importance of Europe as a cultural fountainhead, see Maurie D. McInnis et al., *In Pursuit of Refinement: Charlestonians Abroad, 1740–1860* (Columbia: Univ. of South Carolina Press, 1999) and McInnis, "Politics of Taste."

6. I would like to thank C. Patton Hash, formerly research consultant, at the South Carolina Historical Society for sharing his St. Philip's research with me. Hash compiled a list of newspaper articles concerning the burning and reconstruction of St. Philip's and a summary of the contents in many of the vestry and congregational meetings. *Charleston Courier,* Feb. 16, 1835; *Charleston Mercury,* Feb. 16, 1835.

7. For more on the original St. Philip's, see Louis P. Nelson, "The Material World: Anglican Visual Culture in Colonial South Carolina" (Ph.D. diss., Univ. of Delaware, 2001), especially 243–54. Edmund Burke, *An Account of the European Settlements in America,* 2 vols. (London, 1777), 2:258, quoted in Frederick Dalcho, *An Historical Account of the Protestant Episcopal Church in South Carolina* (Charleston, S.C.: E. Thayer, 1820), 123. Robert Mills, *Statistics of South Carolina Including a View of Its Natural, Civil, and Military History, General and Particular* (Charleston, S.C.: Hurlburt and Lloyd, 1826), 405.

8. *Charleston Courier,* Feb. 16, 1835; the *Circular of the Congregation of St. Philip's Church* was printed in broadside form and was printed in full in the *Charleston Mercury,* Feb. 27, 1835, and the *Charleston Courier,* Mar. 4, 1835.

9. *Southern Literary Gazette* 1, no. 2 (1828): 166–71; *Charleston Mercury,* Feb. 17, 1835.

10. The estimation of wealth and status and church affiliation are detailed in William H. Pease and Jane H. Pease, *The Web of Progress: Private Values and Public Styles in Boston and Charleston, 1828–1843* (New York: Oxford Univ. Press, 1985), 237.

11. St. Philip's Vestry Minutes, Feb. 16, 1835, South Carolina Historical Society (hereafter cited as SCHS). It is also possible that the Mr. Middleton named was Nathaniel's father, Arthur, who was also active in church affairs. Reverend Paul Trapier, "Incidents in My Life: The Autobiography of the Rev. Paul Trapier, S. T. D. with Some of His Letters," in *Publications of the Dalcho Historical Society of the Diocese of South Carolina,* ed. George W. Williams (Charleston, S.C.: Dalcho Historical Society, 1954), 26.

12. *Charleston Courier,* Mar. 4, 1835; the fire at York-Minster and the reconstruction of the choir by Robert Smirke are discussed in the *Monthly Supplement of the Penny Magazine,* Dec. 31, 1832.

13. St. Philip's Vestry Minutes, Feb. 18, 1835; St. Philip's Congregational Minutes, Feb. 23, 1835, SCHS; for more on

the clearing of the old site and the construction of a temporary building, see St. Philip's Vestry Minutes, Feb. 18, 1835; St. Philip's Congregational Minutes, Feb. 23, and Mar. 12, 17, 1835; *Charleston Courier,* May 5, 1835; "St. Philip's Church," *Southern Literary Journal and Magazine of the Arts,* 1, no. 5 (Jan. 1836): 365; *Charleston Mercury,* Apr. 21, 1835; *Charleston Courier,* Apr. 25, 1835.

14. *Charleston Courier,* June 12, 1835, reported the various resolutions and proceedings of city council with regard to the widening of Church Street; the resolution adopted by the vestry as a response to city council can be found in St. Philip's Vestry Minutes, May 19, 1835, SCHS, and *Charleston Courier,* June 12, 1835; Report of Mitchell King to the Commissioners for Opening and Widening Streets, Lanes and Alleys, June 6, 1835, SCHS; the report is also printed in the *Charleston Courier,* June 12, 1835.

15. *Charleston Mercury,* June 16, 1835; for more about the composition of city council and its change over time, see Jane and William Pease, *Web of Progress,* 181–82. For the years 1828–32, 1833–39, and 1839–44, respectively, merchants comprised 22, 52, and 64 percent of the city council; mechanics, 12, 5, and 0 percent; professional men, 51, 31, and 20 percent. The shift in status was, in the same periods, from 65 to 49 to 31 percent; those of notable wealth decreased similarly from 49 to 38 to 31 percent. Taken from Pease and Pease, *Web of Progress,* 314 n. 32. It appears that the commissioners in 1835 included John Julius Pringle and James Reid Pringle, members of St. Michael's vestry; Joseph Manigault, Joshua W. Toomer, and William Mason Smith, members of St. Philip's vestry; Henry Horlbeck, whose affiliation is unknown but whose sister-in-law is listed as a pew holder at St. Philip's; and Mitchell King, a member of First Scots. According to the 1835 city directory, the intendant of the city was Dr. Edward W. North; the wardens were John M. Van Rhyn, Thomas Middleton, Neill M'Neill, Jacob F. Mintzing, William H. Inglesby, Col. John Bryan, Col. Charles E. Miller, George Henry, George B. Eckhard, R. W. Seymour, Charles Graves, and John Magrath.

16. *Charleston Mercury,* June 17, 1835; *Charleston Mercury,* Sept. 28, 1835; for letters in support of St. Philip's building only twenty-two feet behind its former position, see *Charleston Mercury,* Aug. 10, 17, 1835, and *Charleston Courier,* Aug. 13, 1835; a plat drawn by Charles Parker, city surveyor, shows the old line where the church was located and its new position after construction was completed. This plat

also designates the land under the west portico as public. Charleston County, Register Mesne Conveyance, U10, 590.

17. St. Philip's Congregation Minutes, July 19, 1835, SCHS. In 1822, Wesner designed and supervised extending the galleries on each side, adding pews and altering the stairs. St. Philip's Vestry Minutes, Nov. 16, 1822. In 1826, Mills worked on repairing a large fissure in the northwest corner of the church. St. Philip's Vestry Minutes, Apr. 3, 9, 1826, SCHS.

18. St. Philip's Vestry Minutes, Aug. 17, 1835.

19. St. Philip's Vestry Minutes, Mar. 27, 1835. Dalcho, *Account of the Protestant Episcopal Church,* 120–21.

20. For more on the painting, see *Charleston Courier,* Apr. 9, 1835; *Charleston Mercury,* Apr. 9, 1835; *Charleston Courier,* May 27, 1835. White's painting was purchased by a "gentleman" from Charleston for two hundred dollars; "St. Philip's Church," *Charleston Gospel Messenger* 12, no. 137 (May 1835): 156. Amateur artist Thomas Middleton also painted a view of the old interior.

21. For more on the debate over the great piers, see "On Re-building St. Philip's Church," *Charleston Gospel Messenger* 12, no. 137 (May 1835): 141; "On Re-building St. Philip's Church," *Charleston Gospel Messenger* 12, no. 138 (June 1835): 168; "On the New St. Philip's," *Charleston Gospel Messenger* 12, no. 140 (Aug. 1835): 240; *Charleston Courier,* May 6, May 13, June 13, June 21, 1836.

22. "On the New St. Philip's," *Charleston Gospel Messenger* 12, no. 140 (Aug. 1835): 240; "On Re-Building St. Philip's," *Charleston Gospel Messenger* 12, no. 138 (June 1835): 168.

23. *Charleston Courier,* May 13, 1836, reported on the earlier vote taken by the committee, but the results of that vote did not appear in either the vestry minutes or the congregational meeting minutes; the proceedings of the laying of the cornerstone were printed in the *Charleston Courier,* Nov. 12, 1835, and the *Charleston Gospel Messenger* 12, no. 144 (Dec. 1835): 379; "St. Philip's Church," *Charleston Courier,* May 6, 1836; "St. Philip's Church," *Charleston Courier,* June 8, 1836.

24. "St. Philip's Church," *Charleston Courier,* May 13, 1836.

25. "St. Philip's Church," *Charleston Courier,* June 13, 1836. One has to doubt the accuracy of the information regarding the original intention of St. Philip's to be based on St. Martin's in-the-Fields. St. Philip's was begun in 1710–11,

and services were held there as early as 1723. St. Martin's, on the other hand, was only about sixteen feet above its foundations in 1723; its design was not submitted until 1720. It thus seems unlikely that Charleston's St. Philip's was based on St. Martin's in-the-Fields. For more on St. Martin's, see Terry Friedman, *James Gibbs* (New Haven: Yale Univ. Press, 1984), especially chapter 4, "St. Martin's in-the-Fields," 55–86. At the June meeting of the congregation, a resolution was passed dispensing of the heavy pillars and replacing them with an interior as much like St. Martin's in-the-Fields as possible. St. Philip's Vestry Minutes, June 20, 1836, SCHS.

26. For more on Robert Mills in Charleston, see Rhodri Windsor Liscombe, *Altogether American: Robert Mills, Architect and Engineer, 1781–1855* (Oxford: Oxford Univ. Press, 1994), especially chaps. 1 and 4. *Charleston Courier,* May 11, 1836.

4

A PUBLIC HOUSE FOR A NEW REPUBLIC

THE ARCHITECTURE OF ACCOMMODATION AND THE AMERICAN STATE, 1789–1809

A. K. SANDOVAL-STRAUSZ

When George Washington decided on the eve of his presidential tours of 1789–91 to refuse private offers of lodging and stay only at public houses, he knew that it would be at the cost of considerable personal discomfort. Shortly after taking office, Washington had begun planning an official journey through the infant republic "to acquire knowledge of the face of the Country the growth and Agriculture thereof and the temper and disposition of the Inhabitants towards the new government." In fact, the primary reason for the tours was political. It had been more difficult than expected to secure ratification of the Constitution of 1787, a development which highlighted the fragility of the national state and led many to speculate that it would soon collapse. Washington's hope was that by making personal visits to communities throughout the nation, he could use his astounding popularity to solidify the authority of the federal government. The success of the tours was heavily dependent upon the deployment of the president's status as a unifying na-

tional icon, and Washington, with his keen political instincts and preoccupation with personal comportment, surely understood that his every action would be freighted with symbolic significance. His decision was based on the belief that if he accepted private hospitality, even from members of his own family, he risked the appearance of favoritism and compromised the proper impartiality of his office.[1]

The prospect of staying at public houses could not have been a pleasant one, though, since the largely primitive character of American public accommodations was familiar to the well-traveled Washington, as it would have been to many of his compatriots. The nation's inns and taverns[2] had for many years elicited regular torrents of invective from diarists and travel writers for their filth, fleas, poor food, indifferent service, and frequent overcharging. An American army officer exasperated by the "wretched bed" which awaited him at a Massachusetts tavern in 1789 expressed a widely held frustration when he ranted, "Why cannot the people of this country treat themselves at least as well as they do their brutes, & live a little more like rational beings?" The president nonetheless continued to observe his stated rule, despite the low quality of the taverns at which he slept and the constant temptation of a clean and comfortable private bed. In the end, Washington's presidential tours were extraordinarily successful, increasing the prestige of the presidency, fostering popular faith in the federal government, and binding the states into a nation by cultivating a collective American sense of identity.[3]

The tours also marked the starting point for the emergence of the American hotel.[4] When Washington first took office in 1789, the finest public house in the United States was a three-story building about fifty feet long on a side, containing perhaps twenty rooms and valued at roughly fifteen thousand dollars. Two decades later, in 1809, the nation's leading public accommodation occupied an enormous seven-story edifice which covered nearly an acre of land, comprised over two hundred rooms, and cost more than half a million dollars. These years, in other words, saw the emergence of a new order of American public accommodation distinguished by its external architecture, internal arrangement, and particular social character. Yet the hotel was by no means just a new architectural form. It was a new way of understanding, creating, and marketing social space that was occasioned by new political and human geographies resulting from the establishment of a federally structured nation-state by the Constitution of 1787. Indeed, the rapid escalation in the architecture of accommodation reflected a transformation not only in the way American communities dealt with travelers but also in the way they organized their own social, economic, and political pursuits. A closer look at this transformation reveals the origins of one of the most familiar building types on the American landscape and illuminates the complex relationship between travel, sociability, and governance in the early republic.[5]

Eighteenth-century Americans expected little of their public houses architecturally. George Washington suggested as much when in 1789 he paid a Connecticut establishment a decidedly backhanded compliment by observing that it had "a good external appearance (for a Tavern)." The vast majority of the hundreds of taverns in British North America were kept in dwelling houses or other structures which had been built, and continued to be used, for other purposes. As a result, rather than corresponding to any particular academic style, they followed the vernacular architectural idioms of the locality and were usually visually indistinguishable from private homes or shops (figs. 4.1 and 4.2). Even the much-celebrated hanging tavern sign often

Fig. 4.1. Just as early American inns and taverns existed within regionally specific architectural idioms, they were represented with well-understood tropes. In this lithograph, the Spread Eagle Tavern in Stafford, Pennsylvania, is marked by a hanging sign and a stagecoach full of travelers. Courtesy of the Library of Congress.

Fig. 4.2. On well-traveled roads or near cities, colonial-era public houses often were of more substantial construction. The Green Dragon Tavern outside Boston was of brick in the style of the large urban dwellings of the region. Courtesy of the American Antiquarian Society, Worcester, Massachusetts.

failed to compensate for the tavern's architectural anonymity, and eighteenth-century wayfarers were frequently unable to find shelter without the assistance of local residents. Purpose-built public houses mostly awaited the final third of the century, when merchants in the largest cities financed a few substantial establishments, typified by Philadelphia's City Tavern (fig. 4.3). But for the most part, the desire for elegant accommodations was satisfied by converting the mansions of the colonial elite to public use, as with New York City's renowned Fraunces Tavern. Neither case, however, represented a significant departure from the basic architectural continuity of the American tavern. The relatively humble dimensions of eighteenth-century public houses were also discernible in their assessed values. For most taverns that assessment was between several hundred and a few thousand dollars; socially eminent inns averaged well under ten thousand dollars, and even purpose-built establishments in

Fig. 4.3. Philadelphia's City Tavern (1772), seen here in a detail from William Birch's print of the Bank of Pennsylvania, was a purpose-built structure but was modeled on the residence of one of its subscribers rather than representative of a distinctive vernacular style of public house. Courtesy of the Library Company of Philadelphia.

the first rank of prestige and elegance apparently never exceeded fifteen thousand dollars.[6]

Internally, colonial taverns were typified by relatively small and unspecialized interior spaces and shared sleeping quarters. In eighteenth-century Virginia they averaged six to ten rooms total, a size which recent studies of taverns in Massachusetts and Philadelphia suggest was close to the norm in the colonial period. A tavern's kitchen, bar, public rooms, family quarters, and sleeping areas thus had to be distributed among a fairly small number of available spaces, and local patrons were consequently accustomed to drinking and talking cheek by jowl. Travelers, however, were rather less fond of the close quarters, which obliged them to share rooms and even beds with fellow guests. This practice was particularly resented by respectable wayfarers, who complained constantly about being forced into such close contact with the unclean bodies and rude manners of tradesmen and laborers. One traveler complained that "after you have been some time in bed, a stranger of any condition (for there is little distinction), comes into the room, pulls off his clothes, and places himself, without ceremony, between your sheets." Another wrote in his diary about drunk and staggering tavern patrons who "kept up the Roar-Rororum till morning," as a result of which he "watched carefully all night, to keep them from falling over and spewing upon me." The American colonies were also home to a few public houses whose keepers aspired to a higher level of refinement and arranged their premises accordingly. Establishments like Fraunces' Tavern or the Raleigh Tavern in Williamsburg distinguished themselves by having more meeting rooms and offering private quarters, but even the best of these had no more than a few public rooms and evidently never contained more than fifteen or so guest chambers. Taverns existed within a fairly stable tradition of architecture and material culture, and thus remained relatively small and undifferentiated.[7]

The earliest American hotels, by contrast, were designed to dominate the landscape. These grand public houses, which began to appear in the 1790s, represented a dramatic departure from the norms which had characterized public accommodations since the

Fig. 4.4. Nicholas King's 1799 drawing of the Union Public Hotel in Washington, D.C., emphasized its sophistication by contrasting it with the rusticity of the shack and oxcart in the foreground. The White House is faintly visible at center left. Courtesy of The Huntington Library, San Marino, California.

beginnings of European settlement nearly two centuries earlier. The first of these was the Union Public Hotel (fig. 4.4), which was begun in 1793 in the new Federal City at Washington. The hotel was easily the largest privately owned structure in the city, fronting 120 feet by 60 feet deep and rising to a height of about 70 feet. As a presence on the emergent cityscape, it was rivaled only by two nationally important and architecturally ambitious structures—the White House and the Capitol. The construction of the nation's second hotel began in New York City the following year. The City Hotel (fig. 4.5) fronted 80 feet on Broadway and extended 120 feet back into its lot. Like its Washington counterpart, it surpassed practically all the other buildings in the city. The City Hotel stood taller than all but the spires of the metropolis' largest churches, and among private buildings it was exceeded in value only by the newly built headquarters of the New York Stock Exchange on Wall Street. The first hotels evidently inspired similar efforts elsewhere, for in the following years, architects and merchants in at least three American cities drafted plans and raised funds for the construction of hotels of their own. It was not until some years later, however, that the hotel reached its Federal-era apotheosis in the form of the Exchange Coffee House in Boston (fig. 4.6). This remarkable edifice, which began construction in 1806, was in the form of an irregular trapezoid averaging about ninety feet on a side, surmounted by a dome whose apex attained a height of over one hundred feet. (This exceptional feature proved its downfall: when an attic fire started in 1818, there were no ladders in Boston long enough to reach the flames.) The construction of public accommodations on such a greatly enlarged scale required the expenditure of unprecedented amounts of money. The Union Public was budgeted at fifty thousand dollars, and the City Hotel was said to have cost in excess of one hundred thousand. By the same token, when in 1796 Charles Bulfinch, Boston's leading architect, sought investors for a hotel in the

Fig. 4.5. The City Hotel in New York City (1794) was perfectly suited to the economic logic of commerce and real estate and the Gotham elite's desire for social exclusivity, making it the most successful of the first generation of American hotels. Courtesy of the Regenstein Library, University of Chicago.

Fig. 4.6. The Boston Exchange Coffee House displayed a neoclassical sensibility and required an immense capital investment. It was among the largest buildings of the early national period. Courtesy of the Regenstein Library, University of Chicago.

city, he offered shares worth seventy thousand dollars. And little over a decade after the planning of these structures, the Exchange Coffee House made even these figures seem relatively trifling when its building costs surpassed the staggering sum of five hundred thousand dollars.[8]

The interior spaces of the first hotels displayed an equally sharp contrast with previously existing American public houses. The newer form was characterized by an elaborate internal arrangement devoted particularly to substantial public rooms and numerous private bedchambers. The Union Public Hotel's four stories included a main floor of eleven separate rooms, a second floor with several substantial halls (the largest of which was seventy-seven by forty-five feet), and an unfinished basement reportedly suitable for another forty "useful rooms." While no floor plans of the hotel survive, an episode in the life of the structure suggests the impressive character of its internal spaces: when the Capitol was burned by British forces during the War of 1812, the Madison administration decided that the hotel's public rooms offered the best available facilities for the accommodation of Congress, which held session at the Union Public for fourteen months in 1814–15. The City Hotel in New York was likewise designed with exceptionally tall main and second stories to house a ballroom, public parlors, a bar, stores, offices, and a circulating library—the largest in the United States at the time. The hotel also offered a great many private bedrooms, with most of the building's 137 rooms devoted to lodgings for overnight guests. The City Hotel thereby established a precedent which soon became a standard feature of American hotels: the truly private sleeping room. Benjamin Latrobe's 1797 plan of a hotel and theater complex for the city of Richmond exhibited similar features, and while the project ultimately went unbuilt, his architectural drawings provide remarkable insight into the visions of the first generation of hotel builders. The design for the ground story (fig. 4.7) called for a hotel (shown in two sections to either side of the central theater space) composed of elaborate, subdivided spaces with such purpose-specific labels as "supper room," "liquor bar," "coffee bar," and "private dining room." The upper floors contained a "servants lobby," "ladies dressing room," a place for "private card parties," and numerous rooms marked "chamber." Less than a decade later, the Exchange Coffee House outstripped even Latrobe's extravagant plans and eclipsed all previous public houses. The hotel, built to the designs of Asher Benjamin, had a stunning interior constructed around a ninety-five-foot-tall atrium, each of whose five galleries was supported by twenty Doric or Corinthian columns, and which culminated in a glass-domed observatory complete with a built-in telescope. With respect to guest quarters, the Exchange reportedly contained no fewer than 170 bedchambers.[9]

The tremendous size, distinguished architecture, and enormous expense of these structures indicate a deliberate attempt to create a new class of public houses which would stand unmistakably apart from their predecessors. The magnitude and aesthetics of the first hotels in absolute terms, moreover, bespeak an effort to make them into a particular sort of public

monument. Though explicit statements of purpose have not survived as part of the historical record, a reading of the structures and the historical context of their creation suggest as much. The very act of building on such a grand scale would have been a potent symbolic gesture under any circumstances, but was particularly so in the United States of the 1790s, with its economy only recently recovered from the postwar recession and many city districts still showing the heavy damage caused by British occupation. The gesture was heightened by the siting of the hotels in important locations: the Union Public on a hill not far from the Capitol and White House, the City Hotel on a prime section of Broadway, and the Exchange Coffee

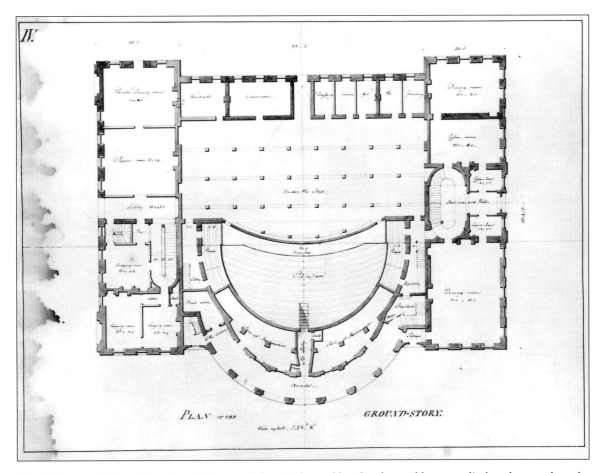

Fig. 4.7. Benjamin Henry Latrobe's 1797 proposal for a Richmond hotel and assembly rooms displays the complex subdivision and purpose-specific assignation of space that characterized hotel interiors. Courtesy of the Library of Congress.

House on its own block in Congress Street. Furthermore, the first generation of hotels was conspicuously the work of the most important architects of the early national period. In addition to Benjamin Latrobe, Charles Bulfinch (whose 1796 attempt to build a hotel in Boston was thwarted only by the recent financial collapse of his brilliant Tontine Crescent project), and influential treatise-writer Asher Benjamin, there was Union Public Hotel architect James Hoban, who had also designed the White House. The financial arrangements required by the first hotels were highly complex in ways which quite transcended the sheer volume of capital which had to be mobilized. The building of the Union Public Hotel involved a huge lottery and a national advertising campaign, and the City Hotel was underwritten by ten of New York's leading merchants, bankers, and lawyers, backed in turn by a larger number of smaller investors. By the same token, Bulfinch's hotel was to have been paid for through the public sale of two hundred shares of stock, and a 1795 hotel project in Newport brought together no fewer than forty-six of the town's leading citizens.[10]

The first hotels did some very important material and ideological work in the early American republic. The clearest example of this was in the realm of economic life. The occupations and enthusiasms of the first generation of hotel builders suggest specific rationales for their elaborate deployments of money and masonry. Almost without exception, these men were dependent for their livelihoods upon transatlantic commerce, with merchants comprising an overwhelming majority and their lawyers making up almost all of the remaining number. Their common interest in public accommodation grew logically out of their shared commitment to trade. In the Atlantic world of the late eighteenth century, and particularly within North America, the great majority of people who traveled from place to place did so for commercial reasons. The masses of seamen who manned merchant fleets, supercargoes who oversaw the delivery of shipments, and trade legations in search of new markets were the primary clientele for the public houses which dotted the harbor districts of the nation's ports. Inland, the roadside inns of the new nation were heavily patronized by peddlers, migrants, and merchants,

and by farmers and drovers on their way to market. The merchants behind the first hotels understood public accommodations as components of the networks of trade and transportation essential to their livelihoods. Indeed, many of them were also deeply involved in building internal improvements—turnpikes, bridges, canals, and the like—as part of a collective effort to provide the United States with the kind of physical infrastructure necessary for the development of a profitable internal and transnational economy.[11]

Hotels thus served three complementary purposes. Functionally, they facilitated trade by providing shelter and refreshment to an elite traveling public. Visually, their imposing architecture symbolized commerce and valorized its pursuit in a nation which was still overwhelmingly agrarian. Financially, the grandeur of early hotels was intended to increase the value of surrounding property at a time when speculative building was becoming popular among urban landholders. Notably, Samuel Blodget Jr., the man behind the Union Public Hotel, was one of the largest land speculators in Washington, and the City Hotel's managing board included several active traders of New York real estate. As a public accommodation for commercial travelers, as a monument to mercantile might, and as a spur to the price of land, the hotel made perfect economic sense as the successor to the tavern in an age of expanding market capitalism.[12]

The hotel's internal architecture likewise signaled changes in the role of the public house in the closely related realms of governance and economy. The inns and taverns of America had always embodied a tension between their two basic purposes: accommodating travelers and selling drinks. In point of fact, state and local authorities only authorized public houses to exist as part of an explicit *quid pro quo* in which the privilege of retailing alcoholic beverages was granted in exchange for a promise to provide wayfarers with shelter, food, and refreshment. In actuality, however, publicans usually catered to a local drinking public while maintaining only minimal facilities for visitors. In the words of one historian of colonial public houses, "tavernkeepers invested in chairs rather than beds." In a reversal of that parochial orientation, the numerous bedchambers of the emergent hotel form both manifested and symbolized a newfound dedication to the needs of travelers. This new public house thus retained its traditional function as community gathering place and at the same time emphasized a decidedly translocal orientation which connected it with a larger economy of human motion. In the broadest sense, this was part of a late-eighteenth-century market-driven reconceptualization of architecture which saw individual sites as connected to others beyond their sight and control and thus as dependent parts of more complex networks of "system and flow."[13]

American hotels were also part of longer historical trajectories of metropolitanism, consumption, and gentility in the Atlantic world. Indeed, this was only the latest in a series of transformations which the Anglo-American public house had undergone over the previous two centuries. In England, differentiations among public houses were codified and reinforced in the late sixteenth century, when a new licensing law created a hierarchy of alehouses, taverns, and inns, each with its own duties, tax liabilities, and implicit social status. The second half of the seventeenth century saw the rise of the coffeehouse, an institution whose commitment to stimulation rather than intoxication reflected the values of a rising mercantile class and served as the locus of an emergent bourgeois public sphere in which the citizenry found a voice to discuss and criticize the actions of the state. And in the latter eighteenth century, the word "hotel" was first applied to converted mansions, large inns with attached assembly rooms, and purpose-built structures which established the design context for the American hotel. In British North America, the driving force behind changes in public houses was a provincial culture of metropolitan aspiration: in much the same way as had happened in the new towns of the English urban renaissance, American colonial elites sought to demonstrate their status and sophistication by fashioning local facsimiles of the royal court in London.[14]

The creation of elegant public spaces became important in an age when refinement in manners and material culture was the most commonly used referent by which Americans demonstrated their own social standing and evaluated that of others. After all,

Fig. 4.8. Latrobe's conceptual sketch for the hotel ballroom reflected his European training and its deployment in support of the local plantation aristocracy's pursuit of personal refinement and social status. Courtesy of the Library of Congress.

proper surroundings were needed for the deployment of the fashionably dressed bodies, cultivated comportment, and witty repartee which served as the social currency of the American *bon ton*. Latrobe's conceptual sketch of his proposed hotel's grand assembly room (fig. 4.8) was an architectural paean to spectatorship and self-display; it may also have been a patriotic attempt to elevate the nation's cultural taste, which was new and relatively coarse. As drawn, the room was brightly illuminated by numerous chandeliers and fitted with long, Versailles-inspired mirrors to enhance and multiply its long lines of sight, providing the ideal courtly setting for the men and women in the image, dressed up in their finest attire and ready to see and be seen. From a business perspective, the publican who could provide appropriate venues for balls, dancing assemblies, and other genteel entertainments might expect a substantial return on his investment. Indeed, it had been in this context that Philadelphia's City Tavern and the other elite public houses of the late eighteenth century had been constructed. But it was the hotel which definitively made opulent decor into a capital good, using wainscoting, drapery, and crystal to attract a handsomely paying clientele while signaling to people of more humble means that they did not belong.[15]

The genteel credentials of the hotel were amplified by the way it offered privacy in public, allowing people to enjoy the benefits of public sociability while simultaneously enabling them to finely modulate the character of the social space they occupied. Polite society in eighteenth-century British America was constituted in private settings as much as it was in public. Indeed, many thought that it was the very privacy of salons and clubs that made possible the highest level of thought and discussion, since only in familiar company could one challenge a person's ideas without the risk of giving offense. In the mixed-class environs of the tavern, where for most of the century patrons of a single establishment varied widely in their social standing, roiling issues of status and honor made this much more difficult. There, interactions between self-identified superiors and their grudging inferiors had to be mediated by an array of rituals and performances, and even these constantly threatened to collapse into open antagonism and even physical violence. Yet whatever the misgivings of the genteel about the limitations of public space, a retreat into private quarters was not an option. Citizenship in the early republic was still heavily dependent upon comportment, persuasion, and deference, and thus personal appearances in public were a *sine qua non* of virtuous social and political participation. Moreover, private sociability itself became a serious political issue in the 1780s and 1790s. Republicans and their radical allies found political leverage in the idea that the Federalist elite's closed meetings and private entertainments threatened the republic with a reversion to the secrecy and corruption of the courts of Europe. The controversies over societies and clubs like the Cincinnati and the Sans Souci were only the most obvious manifestations of this debate. The hotel mediated these difficulties by substituting spatial separation for performance as the mode of defusing the social tensions previously endemic to American public houses. The availability of multiple parlors, meeting halls, ballrooms, coffee rooms, and bars allowed for compartmentalized public sociability. Whatever the cause of discord among patrons, from social rivalry to political infighting, it was now possible to move to another part of the hotel whenever some people decided that others had crossed the line between mingling and intrusion. A similar principle was at work in the sleeping areas of the hotel, which shielded travelers and other guests against being incommoded by the presence in their rooms or beds of strangers or other objectionable sorts. Notably, this type of stratagem typified an age in which social difference was increasingly articulated through physical separation and both ambition and degradation were expressed spatially and visually.[16]

The regendering of public accommodations was also a fundamental part of the creation of the American hotel. While women were no strangers to the insides of taverns, for most intents and purposes these were strongly male-gendered milieux in which the purchase and consumption of strong drink functioned to reinforce fellowship and reciprocity among men. Women served mainly as labor or agreed-upon sexual objects, and as a result, taverns could be very unwelcome places for female patrons. A Pennsylvania hospital matron suggested as much in 1756 when she wrote disgustedly of the leers of tavern customers who assumed her to be the kept woman of her male traveling companion. A quarter century later, Katherine Farnham Hay wrote to her sister upon being left in a New York tavern that her male escort had been "very uneasy" about leaving her unaccompanied, adding, "I was in great distress, but what could I do in a publick House, no person to take care of me[?]" The first hotels were characterized by a very different pattern of sociability which extended to public houses the increasing presence of respectable women outside the home. The participation of women in American public life had been on the rise throughout the eighteenth century, with the proliferation of dancing assemblies, salons, and tea tables indicating that a small elite had built on European precedents and made the public sphere come to them. It is tempting to interpret the inclusion of women in the hotel public only as a sign of greater equality or progressive social change. But a closer look at the politics at century's end suggests that the provision of heterosocial space was also part of an exclusionary dynamic in which respectable women marked the spaces they occupied as refined and worthy of deference. The Federalists especially had been successful in deploying respectable women in order to establish the legitimacy of their public meetings over those of their Republican political rivals. By the early nineteenth century, women had become such an expected presence in the nation's leading public houses that gendered anxiety took a notably different form from what it had been in the tavern. When an observer suggested in 1809 that the Exchange Coffee House should "put up Venetian blinds, or lattice work, between the pillars of the colonnade, to secure the ladies from impertinent observation," it was clear that the presence of spectators of an inappropriate social status was defined as the problem; there was no longer any question that women belonged in the halls of these new public houses.[17]

The symbolic meanings expressed by hotel builders through architecture did not go unnoticed or unanswered, though the response came in a different language than that of bricks and mortar. For as the hotel builders surely realized, as a mode of discourse, grand architecture had the advantage of exclusivity. After all, unlike other methods of communication, such as speech making, pamphleteering, and rioting, large-scale construction was available only to Americans with access to the capital and financial instruments required to dramatically modify the built environment. Hotel buildings were impossible to ignore, and they elicited constant commentary—in this sense their creators had achieved at least part of their rhetorical objectives—but this was often by way of criticism. In fact, it was in the response to hotels that one finds the most explicit evidence of the linkage between their architectural form and particular cultural and economic messages. The grand opening of the City Hotel, for example, drew scorn from New York's radicals, who described the event as the haunt of would-be aristocrats who favored "the ancient Colony system of servility and adulation." The Union Public Hotel meanwhile became a symbol of the folly of speculation. One visitor to Washington, told of the lottery bankruptcy which had left the structure unfinished six years after its cornerstone was laid, suggested that perhaps "hotel" was an acronym for *hic omnes turpitudine excedit longe* ("here all baseness is

taken still further") and referred to the ethics of the building's creator. Indeed, the collapse of the speculative scheme with which the Union Public was financed generated such widespread hostility toward Samuel Blodget that he was still busy defending himself in print a decade later. It was the Exchange Coffee House, however, which inspired the most polemics. Criticism of the structure was constant, and was seen as coming from the common citizenry; this led the *Port Folio*, an elitist journal edited by Federalists, to publish a belletristic poem attacking critics as "that herd, who, striving to abuse . . . with malignant lip asperse thy name." Even more notably, and in a tone reminiscent of earlier attacks on the Union Public, when the Exchange Coffee House burned down in 1818, some observers openly gloated over the destruction of an edifice "erected during the most perfidious periods of speculation . . . [which] arose on the ruins of many industrious citizens" and bore "evidences of the fallacious promises, which were too successfully practised on the credulous tradesmen." The palpable class tension evident here highlights the fact that short of outright vandalism or arson (an expedient which had ample precedent previously and thereafter), the common people could find a victory over such architectural statements only through the buildings' decrepitude or destruction.[18]

A key question remains, however: Why did the hotel appear at the time it did? The economic and social imperatives which undergirded this new type of public house were by no means new to the 1790s. How, then, to account for that decade's sudden enthusiasm for hotel building? The short answer is that the creation of the hotel was occasioned by the establishment of the United States federal government under the Constitution of 1787. The election of the first president, the founding of a national capital, and the activity of federal appointees and other agents of the new American state were responsible—and in the case of the first hotel, solely responsible—for the advent of a new order of public accommodation. More generally speaking, the hotel was also at its inception a response to the spatial logic of representative government as it emerged in the United States. One can reasonably interpret the hotel as a vernacular architectural form which was part and parcel of the project of American nationhood.

There is every reason to suppose that this link between governance and public houses was conscious and intentional, since a close identification between the two would have been entirely intuitive to the citizens of the early American republic. Taverns had by then served as the preeminent loci of political life in British North America for well over a century. In colonial New England, they emerged as centers of popular opposition to the religious and royal authority emanating from the meeting-house and the governor's mansion. And in the decade before the outbreak of the Revolutionary War, taverns became the principal gathering places for organized resistance to the Crown. The postwar years saw a continuation of public-house politics, as evidenced by frequent announcements of tavern meetings for the purpose of discussing news from abroad, selecting candidates for municipal office, and giving campaign speeches. When Americans began to plan and build public houses on an unprecedented scale, then, they surely did so with the expectation that these would be pivotal sites in the new nation's political life.[19]

The relationship between the hotel and the American state began with the election of George Washington to the newly established office of president. Washington's elevation to head of state in 1789 meant that the United States could for the first time be embodied in a single human being. While the notion of corporealized nationhood seems fanciful at the dawn of the twenty-first century, in the late eighteenth most lands in the Western world were still led by monarchs whose physical presence was ideologically identical with their nations. Even in the world's sole republic, only congressional opposition prevented Washington from being inaugurated as "His Highness." The president's presence invariably caused a public sensation. His inauguration packed the streets of New York City, where people gathered flowers for him and where the letters "GW" were emblazoned on doors, pinned onto clothing, and engraved upon personal effects. The visits Washington made on his presidential tours were momentous events in the community life of cities and towns, occasioning elaborate preparations for the reception and honoring of "the Man who unites all hearts" or "Columbia's favourite Son," as banners welcoming the president often called him. Many towns staged highly choreographed processions. In New York, Boston, Salem, Newburyport, and countless other towns and settlements, local authorities posted broadsides informing the community of the proper procedures and sequence of groups in the planned parade. Daytime festivities were frequently followed by large public dinners complete with long rounds of toasts. In Newport, Rhode Island, these included "Prosperity to the Constitution of America," "The Memory of the deceased Patriots and Heroes of our Country," and, after Washington took his leave, "The man we love." Evening entertainments were also common, as in Charleston, South Carolina, where Washington attended a dancing assembly at which, he recalled, "the ladies were all superbly dressed and most of them wore ribbons with different inscriptions expressive of their esteem and respect for the President such as: 'long live the President,' etc."[20]

George Washington's presidential travels offer a convenient and compelling point of origin for the development of the American hotel. The tours accentuated the importance of public accommodations to the political life of the new republic while simultaneously demonstrating the inadequacy of the nation's inns and taverns. Indeed, it was apparent from the outset that there was a problem: so many people traveled to New York to witness the inauguration that the city's taverns and boardinghouses were quickly overwhelmed, forcing many visitors to put up in adjacent settlements or to sleep outdoors in hastily improvised campgrounds. Washington's subsequent presidential tours made plain that the problem was national in scope. His determination to be accommodated and entertained in public houses revealed their shortcomings not only as travel accommodations but also as centers of local sociability. While the president was pleased with some of the taverns at which he stayed, during the last third of his northern tour he became increasingly dissatisfied with them, noting in his diary that several were "indifferent" and on other occasions that the previous night's tavern was "not a good house," though he did recognize when "the People of it were disposed to do all they cou'd to accommodate me." Travel conditions on Washington's southern tour of 1791 were even less satisfactory. In addition to the usual uneven quality of public houses there were many instances in which none were available at all. Traveling in North Carolina, he complained that though he wished to get out of the rain, "the only Inn short of Hallifax having . . . no Rooms or beds which appeared tolerable, & everything else having a dirty appearance, I was compelled to keep on." Further into the journey, Washington grumbled that "the accomadations on the whole Road [to Savannah] we found extremely indifferent—the houses being small and badly provided either for man or horse."[21]

The presidential visits fostered widespread community self-consciousness regarding the adequacy of local accommodations. Washington's hosts were clearly at pains to honor him properly despite their humble fortunes. The president realized that in some instances he was being put up at private residences which had been temporarily deemed public houses specifically for him. Similar arrangements were frequently made for public dinners and receptions: in preference to the local tavern, some towns occupied people's homes or built temporary structures for the reception of the president. At least one account of the president's visit indicates that a collection was taken up in order to secure enough silverware and dishes to serve him. More generalized were feelings of chagrin at not having been able to provide Washington with more elegant surroundings: reception committees in Newport and Marblehead openly expressed their regrets in their addresses to the president, and one Exeter resident published an open letter taking his fellow townspeople to task for their meager efforts. At one point, the governor of South Carolina wrote directly to Washington to "apologise . . . for asking you to call at a place so indifferently furnished."[22]

Washington's difficulties with public houses were an early sign that the new American state would have distinctive spatial requirements, in particular the need to accommodate the officers of the federal government. (The construction of a new presidential residence every time the government moved to a new city

was one indication of this.) More generally, the need for substantial travel accommodations was immanent in the human geography of American governance. The principle of deliberative democracy on the basis of geographic representation required by its very nature that individuals from across a larger territory gather at a single location in order to discuss and resolve matters of public importance. The choice of terminology for these meetings suggested as much: "congress," a Latinate term meaning literally "moving together." Even before the hotel age began in earnest, important predecessor forms appeared in each of the cities that served as the nation's capital. Shortly after the inauguration, a large group of leading merchants met to arrange for the building of a huge new public house on Wall Street for use as a central stock exchange and mercantile clearinghouse. Likewise, several months after the transfer of the national government from New York to Philadelphia in late 1790, a Pennsylvania merchant and an innkeeper arranged to purchase a defunct school building, which they successfully converted into the city's preeminent place of accommodation. It had for years been commonly known, however, that by 1800 the entire federal government would be permanently moved to a new national capital on the banks of the Potomac—and it was there that the nation's first hotel was commenced in 1793.[23]

The origin of the Union Public Hotel highlights the importance of the state in hotel building because it was the federal government that created the need for the structure, established its site, authorized its originator, and supported its financing. The Union Public was from its inception part of the federal government's creation of a national capital at Washington. The hotel was the brainchild of Samuel Blodget, whom the president appointed in 1791 as supervisor of buildings and improvements for the Federal City. Blodget determined that the new city urgently needed a public house to accommodate legislators and other visitors, and proposed that an enormous lottery—the grand prize of which was to be the hotel itself—be used to raise the required funds. He received the necessary permission from the city commissioners in January 1793 and began an aggressive publicity and sales campaign which worked so well that the building's cornerstone was laid in an elaborate ceremony in time for that year's Fourth of July celebrations. The influence of the hotel extended far beyond its immediate vicinity, however. Because Blodget advertised the lottery extensively in numerous commercial newspapers, the project was made known to merchant communities across the nation, and the quick succession of subsequent projects suggests that published lottery notices were instrumental in propagating the idea of building large-scale public accommodations across the United States.[24]

Subsequent hotel projects had analogous origins and a similar dependence upon governments. The provisions of the Constitution of 1787 provided for a dual sovereignty embodied in the simultaneous existence of federal and state legislatures meeting in their respective capitals, and it was thus no coincidence that the nation's second, third, fourth, and fifth hotels were built or planned for New York City, Newport, Boston, and Richmond, all of which were state capitals at that time. The planning and construction of hotels in these capital cities thus demonstrated the political logic of federalism being inscribed upon a new order of public accommodation. The originators of these projects were dependent upon their state representatives for legal support. The members of New York's Tontine associations twice had to obtain state aid in the form of acts of incorporation, as did the builders of the Exchange Coffee House. Similarly, the merchant community of Newport needed the General Assembly of Rhode Island to raise money for its wharf and hotel project. From the outset, then, federal and state officers and agencies provided indispensable support to the transformation of public accommodation. While it would be an exaggeration to call the hotel a product of governance, neither can it be understood separately from the early American state which fostered it.[25]

The link between architecture and the new American state was not lost on contemporary observers. "In respect to their buildings," Henry Wansey wrote in 1794, "I date a new era from their acceptance of the federal constitution. They then began to feel themselves united as a nation, and all their public works and undertakings seem to have commenced in a more important style." The American hotel, however, man-

ifested this link in a way that transcended mere style. In very real ways, the act of creating the nation's first hotels paralleled the integration of local communities into a national polity. It had been George Washington who first used travel in the service of American nationalism, establishing symbolic ties between local political communities and the greater national project. The hotel articulated these ties in physical space in the form of a new architecture of accommodation which reflected and reinforced the evolving American political ethos. Taverns had served as the centers of public life in colonial America, but these public houses remained primarily local institutions which were ill-suited by their very architecture to the exigencies of national politics. It was the hotel, which linked active local publics to one another through the networked itineraries of a traveling citizenry, that was to become the archetypal public house of the nineteenth-century United States.[26]

The hotel form did not become immediately dominant, though the future unmistakably belonged to it. To be sure, many hotel projects went unbuilt. The tavern remained for some time the most common type of public house, and many travelers preferred the private quarters of the boardinghouse. But signs of change were not long in coming. Soon after the appearance of the first hotels, tavernkeepers began adopting new standards of hospitality. Even as it stood unfinished, for example, the Union Public Hotel inspired a host of local imitators who, though they lacked the funds needed to build on a comparable scale, nonetheless provided Washington with well-appointed public accommodations. Publicans began to use the availability of private rooms as a way to distinguish their houses from lesser establishments. A Philadelphia innkeeper explained to his English guest in 1798 that in his establishment "every lodger had a room to himself," and some years later another promised his patrons "that so much desired gratification, *a single bed room.*" The new form also registered linguistically, as numerous taverns and converted mansions were reopened as hotels and the use of the word increased dramatically in city directories and newspapers.[27] But it was the new building type that emerged out of the particular circumstances of the two decades after 1789 that would be the ascendant form of American public house. The development of the hotel after 1809 was interrupted by the dislocations and disruptions of the War of 1812, but as embargo, recession, and conflict gave way to peace and prosperity, a new wave of hotel building followed. Hotels proliferated rapidly across the national landscape and diversified into new types as they were redeployed in very different places and conditions. Yet however numerous and varied they became, their basic architecture, economic role, spatial practices, and political uses were derived from the first generation of American hotels.[28]

The American hotel arose from a complex interaction of architectural, economic, political, social, and geographic factors. However deep these roots, it is essential to remember human agency and historical context. Every aspect of creating the first hotels reflected the kind of deliberate effort, careful calculation, and consistent vision appropriate to a major cul-

tural statement. The tremendous size and grand architecture of the first hotels stood in sharp contrast to the nation's taverns, marking a dramatic departure from long-established standards of public accommodation. The economic imperatives which underlay these hotels were powerful and readily apparent, and the merchants who led the construction efforts mobilized huge amounts of capital through incorporation, shared investment, and national financial networks. The hotel form expressed controversial ideas about social hierarchy, self-display, and material value that were so clearly and widely understood as to provoke angry exchanges over their implications. The federal and state governments of the United States played a crucial role in fostering, structuring, and enabling this creative process, making them into midwives at the birth of the hotel age. The result was nothing less than a new paradigm for public houses, public space, and public life in America.

Notes

1. Don Jackson and Dorothy Twohig, eds., *The Diaries of George Washington* (Charlottesville: Univ. Press of Virginia, 1979), 5:453; T. H. Breen, "The Bumpy Path to a New Republic," *New York Times,* Feb. 14, 1999. Washington only made reference to this policy in letters declining such offers. While the formal tone of these leaves room for slight uncertainty about his motives, other incidents around this time suggest an ongoing effort to minimize any suggestion of favoritism. See George Washington to John Hancock, Oct. 22, 1789, in W. W. Abbott and Dorothy Twohig, eds., *The Papers of George Washington* (Charlottesville: Univ. Press of Virginia, 1993), 4:212–14; George Washington to William Washington, Jan. 8, 1791, in Abbott and Twohig, *Papers of George Washington* 7:211; Jackson and Twohig, *Diaries of George Washington* 5:491, 497.

2. Hereafter these will be referred to as taverns (except where style calls for more variety) because "tavern" was the more common appellation and has been the favored term historiographically. Americans in the early national period made no meaningful distinction between the two terms; Washington, for example, used both in a single sentence

thus: "After dinner through frequent light Showers we proceeded to the Tavern of a Mrs. Haviland at Rye; who keeps a very neat and decent Inn." Jackson and Twohig, *Diaries of George Washington* 5:461. Note that boardinghouses were not public houses at all: while they did provide shelter to travelers, it was on a purely private basis, without a license and therefore without any legal duty to accept guests or privilege of selling alcohol.

3. Robert Hunter Jr., *Quebec to Carolina in 1785–1786* (San Marino, Calif.: Huntington Library, 1943), 200, 274–86; Henry Wansey, *Journal of an Excursion to the United States of North America* (London, 1794), 40, 51–54, 100–110; Francis Baily, *Journal of a Tour in Unsettled Parts of North America in 1796 and 1797* (London, 1856), 129–30; Charles William Janson, *The Stranger in America* (London, 1807), 85; Marquis de Chastellux, *Travels in North America in the Years 1780, 1781, and 1782,* ed. Howard C. Rice Jr. (Paris, 1786; reprint, Chapel Hill: Univ. of North Carolina Press), index. By century's end, complaints about taverns had become such a cliché in British accounts that one author prefaced his own travel narrative by declaring that he

would omit them entirely: John Davis, *Travels of Four Years and a Half in the United States of North America* (London, 1803), 2. See also Sharon V. Salinger, *Taverns and Drinking in Early America* (Baltimore: Johns Hopkins Univ. Press, 2002), 211–16; Charles H. Sherrill, *French Memories of Eighteenth-Century America* (New York: Scribner's, 1915), 227; Kym S. Rice, *Early American Taverns: For the Entertainment of Friends and Strangers* (Chicago: Regnery Gateway, 1983), 41–42; "The Journal of Colonel John May, of Boston, 1789," *Pennsylvania Magazine of History and Biography* 45 (1943), 120; David Waldstreicher, *In the Midst of Perpetual Fetes: The Making of American Nationalism, 1776–1820* (Chapel Hill: Univ. of North Carolina Press, 1997), 117–26.

4. The French word *hôtel,* which referred to a large public building or nobleman's residence, was borrowed in the 1760s by the English, who used it to signify a superior sort of inn; the term began to appear in American usage in the following decade, and by the early 1790s was frequently used to indicate an especially fine public house. See *The Oxford English Dictionary* (Oxford: Oxford Univ. Press, 1989), 7:427. For vernacular American usage, see Folders 1790–1810, W. Johnson Quinn Collection, New-York Historical Society, New York City (hereafter cited as Quinn Collection), or search for "hotel*" on the Library Company of Philadelphia's CD-ROMs of the *Pennsylvania Gazette.*

5. Peter Thompson, *Rum Punch and Revolution: Taverngoing and Public Life in Eighteenth-Century Philadelphia* (Philadelphia: Univ. of Pennsylvania Press, 1999), 149–53. New York's City Tavern and Boston's Royal Exchange Tavern were also among the finest public houses of the day, but they did not differ materially in size, cost, or architecture from their Philadelphia counterpart; *Columbian Centinel* (Boston), Nov. 7, 1818.

6. See, for example, Davis, *Travels,* 127–30; Rice, *Early American Taverns,* 74; Jackson and Twohig, *Diaries of George Washington,* 5:494; Barbara G. Carson, "Early American Tourists and the Commercialization of Leisure," in *Of Consuming Interests: The Style of Life in the Eighteenth Century,* ed. Cary Carson, Ronald Hoffman, and Peter J. Albert (Charlottesville: Univ. Press of Virginia, 1994), 374, 382–95. The City Tavern, for example, was said to have been modeled on the country home of one of its subscribers, and Fraunces Tavern was originally the residence of the merchant and politician Stephen de Lancey: Thompson, 148–50; Rice, *Early American Taverns,* chap. 9; Donna-Belle

Garvin and James L. Garvin, *On the Road North of Boston: New Hampshire Taverns and Turnpikes, 1700–1900* (Concord: New Hampshire Historical Society, 1988), 19–20; *The Direct Tax of 1798* (volume held at the Massachusetts Historical Society, Boston); Samuel Adams Drake, *Old Boston Taverns and Tavern Clubs* (Boston: W. A. Butterfield, 1917), appendix.

7. Colonial Williamsburg Foundation, *A Study of Taverns of Virginia in the Eighteenth Century* (Williamsburg, Va.: Colonial Williamsburg Foundation, 1973), 8; David W. Conroy, *In Public Houses: Drink and the Revolution of Authority in Colonial Massachusetts* (Chapel Hill: Univ. of North Carolina Press, 1992), 47–48; Thompson, *Rum Punch and Revolution,* 56–60; Rice, *Early American Taverns,* 102–6; "Biographical Sketch of Waightstill Avery," *North Carolina University Magazine* 4 (1855): 249; Davis, *Travels,* 327; Wansey, *Journal of an Excursion,* 196.

8. Irving Atkins, "Blodget's Hotel, Federal City, 1793–1836" (unpublished 1981 manuscript held at Massachusetts Historical Society), 5; W. Harrison Bayles, *Old Taverns of New York* (New York: Frank Allaben Co., 1915), 314, 326, 331, 337, 353, 371; James Grant Wilson, *The Memorial History of the City of New York* (New York, 1892–93) 3:150–51; Harold Kirker, "The Boston Exchange Coffee House," *Old-Time New England* 52 (1961), 11–13.

9. Atkins, "Blodget's Hotel," 9–15; For a sense of the variety of uses of the City Hotel's spaces in its early years, see New York City directories for 1794–1810; Folders 1795–1810, Quinn Collection; George Gates Raddin Jr., *An Early New York Library of Fiction* (New York: Wilson, 1940), 11; Meryle R. Evans, "Knickerbocker Hotels and Restaurants, 1800–1850," *New-York Historical Society Quarterly* 36 (1952): 382–83; Benjamin Henry Latrobe, Presentation drawings, Prints and Photographs Division, Library of Congress; Charles Shaw, *A Topographical and Historical Description of Boston* (Boston, 1817), 229–33. By the same token, the Sans Souci Hotel in Ballston Spa, New York, probably the nation's first resort hotel, had nearly one hundred guest rooms when it opened in 1806. See Nancy Goyne Evans, "The Sans Souci, a Fashionable Resort Hotel in Ballston Spa," *Winterthur Portfolio* 6 (1970): 117.

10. Atkins, "Blodget's Hotel," 3; Evans, "Knickerbocker Hotels," 382–83; Kirker, "Boston Exchange Coffee House," 11–13; Latrobe, Presentation drawings; Bayles, *Old Taverns of New York,* 372; Tontine Coffee House Papers, New-York

Historical Society; *Columbian Centinel*, Sept. 14, 1796, p. 2 c. 1; *Acts of the General Assembly of Rhode Island*, Jan. 1795.

11. For a more detailed biographical account of the nation's first hotel builders, see A. K. Sandoval-Strausz, "Why The Hotel? Liberal Visions, Merchant Capital, Public Space, and the Creation of an American Institution," *Business & Economic History* 28 (1999).

12. Atkins, "Blodget's Hotel," 5; City Hotel board members list from Bayles cross-referenced with person catalog at New-York Historical Society; Elizabeth Blackmar, *Manhattan For Rent* (Ithaca: Cornell Univ. Press, 1981), 35–38, 186.

13. G. Thomann, *Colonial Liquor Laws* (New York, 1887); Conroy, *In Public Houses*, 88; Dell Upton, *Architecture in the United States* (New York: Oxford Univ. Press, 1998), 197–99.

14. Peter Clark, *The English Alehouse: A Social History, 1200–1650* (London: Longman, 1943); *Aytoun Ellis, The Penny Universities: A History of the Coffee-Houses* (London: Secker and Warburg, 1956); Jürgen Habermas, *The Structural Transformation of the Public Sphere*, trans. Thomas Burger (Darmstadt, 1962, Cambridge, Mass.: MIT Press, 1989); Steve Pincus, "'Coffee Politicians Does Create': Coffeehouses and Restoration Political Culture," *Journal of Modern History* 67 (1995); F. H. W. Sheppard, ed., *Survey of London*, vol. 36, *The Parish of St. Paul [and] Covent Garden* (London: London City Council, 1970), 1–11; W. Ison, *The Georgian Buildings of Bath* (London: Faber and Faber, 1948), 92–98; Peter Borsay, *The English Urban Renaissance: Culture and Society in the Provincial Town, 1660–1770* (Oxford: Oxford Univ. Press, 1989). It was in provincial English towns like Bath and Leicester that purpose-built accommodations referred to as "hotels" began to be built some years before their appearance in America. While these Georgian structures were surely the antecedents of hotels in the United States, they were less public houses than private clubs with assembly rooms, and it was the American hotel which became the standard form globally in the nineteenth and twentieth centuries. See Nikolaus Pevsner, *A History of Building Types* (Princeton: Princeton Univ. Press, 1976), 176; Paul Groth, *Living Downtown: The History of Residential Hotels* (Berkeley: Univ. of California Press, 1994), 38.

15. Richard Bushman, *The Refinement of America: Persons, Houses, Cities* (New York, 1992); Thompson, *Rum Punch and Revolution*, 151–52.

16. David S. Shields, *Civil Tongues and Polite Letters in British America* (Chapel Hill: Univ. of North Carolina Press, 1997), chap. 6 and pp. 311–14; Thompson, *Rum Punch and Revolution*, chaps. 3, 4; Waldstreicher, *In the Midst of Perpetual Fetes*, 136; Edwin G. Burrows and Mike Wallace, *Gotham: A History of New York City to 1898* (New York: Oxford Univ. Press, 1999), 315–23; Bushman, *Refinement of America*, 160–63. This subdivision of space was also an early manifestation of a more generalized transition in American architecture in the early republic toward one-to-one matching of spaces and people. See Dell Upton, "Another City: The Urban Cultural Landscape in the Early Republic," in *Everyday Life in the Early Republic*, ed. Catherine Hutchins (Winterthur, Del.: Henry du Pont Winterthur Museum, 1994), 85–93.

17. Thompson, *Rum Punch and Revolution*, 40–41, 46; Rice, *Early American Taverns*, 21, 49–56, 106; Salinger, *Taverns and Drinking*, 220–26; Eve Kosofsky Sedgwick, *Between Men: English Literature and Male Homosocial Desire* (New York: Columbia Univ. Press, 1985); Conroy, *In Public Houses*, 320; Thompson, *Rum Punch and Revolution*, 89–90, 98–99; Rice, *Early American Taverns*, 75; Bushman, *Refinement of America*, 440–46; Waldstreicher, *In the Midst of Perpetual Fetes*, 80–85 ("The emergence of women in these genteel celebrations helped an aristocracy desperate to naturalize their social eminence to secure control over public space."), 169–72, 234–36; Kirker, "The Boston Exchange Coffee House," 12.

18. *New York Journal*, Feb. 25, 1797; see also *Washington Gazette*, Sept. 28, 1796; *New York Gazette*, May 19, 1796; Duc de la Rouchefoucauld-Liancourt, *Voyage dans les Etats-Unis d'Amérique* (Paris, 1798), 2:326; Janson, *Stranger in America*, 203; Samuel Blodget Jr., *Economica: A Statistical Maual for the United States of America* (Washington, 1806), I–iii; *Port Folio* 11:452–53; Boston *Independent Chronicle*, Nov. 11, 1818. For a classic example of colonial-era house assault, see Peter Orlando Hutchinson, *The Diary and Letters of Thomas Hutchinson* (Boston, 1884), 67, 72. For hotel assaults arising from the conflict over the expansion of slavery, see "Memorial of the New England Emigrant Company, Praying Indemnification for the destruction of property at Lawrence, Kansas, May 21, 1856," Mis. Doc. No. 29, 37th Cong., 3d sess., and *Frank Leslie's Illustrated Newspaper*, Dec. 12, 1864, 200.

19. Conroy, *In Public Houses*, chaps. 4–6; Carl Bridenbaugh, *Cities in Revolt: Urban Life in America, 1743–1776*

(New York: Knopf, 1955), 358: "If the American Revolution was 'cradled' in any place, it was in the urban public houses." See, for example, the published notices collected in Folders 1780–1790, Quinn Colllection.

20. Burrows and Wallace, *Gotham,* 296; Jackson and Twohig, *Diaries of George Washington,* 5:474; Massachusetts Historical Society, Broadsides, 1789, 1791; Richard Gerry Durnin, "Presidential Visits to Salem," in *Essex Institute Historical Collections,* July 1964, 345; Burrows and Wallace, *Gotham,* 294; transcripts of addresses to George Washington from his visit in 1790, in manuscript box "George Washington," Newport Historical Society, Newport, R.I.; Douglas Southall Freeman, *George Washington* (New York: Scribner's, 1954), 6: 314–15.

21. Burrows and Wallace, *Gotham,* 296; Jackson and Twohig, *Diaries of George Washington* 5:493–97; 6:98–169, esp. 113–21, 134, 147, 158, 160.

22. Transcripts, Newport Historical Society; Richard Bayles, *History of Providence County* (New York, 1891), 514; Abbott and Twohig, *Papers of George Washington* 6:284; Exeter *Gazetteer,* Nov. 7, 1789; Jackson and Twohig, *Diaries of George Washington* 6:127.

23. Damie Stillman, "City Living, Federal Style," in Hutchins, *Everyday Life in the Early Republic,* 143–44; Tontine Coffee House Papers, 1789–1823, New-York Historical Society; *Pennsylvania Magazine of History and Biography* 46 (1944): 169. While an argument could be made that the Tontine Coffee House or Oeller's could just as well be deemed the nation's first hotel, I submit that the explicitly stated purpose of the founders of the Tontine Coffee House was to establish a merchants' exchange and that Oellers', as a refitted school building, cannot properly be read as an architectural prototype. More importantly from an analytical point of view, either of these claims would still be compatible with my larger argument about the linkage between public houses and the location of the national government.

24. Atkins, "Blodget's Hotel," 3–9. See, for example, *Newport Mercury,* Apr. 1, 1793, and especially the *Columbian Centinel* (Boston), Mar. 6, 1793: "Tickets may be had of Col. William Dickens, City Treasurer of Washington; of Thayer and Bartlet, of Charleston, S.C., Gideon Dennison, Savannah, Messrs. James West, and Co., Baltimore; of Mr. Peter Gilman, Boston, and at such other places as will be hereafter published."

25. Tontine Coffee House Papers, New-York Historical Society; "An act to incorporate . . . the Exchange Coffee-House," *Acts of the Massachusetts Assembly,* June 1807; *Acts of the General Assembly of Rhode Island,* Jan. 1795. The relationship between the state and the physical space it occupies raises issues similar to the ones at stake in James Sterling Young's *The Washington Community 1800–1828* (New York: Columbia Univ. Press, 1966). While one must be careful with counterfactual history, questions might be asked as to whether the completion and use of the Union Public Hotel might have created a more unified lodging space for legislators near the Capitol and propelled the political geography of Washington in a direction very different from the one Young describes.

26. Wansey, *Journal of an Excursion,* 226. Analogous dynamics in the process of nation building are explored with respect to the mails in Richard R. John's *Spreading the News: The American Postal Service from Franklin to Morse* (Cambridge, Mass.: Harvard Univ. Press, 1995), celebration and reportage in Waldstreicher's *In the Midst of Perpetual Fetes,* and literary culture in Shields's *Civil Tongues and Polite Letters,* esp. 321–22.

27. W. B. Bryan, "Hotels of Washington Prior to 1814," *Records of the Columbia Historical Society* 7 (1904): 71–106; J. Thomas Scharf and Thompson Westcott, *History of Philadelphia, 1609–1884* (Philadelphia, 1884), 980–98; I. N. Phelps Stokes, *Iconography of Manhattan Island, 1498–1909* (New York, 1967), 6:456–64; *Newport Mercury,* July 20, 1805; Davis, *Travels,* 39; *New York Evening Post* clipping, "Hotels" folder, exhibition notes for "The Larder Invaded," at the Library Company of Philadelphia; Folders 1790–1810, Quinn Collection.

28. This interpretation puts me into disagreement with Barbara Carson's claim that "the impression of change [in public accommodations] during the Federal period was simply a matter of a numerical increase in facilities." She does acknowledge that a "few influential projects stand out for their technological innovations or their levels of capitalization and scale for greater profit." But this characterization elides the architectural and sociospatial novelty of the first hotels and underplays the fundamental continuity between these structures and later hotels. See Carson, "Early American Tourists and the Commercialization of Leisure," 382.

5

THE PRODUCTION OF GOODWILL

THE ORIGINS AND DEVELOPMENT OF THE FACTORY TOUR IN AMERICA

WILLIAM LITTMANN

W. K. Kellogg began to offer public tours of his corn-flake factory in 1912. Despite their cost, Kellogg believed these tours were worthwhile because they impressed tourists with the vast size and sanitary conditions of his new Battle Creek, Michigan, plant (fig. 5.1). Much to Kellogg's delight, the factory soon became one of the region's leading attractions. In seven decades, six million adults and schoolchildren passed through the four-story-tall brick plant and witnessed the miraculous transformation of ordinary corn into breakfast.[1] Despite the enduring popularity of the Kellogg tour, the company closed the factory to outsiders in 1986. Not only did the tours disrupt production, Kellogg believed that spies for other cereal manufacturers were using them to steal trade secrets. Battle Creek residents and devoted customers could not hide their disappointment when they heard that the company would halt the tours. One visitor who came on the tour's final day told a reporter, "Until now this had been a friendly place. Now it will be part

Fig. 5.1 The 1912 booklet, *A Trip Thro' Kellogg's*, describes the first public tour of the Kellogg Company factory in Battle Creek, Michigan.

of some mysterious corporate structure. The cereal will be the same, I guess, but the feeling won't be the same when I sit down to eat breakfast."[2]

For more than a century, factory tours have offered the public a rare view of America's largest manufacturing facilities. This chapter focuses on the growing popularity of factory tours among manufacturers after 1890 and how the tour helped Progressive Era Americans come to terms with the social and cultural transformations caused by the rise of mechanized production and develop trust in the corporations that had come to dominate economic life. By the time of the Great Depression, most elements of the tour had become standardized, with established ways of proceeding through the factory and stock views of workers, machines, and products.[3]

Factory tours helped the public gain a better understanding of the mammoth new industrial facilities that had sprung up on the outskirts of American cities. Before 1880, most manufacturing took place near the city center, which allowed the public to become familiar with the layout of factories and the day-to-day activities of manufacturing. The increasing scale and suburbanization of industry between 1880 and 1920, however, made factories and mills inaccessible to much of the public.[4] The enormous buildings scattered on vast tracts of land miles from the urban core became enigmatic worlds unto themselves, perhaps only glimpsed from passing trains or in photographs in mass-market magazines. The factory tour invited Americans back onto the factory grounds for a brief view of the buildings where corporations mass-produced the consumer goods that filled homes and workplaces.[5]

The effort to open up the factory came in part as a response to the work of muckraking journalists, who offered a far less optimistic picture of the world behind the walls of the plant. Critics of industrialization, including Lewis Hine and Upton Sinclair, depicted the hazardous conditions inside factories, especially the effects of industrial labor on women and children. The factory tour can be best understood as a rebuttal to such criticisms, one that suggested that the plant was indeed a good place to work—better, in fact, than the homes and neighborhoods in which workers lived.

Turn-of-the-century Americans found themselves faced with two contradictory images of what occurred on the grounds of the plant—the paradise displayed on the tour or the dangerous and decrepit environment described by muckrakers.

The success of the factory tour depended on having visitors believe there was a direct correlation between the physical condition of the factory buildings and the less tangible social and economic conduct of the corporation. The gigantic size of a manufacturing plant, for example, was used to symbolize more abstract ideas about the company's stability and its capacity to respond quickly to consumer demand.[6] Visits through well-lit and well-ventilated workrooms similarly communicated the firm's benevolent treatment of its employees. This belief that the factory could represent the behavior of the corporation led many firms to make physical changes to the factory environment, adding lavish reception rooms and museums, and installing glass windows and platforms so that visitors could better see certain phases of factory production.

Early Factory Tours in America

The first large-scale industries in America occasionally offered trips through the plant, though these were informal and only granted to distinguished visitors. Literary and political figures, such as Charles Dickens, Davy Crockett, and John Greenleaf Whittier, came to Lowell, Massachusetts, in the mid-nineteenth century to see the gigantic mills rising up along the banks of the Merrimack River. The tours helped allay suspicions that the importation of the factory system to the United States would turn cities into blighted and smoke-filled landscapes resembling Manchester and other English industrial centers. Vivid accounts of the great mills of Manchester and the cruel conditions within them circulated widely in the United States at this time. Many American critics of industrialization believed that participation in the factory system would quickly create an immoral and debased working class who would be unfit to participate responsibly in a democratic system of government.[7]

Representatives for the Lowell mills took their guests on a lengthy tour through individual rooms for weaving and spinning and through the print works along the river's edge. The owners made sure the yards and buildings looked their best for visitors, who often noted the charm of such touches as the placement of flower boxes in mill windows. Guests often noticed the lack of grime upon the brick walls of the mills, a testament to the benefits of waterpower over the sooty steam engines that drove the looms in Manchester. Inspections of the well-maintained residential quarters of the operatives often helped quell reservations about the presence of women in the industrial landscape. The location of these mills in the bucolic countryside of New England offered hope that the new nation might be able to reap the economic benefits of large industry without creating urban slums.[8]

The cleanliness and architectural regularity of Lowell's industrial and residential landscape led many visitors to believe that workers benefited from their toil in the mills. The English novelist Anthony Trollope visited Lowell during the Civil War and noted that the multistory brick mills resembled less the Manchester of his native country and more a handsome campus. In his *North America*, published in 1862, Trollope wrote that the "workmen and workwomen in Lowell . . . are taken in, as it were, by a philanthropical manufacturing college, and then looked after, and regulated more as girls and lads at a great seminary, than as hands by whose industry profit is to be made out of capital."[9] Swedish writer Fredrika Bremer similarly believed that the attractive buildings of Lowell revealed larger truths about the conditions of labor in the mills. After viewing the Lowell mills from a distant hill on a cold February night in 1850, Bremer wrote that the "manufactories of Lowell, lying below in a half circle, glittering with a thousand lights, [were] like a magic castle on the snow-covered earth. And then, to think and to know that these lights were . . . not merely pomp and show, but they were actually symbols of a healthful and hopeful life in the persons whose labor they lighted; to know that within every heart in this palace of labor burned a bright little light, illumining a future of comfort and prosperity which every day and every turn of the wheel of machinery only brought the nearer."[10]

The Rise of Tours for the General Public, 1890–1930

Formal and regularly scheduled tours for the general public only began during the closing decades of the nineteenth century. The H. J. Heinz Company of Pittsburgh, Pennsylvania, and the National Cash Register Company (NCR) of Dayton, Ohio, pioneered the large-scale tour, opening their plants to large numbers of tourists in the 1890s. The Heinz Company's hour-long tour was typical of the time. Offered four times each day, it began at the plant's "model stable," a three-story fireproof brick structure that contained such devices as an electric machine that automatically fed, watered, and brushed horses. The tour then wound through the printing department, the box- and can-making departments, the Time Office (where workers clocked in and out), the power house, the employee dining room, the Baked Bean Building, the preserving kitchens, the Pickle Bottling Department, and, finally, the auditorium. Each stop focused on a sublime or dramatic aspect of the plant. The Time Office building, for example, was a miniature replica of the Library of Congress in Washington, D.C.; the Pickle Bottling Department offered a view of several hundred women in identical white caps and aprons stuffing pickles into glass bottles. The unexpected smells and sounds of production—including the odor of cooking tomatoes and the harsh racket of can manufacture—only added to the thrilling quality of the excursion.[11]

Heinz and NCR soon discovered that the tours were invaluable in establishing name recognition among consumers. "If I were asked for an opinion on the best advertising the NCR has done, I should answer 'Factory Visitors,'" noted one of the manufacturer's officials.[12] Following the example set by the two firms, dozens of large manufacturing plants quickly instituted tours between 1900 and 1920, including the Ford Motor Company factory in Highland Park, near Detroit, Michigan; the Shredded Wheat Company plant in Niagara Falls, New York; the Swift and Armour meatpacking facilities in Chicago; and the Hershey Chocolate factory in Hershey, Pennsylvania. At the same time, such tours grew increasingly popular with consumers. By the 1920s, more than two hundred thousand tourists were passing through the Armour plant and Ford's Highland Park factory each year. Manufacturers liberally distributed to each guest postcards and booklets describing the tour so that friends and family might enjoy learning about modern manufacturing techniques. The Postum Cereal Company of Battle Creek, for example, gave visitors postage stamps and postcards featuring the major buildings of the plant so that guests could immediately write home about their trip and what they saw in the magnificent Grape-Nuts factory. (fig. 5.2).[13]

Fig. 5.2. Visitors to the Postum Cereal Company factory in Battle Creek at the turn of the century received postcards bearing the image of the plant.

The factory tour helped fix the location of industrial corporations in the public's mind. Before the late nineteenth century, customers had become accustomed to buying locally made goods; new forms of mass production, however, concentrated manufacturing activities in certain cities, often located thousands of miles from the consumer. The tour aimed to prove that the industrial corporation was not a distant entity driven only by profit and market domination, but was instead composed of caring employees toiling in actual offices and factories.[14] The constant promotion of the tours led many Americans to know cities for only the consumer goods they produced. Battle Creek became largely known as the location of Kellogg and Postum factories. Niagara Falls was known not only as the location of the great waterfall but for the great Shredded Wheat plant nearby. An advertisement for Shredded Wheat suggested that the public might be as impressed by the factory as by the waterfall, calling the plant one of the two "Wonders of Niagara, Scenic and Industrial."[15]

Rapid changes in the scale and design of factories in the Progressive Era contributed to the public's fascination with industrial landscapes. In the early 1870s, the nation's largest plants may have employed only four to five hundred laborers, while by the time of the First World War, plants with more than ten thousand workers were not uncommon. A revolution in factory-construction methods, including the use of sawtooth roofs, large expanses of windows, and reinforced concrete, dramatically altered the appearance of factory buildings. At the same time, the increasing preference among manufacturers for single-story buildings combined with the effort to achieve economies of scale led to ever larger industrial sites filled with dozens of buildings sprawled over hundreds of acres of land. Manufacturers soon discovered the high cost of constructing such mammoth plants in congested urban settings and instead looked for cheap land on the city edge. In the undeveloped suburbs of such cities as Chicago, St. Louis, and Detroit, corporations acquired property in order to guarantee unlimited expansion.[16] Yet this shift in industrial location removed the factory from the daily life of those who lived downtown. Work inside the factory became a mystery to many Americans, a thing apart from ordinary life.[17]

In his 1906 novel *The Jungle,* Sinclair summed up the astonishment and interest that many Americans felt at this time about these new industrial zones. In the following excerpt, Sinclair describes one worker's long journey to a steel mill in South Chicago in an effort to find work:

The steel works were fifteen miles away, and as usual it was so contrived that one had to pay two fares to get there. Far and wide the sky was flaring with the red glare that leaped from rows of towering chimneys—for it was pitch dark when Jurgis arrived. The vast works, a city in themselves, were surrounded by a stockade; and already a full hundred men were waiting at the gate where new hands were taken on. . . .

The great mills were getting under way—one could hear a vast stirring, a rolling and rumbling and hammering. Little by little the scene grew plain: towering, black buildings here and there, long rows of shops and sheds, little railways branching everywhere, bare grey cinders underfoot and oceans of billowing black smoke above. On one side of the grounds ran a railroad with a dozen tracks, and on the other side lay the lake, where steamers came to load.[18]

The tours capitalized on the public's interest in the immense new plants. In tours and in advertisements, industrial firms were quick to dispense figures that illustrated the plant's size and output. Publicists for Shredded Wheat, for example, informed customers that builders used three thousands tons of steel, four million bricks, ten tons of putty, and thirty-five tons of paint in the construction of its factory.[19] This emphasis on scale aimed to dispel fears that the new industrial corporations were irresponsible, "fly-by-night" businesses that would disappear without fulfilling orders or adhering to return policies.[20] The linkage between physical magnitude and product quality was summed up in a 1920 article in *Printers' Ink Monthly*, a public relations trade magazine, which stated, "We have inherent respect for a piece of merchandize when we know that its home is a great establishment, spread out over one corner of a county and giving employment to thousands upon thousands of workmen. We are duly impressed by batteries of smoke-stacks and immense factory buildings that reach into dim perspective."[21]

Shaping Corporate Image through Public Tours

The factory tour helped industrial corporations defend themselves against Progressive Era criticisms about workplace conditions and their increasing control over the economy. Crusading journalists such as Edward Markham and William Hard portrayed the dangers of factory employment, offering chilling portraits of work inside the new steel plants, textile mills, and coal mines. The now-classic photographs by Hine showed children—seemingly aged beyond their years—toiling within dim workrooms and tending mammoth, fast-moving machinery. In *The Jungle*, Sinclair offered the following description of a Chicago fertilizer plant that processed animal byproducts from a nearby slaughtering house:

Here they dried out the bones—and in suffocating cellars where the daylight never came you might see men and women and children bending over whirling machines and sawing bits of bone into all sorts of shapes, breathing their lungs full of the fine dust, and doomed to die, every one of them, with a certain definite time. . . . In the corridors and caverns where it was done you might lose yourself as in the great caves of Kentucky. In the dust and the steam the electric lights would shine like far-off twinkling stars . . . according to the colour of the mist and the brew from which it came.[22]

The harmful conditions in manufacturing exposed by Sinclair and other muckrakers led to public support for legislation aimed at improving work environments in factories. Such laws included the Pure Food and Drug Act and the Meat Inspection Act, passed in 1906 and 1907. Frequent antitrust suits by state and federal governments between 1890 and 1930 broke up many industrial firms in an attempt to restore greater competition among businesses.[23]

The factory tour by Heinz and other manufacturers offered Americans an image of factory life that differed greatly from that of the muckrakers. The tours, in essence, argued that the public "could see for themselves" the true conditions within the high walls that surrounded the factory. Firms often used architectural imagery to communicate that they concealed nothing from the public, as in the Shredded Wheat advertisement that depicted the Niagara Falls plant as the "factory with a thousand windows." A 1907 souvenir postcard bearing an image of the plant promoted its sanitary quality of production, stating, "Shredded Wheat—The cleanest and purest of all cereal foods, made in the cleanest, most hygienic food factory in the world" (fig. 5.3).[24] Manufacturers often used the tour to show that the plant could be a place of beauty and refinement. Guides often pointed out that the company provided gardens and well-decorated lounges for workers, providing a respite from the noise and dirt of the factory floor. The Postum plant tour, for example, began with a visit to owner C. W. Post's extensive art collection, which was kept on the top floor of the administration building.[25]

Manufacturers planned tours with all the precision and forethought they put into arranging production

Fig. 5.3. A 1907 postcard promoting the sanitary conditions at the Shredded Wheat factory in Niagara Falls, New York.

lines. By the turn of the century, many firms had created detailed room-by-room directions for visitors. General Electric (GE) management, for example, developed strict guidelines for the tour of the Schenectady (New York) Works that proscribed the use of certain staircases and entrances and the direction of movement through specific departments (map 5.1). By offering each person the same choreographed sequence of experiences, companies believed they could elicit a predictable response of respect for the company.[26] In order to improve their communication with visitors, leading companies hired full-time professional tour guides. NCR president John H. Patterson once boasted that the company had a "school for guides at the factory and they are taught what to say and where

to say it." The gender of guides was often linked to the type of product made at the plant. Manufacturers of food products and consumer goods for the home often employed female guides in an attempt to make the factory less threatening; firms that made large machinery hired young men to usher tourists through what appeared to be a dangerous environment.[27]

While corporations invited the public into the plant, they never offered tourists a full view of all productive activities at the site. To avoid the threat of industrial espionage, many tour guides refused to reveal specific information about the processes and materials used in manufacture. When the spokesman for one Massachusetts industrial firm described in 1919 his company's tour for the general public, he said, "The plan was to see that they were impressed with the extent of the work without letting them see what the work really was. Long vistas were shown from a distance but the really vital points of the plant were avoided."

A 1926 tour for journalists through the GE Schenectady Works passed through only about 10 percent of the major buildings at the site. The tour focused on those departments in which the most spectacular and technically advanced forms of production occurred, including the assembly of complicated switchboards and cable manufacture, leaving out warehouses, carpentry shops, and several foundries (map 5.2). The highlight of the trip was a visit to Building 60, an

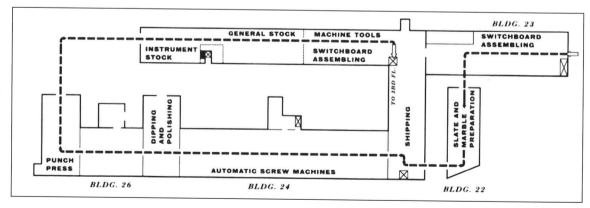

Map 5.1. The route for visitors to the GE Schenectady Works moved through the first floor of the Switchboard manufacturing department in 1913. Delineated by Brett McFadden.

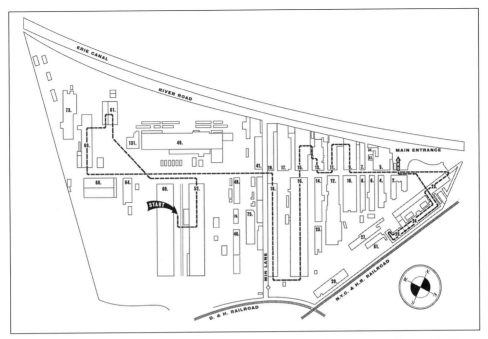

Map 5.2. The route for visitors at the GE factory in Schenectady in 1904. Delineated by Brett McFadden. Illustration drawn from *The Schnectady Electrical Handbook* (Schenectady, N.Y.: General Electric Co., 1904).

eight-hundred-foot-long machine shop where more than a thousand workers assembled giant steam turbines. Because the building was one of the first machine shops in the United States to have all its machinery powered by electricity—and thus avoided the belting and shafting common to most industrial settings—it demonstrated the value of the electrical motors and other products invented and produced by GE. Like most factory tours, the one offered by GE routinely avoided the buildings containing white-collar workers. Even though administrative coordination of the plant was as essential to a manufacturer's success as activities on the shop floor, the rooms filled with typists, telephone operators, draftsmen, and managers were all but invisible to outsiders.[28]

Some meatpacking firms tried to divert attention away from the gruesome realities of meat preparation and instead had focused their tours on more hygienic and placid settings. In the 1930s, tours of one major meatpacker, for example, concentrated on the sliced-bacon department, where visitors saw a largely female and American-born work force arrange, weigh, and wrap bacon slices. The women worked at comfortable tables in heated rooms—conditions that contrasted with the cold and windowless settings where much of the real meatpacking work occurred. Though most of meat production was handled by African American workers or employees of Eastern European descent, meatpacking firms believed that visitors to the plant would feel more comfortable if they saw only white laborers touch meat products.[29]

Physical Changes to the Plant to Improve the Tour

Companies fitted the plant with ramps, platforms, bridges, and other devices to give tourists elevated views of production and keep them out of the way of hazardous machinery. At Highland Park, Ford constructed special railings to allow visitors to observe a final stage of automobile manufacture, the chassis and body assembly. Meatpacking firms installed large windows in some departments to help tourists better see their impressive methods of meat production.

Executives at the GE Schenectady Works considered a plan to put special exterior windows in a refrigerator-assembly building so that passengers on nearby trains could glimpse the work inside. Before rejecting the plan in the 1920s, the executives deliberated about asking the railroad "to slow their trains a bit as they go by" so that riders might get a better view of the refrigerator assembly line.[30]

Company architects might arrange the main entrance of a plant to keep foreign-born workers out of sight to visitors. An architect writing in a trade journal for factory owners in 1924 offered one example of why one might decide to build two gates to separate the female clerical staff from the plant's unskilled work force, whom he described as being of "rather a rough type." "Had the factory employees been of a higher type [the architect] could have made a single entrance serve the entire plant, thus economizing valuable space," he wrote. "But as it was, a single entrance was out of the question. The women employees would have been subject to annoyance from the men . . . and visitors to the plant would have been unfavorably impressed by an entrance which could not have been kept presentable."[31]

Many manufacturers inserted distinctly nonindustrial building types into the plant grounds in an attempt to burnish the company's image. Reception rooms, where the public gathered before tours, often resembled the public spaces of elite homes. Many of these rooms contained grand fireplaces, thick carpets, ornate lamps, and paintings of company officials. Guests could examine company products arranged in glass cases or peruse the liberal supply of in-house publications and company brochures. The lavish Postum Cereal Company reception room was decorated in a medieval English style, and, according to its management, it had a "quaint beauty" in the "midst of the humming factory" (fig. 5.4). The design of the reception room often reflected the company's current public relations campaign. The Gruen watchmaker plant in Time Hill, Cincinnati, for example, used a half-timbered medieval revival design for its reception area, complete with beamed ceilings and period furniture, to reinforce the fact that the company imported watch movements from Switzerland. The firm

described the room as a place "where the Guild brethren of old might have sat on a crisp Swiss evening eating cheese and sipping sack."[32]

Factory museums often were installed in spaces adjacent to reception areas. Usually no larger than a single room, these museums educated visitors about the company's rich past and longstanding effort to provide quality goods. In the reception area of the Dennison paper box company of Framingham, Massachusetts, for example, the company displayed the knives, rulers, and cobbler's bench that founder Aaron Dennison used to make his first paper box. Larger historic objects were placed on the factory grounds and became obligatory stops on plant tours. Visits to the McCormick Reaper Works in Chicago during the 1920s included a view of a large flat-topped boulder that had been brought to the plant from the Virginia farm of company founder Cyrus McCormick. The firm's public relations department claimed that McCormick used the boulder as an anvil block to create parts for the first mechanical reaper—and thus referred to the rock as the company's "first factory."[33]

Manufacturers moved entire historic structures to the factory if they believed the building would symbolize for visitors the simple and virtuous beginnings of the firm. The Walk-Over shoe company, for example, reconstructed the "tiny shack" where former president George Keith made his first pair of shoes. Even though it was surrounded by modern industrial buildings, executives hoped the modest one-room

Fig. 5.4. The reception room for visitors to the Postum Cereal Company factory in 1916.

structure would keep the company from "drifting too far away from the ideals" that guided the first employees of the firm. Heinz appears to have been a pioneer in the placement of historic buildings on plant grounds. In 1904 the company moved to the factory a two-story brick house where in 1869 founder Henry J. Heinz started the enterprise. In an attempt to generate publicity, the manufacturer loaded the structure on a barge and slowly floated it five miles down the Allegheny River to Pittsburgh. Company officials placed the house in a "hallowed spot" near the main entrance, where it could be visited by tourists.[34] In an early 1920s advertisement, the company explained the structure's importance to Heinz, saying, "When you visit the 'Home of the 57' you see the little 'House where we began'—surrounded, overshadowed by larger modern buildings. To the visitor the little house may seem but an interesting relic—a thing of purely historical interest, signifying growth and prosperity. To us, this homely little brick building stands as a symbol—a constant reminder of the ideals established there, the principles on which the Heinz business has been built."[35]

The display of such artifacts at the plant presented visitors with a celebration of a preindustrial past, even though most of the tour focused on the company's technological sophistication. The "House where we began" was an icon of an earlier age of small-scale production, when objects were made by hand and owners were on close terms with workers and with their customers. These artifacts referred to a time when an inventor could achieve national success through sheer intelligence and drive. Such objects obfuscated the fact that economic triumphs in the industrial era were more likely the result of corporate orchestration of enormous numbers of workers, distant raw material sources, and complex financial markets.[36]

Corporate Displays of Labor

To respond to questions about the treatment of workers, manufacturers emphasized how they provided employees with clean and ventilated work spaces, lockers, sinks, and sports and educational facilities. Many of these structures were for women employees, whom male executives and social critics feared were more like-

ly to be harmed by the exhausting work of factory production. The impressions of an enthusiastic visitor to the Heinz plant suggested that the public believed the company treated its female work force well: "Before the visitor . . . leaves, many things should pass his inspection, such as the cleanliness of the buildings and workrooms—the outside of them even is washed once a year—the clean and tidy appearance of the girls who work there, their blue uniforms and white caps, the rooms where they have their hands manicured, the flower boxes in the windows . . . and many other features."[37]

Manufacturers disagreed whether the constant traffic of visitors would disrupt workers or increase productivity. Some experts believed that tours allowed for increased supervision of labor by company guides and that men and women would work more diligently if constantly observed by the public. Early tours offered at the Ford Highland Park plant were termed a

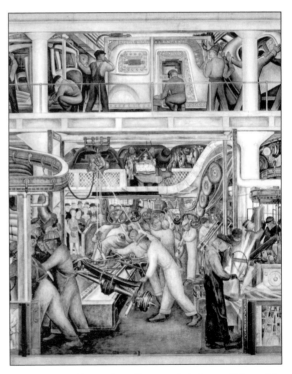

Fig. 5.5. Detail, South Wall, *Detroit Industry,* Diego M. Rivera (1932–33). At the left, visitors to the Ford Motor Company River Rouge plant stand behind a wall and watch the assembly line. Photograph © 1996. Gift of Edsel B. Ford. The Detroit Institute of Arts.

"nuisance" because visitors diverted the attention of the assembly-line workers. Henry Ford responded to this problem by merely increasing the sheer number of tourists. Ford remembered that the company "let so many go through after that, for a while, that they ceased to be a novelty. In a little while no workman would look at a visitor."[38]

Tourists frequently looked at employees from behind glass or down upon them from platforms and other raised viewing sites, intensifying the social distance between tourists and workers. Often dressed in matching uniforms, workers seemed anonymous and interchangeable—thus not unlike the machines sharing the same floor space. The class distinctions between viewers and workers is captured in such representations of the factory as Diego M. Rivera's *Detroit Industry,* his mural of the production line at the Ford River Rouge plant (fig. 5.5). Standing behind a protective wall, the well-heeled tourists in this mural observe a shop floor filled with bustling workers attired in overalls. The prim onlookers look uncomfortable and physically inert compared to the energetic and determined men on the production line.[39]

Though corporate executives found that the factory tour helped improve the public image of manufacturers, critics of industrialization argued that it was impossible for tourists to fully comprehend the experience of factory work after a brief visit. In her classic 1910 study of working-class life in Homestead, Pennsylvania, Margaret Byington noted how visitors might interpret dramatic scenes of steel production in vastly different terms than workers. "The onlooker, fascinated by the picturesqueness of it all, sees in the great dim sheds a wonderful revelation of the creative powers of man," she wrote. "To the worker this fascination is gone; heat and grime, noise and effort are his part in the play."[40]

Changes in Factory Tour Practice, 1930–1970

In the middle decades of the twentieth century, many manufacturers found that the public increasingly grew bored with just observing the everyday operation of the factory. Americans wanted more than just scenes of production and bustling workrooms. To accommodate these desires, factory tours after the Great Depression began to focus on entertaining visitors during their trip through the plant. One public relations expert summed up this trend in the 1950s, noting that "most people would rather watch a show than study statistics," and thus the best plant tour "spices open houses in its plant communities with down-to-earth showmanship."[41] Manufacturers in the 1930s also began to adjust the message of their tours so that they promoted the benefits of free enterprise and attacked New Deal–era attempts to regulate business. While the public generally became more accepting of corporate capitalism in the previous decade, the depression triggered yet another wave of hostility toward big business. One textbook on public relations noted that "more and more companies are slanting plant tours to make visitors appreciate the fact that only in a free economy is it possible for a business to achieve what visitors have observed on their tours."[42]

At the same time, manufacturers attempted to promote themselves as good neighbors to residents who lived near the plant. Corporations made an extra effort to give special tours to leaders in the community, most often teachers, members of the clergy, and heads of business organizations. Many tours reminded visitors about the company's invaluable impact on the local economy and the jobs it provided to residents. The Standard Oil Company distributed a pamphlet to visitors at its Richmond, California, refinery that noted that it supported the community through its tax burden and by purchasing goods from local suppliers. The pamphlet went on to say that Standard Oil hoped the tour provided "factual evidence of the company's sincere efforts to do a good job as a citizen, and as an employer and as a competitive member of the oil industry. We hope that your visit has . . . given you a better understanding of modern American business and how it operates to the benefit of all of the public."

After the 1950s, companies used the tour to address the environmental impact of industry on the local community. The tall chimneys discharging black smoke and the traffic jams at the end of work shifts had come to be seen not as signs of prosperity, but as a nuisance for host cities. By 1978, the magazine *Industry Week* noted that a chief motivation behind tours was to "counter anti-business attitudes such as extreme consumerism or environmentalism."[43]

Decline and Transformation of Factory Tours, 1970–2000

Like the Kellogg plant in Battle Creek, many of the most popular tours came to an end in the 1970s and 1980s. Concerns about sabotage, hygiene, and safety halted the tours at the Hershey and Ford River Rouge plants. Heinz stopped allowing visitors into its Pittsburgh facility in 1972, following a series of lawsuits from tourists injured at the factory. In addition, the flight of industry from the United States to countries with cheaper labor and less government regulation generally reduced the number of large factories available for public inspection. Not all companies gave up factory tours, however. Nearly three hundred firms still offered factory tours in the late 1990s; they were especially popular with smaller industries that did not have extensive advertising budgets but instead depended on word-of-mouth publicity.[44] Other manufacturers explored new technologies that allowed them to educate the public about production without admitting them to the plant. The Dole Food Company, for example, created a web site that used a cartoon character named Sammy-Salad-in-a-Bag to show how lettuce makes its way from the field to the supermarket. This "virtual tour" offered scenes of workers operating machines that dice, wash, and dry lettuce in Soledad, California.[45]

The most successful replacement for the plant tour appears to be corporate visitor centers that offer staged reproductions of the production process. The substitute for the Hershey plant tour is Chocolate World, an entertainment complex and gift shop that invites visitors to take a twelve-minute trip in automated cocoa bean–shaped carts through a series of scenes recreating the manufacture of chocolate. In this ride, the visitor experiences production from the bean's point of view and thus personally goes through a simulation of the roasting and chopping process. These new visitor centers are extremely popular with tourists. In 1997, more than sixty thousand visitors traveled to Hormel Foods Corporation's Spamtown USA, while nearly a million individuals toured the World of Coca-Cola in Atlanta. The following year, Kellogg opened Cereal City USA in Battle Creek as a replacement for tours of its main plant. Here cereal enthusiasts could enjoy the "corporate heritage gallery" containing historic advertisements and products; see a musical play performed by giant bowls and spoons; and enter the Digestive Tunnel, a fun house-like series of rooms and passageways that mimics the shape of the human intestinal tract. Like the Hershey exhibit, Cereal City offers a "stylized representation" of its production line that incorporates equipment from the real plant.[46]

The development of such corporate visitor centers is in many ways a fitting conclusion to longstanding trends in factory tour practice. Many of the major public tours in the early decades of the twentieth century at such firms as GE and Heinz and at meatpacking plants offered visitors an idealized and often comforting vision of factory labor. Even in these mediated views, however, visitors gained some understanding of the mass quantities of human labor power needed to make common consumer goods. The new corporate visitor centers, however, present a production landscape that operates with little or no assistance from labor. Cornflakes and chocolate bars float automatically from one machine to the next toward completion. With these dioramas, corporations obscure the human realm of factory production and thus ignore the contributions of working men and women who toil in real manufacturing settings in the United States and abroad.

Notes

1. On the Kellogg Company tour, see Mary Butler, Frances Thornton, and Martin Ashley, *The Best to You Each Morning: W. K. Kellogg and Kellogg Company* (Battle Creek, Mich.: Heritage Publications, 1994), 34–49; Damon Darlin, "Kellogg Is Snapping Its 80-Year Tradition of Plant Tours," *Wall Street Journal,* 10 Apr. 1986.

2. James Barron, "Nothing Sacred: Kellogg Ends Tours," *New York Times,* 13 Apr. 1986.

3. The rise of the public factory tour in the United States has received relatively little attention in studies of American business and culture. Brief remarks about factory tours can be found in Susan Strasser, *Satisfaction Guaranteed: The Making of the American Mass Market* (New York: Pantheon Books, 1989), 113–15; Roland Marchand, *Creating the Corporate Soul: The Rise of Public Relations and Corporate Imagery in American Big Business* (Berkeley and Los Angeles: Univ. of California Press, 1998), 255–62; David Nye, *American Technological Sublime* (Cambridge: MIT Press, 1994), 127–29; John Jakle, *The Tourist: Travel in Twentieth-Century North America* (Lincoln: Univ. of Nebraska Press, 1985), 30–36.

4. This chapter focuses on tours for the general public as distinguished from the general practice of "factory visiting" common in the manufacturing trade during the nineteenth century, when many plant and shop proprietors welcomed customers, fellow mechanics, and businessmen onto their premises. Though there was always concern about guests stealing trade secrets, many firms considered the practice helpful, since visitors might bring information about business opportunities and new manufacturing technology. For more on these informal tours, see Philip Scranton, *Endless Novelty: Specialty Production and American Industrialization, 1865–1925* (Princeton: Princeton Univ. Press, 1997), 30–33, 39, 208–89, 314.

5. John R. Stilgoe, "Moulding the Industrial Zone Aesthetic: 1880–1929," *Journal of American Studies* 16, no. 1 (Apr. 1982): 8–14; Daniel Nelson, *Managers and Workers: Origins of the New Factory System in the United States,* 2d ed. (Madison: Univ. of Wisconsin Press, 1995), 11–25.

6. On the goal of advertising to offer the idea of stability, see A. Rowden King, "The Factory and Its Relation to the Advertising Department," *Printers' Ink* 62, no. 11 (Sept. 15, 1910): 30–35.

7. On descriptions of Manchester and concern about the impact of industrialization on United States cities, see the introduction to Michael Brewster Folsom and Steven D. Lubar, eds., *The Philosophy of Manufactures: Early Debates over Industrialization in the United States* (Cambridge: MIT Press; North Andover, Mass.: Merrimack Valley Textile Museum, 1982), xix–xxxiii.

8. On early-nineteenth-century tours of the mills of Lowell and how they were understood as signs of forthcoming American industrialization, see Charles Cowley, *Illustrated History of Lowell,* rev. ed. (Boston: Lee and Shepard, 1868), 78–80; Arthur L. Eno Jr., ed., *Cotton Was King: A History of Lowell, Massachusetts* (Somersworth, N.H., New Hampshire Publishing, 1976), 240–41; John F. Kasson, *Civilizing the Machine: Technology and Republican Values in America, 1776–1900* (New York: Penguin Books, 1979), 55–106; Thomas Bender, *Toward an Urban Vision: Ideas and Institutions in Nineteenth-Century America* (1975; reprint, Baltimore: Johns Hopkins Univ. Press, 1982), 21–93; Dona Brown, *Inventing New England: Regional Tourism in the Nineteenth Century* (Washington, D.C.: Smithsonian Institution Press, 1995), 20; Margaret Crawford, *Building the Workingman's Paradise: The Design of American Company Towns* (London: Verso, 1995), 11–28; Nye, *American Technological Sublime,* 112–15.

9. Eno, *Cotton Was King,* 241.

10. Fredrika Bremer, *The Homes of the New World: Impressions of America,* trans. Mary Howitt (New York: Harper and Brothers, 1858), 1:209–10.

11. On the Heinz tour, see Robert Alberts, *The Good Provider: H. J. Heinz and His 57 Varieties* (Boston: Houghton Mifflin, 1973), 90–126; Marchand, *Creating the Corporate Soul,* 255–58; Eleanor Foa Dienstag, *In Good Company: 125 Years at the Heinz Table* (New York: Warner Books, 1994), 34–37, 118; Roland Cole, "How Heinz Advertises Idea Behind Plant and Product," *Printers' Ink Monthly* 5, no. 2 (July 1922): 19–20, 94; Strasser, *Satisfaction Guaranteed,* 121–23.

12. A tour of the NCR plant is described in *A Trip Through the Factory* (Dayton, Ohio: National Cash Register, 1903) and in Lena Harvey Tracy, *How My Heart Sang: The Story of Pioneer Industrial Welfare Work* (New York: Richard R. Smith, 1950), 151–57. The quote about the NCR tour is from Roy W. Johnson and Russell W. Lynch, *The Sales Strategy of John H. Patterson* (Chicago: Dartnell, 1932), 114.

13. A growing interest among Americans in recreational tourism contributed to the popularity of tours. In the late nineteenth and early twentieth centuries, leisure travel became increasingly more available to the upper and middle classes, a trend spurred by rising prosperity, reductions in the work week, and improved train service. Guidebooks and popular magazines of the time regularly published vivid descriptions of the layout and activities within large factories. From the beginning, companies believed that entire families

should enjoy the tours and, as a result, women and children appear to have comprised a large percentage of total visitors. On tourism and the growing popularity of factory tours in the United States, see Strasser, *Satisfaction Guaranteed,* 113–15; Budgett Meakin, *Model Factories and Villages: Ideal Conditions of Labour and Housing* (London: T. Fisher Unwin, 1905), 112–18; Donna Braden, *Leisure and Entertainment in America* (Dearborn, Mich.: Henry Ford Museum and Greenfield Village, 1988), 287–96; Stilgoe, "Moulding the Industrial Zone Aesthetic," 8–14; Cole, "How Heinz Advertises," 20; Marchand, *Creating the Corporate Soul,* 255–60.

14. On the public perception of industrial corporations between 1880 and 1930, see Strasser, *Satisfaction Guaranteed,* 6–28; Marchand, *Creating the Corporate Soul,* 1–10, 21–31.

15. Strasser, *Satisfaction Guaranteed,* 113.

16. Nelson, *Managers and Workers,* 3–25; Graham Romeyn Taylor, *Satellite Cities: A Study of Industrial Suburbs* (New York: D. Appleton, 1915).

17. Nye, *American Technological Sublime,* 124–28.

18. Upton Sinclair, *The Jungle* (1906; reprint, New York: Penguin, 1986), 245–46.

19. Strasser, *Satisfaction Guaranteed,* 113–14.

20. King, "Factory," 30.

21. Nye, *American Technological Sublime,* 109–38; Stilgoe, "Moulding the Industrial Zone Aesthetic," 5–24. The quote is from Marvin Murrey, "Humanizing the Picture of the Factory," *Printers' Ink Monthly* 1, no. 3 (Feb. 1920): 63.

22. Sinclair, *Jungle,* 154.

23. Richard Hofstadter, *The Progressive Movement, 1900–1915* (Englewood Cliffs, N.J.: Prentice-Hall, 1963), 1–15; Marchand, *Creating the Corporate Soul,* 7–47; Daniel Rodgers, "In Search of Progressivism," *Reviews in American History* 10, no. 4 (Dec. 1982): 113–32; G. H. Dickinson, "Why Big Corporations Need Advertising," *Printers' Ink* 66, no. 7 (Feb. 17, 1909): 24–25.

24. The quotes from the Shredded Wheat publicity material come from Strasser, *Satisfaction Guaranteed,* 113, 115. On the NCR tours, see Crawford, *Building the Workingman's Paradise,* 55.

25. Marchand, *Creating the Corporate Soul,* 255; King, "Factory," 30–35.

26. Routes and descriptions of tours can be found in *Ford Factory Facts* (Detroit: Ford Motor Company, 1915);

"Route for Visitors," General Electric Company, Plan no. 01554, 1904, Building and Grounds Department, General Electric Schenectady Works, Schenectady, New York; *The Schenectady Electrical Handbook: Being a Guide for Visitors from Abroad Attending the International Electrical Congress* (Schenectady, N.Y.: General Electric, 1904); "Outline of Visitors' Route Through the Switchboard Department," Image no. 230373, General Electric Photographic Archives, Schenectady Museum, Hall of Electrical History, Schenectady, New York (hereafter known as Hall of Electrical History); "Route for Visitors," Oct. 11, 1900, Series M/I, box 7, McCormick Collection, State Historical Society of Wisconsin, Madison.

27. On guides at plants, see Dienstag, *In Good Company,* 118; Tracy, *How My Heart Sang,* 152; Leon Thomas, "Hanging Out the Factory Latch String," *Factory* (Oct. 1919): 769–71. Patterson's comments of 1911 can be found in Johnson and Lynch, *Sales Strategy,* 120.

28. The quote about showing the plant is from Thomas, "Hanging Out the Factory Latch String," 771. On the tour of the General Electric plant, see Charles M. Ripley, *Romance of a Great Factory* (Schenectady, N.Y: Gazette Press, 1919); Nelson, *Managers and Workers,* 22; *Trip through Schenectady Works of the General Electric Company by Members of the First Pan American Congress of Journalists, April 24, 1926,* pamphlet, Hall of Electrical History.

29. Roger Horowitz, "'Where Men Will Not Work': Gender, Power, Space, and the Sexual Division of Labor in America's Meatpacking Industry," *Technology and Culture* 38, no. 1 (Jan. 1997): 204–6.

30. Terry Smith, *Making the Modern: Industry, Art, and Design in America* (Chicago: Univ. of Chicago Press, 1993), 155; Meakin, *Model Factories and Villages,* 116–17; "Monthly Report from Steever to Simmons, March 13, 1926," Hall of Electrical History.

31. F. Morse Holcomb, "How to Work with Your Architect," *Factory* 33, no. 1 (July 1924): 44.

32. Murrey, "Humanizing the Picture," 65–66; Marchand, *Creating the Corporate Soul,* 255. The description of the Gruen reception room is in Robert Bostick, "Reflecting the Product in the Reception Room," *Printers' Ink Monthly* 5, no. 5 (Oct. 1922): 29–30.

33. On the general rise of the factory museum and its uses, see Roy Johnson, "Have You a Factory Museum?" *Printers' Ink Monthly* 5, no. 3 (Aug. 1922): 25–26; John Allen

Murphy, "How You Can Use a History in Your Business," *Printers' Ink Monthly* 9, no. 3 (Sept. 1923): 27–28, 90; Don Gridley, "History as a Factor in Good-Will Advertising," *Printers' Ink Monthly* 12, no. 1 (Jan. 1926): 44, 133–34; Meakin, *Model Factories and Villages,* 112–13; *Harvester World* 1, no. 3 (Dec. 1909): 24.

34. The establishment of the "house where we began" is described in Alberts, *Good Provider,* 153–56; Dienstag, *In Good Company,* 23. An advertisement depicting the house is in the *Saturday Evening Post,* Aug. 17, 1918, 69.

35. Thomas, "Hanging Out the Factory Latch String," 770; Cole, "How Heinz Advertises," 20.

36. On the general obfuscation of the factory from customers, see Alan Trachtenberg, *The Incorporation of America: Culture and Society in the Gilded Age* (New York: Hill and Wang, 1982), 130–39; Stuart Ewen, *Captains of Consciousness: Advertising and the Social Roots of the Consumer Culture* (New York: McGraw-Hill, 1976), 77–80.

37. Cole, "How Heinz Advertises," 100.

38. Meakin, *Model Factories and Villages,* 112–18. Ford's comments are recorded in Allan Benson, *The New Henry Ford* (New York: Funk & Wagnalls, 1923), 136.

39. On the reinforcement of class distinctions through spatial separation and elevation, see Nye, *American Technological Sublime,* 128–29; Dean MacCannell, *The Tourist: A New Theory of the Leisure Class* (New York: Schocken Books, 1976), 57–76.

40. Margaret Byington, *Homestead: The Households of a Mill Town* (1910; reprint, Pittsburgh: Univ. of Pittsburgh Press, 1974), 172.

41. On increased showmanship in public relations, see John Aspley, ed., *The Dartnell Public Relations Handbook* (Chicago: Dartnell, 1961), 317–18; Glenn Griswold and Denny Griswold, eds., *Your Public Relations: The Standard Public Relations Handbook* (New York: Funk & Wagnalls, 1948), 531–59. The quote is from Rex Harlow and Marvin Black, *Practical Public Relations* (New York: Harper and Brothers, 1952), 194–95.

42. The quoted material is from Aspley, *Dartnell Public Relations Handbook,* 308. On this effort to promote free enterprise, see Griswold and Griswold, *Your Public Relations,* 525–28; Marchand, *Creating the Corporate Soul,* 235–45.

43. A description of the Standard Oil tour of Richmond, California, and quotes from the tour pamphlet are in Aspley, *Dartnell Public Relations Handbook,* 325–26. Environmentalism and how to fight it is addressed in Lad Kuzela, "Plant Tours that Pass the Test," *Industry Week* 198, no. 3 (Aug. 7, 1978): 46. Other sources for using tours to improve relations with the public are Fred Jolly, "How We Did It: Barber's Day at Caterpillar Tractor Company," *Public Relations Journal* (Oct. 1950): 11; Louis Lundborg, *Public Relations in the Local Community* (New York: Harper and Brothers, 1950), 95–107; Harlow and Black, *Practical Public Relations,* 192–93.

44. Carl Quintanilla, "Planning a Vacation? Give Some Thought to Spamtown USA," *Wall Street Journal,* May 1, 1998; Jim Treece, "Will Plant Tours Go the Way of the Tail Fin?" *Business Week,* Apr. 10, 1995, 30D; "Windows on the Workplace," *Wall Street Journal,* Sept. 16, 1997; Karen Axelrod and Bruce Brumberg, *Watch It Made in the U.S.A.* (Santa Fe, N.M.: John Muir Publications, 1997).

45. "Tour of a Fresh-Cut Salad Factory," Dole Food Company, Inc., web site, http://www.dole5aday.com/about/factory/factory.html.

46. Quintanilla, "Planning a Vacation?"; Axelrod and Brumberg, *Watch It Made in the U.S.A.*

6

SIDEWALKS AND STORE WINDOWS AS POLITICAL LANDSCAPES

JESSICA SEWELL

Pedestrians on the streets of San Francisco, California, during the last week of August 1911 would have noticed that store windows were overwhelmingly filled with wares in shades of yellow ranging from the lightest lemon to deep mustard. Mixed in with the familiar window cards marking prices and proclaiming quality were hand-lettered cards supporting women's suffrage and copies of an elegant poster, once again in shades of yellow, showing a chic young suffragist, haloed by the sun setting over the Golden Gate, holding a banner reading "Votes for Women" (fig. 6.1).

In the spring of 1911, California suffragists embarked on the largest woman suffrage campaign yet in the long struggle for women's voting rights in America.[1] In this campaign a broad-ranging coalition of suffragists, ranging from the waitresses and other working women of the Wage Earners Suffrage League to the upper-class ladies of the Club Women's Suffrage League, worked together, using a wide variety of political tactics in their successful battle for the right to vote. This campaign pioneered or expanded the use of many tactics of visibility, including advertising posters

Fig. 6.1. Votes for Women, poster by B. M. Boyé, 1911. This was the winner of a highly publicized poster competition sponsored by a coalition of San Francisco woman suffrage organizations and was the primary image used in the 1911 campaign. From College Equal Suffrage League of Northern California, *Winning Equal Suffrage,* frontispiece.

and signs; the use and sale of suffrage items such as stationery, lapel buttons, and baggage stickers; street speeches; and a storefront office dedicated to selling suffrage. In San Francisco, many of these tactics were focused on the downtown shopping district, which was also the location for the majority of suffrage organization offices. In redefining this district as a space of political action, suffragists not only took advantage of their access to this important space in the center of the city, an access which they had gained as consumers, but also borrowed the techniques of persuasion that had been used on them by downtown businesses. The takeover of show windows was the first, and arguably the most striking, of the tactics that used the downtown shopping landscape as an arena of political action and borrowed that district's techniques of persuasion.[2] Several social and physical attributes of show windows and sidewalks in San Francisco's downtown shopping district made them a fruitful ground for women to argue for the right to vote.

The Downtown Shopping District

In 1911, downtown shopping districts, and the department stores which were their anchors, were relatively new features of American cities. With the increased use of mass-produced goods, especially clothing, in the nineteenth century, women increasingly provided household goods to the family by buying them from large shops rather than producing them at home or buying them from small local providers. Though urban shopping districts existed before the second half of the nineteenth century, the modern shopping district as a special, spectacular destination and shopping as a form of amusement did not fully come into being until the invention of the department store. Department stores were built in most major cities in the United States only after 1870, and in smaller cities somewhat later.[3]

San Francisco had several large dry-goods stores before the opening of the Emporium in 1896, but at least one shopper believed that the Emporium was "run on a new plan for San Francisco—a great department store—with everything in it imaginable."[4] By 1911, San Francisco had several other large and modern department stores, including the White House and the City of Paris. These were at the heart of an active downtown shopping district, which had been rebuilt in renewed form out of the ashes of the 1906 earthquake and fire.

Department-store owners conceptualized the downtown shopping district as a largely segregated female space in which mostly middle-class women did the work of consumption—shopping for the family and themselves. One department-store owner went so far as to call his store an "Adamless Eden."[5] Department stores were imagined by their owners as complete female worlds, self-contained cities providing a wide range of goods and services, including, in the case of the Emporium in 1910, "a parlor with papers, periodicals and writing materials; a children's nursery; an emergency hospital, with trained nurse in attendance; a Post Office Station; a Western Union telegraph office; a theater-ticket office; a manicuring and a hair-dressing parlor and a barber shop; public telephones; a lunch room; an information bureau; [and] always some free exhibition in the art rooms."[6] This range of goods and services all provided under one roof theoretically made it possible for women shoppers do all their downtown errands without ever stepping foot out of the store. The wide variety of shops outside and even most of the nonretail services of the downtown, such as the post office, hair dressers, and restaurants, were duplicated within department stores.

Although historians have taken a critical view of department stores, examining labor and gender politics within them, they have generally accepted the store owners' assessment of the gendering of this landscape. Because historians have focused not on the shopping landscape as a whole, but rather on the interiors of the large, modern department stores anchoring all turn-of-the-century downtown shopping landscapes, they have missed the complex and less clearly gendered landscape that surrounded the stores.[7] Examining how the store was experienced within the daily practices of women shoppers reveals the inadequacy of the gender-segregated model.

Department stores were conceived of as female-gendered islands in the male city. They supposedly provided shoppers with all the services and even experiences of the larger city, without the perils attendant to sharing space with unknown men and people of lower classes. However, in practice, to get to these islands of consumption, women took to the streets. Women walked or took streetcars, which they shared with men, to get downtown. Once there, they walked from store to store along the sidewalks of that district, window-lined worlds of vicarious consumption that were neither as controlled nor as segregated as the world inside the department store.

Department stores were only part of a larger downtown shopping landscape (fig. 6.2). They were surrounded then, as today, by a wide array of smaller shops and other businesses, providing a smaller, more specialized range of products and services. These stores shared the sidewalk with department stores, and their show windows helped to create a largely unbroken facade of glass along that sidewalk, a screen of seductive displays that mediated between the sidewalk

Fig. 6.2. South side of Market Street between Fourth and Fifth Streets, 1909. From the left, the buildings are the Pacific Building, the Commercial Building, and the Emporium department store. Courtesy of the Bancroft Library, University of California, Berkeley.

and store interiors, attempting to draw strolling shoppers inside to buy.

The sidewalks on which the windows faced were frequented not only by women shoppers but also by men and women for whom the sidewalk was part of the landscape of office work, as well as people who came downtown to go to the theater and to eat at popular cafés and restaurants. Turn-of-the century downtown shops and offices shared many of the same requirements, such as high accessibility by public transportation, a dense concentration of people and businesses, and proximity to banks.[8] Geographers and planners who studied the central business district (CBD) in American and European cities in the 1950s and 1960s found that department stores, women's clothing stores, and related shops were heavily concentrated in the CBD, as were financial and other offices.[9] Martin Bowden's historical study of the San Francisco CBD showed that this concentration was true not only in the twentieth century but also in the latter half of the nineteenth century.[10] Within the CBD, the zones occupied by shops and offices were not identical but usually overlapped.

In San Francisco in 1911, the businesses that made up the downtown shopping district were concentrated in a roughly triangular area defined by Mason, Bush, and Market Streets. Map 6.1 shows the location of dry-goods, clothing, ladies' furnishing goods, and millinery businesses listed in the 1911 directory. A number of these businesses, including the Emporium, Hale's, Prager's, and Roos Brothers' department stores, were located along Market east of Fourth Street. The remainder of the trade was in the area between Kearny and Powell and Sutter and Market. Grant Avenue housed several large stores, including the White House, Davis-Schonwasser and Company, I. Magnin, and the "Tiffany's of the West," Shreve and Company. Other major dry-goods and department stores included the City of Paris, at Stockton and Geary on Union Square, and the Lace House, a block away on Stockton and O'Farrell.

The office landscape was concentrated along Montgomery, California, and Market Streets, as can be seen in the mapping of attorneys, brokers, money brokers, and insurance agents in map 6.1. Several buildings contained large numbers of attorneys' offices, including buildings along Market street at Mason, Powell, Fourth (two buildings), Grant (three buildings), Kearny (five buildings), and Montgomery (four buildings).

Though the areas encompassed by the shopping and office districts were not identical, they overlapped on the stretch of Market Streets between Third and Seventh Streets and, to a lesser extent, along Grant and Kearny. These areas of overlap were targeted by the show window campaign as well as the majority of suffrage street speeches and other suffrage uses of the sidewalk realm. For example, the corners of Market and Seventh, Market and Fifth, and especially Market at Grant and at Stockton, were sites of regular suffrage street speeches. Many speeches were also given along Mission Street in the Mission District, a major local shopping district that served a middle- and working-class neighborhood.[11]

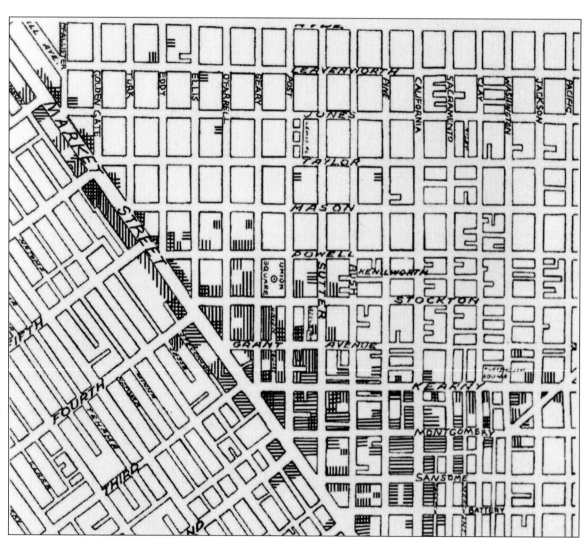

Map 6.1. Location of businesses of the downtown shopping landscape and the downtown office landscape, 1911. Horizontal lines represent dry goods, ladies' furnishing goods, and millinery businesses listed in the 1911 *Crocker Langley San Francisco Directory*. Vertical lines represent brokers, money brokers, insurance agents, and attorneys listed in the 1911 *Crocker Langley San Francisco Directory*.

Fig. 6.3. View north on Powell and east on Market, c. 1910. Flood building at center. Courtesy of the Bancroft Library, University of California, Berkeley.

This overlapping of business and retail functions was made possible by the combination of both in a single building. Because ground floor locations, essential to shops, were not as important for offices, landlords found it financially efficient to rent their ground-floor spaces to shops. The standard building type within the downtown shopping district reflected this real estate situation, combining shops on the ground floor with several stories of offices above. This building type predominated along the stretch of Market Street most shared by the shopping and office landscapes. Even the Emporium had offices in its facade, though selling floors behind. The female-gendered shopping space and male-gendered office space were well segregated within these buildings, which generally had separate entrances for shops and offices and no communication between these two sections of the building.

In spite of the strict segregation of space within each building, the effect of this building type was to encourage an active mix of sexes. The sidewalk in front of these buildings, traveled both by men en route to offices and women walking between stores, functioned as simultaneously part of the primarily male-gendered landscape of white-collar work and the primarily female-gendered landscape of shopping. Photographs of the streets of San Francisco's shopping district reveal a mixed crowd, with business-suited men and groups of women sharing the sidewalk (fig. 6.3).

The significance of this sharing is not just that both men and women used the sidewalk, as men and women shared space in many parts of the city. Men worked as managers and clerks in downtown stores, for example, and many downtown offices had female clerical staff. However, these spaces were imagined as single-gender, with the gender served in each space predominating—the businessman for the office landscape and the female shopper for the stores. Spaces were imagined as part of a male or a female realm, and those who trespassed those boundaries were considered exceptions to the rule, free to enter that space, but not to conceive of it as theirs. In contrast to these functionally mixed-gender, ideologically single-gender spaces, downtown sidewalks were simultaneously part of two different landscapes, the emphatically female-gendered landscape of shopping and the strongly male-gendered landscape of business. Both men and women could imagine the sidewalk as theirs, and this made it a different kind of mixed-gender space.

Suffrage Uses of the Downtown Shopping Landscape

The mixed-gender nature of the public space of the sidewalk provided women a legitimate space for political speech both to other women and to men. Equally important, it also accustomed both men and women to a joint occupation of public space, which helped make shared participation in public life more imaginable. That this particular public space was in the central district, the symbolic heart of the city, made it that much more significant. As women shared this central public space with men, the idea of sharing power and responsibility in the public sphere became more imaginable, as articulated by Fannie McLean, a Berkeley schoolteacher and suffrage activist, in a speech to members of women's clubs during the 1911 campaign: "The woman of today takes a larger and more gracious place in the world. We are now co-thinkers and co-workers with man, in the same world, living in the same houses, using the same public conveyances, attending the same colleges, buying our food and clothing at the same shops; and why not be co-voters as to the management of this common environment and as to the basic principles of the democracy which produces this environment."[12] In this speech, McLean argues that women should have an equal control over the spaces they share, rather than remaining powerless because they are voteless. It is only when women share space with men, rather than using it without having a cultural claim to it, that this argument can be made.

Because the sidewalk was both a space in which women had the authority to act and a space frequented by men, it was a prime site for women's suffrage activity, which focused on the necessary task of getting men to vote for women's voting rights. Furthermore, the sidewalks and streets of the center city, especially Market Street, were a common site of other political speech and civic displays, including parades, rallies, and speeches. This downtown sidewalk and street became a prime site for many women's suffrage strategies, including the window display campaign, both because of the downtown sidewalk's political salience and because of women's access to it, legitimized by their role as consumers.

The 1911 Woman Suffrage campaign in California was the largest yet in the long struggle for women's voting rights in America, and much broader than the unsuccessful 1896 California campaign. At the turn of the century, suffragists were working to get the vote on a state-by-state basis, working to pass amendments to state constitutions rather than focusing on a federal amendment. Though a federal amendment was proposed in 1878, by Senator A. A. Sargent of California, whose wife was a prominent San Francisco suffragist, it had been rejected numerous times and was not even considered by Senate or House committees between 1896 and 1913.[13] In this hostile federal atmosphere, suffragists turned to the states, hoping to build women's rights and influence piecemeal in order to eventually win suffrage on the federal level. By 1911, women had the vote in only five states: Wyoming, Colorado, Idaho, Utah, and Washington.[14] The California campaign helped to turn the tide, and California's 1911 victory was followed by Oregon, Kansas, and Arizona in 1912, Illinois in 1913, Montana and Nevada in 1914, and by several other states soon afterward. These state victories helped lead to the passage of the federal amendment in 1920.

In California in 1911, suffragists fought first to get a referendum on suffrage on the ballot, and once they had achieved this, had less than three months to convince the men of the state to vote for it. A broad-based coalition of San Francisco suffragists worked together in this effort, using a wide variety of political tactics in their successful battle for the right to vote. Some of these strategies included speaking to unions and women's clubs, putting on plays, sending frequent press releases to the papers, canvassing door to door, and advertising through posters, postcards, and pins. Many of the most interesting strategies, which the suffragists themselves thought were crucial to their victory, are those which used the downtown shopping landscape.

For example, on one well-advertised day suffragists sold postcards on major street corners throughout the downtown area, as well as in front of the entrances to department stores and major office buildings.[15] More than half the street speeches made by suffragists in San Francisco during the 1911 campaign also took place at major intersections along Market Street. The street speech campaign climaxed the night before the election, when Lillian Nordica, a famous opera star, sang and spoke in favor of suffrage from a car in Union Square, the symbolic center of the shopping district. Suffragists even set up shop in a storefront just a few doors down from the Emporium, decorating their window with yellow placards and posters, yellow chrysanthemums, and "Votes for Women" banners, pulling sympathizers in with the "constant distribution of leaflets on the sidewalk in front of the store, day and evening, until 9 P.M."[16] In addition, Market Street near Fourth, "the largest business center of the city," was the site of the most prominent piece of suffrage advertising, a blazing "large, permanent, electric sign" reading "Votes for Women."[17]

In emphasizing public visibility and making use of the techniques of modern advertising California suffragists were following British examples, which were also being studied and followed in other states, particularly New York. As in San Francisco, British suffragettes used storefronts as offices, decorating their windows with suffrage posters and books.[18] British suffragettes also convinced shops to display clothing and accessories in the British suffrage colors, purple, white, and green, in preparation for a Hyde Park march in 1908, though this was done primarily to "expedite shopping," as suffragettes were to dress entirely in suffrage colors for the march.[19] Californians also learned from British suffragettes' use of signature colors, their use of pageantry, and their use of advertising posters and postcards.[20] In their use of posters, in particular, California suffragists explicitly followed the British example.[21] In conjunction with a competition to design a poster for the California campaign, the *San Francisco Call* published images of several British suffrage posters as models.[22] British suffragettes also printed some of their posters on yellow paper for use in the California campaign, although California suffragists were concerned about the militancy of many images used in Britain and in the eastern United States.[23]

The Show Window Campaign

Of all of the tactics using the downtown shopping district and the space of the sidewalk, the show window campaign most explicitly engaged the commercial nature of this landscape. In this campaign, stores throughout the Bay Area, but especially in San Francisco's downtown shopping district, decorated their windows in yellow, the suffrage color, "the florist's by having flowers of the suffrage color, the milliner's and the dry goods by hats and goods of our color, the stationer's by filling the window with suffrage books and periodicals."[24] A member of the College Equal Suffrage League described the scene:

> Shopwindows, from one end of the city to the other, blossomed in every known shade of yellow, and to point the reason for the color, copies of the prize poster, in dull olives and tan, lightened with yellow and flame, gave the campaign cry "Votes for Women." . . . One large furniture store gave two great front windows to a beautiful autumn color scheme in browns and yellows, and one book shop put up several dozen copies of the prize poster and filled his window-shelf with copies of such books as Olive Schreiner's "Woman and Labor," and Miss Addams' "Newer Ideals of Peace." . . . The city wore the color that was soon to be the color of success.[25]

For the most part, suffragists were not themselves shop owners or managers, so they gained access to the store windows through their social connections and purchasing power. According to the official committee report on the window display campaign, the committee chairman "was a member of a family long known in the city. She started a list with the signatures of some of the most important firms in San Francisco, and each consent, of course, made the next easier to win."[26] Suffragists encouraged the participation of store owners not only through personal contacts but also through use of the mass media. They published the names of prominent stores that were participating in the campaign in the daily newspapers in advance of the display week to pressure nonparticipants to sign on.

In the window display campaign, suffragists took advantage of the conventional department-store practice of providing space to women's clubs and church groups for charity activities. For example, the July 4, 1903, *Dry Goods Reporter* described a church apron sale held in a Minnesota department store. The store built and decorated a booth for the sale in a corner of the store, served coffee and lunch to the women working at the sale, and advertised the sale heavily. "The visitors to the sale, and to the store as the booth was in our store, could not fail to attend to the special sale we conducted," the manager wrote. "This is where we re-alized returns for the advertising and for granting the ladies the privilege of conducting their sale in our store.... A very impressive impression was created favorable to our store."[27] This sale and similar in-store charity activities reported in the *Dry Goods Reporter* and the *Modern Grocer* were touted for creating good will, extra trade, and advertising for stores. Women's clubs' public, though nonpolitical, use of store space set a precedent for suffrage club's political use of store space. For store owners, promoting suffrage in their window displays simply continued a policy of accommodating female consumers, treating the store as the "women's club" it was often described as being. It also was a way of attracting the middle-class women who were major suffrage boosters, and competing with stores which did not sign on to the campaign.

The Emporium went the furthest, providing space within the store for a demonstration booth at which a suffragist, Miss Bagley, sold and served "Equality Tea," talking "the advantages of political equality to all who will listen to her." She also distributed two hundred "Votes for Women" buttons to Emporium employees.[28] The Emporium had also been supportive in the 1896 campaign, when suffrage headquarters were in an office in the store's facade. Its management at that time placed "a number of artistic hand-painted placards in every prominent portion of the interior of the building" inviting shoppers to visit the Woman Suffrage Association office.[29]

Suffrage Use of Retail Strategies

By the 1910s, suffrage was sufficiently popular that many advertising campaigns used suffrage wording and imagery to sell to women. One notable example is a 1913 Shredded Wheat advertisement, topped by the banner slogan "Votes for Women." This ad shows a woman in front of a ballot box, holding a square of shredded wheat, and the text reads in part "twenty million women have voted for the emancipation of American womanhood by serving Shredded Wheat in their homes."[30]

In another example, a 1915 advertisement used the slogan "Most Women Vote for Knox Gelatine"

Fig. 6.4. Knox Gelatine advertisement, 1915.

(fig. 6.4). The accompanying illustration shows two women, one in an apron and the other in a smart suit and hat, putting ballots labeled "vote" into the ballot slot at the top of Knox Gelatine boxes.[31] The use of two female figures, both the housewife and the woman dressed for public space, possibly a working woman and certainly a modern woman, shows an acceptance of women in public, as long as the modern women continue to cook (with Knox Gelatine). Both of these ads equate the sorts of everyday choices women make as shoppers with the decisions they make as voters; voting is just another form of shopping, appropriate for savvy modern women (though potentially equally manipulable by advertising). The incorporation of suffrage rhetoric into advertising underscores the buying power of prosuffrage women and the economic desirability for a shop owner to align himself with suffrage.

Contemporary advertising practices were also used by California suffragists to promote their political position. The use of a single color and the repetition of the Votes for Women poster, which was posted throughout the state and reproduced on stickers and postcards (fifteen thousand of each), were explicitly patterned on contemporary retail practices. The official report of the committee on design wrote that "the psychology of advertising teaches us to repeat, with slight variations, a familiar design until the public eye is caught by the manifold repetitions of the same arresting idea."[32] The prize poster, the slogan

"Votes for Women," and the color yellow were all repeated to such an extent that some suffragists eventually found the color "violent and pestilential" and wished that they might have chosen "a new and prettier color."[33]

Window displays as well as other forms of advertising used repetition heavily. The major display strategy for windows of this era is patterned repetition. Model window after model window was organized entirely out of handkerchiefs, shoes, canned goods, or other commodities, arranged to create a striking visual effect. Repetition was also created through the use of a single color. Windows, interior displays, and sometimes even entire stores were often decorated in shades of a single color, creating an image that simultaneously expressed unity and harmony through color and abundance through a variety of objects and shades.

The repeated use of a single color is a marketing technique that was particularly associated with department stores. Historian William Leach described this 1907 use of the color green at the New York store Greenhut's: "Carpets, side walls, stool seats, and desk blotters wore different shades of green; window backgrounds were green velvet, and the store attendants dressed in green; there were green stationery, green stock boxes and wrapping paper, green string, even green ink and green ribbon for the green store typewriters."[34] Suffragists adopted this single-color marketing ploy when they decided on the color yellow as a unifying motif for all material related to the California suffrage campaign. In choosing a color to unify the campaign, they were specifically adopting the tactics of modern marketing—specifically, of modern department-store marketing.

Alice Park, a Palo Alto suffragist, wrote that they chose yellow because "we knew the suffragettes in England tried to catch the eye with colors and our yellow was easier to use than their purple, white, and green. . . . We said it was the most beautiful color in the world, and especially in the golden state; that California owed its life to the gold in the hills; that the golden poppy is the state flower; that the golden orange grows here, and golden grain."[35] Yellow had also been used as a suffrage color in the United States since 1887 and had been used in Washington state, where suffrage had

been won in 1910.[36] Yellow was repeated in suffrage posters, pins, sashes, banners, stickers, displays, postcards, flower packets (of yellow flowers), and other paraphernalia. The color yellow and the official suffrage poster, the result of a highly publicized competition, were the unifying symbols of suffrage in the show window campaign and throughout the entire suffrage battle. In the window campaign individual merchants chose which yellow goods to display, but the color and poster marked the display of goods as part of a political display as well as a commercial one.

Show Windows

Windows were a useful site for suffragists' activity because of their ambiguous status as neither fully part of the street and sidewalk realm they spoke to nor the (female-gendered) store realm they were attached to and controlled by. The ambiguous status of show windows is visible not only in their use as a forum for speaking to passersby through display and window cards but also in the design of the windows themselves.

By the time of the suffrage campaign of 1911, show windows were visually, and in many ways physically, separated from the interior of the store. Books and articles on window decorating, as well as photographs of window displays, show the nearly universal use of a background screening the window from the store, so that the window functions as an autonomous space. In contrast to this solid background, the glass which separated the window from the sidewalk was made as invisible and immaterial as possible. The display space in the window had to appear as if it shared the sidewalk with the viewer so that displays could appeal directly to potential customers and draw them into the store. Multiple articles and words of advice in trade journals, as well as advertisements for prefabricated shop fronts and window fixtures, emphasized the importance of windows to attracting customers. More than one advertisement showed immaterial window glass pierced by giant hands reaching out to grab customers on the sidewalk (fig. 6.5).[37]

In order to keep the window glass perfectly clear and immaterial day and night, lighting was carefully planned to minimize glare while fully illuminating the goods in the window. Windows fogging or frosting also obscured this transparency. According to a 1914 article for shopkeepers, a clear window served as "the oasis in the desert and will attract that passer-by." In contrast, "a frosted window glass is worse than having no show window at all. It is a silent witness that the store is not as progressive as it might be."[38] This problem was addressed by circulating outside air into the window display space and sealing the back wall of the window to separate the air in the window from the air in the store (fig. 6.6). With this scheme, the window was not only visually continuous with the sidewalk because of the transparency of the plate glass, but even its air circulation made it one with the outside.

Fig. 6.5. Onken Younits advertisement, 1911.

The plan of store fronts also increasingly emphasized the link between window and sidewalk (fig. 6.7). Store entrances were usually recessed, the entry door aligned with the plane of the opaque back of the windows. These plans brought the street into the building on the ground floor, blurring the line between interior and exterior. This line could be drawn either at the front of the plate glass windows, with the windows as part of the interior, or by the opaque window backs and the entry door, with the windows as exterior. The space between the window fronts and the plane of the entry was primarily controlled from inside, but visually it was continuous with the sidewalk, and shop owners saw themselves as financially benefiting from emphasizing the continuity between sidewalk and window.

Thus, show windows were marked as an ambiguous space, part of a store yet focused on the street. Through lighting, air circulation, enclosure, and plan, windows were constructed as not properly interior to the store, but as a special, protected element of the public sidewalk landscape. The ambiguous status of show windows, combined with their conventional use as a space of (commercial) speech to passersby, made them an ideal forum for women, who were associated with the interior space of the store, to speak to the mixed crowd that frequented the sidewalks of the downtown shopping district. Suffragists saw the potential in show windows as a space of communication to crowds, made use of the advertising tactics developed by retailers to catch the eye of the masses, and exploited their status as consumers to gain access to the windows and use them as a space of political, rather than commercial, speech. In so doing, they pushed the windows further into the public realm of the sidewalk. When used by shopkeepers for commercial speech, windows remained functionally one with the store, serving the commercial space of the interior rather than the more fully public space of the exterior. By using these same windows for political speech, suffragists tipped the balance in favor of the public sidewalk.

With the suffrage windows, store owners signaled their support to their female customers while simultaneously showing goods those customers might want to buy. However, for male window viewers, suffrage windows also implied that the prominent businessmen who owned the stores supported women suffrage, marking it as a political position worth taking. By exploiting their power as consumers, suffragists redefined the windows, making them not only a space of commercial display, but also a space of feminist political speech.

Conclusion

The shopping district was an important space for San Francisco suffragists because it was a public space within which women had standing. Because the shopping district existed for women shoppers and was imagined as a female world, women had a claim to its

Fig. 6.6. System of air circulation for windows. From *The Art of Decorating: Show Windows and Interiors* (Chicago: Merchants Record Company, 1906–9), 227.

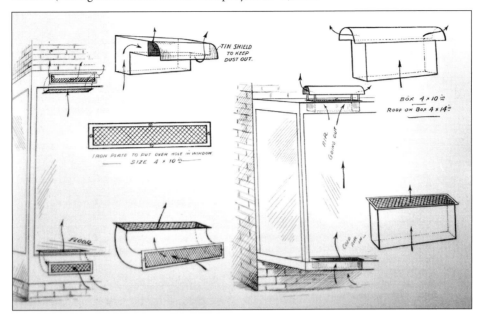

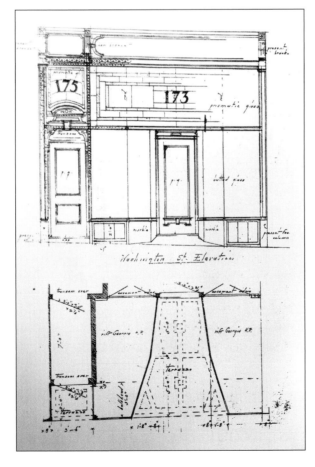

Fig. 6.7. Plan and view of store front, 1907. Entrances to early-twentieth-century stores were typically recessed, so that the door lined up with the rear of the window display space. Note the doors at the back of the window display space, where the windows are separated from the interior of the shop. From Henry L. Walters, "Modern Store Fronts," *Architectural Review* 14, no. 6 (1907): plate 33.

spaces. Women were expected to inhabit the downtown streets, and to consider them theirs. Their power as consumers also gave them access to store windows for the show window campaign.

Though the cultural imagination of the downtown shopping district as a female world gave women power within it, the usefulness of the downtown lay in its *not* being a female world. Rather than being segregated spatially from men in "Adamless Edens," women engaged in a shopping landscape which overlapped and interconnected with men's landscapes of work and transportation. Downtown buildings which combined upstairs offices and first floor shops helped to create a mixed-gender landscape on downtown sidewalks, a landscape which was fully exploited by San Francisco suffragists in 1911. Because the downtown was a mixed-gender space in the symbolic heart of the city, it was a prime site in which to speak to a large number of men and women. Through street speeches, window displays, postcard sales, advertisements, the distribu-

tion of literature, and the shopfront headquarters, suffragists made themselves heard and seen by both voting men and women who could join their cause. Their activities extended beyond the conventional shopping hours into the evening, thus reaching working men and women on the way home from work, as well as evening promenaders and theatergoers.

San Francisco suffragists' use of the downtown shopping district in 1911 illustrates the importance of public space to the public sphere. Though women gained access to that public space as consumers, not citizens, they were able to parlay that access into political power, using their power as consumers to gain access to store windows and to the streets of the downtown. They cannily exploited the nature of downtown spaces, including the public/private ambiguities of show windows and the mixed-gender space of the sidewalk. Using the display and advertising techniques that had been aimed at them by retailers, they sold suffrage to the men and women of California.

Notes

1. Eleanor Flexner and Ellen Fitzpatrick, *Century of Struggle: The Woman's Rights Movement in the United States,* enlarged ed. (Cambridge: Belknap Press, Harvard Univ. Press, 1996), 248.

2. "Show window" is the term used in the retail trades during this period to refer to store windows.

3. William Leach, "Transformations in a Culture of Consumption: Women and Department Stores, 1890–1925," *Journal of American History* 71, no. 2 (1984): 322; Susan Porter Benson, *Counter Cultures: Saleswomen, Managers, and Customers in American Department Stores, 1890–1940* (Urbana: Univ. of Illinois Press, 1986), 31.

4. Annie Haskell diary, June 2, 1896, Haskell Family Papers, Bancroft Library, Univ. of California.

5. Edward Filene, quoted in Benson, *Counter Cultures,* 76.

6. C. E. Cake, "Arranging Goods to Make the Shoppers Buy," *System* 18 (Dec 1910): 593, quoted in Benson, *Counter Cultures,* 76.

7. Benson, *Counter Cultures;* Susan Porter Benson, "Palaces of Consumption and Machine for Selling: The American Department Store, 1880–1940," *Radical History*

Review 21 (Fall 1979): 199–221; Elaine S. Abelson, *When Ladies Go A-Thieving: Middle-Class Shoplifters in the Victorian Department Store* (Oxford: Oxford Univ. Press, 1989); William Leach, "Transformations in a Culture of Consumption"; and Rudi Laermans, "Learning to Consume: Early Department Stores and the Shaping of the Modern Consumer Culture (1860–1914)," *Theory, Culture & Society* 10 (1993): 79–102 all focus on department stores and end their gaze at the inside of the plate glass of the display window. Even Gail Reekie, *Temptations: Sex, Selling, and the Department Store* (St. Leonards, Australia: Allen & Unwin, 1993), and William Leach, "Strategists of Display and the Production of Desire," in *Consuming Visions: Accumulation and Display of Goods in America, 1880–1920,* ed. Simon J. Bronner (Winterthur, Del.: Henry du Pont Winterthur Museum, 1989), 99–132, which discuss display windows at length, do not address the district as a whole or women's use of the sidewalk. Anne Friedberg, *Window Shopping: Cinema and the Postmodern* (Berkeley and Los Angeles: Univ. of California Press, 1993), recognizes the importance of store windows and the downtown shopping district in creating the possibility of a female flaneur, but because her focus is on film theory and the gaze, this book is of somewhat limited use to architectural historians.

8. Richard M. Hurd, *Principals of City Land Values* (New York: Record and Guide, 1911); Cecil C. Evers, *The Commercial Problem in Buildings* (New York: Record and Guide, 1914).

9. The CBD is usually defined either by its high land value or by the concentration within it of businesses which serve the city as a whole, rather than a more local population. See Raymond Murphy, J. E. Vance Jr., and Bart J. Epstein, *Central Business District Studies* (Worcester, Mass.: Clark Univ., 1955); Martyn J. Bowden, "Growth of the Central Districts in Large Cities," in *The New Urban History: Quantitative Exploration by American Historians,* ed. Leo F. Schnore (Princeton: Princeton Univ. Press, 1975); and Hans Carol, "The Hierarchy of Central Business Functions within the City," *Annals of the Association of American Geographers* 50, no. 4 (1960): 419–38. These studies all include both retail and office functions as aspects of the CBD, but none of them comment on the gendering of these functions.

10. Martyn John Bowden, "The Dynamics of City Growth: An Historical Geography of the San Francisco Central District, 1850–1931" (Ph.D. diss., Dept. of Geography, Univ. of California, Berkeley, 1967).

11. *San Francisco Call,* Sept. 14, 1911, p. 7; Sept. 21, 1911, p. 7; Sept. 22, 1911, p. 7; Sept. 23, 1911, p. 13; Sept. 30, 1911, p. 13; Oct. 5, 1911, p. 4; Oct. 7, 1911, p. 13; Oct. 10, 1911, p. 1. I use speeches mentioned in the *San Francisco Call* because of all the daily San Francisco papers, it had the most complete coverage of suffrage matters.

12. Fannie McLean, "Speech to Women's Clubs," carton 9, Fannie McLean Papers, Bancroft Library, Univ. of California (hereafter cited as McLean Papers).

13. Carrie Chapman Catt and Nettie Rogers Shuler, *Woman Suffrage and Politics* (Seattle: Univ. of Washington Press, 1923), 495–96.

14. Wyoming granted the vote to women from its beginnings as a territory in 1869 and was admitted to the union as a woman suffrage state in 1890. The Utah Territory initially granted women the vote in 1870, but Congress negated that right in 1887. When Utah gained statehood in 1896, they granted woman suffrage by means of a constitutional referendum. Colorado amended its constitution to allow women the vote in 1893, and Idaho followed suit in 1896. Fourteen years later, in 1910, Washington became the next state to amend its constitution to give women the vote. For a full chronology, see Marjorie Spruill Wheeler, ed., *One Woman, One Vote* (Troutdale, Oreg.: NewSage Press, 1995), 375–77.

15. "Yes, the Lady with the Postals Wants Both Coin and Vote," *San Francisco Call,* Oct. 5, 1911, p. 7.

16. College Equal Suffrage League of Northern California, *Winning Equal Suffrage in California: Reports of Committees of the College Equal Suffrage League of Northern California in the Campaign of 1911* (National College Equal Suffrage League, 1913), 80.

17. Ibid., 84.

18. Ibid.

19. Lisa Tickner, *The Spectacle of Women: Imagery of the Suffrage Campaign, 1907–1914* (Chicago: Univ. of Chicago Press, 1988), 45–47, 49; Liz McQuiston, *Suffragettes to She-Devils* (London: Phaidon, 1997), 35, 40. Most American suffragists carefully avoided the use of the term "suffragette," preferring the term "suffragist." Because of the radical nature of English tactics, which included breaking windows and other forms of violent protest, "suffragette" came to carry connotations of militancy that American suffragists wished to avoid.

20. Tickner, *Spectacle of Women,* 93.

21. Tickner, *Spectacle of Women;* McQuiston, *Suffragettes to She-Devils;* and Barbara Green, *Spectacular Confessions: Autobiography, Performative Activism, and the Sites of Suffrage, 1905–1938* (New York: St. Martin's Press, 1997) discuss British suffrage tactics in detail. Though San Francisco suffragists did not hold a parade in the 1911 campaign, they did participate in the San Francisco Labor Day parade and made use of banners, which they "carried 'accidentally' through the streets from one headquarters to the other, or for some ostensible reason," attracting "just the right kind and amount of attention," according to Selina Solomons in *How We Won the Vote in California* (San Francisco: New Woman Publishing, 1912), 41. On the Labor Day float, see College Equal Suffrage League of Northern California, *Winning Equal Suffrage,* 96–98, and "Thousands March in Ranks of Labor," *San Francisco Call,* Sept. 5, 1911, pp. 1–2.

22. "Big Posters are Effective Weapons in Luring Votes to Suffrage," *San Francisco Call,* Aug. 23, 1911, p. 7; "Woman—Her Long, Long Fight to Win Back, Illustrated with Posters used by the Women of England in their Battle to Win the Ballot," *San Francisco Call,* Sept. 10, 1911.

23. Tickner, *Spectacle of Women,* 267; College Equal Suffrage League of Northern California, *Winning Equal Suffrage,* 46. The first real success of the British suffragettes came in 1918, when women over age thirty gained the vote. In 1928, the voting age for women in England was lowered to twenty-one.

24. Fannie McLean, "Campaign of Ed," carton 9, McLean Papers.

25. College Equal Suffrage League of Northern California, *Winning Equal Suffrage,* 46.

26. Ibid.

27. "Apron Sale," *Dry Goods Reporter,* July 4, 1903, 69.

28. "Boston Tea Party Is Far Eclipsed by California Women," *San Francisco Call,* Aug. 11, 1911, p. 7.

29. "Food for Mind and Body," *San Francisco Call,* July 25, 1896, p. 6.

30. Ellen DuBois and Karen Kearns, *Votes for Women: A 75th Anniversary Album* (San Marino, Calif.: Huntington Library, 1995), 17.

31. Knox Gelatine advertisement, *Modern Grocer,* Apr. 17, 1915, 15.

32. College Equal Suffrage League of Northern California, *Winning Equal Suffrage,* 46.

33. Ibid., 49.

34. Leach, *Transformations,* 323.

35. Alice Park, quoted in Du Bois and Kearns, *Votes for Women,* 19.

36. Margaret Finnegan, *Selling Suffrage: Consumer Culture and Votes for Women* (New York: Columbia Univ. Press, 1999), 111–16. College Equal Suffrage League of Northern California, *Winning Equal Suffrage,* 49.

37. Onken Younits advertisement, *Modern Grocer,* 1911; Butler Brothers advertisement, *Modern Grocer,* Mar. 4, 1911, 32.

38. "Keeping Frost Off the Display Window," *Modern Grocer,* Dec. 19, 1914, 8.

PART II

IDENTITY

7

HIDING BEHIND TREES AND BUILDING SHELTER WITHOUT WALLS

STICK AND FOLIATE STRUCTURES IN THE CIVIL WAR LANDSCAPE

MARTIN C. PERDUE

As he watched Union soldiers splitting shingles and daubing mud on logs for their winter huts, a reporter for *Frank Leslie's Illustrated Newspaper* mused, "Truly, every man is a Robinson Crusoe to a certain extent."[1] Like the storied castaway, many soldiers during the American Civil War found themselves living in a strange and inhospitable land. Here they improvised shelter on familiar cultural models using the materials at hand and few or no tools. With canvas, sticks, logs, mud, stones, and leafy branches soldiers made homes for themselves in the midst of war. Whether it was a patch of ground with a small tent and a fire or a picketed regimental camp, shaping the nearby landscape gave the men a chance to govern one aspect of their lives during a time of tremendous upheaval and imminent peril. They made the unknown familiar by contriving small shelters with homelike qualities of scale and a degree of comfort. In addition to molding their surroundings to create places of shelter and refuge, some fighting men sought to obstruct the threatening landscape of war by raising barriers of greenery. Tents and shanties were the principal modes of shelter during the war, but of particular interest here are the more obscure structures built by soldiers using trees, hedges, sticks, and leafy branches, from the common and mundane to the rare and elegant.[2]

From 1861 to 1865 more than three million Union and Confederate soldiers lived and fought on contested ground, often far from home. Many of the men who volunteered for service had never before spent any appreciable time away from their family and loved ones. Young recruits undoubtedly suffered some emotional trauma when they were sent off to live for months and even years at a time in distant regions, solely in the company of men. Federal troops, nearly two million strong, often faced the additional strain of fighting on enemy soil. According to historian Reid Mitchell, "The Union soldier, trapped in [an unfamiliar] . . . landscape, surrounded by a civilian population half of it hostile and all of it bizarre, felt tremendous anxiety."[3] One way of dealing with this disorientation was to shape and to structure the camp environment and the surrounding landscape. Another method for coping with the feelings of fear and hostility was to assault the countryside of the enemy directly. As Mitchell has ably demonstrated, the so-called total war that Grant is credited with initiating could not have occurred when it did had it not been for the willingness of the common soldier to set fire to the houses and fields of the South. Evidence of Northern attitudes toward the landscape of the South survives in the etymology of the word "bushwhacker." Originally used to describe someone who blazed trails by literally whacking bushes, the term became curiously inverted during the Civil War to warn that the bushes might conceal dangers of their own. A bushwhacker became someone who attacked suddenly from a place of concealment, an ambusher. Webster's further defines the term as "a guerrilla fighter, especially one on the Confederate side in the Civil War; so called by the Northern soldiers."[4] One New York newspaper printed a sensationalist illustration in 1863 of Confederate pickets disguised as small cedar trees firing on Union troops.[5] From all indications, such attacks were actually rare. Nonetheless, in the minds of Union troops, imminent danger lurked behind the bushes, trees, and rocks of a foreign countryside.

Sometimes these feelings were manifested materially by soldiers in the design and layout of their camps. One Confederate veteran recalled the differences he observed between Northern and Southern camps. Of the Southerner, he wrote, "Each man and his 'chum' picks out a tree, and that particular tree becomes the homestead of the two. They hang their canteens on it, lay their haversacks and spread their blankets at the foot of it, and sit down and lean their

weary backs against it, and feel that they are at home."[6] By contrast, he observed that "the 'Boys in Blue' generally preferred to camp in the open fields."[7] This was clearly a generalization, but it seems to have the germ of observable truth in that many Union encampments were more formally organized and inward looking. Trees offered friendly shelter in one's own homeland while concealing potential dangers for invading strangers.

For months at a time the soldier's material world consisted entirely of the clothes he wore and the things he could carry: his gun, knife; three days rations in his haversack while on march; various cooking and toiletry items; blankets, tarps, and half of a shelter tent. Weather permitting, soldiers slept under the open sky. When it was cold or raining, they took to the tents. The "shelter" or "dog" tent consisted of a piece of cotton drilling, canvas, light duck, or, in a few instances, rubber measuring about five and a half feet square. A series of buttons and buttonholes were arranged along three sides such that two soldiers could join their halves together to make a small tent. Other tents included, from smallest to largest: the "A" or "wedge" tent, the round "Sibley" and "bell" tents, and several sizes of the "wall" or "hospital" tent. As a rule the larger the tent, the less common it was on the front lines.[8]

Fighting was a seasonal activity during the Civil War. From approximately November to February hostilities would cease, for the most part, and the armies of the North and South would encamp for the winter. It was during winter camp, and at the more permanent forts, that most building took place. One observer characterized this wartime interlude as "the most wearing thing in the world, the very essence of ennui."[9] Undoubtedly some of the more elaborate building projects undertaken during this period were conceived as make-work to combat boredom and occupy idle hands. Basic shelter for the winter was improvised by the soldiers themselves, often using only shovels, axes, and knives. The exigencies of wartime camp life fostered innovation as well as adaptation. Iowa infantryman Cyrus Boyd recalled his inexperience as a novice soldier: "One year ago such times as these would have made us all sick. . . . We did not know how to fix our tents and how easy it was to make bunks out of little round poles such as we found everywhere and to sleep off the ground. The experiences of those days learned us much. We can now in two hours after we stack arms have up tents or even build houses and have up good dry bunks ready to sleep."[10]

One building solution, popular with many Union troops, was to "winterize" or "stockade" tents by raising them on a low foundation of horizontal or vertical logs. Still others relied on their knowledge of vernacular construction and frontier life to raise crude plank huts, cabins of horizontal or vertical logs, dugouts, semi-dugouts, and, in a few instances, makeshift shanties of stone. Soldiers learned by example, from one another, and to a degree the Civil War contributed to the dissemination and revival of some vernacular building techniques, in particular, horizontal log construction. Complementing the tents and winter huts were adjunct structures of sticks and foliage.

In their letters, journals, and diaries soldiers made very few distinctions between different kinds of foliate assemblages and often identified them simply with descriptive expressions such as "screens," "hedges," and "rooms" of evergreen. In modern usage the words "arbor" and "bower" evoke images of shady retreat but are vague as to form. For the purposes of discussion and making typological distinctions, I have adopted the provisional terms "arbor" (or "brush arbor"), "walled bower," and "architectural bower."

Without question the most common foliate feature of the Civil War landscape was the simple arbor, or "brush arbor" (fig. 7.1). The arbor is an ancient structure with a wide distribution throughout the world, which makes tracing specific building traditions problematic. The daunting task of studying historical arbors is further limited by the intrinsic impermanence of earthfast structures bearing dead foliage as well as the dearth of pictorial evidence prior to the mid-nineteenth century. Historian J. Daniel Pezzoni addressed these challenges in a recent study of brush arbors in the American South. He found that they "were built by whites and Native Americans as well as blacks; they served varied functions in a variety of contexts; and they have figured in Southern material culture

Fig. 7.1. Gen. George Gordon Meade *(fourth from the right)* and his staff pose before a typical brush arbor in June 1865. Courtesy of the Massachusetts Commandery Military Order of the Loyal Legion and the U.S. Army Military History Institute.

since the beginning of recorded history, if not earlier."[11] During the Civil War brush arbors were built by Confederate and Union troops, by old-stock New England Yankees as well as recent European immigrants, and by African American soldiers.[12]

The basic arbor consisted of four poles set in the ground, forming the corners of a rough square. The posts were cut to a length of about ten to fourteen feet from a tree or large sapling with a fork or crotch at one end. A horizontal pole was set in the forks of each pair of posts and was secured by lashing or simply held in place by the weight of the load. Over these makeshift plates a series of smaller poles were laid perpendicularly. These functioned much like joists to hold the final component of the arbor, a pile of leafy branches and brush. Soldiers now and then conserved labor by incorporating living trees to replace one or more of the pillars. It was a simple matter to enlarge the brush arbor by adding a pair of posts with a crossbeam to one or more sides of the square. The linear, modular nature of this system made it relatively easy to construct arbors that ran the entire length of a range of tents or a company street (fig 7.2).

The first and most practical consideration of building a home-away-from-home in camp was shelter. Arbors afforded protection from the sun's rays while allowing for the passage of cool breezes.

Fig. 7.2. This linear brush arbor offered shade for tents and soldiers at the headquarters of General Butterfield, near Harrison's Landing, James River, Virginia. From *Frank Leslie's Scenes and Portraits of the Civil War* (New York: Mrs. Frank Leslie, 1894), 237. The Albert H. Small Special Collections Library, University of Virginia Library.

A young officer from Rhode Island, Elisha Rhodes, testified to their utility. "We are back in the lines again," he wrote, "and I have an arbor of green boughs to shield me from the sun. The thermometer stands today at 124, and the men are suffering severely."[13] Arbors were used in a variety of placements and arrangements. At another camp Rhodes wrote, "We have fine headquarters with the tents pitched on three sides of a square and opening into an arbor."[14] It was

Fig. 7.3. This partially enclosed arbor functioned as a stable. From Forbes, *Thirty Years After* 1:27. The Albert H. Small Special Collections Library, University of Virginia Library.

also common to build low arbors above tents to supplement the meager shade afforded by canvas. "The men have thick bowers over every row of shelter tents," one Union officer observed.[15] Arbors were also used as stables (fig 7.3). Describing one built against the side of a log hut, Edwin Forbes wrote, "Protection to horses was a necessary consideration as well as to men, and the arrangement of pine boughs against the chimney in the picture was a stable contrived for the sergeant's favorite horse."[16]

Arbors were places to sit and read, write letters, play cards, smoke pipes, and converse. Colonel Higginson, commanding a regiment of former slaves, most from South Carolina and Florida, wrote, "The Camp here, with six 'company streets' of tents looks very pretty, for there is a line of even [*sic*] green awnings before every tent, all uniform—making a sort of little cool bazaar in each company street, under which the men sit and clean their guns, mend their clothes, read their primers &c, & it is all picturesque. Entirely their own idea, too,—one company, my pet Floridian 'G' always foremost in everything, led off also in this—& all the others followed."[17] The space defined by arbors was neither truly indoors nor outdoors, but mediated between the two, much like that of verandas. Indeed, there were a few instances of porches being added to winter huts and military buildings using the techniques of forked posts and poles to support a leafy canopy.[18]

One of the most intriguing aspects of the Civil War arbor lies in its system of construction. Its component parts, the forked post and horizontal pole, were assembled in several ways to suit a variety of purposes in camp life. The forked or multipronged stick in the ground was a useful structure in and of itself. Strictly speaking, the forked stick was not foliate, yet it was integral to the primitive framing system used to support leafy boughs in all Civil War arbors and most bowers. Discussing similar examples from Depression-era Texas, George Ewing described this tradition as "forked stick folkcraft."[19] The upright stick was the basic unit of what might also be called "camp stickcraft." Cyrus Boyd offered the following advice, gained from his war experiences: "On a stick having several prongs driven into the ground near his head [the soldier] can hang his canteen[,] haversack[,] and the last thing he takes off when he goes to bed—his cap will take the highest prong. In case of a night alarm he can put his hand on all his fixtures."[20] Two forked sticks driven into the ground were used to carry the cross-piece of a makeshift lean-to, or the ridgepole of a tent. With variations in scale, this same assembly served many purposes. Documented examples include hitching bars for horses and frames for holding cooking pots over the fire.[21] A sketch in John Billings's *Hardtack and Coffee* apparently shows two soldiers digging a "sink" or latrine.[22] In the background can be seen a half-completed bench consisting of two forked posts and a pole.

A pair of these structures, or in other words four forked posts, could be connected with cross poles to create a sleeping platform (fig 7.4). George Whitman, brother of poet Walt Whitman, wrote home about making a bunk in this fashion: "Maby you think I aint got no bed, but I have, and a bedstead too, made with four croched sticks drove in the ground, . . . and my bed is a genuine corn husk Mattress which I think is a good deal healthier than feathers."[23] A Confederate artilleryman recounted a similar technique for making beds.

"Then we went out and cut small poles and made a bunk, to lift us off the ground," he wrote. "Over the expanse of springy poles we spread sprigs of cedar—and this made a pretty good spring mattress."[24] In some instances planks and nails, scarce commodities during the war, took the place of sticks. Edwin Forbes recounted how bunks in stockaded Sibley tents "were made by driving four posts at the corners, left about a foot above ground, and straight pieces of board fastened and extended from one to the other. Pine boughs were laid lengthwise, and covered with quite a depth of pine needles gathered from the woods; and when over the whole a blanket was spread a most comfortable bed had been completed."[25] A closer examination of such primitive four-posters reveals that they were in fact little more than small-scale brush arbors built low to the ground. In one instance forked sticks held poles and a springy bed of leaves to sleep on, in the other the sticks carried a canopy of green shade.

The very simplicity of these structures is deceptive. It must be emphasized that critical decisions on the nature of shelter were made at some level in the minds of the soldiers. They built in a specific fashion, one that was somehow familiar, comfortable, and culturally

Fig. 7.4. A soldier sits on a bed frame of sticks and poles during the breakup of winter camp near Falmouth, Virginia. Courtesy of the Massachusetts Commandery Military Order of the Loyal Legion and the U.S. Army Military History Institute.

coherent. While the brush arbor and its forked stick folkcraft may have a complex multicultural history, they also contained essential elements of Western architecture in the post-and-beam trabeated system of construction, linear geometry, modular accretion, and cubic form. It is not surprising that architectural theorist Abbé Laugier pictured man's first dwelling, the primitive hut, as something akin to the arbor.[26] With four crude poles and a simple roof, it defined a space of comfortable familiarity. More than any other shelter raised on the battlefield, the arbor most closely approximated the proportions of a traditional domestic bay. By contrast, the largest tents and log shanties offered little in the way of headroom and were notorious for poor ventilation. Like the arbor, the foliate camp bed resembled traditional sleeping furniture. Sleeping off the ground is a cultural behavior that soldiers considered desirable, if not essential. With sticks and leaves soldiers fashioned beds and living spaces that, no matter how crude, embodied important elements of familiar cultural models.

On a larger scale, however, the design of regimental camps was one of the few aspects of the soldier's environment governed by military protocol. Army manuals specified that camps be arranged on a grid plan with about ten company streets, each with its kitchen and officers quarters at one end.[27] In practice campgrounds varied widely, influenced by such things as terrain, reductions in ranks, fatigue, and the more urgent concerns of an army on the move. Soldiers with the time, energy, and inclination could always find ways to improve upon the regimental plan. One aspect of camp design that was not specified in military manuals was the planting of trees and hedge screens (fig. 7.5). When they referred to "planting" it is highly improbable that soldiers were digging up entire root balls to transplant whole trees. In all likelihood they were chopping down small trees close to the ground and inserting them directly in postholes or trenches. By all accounts the preferred tree was cedar because it is hardy and will keep its foliage long after the tree has died. Elisha Rhodes mentioned tree planting, in addition to other foliate structures, at one of his encampments: "We have been fixing up our camp, and we look very fine. . . . Each Company has a street

one hundred and fifty feet long and fifty feet wide. The tents are all on the right hand side and shade trees have been planted. . . . In front we have a hedge and a gateway. Over the gate in an arch of evergreen we have the name "Young Avenue" in honor of the Captain who is serving on the Brigade staff."[28] There are a few surviving photographs showing entire regimental camps surrounded by thick hedges of greenery. Somewhat rare, they were found among the outer defenses of Washington, D.C., and in areas of well-established Federal occupation. As a rule, soldiers were more likely to invest time and energy in building improvements to their camps if they knew they would be staying for a while.

In addition to putting up arbors and moving small trees, soldiers built several types of structures with greenery. Sometimes described as an "evergreen room," the walled bower was one of the more obscure features of the Civil War landscape (fig. 7.6). It consisted of three or four vertical walls of greenery and was rarely roofed. Walled bowers appear in a few ambiguous photographs and drawings betrayed only by their geometric form and the occasional branch projecting at an odd angle. This type of bower seems to have developed, in part, when soldiers built hedges around small plots of ground rather than fencing entire regimental camps. Some of these screens were little more than pole and thatch fences, while others were a bit more ambitious. "Yesterday we enclosed a piece of ground with a hedge of cedar and the officers of our mess pitched three *three* new A tents inside," wrote Elisha Rhodes, describing such an arrangement at one of his bivouacs. "We made a gateway and arched it with boughs and built a green screen in front of our tents. We built beds of boughs and as darkness came on we sat down to enjoy our new homes."[29] Some of these structures appear to have been constructed by planting trees in close order, much like a palisade wall of vertical logs. Others, smaller, more finely crafted, and often roofed, were built by filling in the walls of brush arbors with a pole framework to hold additional foliage (fig. 7.7).[30]

From a utilitarian standpoint bowers and hedgerows offered some shade and cover against winter winds. As one Union officer wrote, "We have planted

Fig. 7.5. A well-constructed hedge screen or foliate wall adjoining a sturdy log hut at the headquarters of the Fifth Army Corps, Army of the Potomac. From George F. Williams, *The Memorial War Book* (New York: Lovell Brothers, 1894), 485.

Fig. 7.7. Detail of a photograph by James F. Gibson taken in May 1862 of Gen. George B. McClellan's tent (not shown), Camp Winfield Scott, in the vicinity of Yorktown, Virginia. Note the arbor/walled bower between the two wall tents. The walls are partially filled with foliage on a trellis framework between the main posts. On the far right is visible the end of what appears to be a large foliate screen or walled bower. Courtesy of the Prints and Photographs Division, Library of Congress.

Fig. 7.6. A walled bower, complete with arched entrance, serves as an enclosure for tents in the background of this engraving. From "Camp Scenes. The Coming Election in the Army," *Frank Leslie's Illustrated Newspaper* 19, no. 473 (Oct. 22, 1864): 69. The Virginia Historical Society, Richmond, Virginia.

a row of cedars around our camp to keep off sun and dust."[31] They also thwarted the prying eyes of friends and foes. Walled bowers most often occur in the context of informal camp life, as a kind of outdoor living room. It is possible that some of these shielded latrines when there were no woods nearby. At least one bower was described as being built solely for a ceremonial occasion. Like the palisades of cedar encircling some camps, the bowers served to define, structure, and enclose a space of temporary seclusion. Reid Mitchell surmised, "The threat from a strange and hostile countryside encouraged men to stick together in their own military communities."[32] It is tempting to theorize that the screens, hedges, and walls of foliage found within and around some Union camps were built by soldiers seeking a temporary respite from the war. They built walls of greenery to repudiate the surrounding inhospitable terrain, to deny, however briefly, the conflict that threatened life and limb far from home.

Soldiers also shaped and enlivened their surroundings by decorating with greenery. From hanging wreaths and strewing garlands to celebrate the holidays to building elaborate bowers for special events, they adapted materials at hand to mark ceremonial occasions. These events served to reinforce the bonds of the military community and to strengthen ties to home by observing the ritual calendar of civilian life. Decorating with greenery, both indoors and out, came into fashion in the mid-nineteenth century and was considered a primarily feminine pursuit. In *The American Woman's Home* of 1869, Catharine Beecher and Harriet Beecher Stowe devoted an entire chapter to ornamental foliage in the house, including such things as Wardian cases for plants, ferneries, rustic frames and plant stands, and decorating with trailing ivy. Horticulturist and architectural pattern-book author Andrew Jackson Downing also remarked that the planting of climbing vines on houses was not done by "architects, masons, carpenters, or those who build the cottage, but always by those who live in it, and make it truly a home, and generally by the mother or daughter, whose very planting of vines is a labor of love offered up on the domestic altar, . . . vines on a rural cottage always express domesticity and the presence of heart."[33]

It was eminently practical for soldiers to use the abundant indigenous flora for building and decorating. Nonetheless, this was only one of several ways in which men altered traditional role-specific behavior, raising interesting questions about notions of gender and domesticity during the war.[34] The association of women with aesthetic sensibility was further emphasized when women came to camp, a common motivation for aesthetic improvement, both architectural and foliate, in winter quarters. Allowing wives and immediate family members to visit camp for extended stays was a privilege of rank.[35] During the winter of 1861 New Yorker Richard Auchmuty casually remarked to his mother, "All the colonels have their wives here, and have built log houses."[36] With wives in camp the officers required private lodgings and the log houses were seen as an improvement over the reinforced wall tents. When the occasion arose some officers would go to great lengths to build elaborate huts. The ranking members of the Twenty-second Michigan boasted board and batten cabins with oversized bargeboards at Camp Ella in Bishop, Kentucky.[37] Officers of the engineer corps built finely crafted log houses, complete with rustic porches and trim. Some of these elegant huts were so fanciful as to belie their true circumstances. Indeed, a few seemed far removed from the battlefield and would have served well as honeymoon cottages or sitting on the grounds of some Chautauqua. Foliage was also used to decorate and improve the aesthetic condition of winter huts. In addition to green fences and plantings about the shanty, some officers embowered their tent or cabin by draping a thick curtain of verdure over the facade. On the whole, however, green decoration of officers' quarters seems to have been somewhat rare. They put their initial energies into making architectural improvements. Decorating with greenery for spousal visitations was a less common afterthought.

The architectural expression of officers' quarters at one extreme tended toward an exaggerated homey charm with front porches, oversized chimneys, and decorative details that seemed incongruous for military camps. The implication was that the presence of women demanded a greater degree of domestic comfort and aesthetic refinement. The corollary belief was that men living together during wartime were more suited to inhabiting shelters that met only simple utilitarian and functional requirements. Perhaps the emphasis on domesticity was in response to underlying feelings of dislocation and insecurity. It is significant that one of the most popular songs among soldiers during the Civil War was "Home, Sweet Home."[38] Undoubtedly there was a heightened sentimental perception of hearth and home felt by those who were separated from their loved ones while living a precarious day-to-day existence. These feelings were voiced by the common soldier in letters, diaries, and song, and exhibited materially by officers when their families came to visit.

Perhaps the least utilitarian and most emblematic structure in the inventory of Civil War foliate constructs was the triumphal arch. The origin of these green arches is a bit obscure, but they undoubtedly have ties to the emblems of martial success of antiquity. Evergreen arches were raised to welcome returning heroes during and following the Civil War and there is some antebellum precedent for this practice. In November 1824 Lafayette was feted during a visit to Virginia. According to one account, "The citizens of the lower end of [Orange] county had erected, with great taste, a triumphal arch immediately at the intersection

Fig. 7.8. The headquarters of Gen. J. H. H. Ward boasted a fanciful arched gate of greenery in this photograph taken February 17, 1864. The facades of the plank winter huts are also decked with evergreens, and smaller arches span the alleys between huts. Courtesy of the Prints and Photographs Division, Library of Congress.

of the road which yet bears the General's name, from its having been the theatre of his military operations. It was adorned with the evergreen of the forest, with which it is surrounded, and with emblems and sentiments most flattering to the General."[39]

Similar arches were sometimes erected at the entrance to company streets in well-organized camps displaying regimental pride. They were frequently decorated with evergreen wreaths framing the company designation or a respected officer's name. Dean Nelson remarked that arches were most often seen in "encampments near Washington, D.C., and other population centers," and that "such garnishments lost favor among those camps that were closer to the breach of war" (fig. 7.8).[40] While this was certainly true, there were also some instances of arch raising in far flung winter camps during holidays, military reviews, and for other special events. Popular holidays at this time were Washington's Birthday, Independence Day, Thanksgiving, and Christmas. The occasions most often observed by soldiers in the field were those that occurred during the months of winter camp, specifically Christmas and Washington's Birthday. During the winter of 1861, Richard Auchmuty observed, "The camps are dressed quite gorgeously for Christmas, with bushes, wreaths, and little gardens."[41] A vignette of camp life during Christmas 1863 printed in *Frank Leslie's* showed three evergreen arches rising above a group of snow covered log huts.[42] The 1862 celebration of Washington's Birthday at Camp Brightwood, Maryland, included exhibitions of tight-rope walking, the firing of heavy-gun salutes, an officer's foot race, sack races, a clam chowder dinner, and a huge bonfire. "A double row of pine trees was planted around the entire camp and hung with paper lanterns," noted Elisha Rhodes. "Company 'D' (my company) had the name of 'Buell' in letters of evergreen extending the length of the Company street or the distance of six tents."[43]

The decorative and aesthetic use of foliage, from wreaths, garlands, screens and plantings to green structures, served as a visual marker for celebrations and ritual occasions. The observance of holidays helped to maintain a sense of connection with the familiar ceremonial calendar and customs of life during peacetime and gave soldiers a chance to relax and give vent to pent up stresses. Contemporary observers noted the cathartic value of holiday festivities during wartime. As one writer put it, "Indeed danger gives a keen relish to all enjoyments, for it must be confessed that the old saying, 'eat, drink and be merry, for tomorrow you may die,' is very much at the bottom of a soldier's life."[44]

Some of the finest ornamental green structures raised during the war were not built for women or to celebrate holidays, but were instead made by soldiers as gifts for their commanders. It should be noted that a very small percentage of the combat troops were career soldiers prior to the outbreak of war. Volunteer regiments and militias made up the first battalions of fighting men. Later in the war additional soldiers were provided through conscription and the offer of enlistment bounties. Militias were public and private quasi-fraternal groups variously organized for paramilitary training and drilling. The volunteer regiments were often assembled independently by prominent individuals with the permission and approval of regional authorities, typically a state governor. Groups of young men, often friends and neighbors, signed up together. As such, volunteer regiments tended to have strong, cohesive, regional identities. After mustering the requisite number of soldiers, the volunteers usually held elections to choose their company and regimental officers.

The relationship between leaders and troops during the Civil War often involved elements of paternalism and patronage. The making and giving of gifts to one's superiors was a military tradition that cemented the ties of reciprocity and interdependence that existed in the volunteer armies. Soldiers built camp furniture, carved pipes and trinkets, sang songs, and performed chores for their favorite officers.[45] In return, the men expected their leaders to keep their best interests at heart. The troops generally despised glory hounds and martinets. Competent officers earned the respect of their soldiers by exhibiting sound military judgment and fearlessness in combat, and by seeing that their men were well cared for. In several cases, men expressed their gratitude with buildings.

The "architectural bower," distinguished from the walled bower in the level of refinement of its overall

Fig. 7.9. A photograph of the architectural bower built for Provost Marshal General Patrick *(seated)* at Warrenton Sulphur Springs near Bealton, Virginia, in late August 1863. Note the tent stakes and guy lines to the left, supporting the wall tent under the bower. Courtesy of the Prints and Photographs Division, Library of Congress.

form and by a display of architectural features more elaborate than simple openings in the walls, was a rare feature of the Civil War landscape.[46] In August 1863, near Bealton in Fauquier County, Virginia, one was built by two companies of the Twentieth New York Volunteers for Provost Marshal Gen. Marsena Patrick as a token of esteem (fig. 7.9). Recent immigrants from Germany, the builders had been misled as to the length of their enlistment and were held back while the remainder of their regiment returned to New York. General Patrick cleared up the misunderstanding and signed their discharge papers. *Harper's Weekly* reported that "these poor Germans had not the means to offer any costly present, but their humble offering was as acceptable to the General as if it had cost thousands."[47] The bower appeared to be a small leafy temple with two arched openings flanking a central column under a pediment. The facade was decorated with a pale floral star in the gable and wreaths hanging from the arches. Judging from photographs, the bower was about fifteen feet high at the ridge and fourteen feet wide and was apparently constructed as a shell around General Patrick's wall tent. The central column may seem to be an awkward feature of the design, but perhaps it served to disguise one of the main tent poles. At least three more architectural bowers were raised about a year later by the Fiftieth New York Volunteer Engineers stationed in City Point, near Petersburg, Virginia. The engineers were exceptional for building bowers and fine rustic work as their ranks were filled with skilled craftsmen, builders, artisans, architects, and engineers.[48]

Perhaps the most elaborate assemblage of decorative foliate structures raised during the Civil War was constructed for the presentation of a sword to General Meade by the Pennsylvania Reserves on August 28, 1863 (fig. 7.10). War correspondent and artist Alfred R. Waud claimed that the giving of swords was nothing more than an excuse to throw a party, which was in keeping with the reciprocal giving between officers and their soldiers. As a rule, greater rank called for a more lavish gift and, in turn, a grander festivity. When a line

Fig. 7.10. The dais and one of the cedar arches built by Richard T. Auchmuty on the occasion of a sword presentation ceremony for Gen. George Gordon Meade. Drawn by Edwin Forbes. From "Presentation of a Sword to General Meade," *Frank Leslie's Illustrated Newspaper* 17, no. 418 (Oct. 3, 1863): 28. The Albert H. Small Special Collections Library, University of Virginia Library.

officer received a sword from the rank and file, Waud wrote, "the opening of a barrel of whisky was considered the right thing."[49] Given his eminent status at the time, the reception for General Meade was suitably grand, although it drew some criticism from the popular press as being overly extravagant and ostentatious.

The foliate decorations built for General Meade's ceremony were designed by Capt. Richard Tylden Auchmuty, an architect who had apprenticed under, and later partnered with, James Renwick.[50] The presentation took place on the grounds of a deserted plantation near Rappahannock Station in Virginia. At each end of the tree-lined drive Auchmuty raised green arches. One was twenty-five feet wide and forty-five feet tall, and the other was described as smaller, "built very heavy to look like an old-fashioned doorway."[51] A triumphal arch of cedar surmounted the dais where the offering was made to General Meade.

Auchmuty also built temporary accommodations for the visiting dignitaries as well as for himself. He described "General Crawford's tent with an arbor in front and a square room behind, made, roof and all, of evergreens so smoothly clipped that it looked like a wall."[52] For Governor Curtin, Auchmuty apparently built a foliate antechamber that he characterized as "a room in front, entered by an arch, [with] two tents opening into it at the corners. The windows were oval and looked like pictures on the wall. The floors were matted, and the main room was furnished with a mahogany sofa, marble table, glass lantern, etc., taken out of the neighboring houses."[53] He further related that they "also built a refreshment room of evergreens, with a canvas roof, thirty by sixty, and thirteen feet high."[54] The trees were hung with two hundred colored lanterns and, following the sword presentation, refreshments were served consisting of "wine, whiskey, ice-cream, and meats having been ordered in Philadelphia for 450 persons."[55]

It would be interesting to know how much Auchmuty's architectural training influenced his design of green structures and how much was due to his observance of other wartime arbors and bowers.[56] His wonderful grouping of green arches, arbors, and bowers functioned as both celebratory decoration and as a tribute to Generals Meade and Crawford and Governor

Curtin. The design and production of such elaborate foliate settings, in addition to the reciprocal gift giving, served to strengthen and define the social order that existed between soldiers and their leaders.

During the American Civil War soldiers employed greenery to serve three distinct, yet sometimes overlapping functions: as shelter, screen, and ornament. With few tools and little hardware, they used the natural materials at hand to shape and mold the enveloping landscape of war. They built walls of foliage to create places, large and small, of privacy and refuge. With the same techniques some built screens to insulate and decorate tents and cabins. During holidays and military ceremonies some soldiers fashioned greenery into decorative wreaths, garlands, and triumphal arches to visually define and celebrate ritual space. In a handful of instances men built elaborate and fanciful bowers for their beloved leaders. All told, these examples of artistry and expertise in foliate design were few and far between. The green structures that suffused the Civil War were the utilitarian brush arbor, its diminutive equivalent the sleeping platform, and their components parts evident in the ubiquitous camp stick-craft. Whether elegant or plain, whimsical or pragmatic, building with sticks and leaves afforded soldiers self-expression and a modicum of control over their surroundings while far from home and loved ones in a strange land fraught with peril.

Notes

1. "Camp Scenes. Army of the James," *Frank Leslie's Illustrated Newspaper* 19, no. 494 (Mar. 18, 1865): 413.

2. The most significant work on vernacular architecture during the Civil War is Dean E. Nelson, "'Right Nice Little House(s)': Impermanent Camp Architecture of the American Civil War," *Perspectives in Vernacular Architecture,* ed. Camille Wells (Annapolis, Md.: Vernacular Architecture Forum, 1982), 79–93. The investigation of material remains of the Civil War below ground has also become a recent topic of interest to historical archaeologists; see, for example, Clarence R. Geier and Susan E. Winters, eds., *Look to the Earth: Historical Archaeology and the American Civil War* (Knoxville: Univ. of Tennessee Press, 1995).

3. Reid Mitchell, *Civil War Soldiers* (New York: Viking, 1988), 132.

4. *Webster's New World Dictionary of the American Language, College Edition* (Cleveland: World Publishing, 1957), 197.

5. "Rebel Pickets Disguised in Cedar Bushes," *Frank Leslie's Illustrated Newspaper* 17, no. 428 (Dec. 12, 1863): 177, 189. In contrast, the Union sniper, heroically portrayed while taking aim from a tree-top perch, was known as a "sharpshooter."

6. Carlton McCarthy, *Detailed Minutæ of Soldier Life in the Army of Northern Virginia, 1861–1865* (Richmond, Va.: Carlton McCarthy, 1882), 196.

7. Ibid., 205.

8. For an excellent comprehensive study of the shelter tent, see Frederick C. Gaede, *The Federal Civil War Shelter Tent,* Civil War Monograph Series No. 1 (Alexandria, Va.: O'Donnell Publications, 2001). For summary descriptions of the variety of Civil War tents, see Francis A. Lord, "Weapons & Equipment—Whether Sibley, 'A,' Wall, or Pup . . . Tents Provided Chief Shelter for the Troops," *Civil War Times Illustrated* 2, no. 5 (Aug. 1963): 30–32; and Les Jensen, "Sibley's Tent," *Civil War Times Illustrated* 20, no. 9 (Jan. 1982): 38–39.

9. "Scenes on the Rappahannock. Erecting Huts for Winter Quarters," *Frank Leslie's Illustrated Newspaper* 15, no. 389 (Mar. 14, 1863): 396.

10. Mildred Throne, ed., *The Civil War Diary of Cyrus F. Boyd, Fifteenth Iowa Infantry, 1861–1863*, with a new introduction by E. B. Long (Millwood, N.Y.: Kraus Reprint, 1977), 123, entry dated Feb. 16, 1863.

11. J. Daniel Pezzoni, "Brush Arbors in the American South," *PAST: Pioneer America Society Transactions* 20 (1997): 25.

12. John U. Rees recently shed light on the history of military arbors and bowers in his article on foliate structures built during the Revolutionary War, "'We . . . got ourselves cleverly settled for the night. . . .': Soldiers' Shelter on Campaign During the War for Independence: Part III,"

Military Collector & Historian 53, no. 4 (Winter 2001–2): 161–69. During the Civil War there were also some tantalizing hints suggesting ethnic preferences for certain foliate structures and landscape features. While bivouacked in Beaufort, South Carolina, Union commander Thomas Wentworth Higginson mused, "I may become a field officer in a literal sense myself & try to make some transplantations round my tent. I hv. already the prettiest trellis of [Spanish] moss to shade the main tent fr. the sun. It was curious to notice, that the only regiment which ever planted anything round it's [*sic*] tents was a foreign one called the Lost Children or Enfans Perdus from the variety of nationalities [German, Irish, and French], the 100th N.Y. They had a little garden round almost every tent." Christopher Looby, ed., *The Complete Civil War Journal and Selected Letters of Thomas Wentworth Higginson* (Chicago: Univ. of Chicago Press, 2000), 168.

13. Robert Hunt Rhodes, ed., *All for the Union: The Civil War Diary and Letters of Elisha Hunt Rhodes* (New York: Orion Books, 1991), 166.

14. Ibid., 238.

15. Richard Tylden Auchmuty, *Letters of Richard Tylden Auchmuty, Fifth Corps, Army of the Potomac,* ed. E. S. A. [Ellen Schermerhorn Auchmuty] (n.p.: Privately printed, n.d.), 114, letter dated Aug. 12, 1863 to "Madgie" from Rappahannock Station, Virginia.

16. Edwin Forbes, *Thirty Years After: An Artist's Story of the Great War,* 2 vols. (New York: Fords, Howard, & Hulbert, 1890), 1:25.

17. Looby, *Complete Civil War Journal,* 137, entry dated Apr. 26, 1863, Port Royal Island, South Carolina.

18. See the engraving of "A Wagoners Shanty," in Forbes, *Thirty Years After* 2:199, and a photograph entitled *Brig. Gen. M. D. Hardin & Staff, at Fort Slocum, Defenses of Washington, D.C., August, 1865,* Negative no. B817-7429, Prints and Photographs Collection, Library of Congress. The arbor porch also shows up in other marginal contexts. See, for example, the illustration of a Cherokee log hut with a shingled porch carried on forked posts in "In the Indian Territory," *Harper's Weekly* 19, no. 959 (May 15, 1875): 396, 406.

19. George Ewing, "Forked Stick Folkcraft," in *Corners of Texas,* ed. Francis Edward Abernethy, Publications of the Texas Folklore Society, 52 (Denton: Univ. of North Texas Press, 1993), 105–13.

20. Throne, *Civil War Diary,* 123–24.

21. An example of a hitching bar was mentioned in *Hospital Transports. A Memoir of the Embarkation of the Sick and Wounded from the Peninsula of Virginia in the Summer of 1862* (Boston: Ticknor and Fields, 1863), 22.

22. John D. Billings, *Hardtack and Coffee; or the Unwritten Story of Army Life* (1887; reprint, Glendale, N.Y.: Benchmark Publishing, 1970), 163.

23. Jerome M. Loving, ed., *Civil War Letters of George Washington Whitman,* foreword by Gay Wilson Allen (Durham, N.C.: Duke Univ. Press, 1975), 72.

24. William Meade Dame, *From the Rapidan to Richmond and the Spotsylvania Campaign: A Sketch in Personal Narrative of the Scenes a Soldier Saw* (Baltimore: Green-Lucas, 1920), 19.

25. Forbes, *Thirty Years After,* 1:129.

26. Marc-Antoine Laugier's *Essai sur l'Architecture,* 1755, is treated in Wolfgang Herrmann, *Laugier and Eighteenth Century French Theory* (London: A. Zwemmer, 1962). On Laugier and other interpretations of original architecture, see Joseph Rykwert, *On Adam's House in Paradise: The Idea of the Primitive Hut in Architectural History,* 2d ed. (Cambridge, Mass.: MIT Press, 1981). Following the war, camp stick-craft, together with other examples of traditional camp lore, entered popular culture in the writings of outdoor sporting enthusiasts such as George W. Sears, alias "Nessmuk," and Daniel Carter Beard. See, for example, D. C. Beard, *Shelters, Shacks, and Shanties* (New York: Charles Scribner's Sons, 1914); Horace Kephart, *Camping and Woodcraft,* facsimile reprint, 2 vols. in 1, with an introduction by Jim Casada (Knoxville: Univ. of Tennessee Press, 1988); "Nessmuk" [George W. Sears], *Woodcraft and Camping,* reprint of *Woodcraft* (1920) (New York: Dover Publications, 1963); and Bernard S. Mason, *Woodcraft & Camping,* reprint of *Woodcraft* (1939) (New York: Dover Publications, 1974).

27. Nelson, "Right Nice Little House(s)," 79.

28. Rhodes, *All for the Union,* 110, letter dated May 21, 1863, from camp near Falmouth, Virginia. A diagram of the camp layout appears on p. 111.

29. Ibid., 88–89, letter dated Dec. 3, 1862, near Stafford Court House, Virginia.

30. A roofed bower, seemingly thatched, appears in the background of an illustration entitled "Southern Ladies Drawing Rations," *Frank Leslie's Illustrated Newspaper* 17, no. 419 (Oct. 10, 1863): 33. A similar structure appears in a

photograph of a militia group, the Zouaves, captioned *Pole and Brush Cottage,* in James J. Robertson Jr., *Tenting Tonight: The Soldier's Life,* The Civil War (Alexandria, Va.: Time-Life Books, 1984), 51.

31. Auchmuty, *Letters,* 63, letter dated June 22, 1862, from camp near New Bridge, Virginia.

32. Mitchell, *Soldiers,* 146.

33. Catharine E. Beecher and Harriet Beecher Stowe, "Home Decoration," in *The American Woman's Home; or Principles of Domestic Science; Being a Guide to the Formation and Maintenance of Economical, Healthful, Beautiful, and Christian Homes* (1869; reprint), American Education: Its Men, Ideas, and Institutions, ser. II (New York: Arno Press, 1971), 84–103; A. J. Downing, *The Architecture of Country Houses* (1850; reprint, New York: Dover Publications, 1969), 79.

34. On gender and the uses of the domestic metaphor during the Civil War, see Reid Mitchell, *The Vacant Chair: The Northern Soldier Leaves Home* (New York: Oxford Univ. Press, 1993); Nina Silber, *The Romance of Reunion: Northerners and the South, 1865–1900* (Chapel Hill: Univ. of North Carolina Press, 1994); and Catherine Clinton and Nina Silber, eds., *Divided Houses: Gender and the Civil War* (New York: Oxford Univ. Press, 1992).

35. Provost Marshal General Patrick complained that the prerogative was often abused, noting in his diary, "Col. Sharp[e] returned this morning & brought his Wife with him, as well as several other Ladies but I have not seen them. They are over at Head Quarters and the Band is playing for them. It is all a farce this business of not allowing ladies to come to the Army when every one that has a friend at Head Quarters can get permission without applying to me for a pass." Diary entry for June 2, 1863, in David S. Sparks, ed., *Inside Lincoln's Army: The Diary of Marsena Rudolph Patrick, Provost Marshal General, Army of the Potomac* (New York: Thomas Yoseloff, 1964), 253.

36. Auchmuty, *Letters,* 20, letter to his mother, Dec. 22, 1861, camp near Minor's House, in Virginia.

37. See William C. Davis, *The Guns of '62,* The Image of War, 1861–1865 (Garden City, N.Y.: Doubleday, for the National Historical Society, Gettysburg, Pa., 1982), 2:187 and 231. Other examples of elaborate officers' quarters for connubial visits can be found in Francis Trevelyan Miller, ed., *The Photographic History of the Civil War* (New York:

Thomas Yoseloff, 1957), 1:47, 2:149, 5:249; and Robertson, *Tenting Tonight,* 50.

38. "Home, Sweet Home" was written by American playwright John Howard Payne (1792–1852) in 1823 during a stay in Paris. Payne wrote a play entitled *Clari, the Maid of Milan* which was purchased by Charles Kemble, manager of Covent Garden Theatre. Kemble asked Payne to rewrite the play as an opera. Payne complied and introduced the words of "Home, Sweet Home" in the new work. The song quickly became very popular and surpassed the opera in fame. See Helen Kendrick Johnson, *Our Familiar Songs and Those Who Made Them* (New York: Henry Holt, 1889), 41–44; and Frank Luther, *Americans and Their Songs* (New York: Harper & Brothers, 1942), 67. According to Bell Irvin Wiley, "Home, Sweet Home" was the most popular song with soldiers of the Confederacy. *The Life of Johnny Reb, the Common Soldier of the Confederacy* (Indianapolis: Bobbs-Merrill, 1943), 152, as quoted in Richard B. Harwell, *Confederate Music* (Chapel Hill: Univ. of North Carolina Press, 1950), 6. "Home, Sweet Home" was a favorite with Union soldiers as well. According to Robertson, "When spirits were at their lowest in the Army of the Potomac in the winter of 1862–1863, bands were forbidden to play the most popular of all Civil War songs, 'Home Sweet Home,' for fear of the devastating effect it would have on the morale of the homesick troops." *Tenting Tonight,* 68. See also the chapter entitled "Home, Sweet Home" in Forbes, *Thirty Years After* 2:265–66.

39. Marie Joseph Paul Yves Roch Gilbert du Motier, Marquis de Lafayette [1757–1834], "General La Fayette in Virginia," *Enquirer* (Richmond, Va.), Nov. 30, 1824. Simon P. Newman discusses an arch built by the women of Trenton, New Jersey, to welcome George Washington during his inaugural journey to New York. It was eighteen feet high, fifteen feet wide, and ten feet long, made of laurel and evergreen with floral highlights. See his *Parades and the Politics of the Street: Festive Culture in the Early American Republic* (Philadelphia: Univ. of Pennsylvania Press, 1997), 47–49.

40. Nelson, "Right Nice Little House(s)," 79.

41. Auchmuty, *Letters,* 20–21, letter to his mother, Dec. 22, 1861.

42. Untitled, uncaptioned illustration in *Frank Leslie's Illustrated Newspaper* 17, no. 431 (Jan. 2, 1864): 232–33.

43. Rhodes, *All for the Union,* 55–56.

44. "Camp Graham and Its Festivities," *Frank Leslie's Illustrated Newspaper* 13, no. 320 (Jan. 11, 1862): 119.

45. See, for example, "A Present for the Colonel," an engraving of a soldier making a chair for his commander, in Forbes, *Thirty Years After* 2:286.

46. To date I have found evidence of only five such structures, though there may well have been others.

47. "The Army of the Potomac. General Patrick's Head-Quarters," *Harper's Weekly* 7, no. 351 (Sept. 19, 1863): 603, 605. General Patrick commented on this situation in his diary; see entries for Aug. 31, 1863, and Sept. 1, 1863, in Sparks, *Inside Lincoln's Army,* 284–85.

48. Information on the architectural bowers built by the New York Volunteer Engineers for their headquarters structure, as well as two bowered surgeon's quarters, can be found in photographs in the Prints and Photographs Collection, Library of Congress, one of which is reproduced in Davis, *Guns of '62,* 247.

49. [Alfred R. Waud], "The Army of the Potomac. A Sword Presentation to General Meade," *Harper's Weekly* 7, no. 353 (Oct. 3, 1863): 635–36.

50. Richard Tylden Auchmuty (1831–1893) was born in New York City, the grandson of a signer of the Declaration of Independence and the only son in a prestigious, well-to-do family. More information on his life and career can be gleaned from the following sources: *The National Cyclopæ-dia of American Biography* (New York: James T. White, 1899), 9:102–3; Allen Johnson, ed., *Dictionary of American Biography* (New York: Charles Scribner's Sons, 1964), 420–21; obituary, Richard Tylden Auchmuty, *American Architect and Building News* 41, no. 918 (July 29, 1893): 61; Auchmuty, *Letters;* Richard T. Auchmuty, "The Need of Trade Schools," *Century Magazine,* n.s., 33, no. 1 (Nov. 1886): 83–92; Annette Townsend, *The Auchmuty Family of Scotland and America* (New York: Grafton Press, 1932), 186–87; and Dennis Steadman Francis, *Architects in Practice, New York City, 1840–1900* (New York: Committee for the Preservation of Architectural Records, c. 1979), 12.

51. Auchmuty, *Letters,* 119, letter to his mother dated Sept. 1, 1863, from Rappahannock Station, Virginia.

52. Ibid., 119–20.

53. Ibid., 120.

54. Ibid.

55. Ibid.

56. There is an ancient, albeit obscure, tradition of designing and building elaborate temporary green structures for celebrations and ceremonies. Jennifer Stead describes some examples of Elizabethan bowers and arbors raised as temporary banqueting houses in "Bowers of Bliss: The Banquet Setting," in *"Banquetting Stuffe": The Fare and Social Background of the Tudor and Stuart Banquet,* ed. C. Anne Wilson, Food and Society, 1 (Edinburgh: Edinburgh Univ. Press, 1991), 126.

8

THE ARCHITECTURE OF SHARECROPPING

EXTENDED FARMS OF THE GEORGIA PIEDMONT

MARK REINBERGER

Prelude: Background

Although far from exhausted as a subject, the architecture of antebellum southern plantations has received significant scholarly attention over the past few decades.[1] Historians have also begun to focus on the landscape and architecture of the postbellum rural South, the architecture of what might be called the extended sharecropping farm.[2] This chapter looks at three such farms in the cotton belt of the Old South, located in a circle of about twenty miles radius around Athens, Georgia, an important regional cotton center in the Piedmont.[3]

For much of the twentieth century, tenant farming, especially sharecropping, defined the American Deep South in a way nothing had since slavery. Sharecropping originated in the period after Reconstruction as a means by which large southern landowners could maximize their profit from the land, minimize their own risk in agriculture, and re-subjugate freed blacks. The system of southern tenantry involved several varieties of economic relationships between landowner and landless worker. The agricultural ladder had four rungs: landowners; renters; croppers; and wage hands, the latter miserably paid and the poorest of the rural proletariat. Among landless tenants, renters were the most independent, paying cash or a fixed amount of cotton to a landlord and providing for themselves fertilizer, feed, seed, and tools for farming. Since fertilizer and seed had to be bought in advance, only families with established credit could be renters.[4]

Sharecroppers furnished primarily their labor; the landlord provided land and equipment for farming. The landlord received half of the crop, minus any debts to the landlord. In sharecropping, a farmer was given the use of a relatively small tract (usually between ten and twenty acres) to produce cotton. The size of the tract depended upon the size of his family and his industriousness; more children who could work meant more acreage, an equation which generated pressure to reproduce. The landowner held farming equipment and mules at a central location and lent them to the cropper.[5] The landowner sold fertilizer, food, and other domestic commodities on credit to the sharecroppers at a central commissary or store. In the fall, after the cotton crop was processed (often at the owner's gin), the owner took his share, and the remainder (minus any debt to the commissary) was the sharecropper's. Many years there was little, if anything, left. On the extended farms described in this chapter, the owners provided all means necessary for farming; the tenants provided only their labor. In other situations, the owners might be absentee (living in town or on other farms), so that the tenants were more independent.[6]

In two Piedmont Georgia counties (Greene and Macon) studied closely in the 1930s, whites owned 95 percent of the land. Over half the whites and 90 percent of the blacks were landless. Of the landless blacks, a quarter were wage hands, another quarter were renters who owned some animals and equipment, and the rest were sharecroppers. Over half of southern tenants, white and black, were sharecroppers. In many ways, sharecropping was more advantageous than slavery to landowners, because they no longer had any legal duty to take care of their tenants, although in many cases owners felt a moral duty that bound both levels of society paternalistically.[7]

Sharecropping as a system might not have been so bad if it had incorporated ideas of progressive agriculture, such as crop rotation, fallow, and erosion control. It was theoretically possible (and indeed happened, especially in the early twentieth century when cotton prices were high) that a sharecropper could produce enough cotton over a period of years to allow him to buy land of his own. However, the almost exclusive cultivation of cotton and the lack of effective erosion control often destroyed the soil to such an extent that sooner or later it became impossible to produce a surplus. The boll weevil, often given as the

cause of cotton's demise, was merely the coup de grâce; for many sharecroppers cotton had already become economically untenable.

After the boll weevil hit northeast Georgia in 1920, cotton production dropped by more than 90 percent. During the 1920s in Greene County, Georgia, 43 percent of blacks and 23 percent of whites left for the cities. One in three farm houses (mostly tenants') were abandoned, and there was a veritable epidemic of farmhouse burnings, so much so that for a time insurance companies stopped writing policies for rural dwellings.[8] A slight improvement came in the late 1920s as farmers learned ways to keep the boll weevil in check, but cotton prices remained low, credit was tighter, and the soil that much less productive. By 1930, sharecroppers could not make ends meet, which doomed them to a downward spiral of debt and poverty. Wholesale exodus from the land continued. Between 1920 and 1990, the number of farms in Georgia dropped from 1.7 million to 121,000, most of that drop happening by 1970. Small sharecropper farms were absorbed into larger farms that were worked by the owners. Many of these diversified into livestock, feed crops and fruits, types of farming that did not require sharecroppers or as many hired hands. After World War II, mechanization reached southern farms, further reducing the need for labor.[9]

The architecture of this milieu has rapidly vanished from the countryside, resulting in the most profound transformation of the southern landscape since the Civil War. Large areas once full of people and houses are now virtually empty, given up to mechanized farming, pasture, or forest. Here and there mostly abandoned farms dot the landscape. Of the three farms presented here, two are inhabited but none are actively cultivated.

Scholars of vernacular architecture often say they aim not so much at the explication of buildings as the lives and thought of the people who created them. They write social, rather than architectural, history, although often their search originates in an aesthetic or intellectual impulse that derives from the buildings or their settings. An almost unbearable tension develops between these two aims when the subject is the architecture of southern sharecropping. On one level it is difficult to find an aesthetic or emotional rationale for studying this architecture: its simplicity elides into coarseness; its builders rarely aimed at any but the cheapest construction; its occupants by and large hated and felt no attachment to it; it embodied no innovative or even particularly interesting design or structural principles; and, finally, it led nowhere. Ninety-eight percent of it has vanished or stands in ruins. Its greatest aesthetic pleasure lies in a romantic proclivity for ruins as generators of "divine melancholy," reminding us of the inevitable passing of all things temporal; that and the modernist aesthetic that finds beauty in the simplicity of this architecture and of the southern landscape which envelops it and often absorbs it through kudzu, termites, and dry rot. In his

1941 classic study of three Alabama sharecropping families, *Let Us Now Praise Famous Men,* James Agee compared it in visual power to Greek Doric architecture.[10] His comments still resonate with an observer of the southern landscape today: "They [sharecroppers] live on land, and in houses, and under skies and seasons, which all happen to seem to me beautiful beyond almost anything else I know, and they themselves and the clothes they wear, and their motions and their speech are beautiful in the same intense and final commonness and purity."[11]

When we move from the aesthetic contemplation of ruins to the lives of sharecroppers, however, we are caught up short by the miserable poverty embodied in this architecture. Aesthetics or intellectual curiosity come to seem callous and a horrible and misplaced

Fig. 8.1. Walker Evans, *Sharecropper Bud Fields and His Family at Home, Hale County, Alabama,* 1935 or 1936. Farm Security Administration, Office of War Information Photograph Collection, Library of Congress Prints and Photographs Division, Washington, D.C.

invasion of the lives of people who would (or mostly, thank heavens, would have) rather be left alone. This dilemma so bedeviled Agee that *Let Us Now Praise Famous Men* consisted largely of anguished acknowledgments that words can never capture, can never do justice to these people that he came to love, and that the attempt to capture their lives simultaneously violated them. The families themselves felt most violated by the photographs taken by Walker Evans that depicted people at the very edge of physical and psychic survival (fig. 8.1). These images conjure up nothing so much as the Nazi Holocaust, then going on in central Europe.[12]

Agee and Walker were northern journalists sent to investigate conditions in the South in the 1930s. Their writing and photographs, like those of many other Depression-era journalists (for example, photographer Margaret Bourke-White and author Erskine Caldwell, who produced *You Have Seen Their Faces*) were inevitably colored by a liberal political point of view and by artistic modernism. Such sources obviously have to be used with caution, because the authors had their own biases and were, in many cases, working for the New Deal federal administration that was attempting to fundamentally change southern culture. Thus they may be suspected of exaggerating the misery of conditions. However, their descriptions of tenants' lives and environment are extremely detailed and remain valuable as documents of the region and period. Similarly, Walker Evans's photos also remain valid documents of the houses and people, even if their subjects were sometimes arranged to fit a photographic negative and better reveal what a room looked like.[13] Other, more "objective," writers of the period, such as Arthur Raper, also acknowledged the terrible poverty but saw salvation in the form of New Deal programs that attempted to alleviate southern poverty.[14]

Nor has the objectivity of W. E. B. Du Bois ever been impugned. Du Bois was the first to study the poverty of the southern tenant farmer and he stressed the personal and social problems that were both cause and effect of the poor condition of housing in the South at the turn of the century. He listed eight characteristics of southern rural tenant houses that he felt weakened both the physical and moral health of the inhabitants: poor light; bad air; lack of sanitary facilities; poor protection against the weather; crowding due to small size; inadequate provisions for storing and preparing food; lack of privacy; and lack of beauty.[15] All these conditions can be observed in surviving tenant houses.

The three farms examined here were originally selected for documentation and study because they were relatively intact, having their big house, some farm buildings and some of the original tenant houses. Serendipitously, they illustrate a variety of relationships of landlord and landless tenant, and their houses illustrate the major types of tenant houses in Piedmont Georgia.

When seen in the context of the farms and their history, the houses illustrate a complex hierarchy in postbellum rural society, a hierarchy reflected in the placement and design of tenant houses and other farm buildings. The layout of the farms and the quality of tenant houses reflected the economic relationship between owner and tenant, but they also reflected personal relationships, which, in turn, affected an individual's or family's place in the rural hierarchy. While things were often bad in the countryside, they were not as uniformly bleak as writers in the 1930s sometimes suggested. Although, the system was without doubt irremediably flawed, much depended on the character of the owner, his particular relationship with individual tenants, and the nature of agriculture on the extended farm. Clues to the quality of tenants' lives lie in the houses and their accouterments.

Establishing the Theme: Shields-Ethridge Farm, Jackson County

The Shields-Ethridge Farm in Jackson County, Georgia, about twenty miles northwest of Athens, presents a typical extended sharecropper plantation. The owner, Joyce Ethridge, has left the farm to a nonprofit foundation to preserve and interpret to the public. It is probably the best-preserved farm in Georgia, if not the entire Southeast, retaining not only about fifty buildings but also all of its equipment from the days of both mules and tractors (fig. 8.2).[16]

The Shields and later the Ethridge families were part of the gentry of Jackson County. Joseph Shields settled in the area about 1830. Like many landowners in the Georgia Piedmont, the Shields came from Virginia with short stops in counties farther east in Georgia. They settled first on land not far from the present farm which was established two generations later by Joseph Roberts Shields. He built a fairly large house in 1866 in a conservative form known as plantation plain style: two-story, single-pile, with a center hall, end chimneys, and rear one-story shed. This form is usually associated with the antebellum period, but quite a number appeared in the immediate postwar period as well. The interior retains much of its exposed woodwork and planking on the floors, walls, and ceilings.

The Shields-Ethridge House introduces an important theme of the sharecropping story, one seen in all three farms: they are tales of three generations. Joseph Robert Shields was a member of the generation that came of age immediately after the Civil War and had to deal with the psychological defeat and economic dislocations of the South at that time. Cotton prices were high at the end of the Civil War but dropped steadily in the 1870s. Prices and production rebounded in the 1880s, but the prosperity was cut short by the severe depression that began in 1893.[17] In the words of one farmer interviewed, that generation "was just making a living." They generally constructed conservative dwellings or were content to remain in antebellum houses. There are very few surviving outbuildings from this generation at Shields-Ethridge: only two log corn cribs and (until its recent destruction) a detached kitchen date from before about 1900.

The next generation faced a different economic reality and had a far different character. Ira Washington Ethridge, who married Joseph Robert Shields's daughter, came to maturity at a time when the South was far more prosperous. Cotton prices and production rose during the first two decades of the twentieth century, reaching a peak during World War I. Boosterism swept the South, like the rest of the nation. Rural roads, bridges, and schools were improved. Rural dwellers (at least the landowners) started getting urban conveniences, such as indoor plumbing and telephones.[18] Ira Washington Ethridge was far more self-confident than his father-in-law, was college-educated in business administration, and came from a family that had roots in Jefferson, the county seat. His daughter-in-law, Joyce Ethridge, remembers him as "a very domineering person, very positive about everything that he did." Ira Washington represented the ascendancy of town wealth and education over the old rural families. In their youth, his generation was inspired by the vision of Atlanta booster, Henry Grady, of a "New South" and a "New Departure," which embraced industry, technology, and commerce as vital adjuncts to the region's agriculture.[19] When this generation came to power in the early twentieth century, tenant farming reached its peak in Georgia. During the depression of the mid-1890s, wealthy families had been able to buy out failed smaller farmers, resulting in fewer, larger holdings and more renters and sharecroppers.[20]

Within a few years of taking over the farm when his father-in-law died in 1910, Ira Washington Ethridge monumentalized the main house with a portico and remodeled the interior. One of the interior changes was the removal of a wall separating the original center passage from one side. This created a very large living room with the entry in one corner and open stairs in another.[21] He also created a formally landscaped and iron-fenced yard at the front, setting the house off from

Fig. 8.2. Shields-Ethridge Farm, Jackson County, Georgia, main house, 1866, with portico and front yard remodeled, 1911.

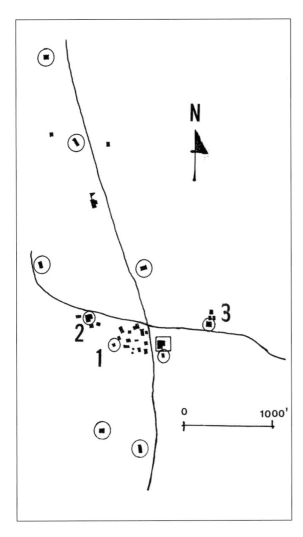

Fig. 8.3. Shields-Ethridge Farm, site layout. Main house enclosed in a square; tenant houses enclosed in circles. The farm building complex is across the road from the main house. Tenant house 1: Schoolteacher's House; 2: Preacher Riley's House; 3: James Jackson's House.

its surroundings. Almost all of the surviving farm buildings and tenant houses date from his period.

Surviving buildings at Shields-Ethridge reflect the changes in southern agriculture in the twentieth century. By 1900 progressive farmers saw the need for crop diversification, so that even before the boll weevil hit Georgia, Ira W. Ethridge had begun producing wheat (the wheat house dates to circa 1911), potatoes

(a concrete block potato house with double insulated walls and roof ventilators stands near the main house), and livestock. The many concrete block buildings and the water tower (for fire protection) also testify to Ira W. Ethridge's technological progressiveness. His concrete block garage (circa 1915) held one of the first cars in Jackson County.

At its heyday in the early twentieth century, the Shields-Ethridge Farm had twelve hundred acres, about average for a Georgia sharecropper plantation of this era. Approximately half of that was held and worked by the owner himself with hired hands. The other half was split between two renters and eleven sharecroppers, about one-quarter white and the rest black. Again, such a distribution of land and race was typical for Georgia in this period. Sharecroppers' fields were generally not fenced, so that the landscape was fairly open.[22]

The layout of the Shields-Ethridge Farm reflected its agricultural and social structure (fig. 8.3). At the center, on nearly the highest spot, stood the main house and its attendant outbuildings.[23] The actual highest spot was across the road and was reserved for the family cemetery, located in the midst of the many farm buildings. Directly across the road from the main house was the commissary, where tenants bought all their domestic supplies and food. Plantation owners usually located commissaries close to the main house, probably for surveillance and security. Nearby stood the blacksmith shop, common mule barn and equipment shed in which animals and plows were kept and repaired for all farmers. Farther back (probably to get its dust and noise away from the main house) was the concrete block cotton gin, built in 1911 (to replace an earlier wooden structure that had burned)[24] and upgraded in 1935 and 1950. Having their own gin placed the Ethridges in the top rank of Jackson County farmers. Smaller farmers in the area used it, giving the Ethridges an additional source of income.

The Shields-Ethridge Farm also retains ten out of thirteen of its tenant houses, an extremely high survival rate. Several of these were clustered at the edge of the central complex with the rest scattered along the roads some distance away. Between lay the fields assigned to the various cropping families.[25]

Tenant houses in Piedmont Georgia generally came in three varieties of plan, with several subtypes in each (fig. 8.4).[26] The simplest was a one-room cabin with a chimney at one end.[27] The most common had a two-room plan, with either a chimney in the center (the "saddle-bag" type) or one or two end chimneys. The two-room variety could be expanded to three or four rooms with either an ell or a shed addition on the rear. The third variety had a central hall, a room to each side, and one or two end chimneys (most commonly only one, that is, only one of the front rooms was heated). It too could be expanded by additions to

the rear. In addition, larger tenant houses of a bungalow type are encountered occasionally. All tenant houses encountered in this study had a single story, although owners' houses in the region (even relatively simple ones) often had a second story. Tenant houses and, before them, slave houses almost never had an upper story.

The vast majority of tenant houses were framed structures, made mostly of circularly sawn two-by-fours fastened together with cut nails. A very few log tenant houses can still be found. Two varieties of framing are present in the houses surveyed. The most common was platform framing in which two-by-four studs (generally spaced about two feet apart) form the wall, which was clad in clapboards. An alternative method employed two-by-four (or slightly larger) posts approximately six feet apart, between which ran two horizontal girts to which vertical planks were nailed on the outside. No tenant houses surveyed had any exterior wall sheathing underneath their siding, even those built in the twentieth century, when sheathing became common in middle-class houses. Generally the framed floor structure stood on brick or stone piers, with the space under the house left open (and used by children and animals).[28] Roofs of surviving houses are almost universally of galvanized steel or asphalt shingles. Old commentaries record wood shingles.[29] They also universally noted leaking roofs, evidence for which can still be seen in most houses.

Room sizes in tenant houses were remarkably consistent among the three farms surveyed. In front rooms, generally one dimension was thirteen feet, with the other ranging from ten to fifteen feet.[30] Thirteen by fourteen and thirteen by fifteen were far and away the most common room dimensions. Rear rooms (often kitchens) were usually smaller, the most common dimensions being fifteen by ten feet. Room size apparently did not play a great role in distinguishing tenant houses, although number of rooms may have in some cases. Room size did distinguish between landowners' homes and those of tenants, however. Not only did owners' homes generally (although not always) have more rooms, but their rooms averaged two to three feet larger in each direction. Among tenant houses on the farms surveyed, neither number of rooms nor

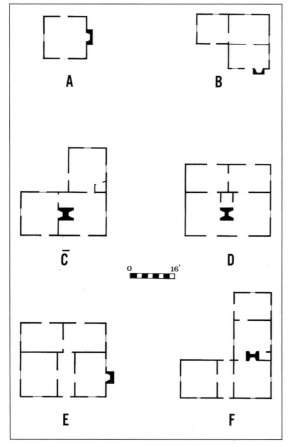

Fig. 8.4. Tenant Houses, plans, all at the same scale. A: one-room house, Nolan's Store; B: Schoolteacher's House, Shields-Ethridge Farm; C: Three-room house, Nolan's Store; D: poorest house, Wynn Farm; E: middling house, Wynn Farm; E: Preacher Riley's House, Shields-Ethridge Farm.

Fig. 8.5. Shields-Ethridge Farm, Schoolteacher's House.

room size correlated with quality of finish or status of house. That is, similar room sizes and numbers could be found in both poorly built and well-built houses.

A major key to the status of a tenant house was the interior finish. Only a very few had plaster, which by the beginning of the twentieth century had become normative in owners' houses. More were sheathed (floors, walls, and ceilings) with pine boards, the warmth and patina of which add immeasurably to the sense of timelessness and simplicity that these houses evoke. However, many were unsheathed; from inside the family looked at the back of the clapboards, a condition that naturally made the houses damp and cold in the winter. In Greene County, 13 percent of houses inhabited by white tenants and 58 percent of those lived in by black tenants were unsheathed.[31]

Three of the tenant houses at Shields-Ethridge illustrate the variety of tenant house types and quality found in the farms surveyed. The tenant house just behind the gin at Shields-Ethridge is called the Schoolteacher's House because in the 1950s its use was donated to the Jackson County School Board for a teacher in the two-room school on the farm (fig. 8.5). Before that, it was a sharecropper's house. With only three rooms (and originally only two), it is the smallest on the farm. At fifteen by eight and fifteen by ten feet, its two original rooms were the smallest of any tenant house surveyed. Originally it was two rooms deep with the entrance on a narrow gable wall, which also accommodates the house's only fireplace. This unusual arrangement, and the fact that the partition between the two rooms was constructed with vertical planks with battens (unique on this farm), make it possible that this house began life with another use or was reworked in some way. The rear room had a cook stove. At some later time an unheated room was added on one side for an additional bedroom. Most commentators noted the inadequacy of heating in tenant houses, especially in the damp of southern winters.[32] Stud framed and clapboarded, the house did have tight interior planking on the walls and board-and-batten ceilings to keep out the cold. It also had glazed sash windows with screens (at least at some point in time), to judge by a multiplicity of tacks on the exterior window frames. Doors were board-and-batten.

With so few rooms, sharecropping families inevitably had to use spaces in more than one way. The front room in the Schoolteacher's House was used as a bedroom and general living room. The rear room obviously served as a kitchen and eating room, but it too had a bed in it. Besides its use as a bedroom, the added side room functioned as a space for quilting, the remembrance of which is confirmed by hanging nails in the ceiling. This space also has nails for clothing hooks, some of them holding empty thread spools so that the nails did not tear the fabric (an expediency commonly found in the houses surveyed).

Like almost all tenant houses surveyed, the Schoolteacher's House had a front porch; in fact, after the addition, two of them, although the one on the side addition had no floor besides the ground. Cedar logs support the porch roofs. Relatively few tenant houses had back porches as well. Just out front of the Schoolteacher's House stood a covered well. All the Shields-Ethridge tenants had their own wells, something not true on all sharecropping farms and a distinct luxury.[33] The Schoolteacher's House was whitewashed, with trim and roof painted red, a common color scheme for tenant houses which, in this case at least, was selected by tenants.

Somewhat larger is Preacher Riley's House, located a short distance from the central farm complex and named for one of the last tenants (who was not, however, a preacher) (fig. 8.6). It had a central passage, two front rooms and a rather large rear ell with a kitchen and adjoining space, about the most expansive plan form of any typical tenant house studied.[34] Like all

houses on the farm, this one is stud framed and covered outside with clapboards. Inside, beaded boards form the ceilings and walls of all rooms. The heated front room functioned as a living room; the unheated one across the hall was the primary bedroom. About twenty years ago, the most recent tenants painted this room, apparently doing so without moving the furniture; the outlines of three beds and two dressers can be made out. Because it was unheated, the room's use may have been limited to certain seasons. Agee discussed this problem: even though a house might have four rooms, only one or two were habitable in all seasons because of lack of heat or screens.[35] The windows in Preacher Riley's House show no evidence of screens, although exterior screened doors (of uncertain date) protected the front and back of the hall.

The rearmost room in the ell clearly functioned as the kitchen. The space in front of it was used for eating but probably also served other functions. Being heated, it may have served as a cold-weather bedroom. Built into a corner is a shelf to hold a bowl and towel for washing, a universal feature in tenant homes.

Finishes in Preacher Riley's House are nicer than those in the Schoolteacher's. Except in the passage, the beaded board ceilings and walls are painted (with several coats stretching back many years), and the front room had a nicer than average fireplace and mantel. Doors are paneled throughout, although without hardware. Most tenant houses had very little hardware beyond hinges, and inspection of doors show that

Fig. 8.6. Shields-Ethridge Farm, Preacher Riley's House.

they never did. For many owners, hardware was an unnecessary expense and there was probably concern that it might disappear when tenants moved, as they often did.[36] The effect of this impermanence and the attitude of owners toward sharecroppers appear in this statement by a landlord:

> The landlord has his troubles as well as the sharecropper does. The destructive spirit that seems to prevail among them is expensive to us. After every tenure the landlord has to spend a lot on repairs and building back what the tenant tore down. Sometimes he knocks down outhouses to burn instead of going to the woods to cut his firewood. I had one man to tear down the kitchen, that was made out of heart timber, for lightwood kindling. In the house I lived in before I moved to town the plastering was better than in the house I live in now—till I put a nigger in there. In one year he smoked the walls black as soot and shot holes all through the plastering. They drunk whiskey and fired shotguns all day Sundays. They break out window lights and expect you to replace them, when sometimes it's pure meanness that prompts 'em. Tom Mullen stayed with me fifteen years, and after he knowed he wasn't going to be there another year, he begun digging up all the flower bushes in the yard that had been there no telling how long.[37]

Preacher Riley's House also had its own cluster of small outbuildings, another sign of fairly high status. Surviving outbuildings include a garage and shed (built circa 1940), an older garage which was probably built as a small barn, a chicken shed, a covered well, and a three-hole privy. Gone is a hog house and its pen. All the tenants of the Ethridges were encouraged to have gardens, a practice forbidden by some of the harsher owners in the South because it cut into food purchases at the commissary. In sharecropping generally, there seems to have been a great variety as to how much livestock and poultry tenants had for their own use.[38] On the Shields-Ethridge Farm, most tenants had some livestock.[39]

The obvious difference in quality of tenant houses (both within one farm and between different farms) raises the issue of the relationship of an owner to his tenants. There seems to have been a large variation in the respect and humanity accorded sharecroppers by owners, and this variation reflected itself in the houses. In 1939, a black sharecropper in Dillon, South Carolina, who was about to move from a one-story shack rented from Mr. Stores to a nicer house owned by Mr. Richards, told the following anecdote: "I sho' will be proud when I kin git moved outen dis here shed. I 'bout freezes to death in de winter, and de skeeters eats me up in de summer. Mister Richards he comed by one day an' look at dis shack an' sez right pert: 'Stores, I wouldn't put stock in a shed lak dat!' Mister Stores he mumbles something bout he ain't got no money to set niggers up a fine hotel."[40]

An unusual house at Shields-Ethridge testifies to the hierarchy that permeated rural life. Fairly close behind the main house was a tenant house and collection of outbuildings built in the 1920s for James Jackson, a black man who was the "main man" of Ira Washington Ethridge (fig. 8.7). James was a sharecropper but he could drive a car and was skilled mechanically. For his talents, he received the best tenant house on the farm (and indeed the most elaborate tenant house surveyed). It had a southern bungalow form, with the entrance through a front gable and porch. The rear also had a porch. Generous, nicely cased windows and deep overhangs with brackets at both eaves and gables distinguished this very unusual tenant house that rivaled those of many small landowners in Jackson County.[41]

James Jackson's House also had outbuildings of unusually large number and size: a very large barn for

Fig. 8.7. Shields-Ethridge Farm, James Jackson's House, with barber shop to left.

a tenant house; two garages, one of which held James's own car; and another small outbuilding used as a barber shop where James spent Saturdays cutting the hair of all on the farm (both black and white), another of his skills and another source of income.

Ira Lanis Ethridge, the son of Ira Washington, represented the third generation at Shields-Ethridge. Born in 1899 and assuming control of the farm in 1935, Ira Lanis presided over the conversion of the farm to livestock, the demise of the sharecropper system, and the downfall of cotton. He built very little at the farm, partly because times were hard and partly because his father had built so much and so well. He improved the gin about 1950 and he built an equipment shed and improved the water tower. By the 1960s, the gin was out of date and could no longer compete with gins that processed machine-picked cotton. He shut it down in 1967, and Joyce Ethridge says she thinks it killed him because he died three years later.

Diminutive Variation: The Wynn Farm, Oglethorpe County

The second farm in this study belongs to Pat Wynn Jr., the third generation of his family to live in this area. It is not clear where the family came from, and they could hardly be considered gentry in the same way the Shields and Ethridges could. Wynn's grandfather was of the generation just after the Civil War ("just making a living") and apparently did not own enough land to endow all his children. Consequently his son, Pat Wynn Sr., moved to a farm near Athens where he sharecropped for another owner. These were good times, and in a few years he had made enough money to buy his own land near his grandfather's place. He bought and expanded a large pyramidally roofed house about 1916 and erected almost all the buildings still standing on the Wynn farm.[42]

Although of more modest scale than Shields-Ethridge, the Wynn Farm (fig. 8.8) has a similar layout. The main house and principal farm buildings stand in a cluster near the center of the land. Six tenant houses were scattered along the roads and back into the fields, located on twenty-five-acre tracts assigned to each sharecropper.

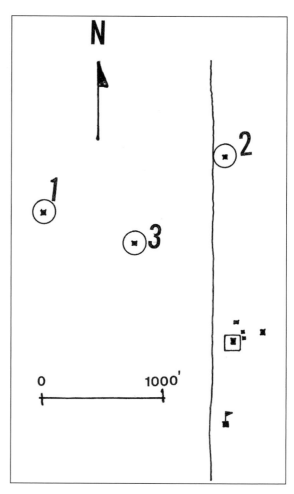

Fig. 8.8. Wynn Farm, Oglethorpe County, Georgia, site layout. Main house enclosed in a square; tenant houses enclosed in circles. Tenant house 1: poorest house; 2: middling house; 3: finest house (Brother's).

The three surviving tenant houses illustrate the social hierarchy of the farm. The poorest was located a long distance from the main house (fig. 8.9). Possibly it was placed there to get it out of sight. It originally was of the "saddlebag" type, consisting of only two rooms with a chimney between. Later a small shed addition of two half-finished rooms was constructed at the rear. During slavery, such dwellings often housed two families, but this practice was largely given up after the Civil War. Indeed, shared dwellings were one of the aspects of slavery most emphatically avoided by free blacks (and, of course, white tenants).[43]

Doors in this simplest of Wynn houses were board-and-batten and had virtually no hardware. Window openings had no sash, but merely board shutters.[44] As in most of the houses inspected, there was no evidence of screens.[45] Each room had a door to the outside and a single window, except one rear room which had only a door. Inside there was no trim and some rooms were unsheathed, having no planking on the walls or ceilings. This house was as roughly built as any surveyed.

A second house was of middling quality and at a middling distance from the main house (fig. 8.10). Originally, it had two rooms (only one had a chimney) and a center passage, with two more, half-finished rooms being added in a rear shed. One of the later spaces was a kitchen with a stove that vented through a brick chimney hung from the roof framing.

Such kitchen additions with stove chimneys abound in tenant houses; tenants originally cooked over a fireplace in one of the front rooms. As in this house, such kitchen additions usually had very low ceilings and very small windows, which made them almost unbearably hot during the summer.[46] The original part of this house has sash windows. Its exterior doors are paneled and have some hardware. Its interior doors are board-and-batten.

The third surviving house on the Wynn farm was located on high ground relatively close to the main house and was distinctly finer than the others (fig. 8.11). It was built by Pat Wynn Sr. for his brother who sharecropped for him. This house had a very unusual and somewhat honorific front porch with a crude pediment. Inside it had four rooms, all nicely boarded and with trim around the doors and windows, a

Fig. 8.9. Wynn Farm, poorest house.

Fig. 8.10. Wynn Farm, middling house, kitchen.

Fig. 8.11. Wynn Farm, finest house (Brother's), front room.

nicety rarely seen in sharecropper dwellings. All the doors were paneled and had hardware. There was even a back porch that provided covered access to the well, a rare convenience in a tenant house.

Climax in a Minor Key: Nolan's Store, Morgan County

At the bottom of the hierarchy of rural tenant dwellings are those at the third farm, Nolan's Store in Morgan County, Georgia (fig. 8.12). The Nolans mostly utilized wage hands working the owner's land. In its layout and the quality of its housing, Nolan's Store remained very close to a slave plantation.

Like the Shields, the Nolans came to Georgia from Virginia in the 1820s. On what would become a two-thousand-acre plantation, they built a plantation plain-style house. The generation after the Civil War remained in this house and their freed slaves became hired workers. Dating from this generation are three tenant houses, two of them frame and across the road from the main house. Another was log and located some distance away. Log tenant houses were probably once common but few survive. Of the dwellings surveyed for this study, these are the smallest and have the fewest amenities. They are virtually indistinguishable from surviving slave quarters in the region. Only the fact that they are stick-built with circularly sawn lumber dates them to after the war. In one of these houses a family shared a single room and half a loft

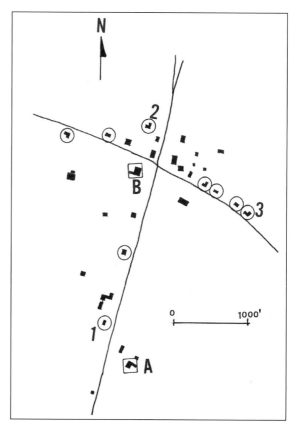

Fig. 8.12. Nolan's Store, Morgan County, Georgia, site layout. Antebellum main house in square A; 1905 main house in square B; tenant houses enclosed in circles. Tenant house 1: one-room house; 2: log house; 3: three-room house.

(fig. 8.13).[47] There was originally no interior boarding on its walls and ceilings. The joists, studs, and backs of the clapboards were merely whitewashed for sanitary reasons. The house's one window had no sash. The only door was of rough boards with no hardware.

Fig. 8.13. Nolan's Store, one-room house.

The next generation of Nolans was more expansive. About 1905 James Alonzo Nolan left the old family house and at the crossroads built a large classical revival house with a wrap-around portico, giving himself much greater prominence in this part of the county. The new house displaced an African American church which had to move to a new site up the road. Nolan's big house became the nucleus of a new community. Across the street he built a very large commissary and back toward the old house he built a gin (no longer standing). The mule barn and blacksmith shop occupied the quadrant diagonally opposite the main house. Nearby in the other directions he erected two sets of tenant houses, lined up like plantation slave cabins of old and visible from the new main house.

The Nolans also had some sharecroppers spread around their vast acreage. Buddy Nolan, the grandson of Alonzo, said his grandfather picked his sharecroppers with care, granting that distinction to only those he felt could produce successfully on their own. He felt that most workers needed the daily supervision that went with being a wage hand. Although some of the sharecroppers at Nolan's Store were white, the wage hands were all black. Several older tenant houses had historically been inhabited by white families, but over the years blacks occupied more and more. Once blacks had lived in a tenant house, white families would not live there.[48]

Several three-room house plans were represented by the newer tenant houses at Nolan's Store. One house is typical and survives in astonishing detail (fig. 8.14). Lived in by African American tenants until 1986, it has a saddlebag plan and a rear kitchen with a stove chimney. It has girt framing and vertical planking, covered later with building paper and asphalt shingles. The vertical siding was painted red at some point in time. Its six-over-six single-hung sash windows were glazed, although screening appears to date from recent times. Inside, the house retains finishes dating back at least into the 1930s. These and surviving accouterments tell much about the tenants way of life.

The right front room was clearly the major entry and living space. The left front room also has a front door, but it was fastened closed quite early because it is sealed over with wallpaper and its threshold shows very little evidence of wear. The entry room has a rough board ceiling and interior wall boarding only on the side wall and part of the front (a commonly seen pattern possibly related to wind direction). The two doors on the house front are paneled; their pegged construction and Greek revival ogee molding indicate that they were salvaged from an older structure. All

Fig. 8.14. Nolan's Store, three-room house, interior of right front room.

other doors in the house have board-and-batten construction. No doors have hardware beyond hinges. Where it occurs, the interior planking in this space was covered with newspapers, dating from 1937 to 1940. This served to further insulate the house and may have had a decorative function as well. Newspapers often covered inside walls in sharecropper houses, especially those lived in by blacks. Where the front wall had no interior boarding, the cracks between the exterior vertical siding were stuffed with rags and the whole covered with burlap to keep out the cold and mosquitoes. At some point after 1940, all the walls were covered with wallpaper, nailed up; three layers of flower prints can be discerned, repaired in places with cardboard. The board floor, usually left exposed in tenant houses, has here been covered with building paper, attached with hundreds of small nails. Over this lie remnant pieces of various linoleum patterns.

The entry and living space had few built-in fixtures. The only original fixture was a high shelf near the door to the kitchen; too high for a washstand, it possibly held a lamp. Nails on the left side of the chimney block probably held coats. Originally heated with the fireplace, a cast-iron and painted tin stove (still in the room) was later installed, its chimney pipe simply run into the fireplace opening. Over the fireplace was the most symbolically important of the house's features, a simple board mantel. Above the mantel, Christmas wrapping paper decorated the wall, along with selected color pages from a Sunday newspaper supplement, most poignantly a furniture store advertisement of a fashionable dining room set and a picture of Jesus the Good Shepherd.[49] James Agee wrote about the almost sacramental quality of the decoration accorded the nicest mantel in tenant houses.[50] Another observer described a similar room thusly in the 1930s:

> Back at the house, Tom opened the door of the living room. A lamp had been lit and a fire made in the silver-painted tin stove. Faded paper covered with tiny pink roses covered the walls. On one side of the stovepipe was a colored picture of Joe Louis sparring with a white man. . . . There was a carpet on the floor and a two-piece living room set, upholstered chair and sofa. Several assorted chairs were in the room. There was a battery radio and a winder phonograph. On the side table were a few china figures of the kind given away as pitch-penny prizes at the fair.[51]

The left front room in the Nolan's Store house evidently served as the primary bedroom. With its front door fastened shut, this room became a private space and had some niceties of finish not seen elsewhere, such as pull blinds and (later) curtains on rods at the two windows. All its walls were covered with interior planking, painted white with here and there pieces of wallpaper. The floor was covered with pieces of linoleum. Mounds of ashes in the fireplace indicate that the room was well heated. Nails with thread spools held clothes. A stick fastened high across one corner probably held either clothes hangers or a curtain that formed a closet. A five foot square of nails in the ceiling may have been for quilting, as in the Shields-Ethridge Schoolteacher's House. It is hard to say which of these front rooms was "better." In many tenant houses, one of the front rooms was treated in a finer manner, although deciphering these relationships is often difficult given the subtlety of the clues, the ruinous state of many houses, and the death of tenants.[52]

The kitchen received a much rougher treatment than the front rooms. It had no interior boarding on the walls and no ceiling, being open into the attic space so that the underside of the galvanized steel roof was visible. The stove formerly stood in the right rear corner where still hangs a brick chimney. Smoke has blackened the walls, ceiling joists, and rafters in this area. A diagonally shaped pantry closet of vertical plank walls fills the right front corner. Inside shelves still hold unopened cans of food and several mason jars of home-canned tomatoes. Hanging on nails are bunches of onions and dried peppers, suggesting that the tenant had a small garden. High shelves also hang above the door to the entry room and in the left rear corner.

Throughout the house stand remnants of much old furniture. Many former tenant houses are filled with junked furniture, reflecting old commentaries that noted the relative abundance of furniture in otherwise very poor households. The reason seems to have been that tenants put what money they had in possessions

Fig. 8.15. John and Suzy Walter's house and yard, Oglethorpe County.

that could be moved from house to house. Landowners were more likely to spend money on houses.[53]

The land around the Nolan's Store houses has grown up so densely that landscape features are no longer visible. Neither privies, wells, nor outbuildings are visible. Probably there were few. Given the houses' proximity, families may have shared a well and privy. They evidently had small gardens, although clearly they did not have land enough to grow much food or to raise livestock.

The houses at Nolan's Store reveal the depths of poverty in southern tenantry. Their small size, rough construction, and the regimentation implicit in the site's arrangement suggest a life-style little changed from slavery. Arthur Raper summarized the situation of such tenants: "The decadence of this civilization is far advanced. . . . The collapse of the plantation system, rendered inevitable by its exploitation of land and labor, leaves in its wake depleted soil, shoddy livestock, inadequate farm equipment, crude agricultural practices, crippled institutions, a defeated and impoverished people. . . . The fatalism which accompanies their low plane of living does to their minds what inadequate food, malaria, and hookworm do to their bodies."[54]

Pastoral Coda: An Affirmative Survival

Nolan's Store testifies to the extreme of southern rural poverty, but another sharecropper house strikes a happier note for an ending. The home of John H. Walter and his wife, Suzy, in southwest Oglethorpe County does not belong to any of the three farms but still houses former sharecroppers and illustrates their way of life (fig. 8.15). Now in their late seventies, they have lived in the house for sixty years. The house was built for her uncle about 1910 by the owner, Mr. Finlay. The Walters sharecropped here until about 1950 when he went to work at the University of Georgia.

As sharecroppers go, the Walters were fortunate. Their soil was good, and Finlay allowed them to plant gardens and corn and raise livestock, so that they could be self-sufficient in food. There was no commissary and indeed the houses on the Finlay land were scattered fairly widely, so that the tenants had a fair degree of privacy and independence. The Walters usually had about ten acres in cotton, five in corn, and one or two in vegetables. They also rotated crops: cotton and corn in alternate years. The land is still fertile, and they still plant about an acre of garden, which, along with chickens and goats makes them still largely self-sufficient in food.

Their house, too, was on the finer end of the sharecropping spectrum. It has three large rooms, all heated, all nicely boarded, and all with paneled doors and hardware. In addition, there is a back porch as well as one on the front. Mrs. Walter still makes brush brooms to sweep her yard, an old-fashioned landscaping technique now practiced by only a few blacks.[55] The Walters still draw water from a well, but they have electricity, a cellular telephone, and a television.

The Walters are like many older blacks in Oglethorpe County. Although they are certainly glad their jobs in town relieved them from the worst of rural poverty, they liked farming; indeed, they say they preferred it to the regimentation of an eight-to-five job. They believe they have lived so long because they work the land and they miss cotton. Their kindness, generosity, and even abundance is obvious to all visitors. They remind us that people with very little power or money can still have much dignity and nobility.[56] Perhaps their lives, their house, and their landscape call into question the validity of modern expectations about material affluence and suggest instead the value in a variety of other riches that in some way helps redeem the poverty and misery inherent in so much of the architecture of sharecropping.

Notes

1. John Vlach, *Back of the Big House: The Architecture of Plantation Slavery* (Chapel Hill: Univ. of North Carolina Press, 1993).

2. George McDaniel, *Hearth and Home: Preserving a People's Culture* (Philadelphia: Temple Univ. Press, 1982).

3. Acknowledgment must go to the work of Gretchen Brock Kinnard, who is writing her masters thesis at the University of Georgia on the typology of sharecropper houses. Other University of Georgia graduate students who helped in the documentation of structures and sites (particularly measured drawings and photography) include Glen Bennett, Corinne Blencoe, Cherie Blizzard, Patricia Deyo, Nicole Diehlman, Richard Drumheller, Alan Durham, Ken Kocher, Paige Labord, Peggy McAllister, Gail Miller, Ashish Mishra, Tom Pfister, Amy Phillips, Gary Porter, David Ray, Paige Weiss, and Monaca Wiggers. I'd also like to thank the reviewers for *Perspectives in Vernacular Architecture* for many helpful suggestions.

4. Arthur Raper, *Preface to Peasantry: A Tale of Two Black Belt Counties* (Chapel Hill: Univ. of North Carolina Press, 1936).

5. Raper, *Preface to Peasantry*, 81–82.

6. On the relationships between owner and tenant, see Jack Temple Kirby, *Rural Worlds Lost: The American South, 1920–1960* (Baton Rouge: Louisiana State Univ. Press, 1987), chap. 4.

7. Raper, *Preface to Peasantry*, 59.

8. Arthur Raper, *Tenants of the Almighty* (New York: Macmillan, 1943), 151–65.

9. Kirby, *Rural Worlds Lost*, especially chap. 2.

10. James Agee and Walker Evans, *Let Us Now Praise Famous Men* (Boston: Houghton Mifflin, 1941), 144.

11. Agee, *Let Us Now Praise Famous Men*, 144. I am indebted to Richard Westmacott for this quote and for general counsel and inspiration in my research on tenant farms. My first stimulus to look at sharecropper farms was an unpublished paper he wrote, "The Not-So-Good Life of the Southern Farmer," read at a conference to honor the centennial of the Savannah Park and Tree Commission, in Savannah, November 1994.

12. Dale Maharidge and Michael Williamson, *And Their Children After Them: The Legacy of Let Us Now Praise Famous Men: James Agee, Walker Evans, and the Rise and Fall of Cotton in the South* (New York: Pantheon Books,

1989) traces the later history of the families about which Agee wrote.

13. Maharidge and Williamson, *And Their Children After Them,* 39. See also Howell Raines, "Let Us Now Revisit Famous Folk," *New York Times Magazine* 25 (May 1980): 31–46, and Michael Connor, "Let Us Now Praise the Story of Alabama Families *Redux*," *Neiman Reports* 43 (1989): 47–49. On Agee, see William Stott, *Documentary Expression and Thirties America* (New York: Oxford Univ. Press, 1973), 290–314. For a critique of Evans's "realism," see James Curtis, *Mind's Truth FSA Photography Reconsidered* (Philadelphia: Temple Univ. Press, 1989), 21–44.

14. Virginius Dabney, "Realities on Tobacco Road," *Saturday Review of Literature* 20 (May 27, 1939): 5; and W. T. Couch, "Landlord and Tenant," *Virginia Quarterly Review* 14 (1938): 309–12. Raper, *Preface to Peasantry.*

15. W. E. B. Du Bois, "The Problem of Housing the Negro," *Southern Workman* 30, no. 7 (July 1901): 390–95; 30, no. 9 (Sept. 1901): 486–93; 30, no. 10 (Oct. 1901): 535–42; 30, no. 11 (Nov. 1901): 601–4; 30, no. 12 (Dec. 1901): 688–93.

16. Most of the information about the Shields-Ethridge Farm comes from Joyce Ethridge, interview with author, Jackson County, Ga., taped July 1997 and noted March 2000.

17. Raper, *Tenants of the Almighty,* 88–119, gives an economic agricultural history for this period. For a briefer review, see Kenneth Coleman, ed., *A History of Georgia,* 2d ed. (Athens: Univ. of Georgia Press, 1991), 225–31.

18. Raper, *Tenants of the Almighty,* 135–42, and Numan V. Bartley, *The Creation of Modern Georgia,* 2d ed. (Athens: Univ. of Georgia Press, 1990), 127.

19. See Bartley, *Creation of Modern Georgia,* 127–47, for a characterization of this period. See also C. Vann Woodward, *Tom Watson: Agrarian Rebel* (New York: Oxford Univ. Press, 1963), 98–99, on the ideology of the New South and the New Departure.

20. Raper, *Preface to Peasantry,* 143.

21. Michael Ann Williams describes this same change being made in houses in southwestern North Carolina during this period, in *Homeplace: The Social Use and Meaning of the Folk Dwelling in Southwestern North Carolina* (Athens: Univ. of Georgia Press, 1991), 99.

22. Merle Prunty Jr., "The Renaissance of the Southern Plantation," *Geographical Review* 45, no. 4 (Oct. 1955): 476.

23. Prunty, "Renaissance of the Southern Plantation," deals with the layout of the postbellum sharecropper plantation versus the antebellum slave plantation.

24. *Athens Banner,* Oct. 1, 1910.

25. Prunty called this pattern a "fragmented plantation." Prunty, "Renaissance of the Southern Plantation," 479.

26. Basic plan types are similar to those discussed in Williams, *Homeplace.*

27. This form was exhaustively studied in Maryland in both antebellum and postbellum examples by McDaniel, *Hearth and Home,* 53–57 and 149–86.

28. Agee and Evans, *Let Us Now Praise Famous Men,* 147.

29. Raper, *Preface to Peasantry,* 65.

30. McDaniel, *Hearth and Home,* 56, notes that the most typical dimension of one-room houses in southern Maryland was sixteen feet.

31. Raper, *Preface to Peasantry,* 63.

32. Agee and Evans, *Let Us Now Praise Famous Men,* 209.

33. Ibid., 129.

34. Ibid., 152, notes that a four-room house was generous for sharecroppers.

35. Ibid., 157 and 174.

36. Arthur Raper, *Preface to Peasantry,* 61, reported that the average length of tenure for landless tenants was two and a half years.

37. Landowner in Seaboard, North Carolina, 1939, in Tom E. Terrill and Jerrold Hirsch, eds., *Such as Us: Southern Voices of the Thirties* (Chapel Hill: Univ. of North Carolina Press, 1978), 68.

38. Agee and Evans, *Let Us Now Praise Famous Men,* 212–17, and Raper, *Preface to Peasantry,* 81.

39. McDaniel, *Hearth and Home,* fig. 11, shows the lot layout for a typical tenant farm complex in southern Maryland. There tenants almost always had their own gardens and livestock.

40. Terrill and Hirsch, *Such as Us,* 79.

41. For the use of the bungalow form as an upscale African American house form, see M. Jeff Hardwick "Homesteads and Bungalows: African-American Architecture in Langstone, Oklahoma," in *Shaping Communities Perspectives in Vernacular Architecture,* ed. Carter L. Hudgins and Elizabeth Collins Cromley (Knoxville: Univ. of Tennessee Press, 1997), 6:21–32.

42. Information from Pat Wynn Jr., interview with author, Oglethorpe County, Georgia, July 1997.

43. Two-room houses shared by two families were described by many observers of slavery, among them Frederick Law Olmsted, in *The Cotton Kingdom: A Traveller's Observations on Cotton and Slavery in the American Slave States,* ed. by Arthur Schlesinger (New York: Alfred A. Knopf, 1953), 31.

44. Board-and-batten shutters without sash were typical in slave times; see McDaniel, *Hearth and Home,* 73.

45. Raper, *Preface to Peasantry,* 65, noted that screens were rare.

46. Agee and Evans, *Let Us Now Praise Famous Men,* 177.

47. This was the normative form of slave house described by McDaniel in *Hearth and Home,* 53–100.

48. Buddy Nolan, interview with author, Morgan County, Ga., June 1997.

49. This same image figures prominently in a story by Alice Walker, "The Welcome Table," in *In Love and Trouble: Stories of Black Women* (New York: Harcourt, Brace, 1973).

50. Agee and Evans, *Let Us Now Praise Famous Men,* 162–65.

51. A black renter in Federal Writers' Project, *These Are Our Lives* (Chapel Hill: Univ. of North Carolina Press, 1939), 51. Locations for the interviews were not given in this book. Many were in North Carolina. For a very complete description of a comparable tenant house in Maryland, see McDaniel, *Hearth and Home,* 149–86.

52. A similar conclusion, but buttressed with much oral history, appears in Michael Ann Williams, *Homeplace.*

53. Raper, *Preface to Peasantry,* 65. See Agee and Evans, *Let Us Now Praise Famous Men,* 150–89, for an excruciatingly detailed description of the interior of a typical sharecropper's house.

54. Raper, *Preface to Peasantry,* viii, 3, and 405; quoted thus in Bartley, *Creation of Modern Georgia,* 176.

55. On swept yards, see Richard Westmacott, *African-American Gardens and Yards in the Rural South* (Knoxville: Univ. of Tennessee Press, 1992), 31 and 80.

56. Vlach, quoting Ralph Ellison, in *Back of the Big House,* 168.

9

Unraveling the Threads of Community Life

Work, Play, and Place in the Alabama Mill Villages of the West Point Manufacturing Company

ROBERT W. BLYTHE

This chapter explores how families in five textile mill villages in Chambers County, Alabama, used both the environments provided for them by the West Point Manufacturing Company and the many nearby spaces that were outside direct company control. The isolated location of the West Point villages, with just one paved road (U.S. 29) connecting them to surrounding communities, profoundly influenced life for workers. The presence of nearby fields, forests, and the Chattahoochee River allowed workers to maintain many aspects of a traditional rural way of life. It also ameliorated some of the worst aspects of the paternalistic regime by providing places for recreation free from management observation. On the other hand, the isolation allowed the company to repel threats to its authority, especially in times of crisis like the September 1934 general strike in the textile industry. Issues of au-

thority and resistance, intended use and actual use, race, and status are at the core of this study. In an effort to uncover the perspectives of mill worker families, I have relied on oral history interviews and published memoirs. By its nature, this kind of evidence tends to represent the views of the more literate and successful members of the mill communities, but it is indispensable in approaching topics that are not covered in company histories, newspaper articles, and other documents.

Most histories of southern textile mills and mill village life have been broad studies that treat the South as a whole or a single important state like North Carolina. These works tend to emphasize broad concepts and trends such as paternalism or southern resistance to labor unions. Broadus Mitchell's pioneering 1921 work, *The Rise of Cotton Mills in the South*, trumpeted the philanthropic motives of the mill founders and cast a long shadow over subsequent histories. From the beginning, southern mills have had their critics—journalists, sociologists, and historians—who took a dim view of the paternalistic system of the southern mills and its effects on workers. The conclusion of most of these analysts was that paternalism stunted the initiative and self-respect of mill families. Finally, under the influence of social history's ascendancy in the last twenty years, historians have restored a considerable amount of agency to the mill families. Increasingly, historians emphasize the role of mill workers in fashioning a unique social world, one characterized by mutual support and based in large part on their rural heritage. This world is seen as pervasively influenced by mill management but also marked by considerable opportunities for self-expression and even resistance. Resistance was most often expressed in spontaneous reactions to specific company abuses rather than in traditional labor organizing.[1]

Historians of the built environment have also recently written of the southern textile mill village. Here the focus has been on the intentions of the mill owners and the architects and landscape designers that they retained to plan and construct the mill village environments. In keeping with the origins of architectural history in art history, the interest of architectural historians tends to flag once the original designer's intent has been realized and people actually begin to occupy the designed spaces. Margaret Crawford's study *Building the Workingman's Paradise* notes that workers were rarely consulted in the planning of company towns, but says little about the day-to-day use of space.[2] Close-grained studies of the intricate social dynamics of individual mill communities are just beginning to appear. Notable among these are Douglas Flamming's book *Creating the Modern South: Millhands and Managers in Dalton, Georgia, 1884–1984* (1992) and Mary Letherd Wingerd's article on Cooleemee, North Carolina, "Rethinking Paternalism: Power and Parochialism in a Southern Mill Village" (1996). Although these recent community studies have added much to an understanding of how the dynamics of authority and deference, class, gender,

and race operated in particular villages, they have not focused much attention on how these dynamics played out in the physical spaces of the mill village. The effort of mill managers to shape worker behavior and the desire of mill families to lead their own lives and express their cultural values were acted out in specific physical spaces. Most of these spaces were provided by the company, but merely by living in them, the mill families put their own stamp on them.

Strung out over a distance of about eight miles in eastern Alabama, just across the Chattahoochee River from Georgia, the five mill villages considered here are (from north to south): Lanett, Shawmut, Langdale, Fairfax, and Riverview. The West Point Manufacturing Company had its origins in the Langdale Mill, established on the Chattahoochee River in 1866, at a

Map 9.1. The five West Point Manufacturing Company mill villages.

time when mills relied on waterpower. In 1892, West Point took over the Riverdale Mill (in the town of Riverview), a water-powered mill on the Chattahoochee that also began operations in 1866. In the economically expansive New South period, the company built three new mills and villages in the area: Lanett in 1894, Shawmut in 1908, and Fairfax in 1917. Several local families, mostly planters, led the move to establish the Langdale and Riverdale Mills in the 1860s; the Lanier family was closely associated with the Langdale Mill from the 1870s on and became a major force in the activities of the West Point Manufacturing Company.[3]

Riverview Village and Langdale Village both began as minimally planned communities, although Langdale in the twentieth century received an overlay of community buildings that gave it a new, more obviously planned, appearance. These first mills were restricted by their need for waterpower to irregular, hilly sites directly on the Chattahoochee River. The local investors who organized the mills at first erected only a handful of small frame houses for their workers and built no community buildings. The houses in both villages were clustered on unpaved streets that followed the topography, winding their way up the hills from the mill.[4]

The first mill employees in this area came, usually as families, from nearby farms in Alabama and just across the river in Georgia. In the wake of the appalling casualties of the Civil War, there were many female-headed households eager for employment of any kind. The example of Elmira Andrews Crowder, a widow who moved to Langdale with her five children in the 1860s soon after the mill opened, was typical.[5] The family labor system quickly became the norm in southern mill villages. The first mill families were accustomed to a preindustrial, rural, southern way of life, characterized by small, largely self-sufficient mixed farms, the church (usually Baptist or Methodist) as the center of both spiritual and social life, and minimal opportunities for formal schooling. Church services, picnics, and revivals were the main events that brought people together. An occasional trip to a market town to trade was about the only other opportunity for exten-

sive social interaction. This way of life, with a few modifications, carried over to the two new mill towns on the Chattahoochee. Ample land allowed families to have kitchen gardens and keep livestock, and the nearby river, creeks, and woods provided fish and game to supplement their diets. The early mill owners, struggling just to keep operating, built no churches. Families worshiped in homes or built their own small sanctuaries.

By the time that the West Point Company decided to build a new plant at Lanett in 1894, living standards in general had risen, good labor was harder to get, and industrial firms were devoting somewhat more attention to their workers' health and well-being. This was also the period when city planning was getting its start as a professional discipline in the United States.[6] The planning of the new villages at Lanett (1894), Shawmut (1908), and Fairfax (1917) reveals much about the company's assumptions concerning the needs and sensibilities of its work force. The middle- and upper-class whites who organized mills looked down on farm families as ignorant and socially backward.[7] They assumed that when these families came to the mills, their needs would continue to be minimal. The company provided detached houses because that was the norm in the rural South. If African Americans were hired, they were housed away from white families. Because nearly everyone walked in a mill town, housing for whites, stores, and churches had to be clustered near the mill. It is no surprise then, that West Point's mill villages were compact communities. Lanett, built in 1894, when city planning was in its infancy, has a gridded street pattern with monotonous rows of identical houses set close to the street. The layout indicates an interest in creating a rationally organized community but little concern for aesthetics or the amenities of community life. As more comprehensively planned, early-twentieth-century company towns, Shawmut and Fairfax were influenced by the planning principles prevailing at the time of their creation.

Designed in 1907 by an unidentified landscape architect,[8] Shawmut bears the imprint of the City Beautiful movement, with its dominant axis, tightly controlled, geometric street pattern, and more

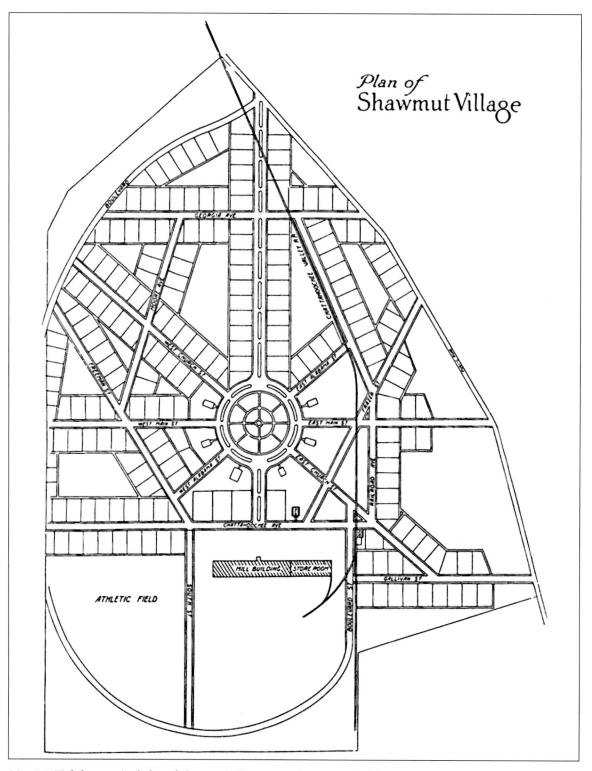

Map 9.2. Tightly organized plan of Shawmut Village, 1907. Courtesy of Cobb Memorial Archive.

Fig. 9.1. Typical frame mill house in Fairfax.

generous house setbacks. The design of Shawmut underscores the production processes and power relationships of southern mill villages (map 9.2). A single principal axis organizes the spaces of the village. It begins at the cotton warehouse, runs through the opening room where the cotton bales were initially processed, and into the three-story brick mill itself, where spinning, weaving, and finishing of cloth took place. The axis then continues directly out of the mill's main entrance, across a circle (meant to be a public park and the focus of community life), and down Lanier Street. Broad Lanier Street, with its landscaped median planted in magnolia trees, was home to the mill superintendent and supervisors. The village school, Baptist and Methodist churches, a motion picture auditorium, and a hotel/cafeteria all faced the circular park, while worker housing was on streets radiating from the circle and streets connecting the rays. Shawmut's design unmistakably establishes the primacy of the mill as the economic engine that drives the village and also emphasizes the importance of the mill managers, living directly opposite the mill on the far side of the circle.

Fairfax was designed by Harvard-trained landscape architect William Marquis, who later had a long career with the Olmsted Brothers firm.[9] Built in 1917, Fairfax shows the impact of the picturesque suburb. Workers' houses are arrayed on a system of gently curving streets surrounding the mill, avoiding straight lines and long vistas. Public buildings are clustered on a looping street facing one end of the mill, while supervisors' houses are in a group facing the opposite end. West of the mill is a large open space, which some residents called the village green.[10] The planning of Fairfax also shows more attention to the mixing of house types on each street to further avoid an appearance of regimentation. The power relationships and hierarchy of the mill village are thus somewhat softened and disguised in Fairfax, as compared to Shawmut, built just nine years earlier. Nevertheless, it is readily apparent that the supervisors' houses are larger and set apart in their own precinct.

In all five villages the houses for mill operatives were freestanding vernacular types typical of the Piedmont South. Side-gabled double-pen houses, gabled-wing houses, pyramidal cottages, and front-gabled bungalows were the most common types. All houses were frame structures, built on brick pier foundations, usually with a front porch, and were originally heated by fireplaces (fig. 9.1).

Many originally were duplexes, with two families living side by side. Water was supplied by a single spigot on the back porch, and each house had an outhouse in the back yard. Most families had vegetable gardens in the back as well as fenced chicken coops. Many families also kept a milk cow or raised hogs. In the words of James Brooks Sr., "You could raise hogs anywhere. The only thing you needed was a hog pen and a hog and some dishwater. Leftover food, dishwater, what have you, you put it in the trough for the hog."[11] The West Point Company built backyard cow sheds and made communal pastures available for the livestock. Following a custom common throughout the rural South, front yards before World War II were dirt, kept tidy with regular sweepings with brush brooms (fig. 9.2).[12]

Through the 1920s, the mill village landscapes closely resembled rural hamlets, and each lot was not unlike a miniature farmstead, with a small frame house, an outbuilding or two, a kitchen garden, and livestock penned or tethered in the back yard (fig. 9.3). A wash shed or a site devoted to wash pots, along with a clothesline and perhaps a pallet for airing bedding were also backyard fixtures. Much more than is common today, back yards in the mill villages were utilitarian rather than ornamental landscapes. Although the rhythms of work were very different from what these rural families had left behind, the physical setting was largely familiar. Additionally, before 1920, the line between work life and home life was not sharply drawn. Small children played in the mills where mothers could keep an eye on them, and workers could leave the mill to attend to household chores.[13]

Like many southern mill companies, West Point employed African Americans in a handful of strictly defined roles. Until the 1970s, blacks were denied inside jobs as spinners and weavers and held no supervisory positions. African American men worked in the mill yard and warehouses, moving baled cotton and loading finished cloth, and as helpers in areas like the machine shop. West Point also hired blacks to build and maintain the houses and infrastructure in its villages—this is one of the few areas where black and white men sometimes worked side by side, although always under the direction of white supervisors. West Point Manufacturing Company also employed a few blacks as skilled craftsmen. It maintained a crew of black stone masons who laid the foundation of the Fairfax Mill, as well as building retaining walls, bridges, and small buildings like the Langdale Boy Scout House. The masons also could moonlight for other employers and were responsible for the impressive seventy-stall dairy barn of the Word Dairy Company on the outskirts of Langdale.[14]

As with its white workers, West Point had to provide housing for its African American employees. In keeping with the racial codes of the period, it did so by establishing separate "Negro villages," located from half a mile to a mile from the respective white villages. Several of these are clearly marked on company plats and can be located today. Because the African American work force at each mill was small, each Negro village had from twenty to forty houses, compared to the three or four hundred in the white villages. Typical is the Fairfax Negro village, noted as being fifty-five hundred feet from Fairfax Mill (fig. 9.4).[15] Houses in the African American villages were smaller (most of them just two rooms), placed closer to the street, and had fewer amenities such as flush toilets. Otherwise, they were similar in construction to the frame houses with brick chimneys that were built for white workers. The overarching principles of segregation and white supremacy were thus encoded in work assignments and in the plans for the mill villages.

As competition for labor increased and living standards improved generally in the first three decades of the twentieth century, West Point made a series of improvements both to the mill houses and to the communities themselves. After building a hydro-electric generating station at Langdale in 1908, the company provided electricity to most of the mill houses. Beginning in the 1920s, company crews installed flush toilets, often creating water closets by framing off a portion of the back porch. Bathtubs and sinks with running water came later, usually in the 1930s.[16]

In December 1929, author Harold Shumway visited these five villages and produced a book that is the best extant first-hand account of village life before World War II. Shumway confirms the ubiquitous

Fig. 9.2. Clarence and Irma Gibson in a typical swept-dirt yard in Langdale, c. 1940. Courtesy of Mrs. Jean Crowder Williams.

Fig. 9.3. Backyard vegetable gardens and outbuildings in Langdale, c. 1906. Courtesy of Cobb Memorial Archive.

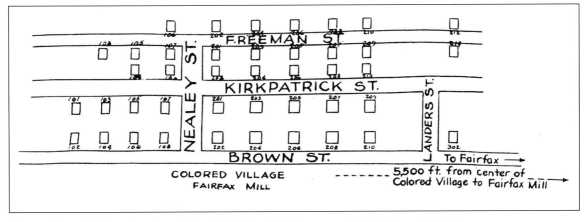

Fig. 9.4. Plan of African American village for Fairfax Mill. Courtesy of Cobb Memorial Archive.

custom of swept-dirt front yards, and noted some with plantings of zinnias and asters. He describes the houses as decent and livable, with adequate space, but certainly no wasted space. The three- and four-room houses he entered typically had bare wood floors, brick fireplaces, screened windows, walls of wallboard painted white and unadorned by pictures, a bed in every room except the kitchen, and straight-backed wooden chairs (fig. 9.5). He notes the presence of running water in each kitchen (often called the stove room), and a water closet directly adjacent. Shumway rarely encountered a bathtub at this period. He noted "evidences of prideful tenancy and evidences of don't-give-a-darn." He was much struck by West Point Manufacturing Company's provision of free electricity to the families, but its use was typically restricted to a bare bulb on a cord in each room. He comments on the presence of a phonograph—in a house where husband and wife both held semi-skilled positions. Although Shumway presents himself as an impartial observer, he takes pains to refute the more extreme condemnations of mill village life.[17]

Shumway noted a "plentiful" supply of black nurses to tend mill workers' children, and he observed "colored mammies all over the place." Other longtime residents have spoken of having African American washerwomen, and one has written that if one washerwoman quit, she could easily hire another by going down by the railroad tracks and asking around. James Brooks recalls seeing streams of black women carrying bundles of dirty laundry away from the mill villages and returning next day with flat boxes of finished laundry. One indication of the pervasiveness of segregation was the construction by the company of a backyard washhouse with its own toilet for at least one manager; the separate toilet meant that the black washerwoman would not need to use the family's toilet inside the house. The trend toward increased employment of black domestics in the 1920s reflects a tightening of control by the mill owners. The older casual practices of allowing small children in the mill as helpers disappeared, and working mothers could no longer come and go to attend to household chores. Not only supervisors, but families where both husband and wife had better-paying mill jobs could afford black

Fig. 9.5. Interior of Lanett mill house showing wallboard and minimal detailing. Courtesy of Cobb Memorial Archive.

domestic help. Denied even the minimal role that was afforded black men in the mills, black women had no employment options outside of domestic work.[18]

West Point began a program of corporate welfare with the construction of a school and library in Langdale in 1896. Like the company's efforts to improve conditions in its houses, the welfare work had multiple motives. Chief among these were a desire for a contented, stable labor force, insurance against discontent that could lead to labor organizing, and a concern for public relations. Around 1900, the company began transplanting shade trees from nearby forests to beautify village streets. The first village nurse was hired in 1918, and soon each village had one. Langdale had a community swimming pool as early as 1920. By the late 1920s, each of the five villages had a school, a moving picture show, a Masonic Hall (used by a number of fraternal and community organizations), a Boy Scout House, and a Girl Scout House, all provided by the company. Blacks were excluded from the white recreation programs, and the company began a separate, more limited recreation program for African Americans in the 1940s. A number of new church buildings also went up in the 1920s, with company financial assistance.[19]

The assemblage of community buildings in the center of Langdale on U.S. 29 represents the company's greatest effort to demonstrate to workers and the world in general its commitment to its employees and their quality of life. Sears Hall, a gymnasium/assembly hall (1928), Lafayette Lanier School (1934), and the Lanier School Auditorium are all substantial, architect-designed buildings in a colonial revival vein. In a prominent location across the road from the school, a memorial to Lafayette Lanier Jr. was erected in 1935, funded by contributions from company employees, local merchants, and textile industry leaders (fig. 9.6).[20] These structures and nearby churches provided the village with a highly visible and ceremonial civic center. From a single vantage point on Highway 29 in Langdale, the observer had a panoramic view that summarized the major elements of southern mill village paternalism. In the background was the mill itself, the economic foundation of the community. Readily apparent on every side were the company's efforts to provide for the spiritual life, education, recreation, and entertainment of its workers. Tying it all together was the Lafayette Lanier Memorial, tangible evidence of the enduring economic and emotional ties between employer and employee. It should be remembered that the company owned everything within this vista except the public highway and the river.

African Americans received much less than whites from the corporate welfare activities of the West Point Manufacturing Company. They were also subject to a strict system of segregation in the mills and the villages. James Brooks tells of the uproar he caused in the 1950s, when he strayed from his post as helper in the

Fig. 9.6. Lafayette Lanier Memorial in the center of Langdale. Courtesy of Cobb Memorial Archive.

machine shop to a spinning room at the Langdale mill. His motive was curiosity about the spinning operations, but his boss soon told him that it was unsafe to venture into whites-only areas of the mill. Similarly, blacks understood that they were in jeopardy if they were seen on the streets of the white villages after dark. Blacks were also expected to be deferential to whites, "to show some type of obedience," as Brooks puts it.[21]

Although the company gave some support to black churches and built schools for black children, including a high school in Lanett, the public facilities in the villages were off-limits to blacks, as they were in any southern town before the late 1960s. By the 1940s, the company had a separate recreational program for blacks, but it had strict limits. James Brooks poignantly observes about the Langdale pool, "I've been in that pool. I went in that pool early—a long time ago. But it was dry and I was scraping paint from the bottom of it to repaint it." Blacks also could see movies, but not even from the balconies of the auditoriums where whites viewed them. Special screenings were held for blacks in their schools.[22]

In the 1920s and 1930s, daily life in the West Point Company mill villages had a strong flavor of southern small town life, with one important difference: virtually every space, public and private, was owned by the company. Life was no different in the comprehensively planned villages like Shawmut then in villages like Riverview that grew without planning. The physical isolation of the villages often ameliorated the effects of company control, but at other times strongly reinforced it. Being surrounded by thousands of acres of forest, meadow, and river provided residents with opportunities to hunt, fish, picnic, and even make and drink moonshine, away from the watchful eye of the company. But, when the company believed that its core interests were at stake, as in the 1934 general strike, it took advantage of the isolation to shut its workers off from the outside world.

Organized social life in the communities centered on churches and the company and, to a lesser extent, fraternal orders like the Masons and the Woodmen of the World. In communities with few cars in the days before air conditioning, much social life was conducted outdoors, particularly on front porches. Older

Fig. 9.7. Lanett baseball field and grandstand. Courtesy of Cobb Memorial Archive.

residents recall the neighborliness and rounds of visiting that characterized the communities prior to World War II. Some entertaining revolved around Sunday school groups or school groups, while adults often held potlucks after church on Sundays, "bringing Vienna sausages, cookies, or whatever you had."[23] Old-timers complain about the indoor orientation of family life today. Lifelong resident Marshall Lane observed that "you spent a little time with your neighbors back then [1930s], but now you only see them when they're doing yardwork."[24]

Public spaces like parks and ball fields were used for both organized and unorganized activity. Each village had a baseball diamond with a wooden grandstand, and the company-sponsored semipro teams of the Chattahoochee Valley League drew large and enthusiastic crowds (fig. 9.7). Teams from each of the five West Point villages plus two or three from mills in Opelika made up the league. Admission to games was a nickel or a dime, and competitive mill superintendents recruited players from all over the state. During vacations from college, Billy Hitchcock, who later played nine seasons in the majors, was a nominal employee of Langdale Mill and received as much as twenty-five dollars for every game he played.[25]

Christmas and the Fourth of July were big times in the villages. As part of the paternalistic bond that it strove to foster, the company provided a gift for each child at gala annual Christmas parties, which continued into the 1950s. Fourth of July celebrations featured barbecues, followed by games, contests, and entertainment. West Point sponsored separate, smaller holiday celebrations for its black workers and their families (fig. 9.8). Underlying all of these events was the understanding that the company's largesse was conditional and could be withdrawn if workers asserted themselves, for example through union organizing.[26]

Over time, certain spots in the white villages became recognized gathering places. In the evenings, men would hang out at the cement bridge over Moores Creek in Langdale, "talking and spitting into the creek," as one resident put it. Young women would promenade in the small park surrounding the Lanier Memorial in Langdale while young men sat on the bank on the other side of the highway watching them. Most socializing was within the particular mill village, although the more adventuresome boys hitchhiked to the other villages looking for dates. Within the bounds

Fig. 9.8. Picnic for African American workers, c. 1950. Courtesy of Cobb Memorial Archive.

of segregation and the paternalistic compact, white mill families felt free to gather and converse in the company-owned, but publicly accessible spaces of the villages.[27]

The West Point Company's proprietary attitude toward space in its villages is exemplified by a story told by Elizabeth Lyons, who grew up near Riverview. She tells of a night in the late 1940s or early 1950s, when white-robed Ku Klux Klan members burned a cross in the front yard of a neighbor, an African American family that had dared to purchase a new, rather than used, automobile. Soon, a large black car arrived on the scene. From it emerged company president Joseph Lanier, who was seen in animated conversation with the Klan leaders. He made it clear to them that he would brook no outside interference with, or public displays against, his people, black or white. The Klan withdrew and never returned.[28]

The use of common spaces for labor organizing activity was wholly prohibited. Historian Janet Irons has characterized the "flying squadron" tactics used by southern textile workers in the September 1934 general strike as a direct threat to the control of public space traditionally exercised by southern elites.[29] The West Point Company's reaction to this threat shows that, when its core interests were at stake, the company exercised an absolute control over its mill town environments.

The 1934 textile strike was the culmination of more than a decade of worker frustration with production speed-ups, the imposition of scientific management, and the elimination of the older, much more flexible blend of work life and family life. The strike began with a July walkout that closed plants in northern Alabama. The West Point Company responded by hiring an undercover operative to pose as a union organizer and give management reports on union sentiment in its mills. The company also bought or borrowed seven machine guns and a supply of tear gas and gas launchers. Workers in the five West Point mills did not join the Alabama walkout. The United Textile Workers of America (UTW) then called a nationwide general strike on August 30, 1934. To spread the strike beyond mills where the union was strong, UTW members used flying squadrons of workers who trav-

eled in cars and trucks. Up to two hundred strikers would suddenly appear at a mill, surround it, and persuade workers to walk out. When rumors reached West Point management that workers from nearby LaGrange and Columbus, Georgia, might attempt flying squadron tactics at its mills, its reaction was swift and brutal. The company had eight hundred of its employees commissioned as special deputies or special policemen and established roadblocks on U.S. 29 at Lanett and Fairfax. All vehicles attempting to enter were stopped and searched. With cotton bale barricades and armed guards, West Point effectively isolated its five thousand workers from any outside influence until the strike was abandoned by the UTW's national leaders on September 23.[30]

When labor organizing was not the issue, West Point pursued a pragmatic approach to controlling the everyday, off-the-clock behavior of workers and families in its mill villages. There is anecdotal evidence that Shawmut had a set of written rules of behavior, although no copies of rules have been discovered for any of the five villages. Former Fairfax school teacher Eloise Echols Gray reports that teachers (whose salaries were paid by the company) were expected to lead "admirable lives." She was chastised for playing rook with some friends until the hour of 10:00 P.M. in the parlor of her teachers' dormitory; following that, she did all her entertaining on the front porch, no matter what the weather. James Hooks relates a story of a Shawmut man who beat his daughter with a rope for coming in late on a Saturday night; the company fired him and moved him out of his house by sundown Sunday.[31]

The key considerations for the company were keeping the mills running efficiently (under its unfettered control) and suppressing public disorderly conduct. Drinking was widespread, but tolerated, as long as it did not result in chronic absenteeism or public disturbances. As longtime Langdale resident Annie Hawkins put it, "On Saturday night after these people had worked twelve hours a day, six days a week, they got some rowdy sometimes on Saturday night. It's notorious for drinking in a mill village, too, because it's hard, it's hard." Homemade whiskey (moonshine) was brewed along many nearby creeks and was readily

Fig. 9.9. Nannie Pearl Snuggs enjoying an outing on the banks of the Chattahoochee River, c. 1910. Courtesy of Mrs. Jean Crowder Williams.

available. The company discouraged public intoxication, and the village constable (a company employee) would get a drunken man off the streets and back to his home, if possible. Drinkers or teetotalers, the men were needed on the job on Monday morning. In fact, one of the tasks of the village nurse was to go around on Monday morning and roust the hung-over men out of bed and get them in to the mill.[32]

Honky-tonks, roadhouses, and dance halls provided places for men and women to escape the confining atmosphere of a company town to relax and have fun. Some drinking establishments operated in private residences in Chambers County. Just across the Chambers County line in Lee County, Alabama, were several roadhouses and dance halls. Club Blanton, in the community of the same name, was variously described in interviews as a "beer joint," a "honky-tonk," and a "house of ill repute." Club Blanton and another road-houses catered to farmers and soldiers as well as mill workers. There were also honky-tonks in the black communities, which operated in private houses.[33]

The location of the West Point mills along an isolated stretch of the Chattahoochee River on the Alabama–Georgia border had significant effects on the way of life and even the self-image of residents. With the river and acres of rural countryside close at hand, mill families had plenty of places to go to fish, hunt, swim, boat, camp, and picnic—all away from the observation of mill managers. Some families built cabins on is-lands in the river, while others pitched tents on its banks. Children used bateaux to paddle between the islands. The river, and especially a picnic spot known as Granny White Springs, feature prominently in the reminiscences of older residents when describing recreation (fig. 9.9). The hydropower dams at Langdale and Riverview allowed stretches of the river to be drained, and locals could gather fish with baskets at certain times.[34] In any environment, especially one so firmly under an employer's control, "third places" add to the psychological health and satisfaction of workers.

The Georgia-Alabama border mostly follows the west bank of the Chattahoochee, but there are small portions of the west bank that are in Georgia. A portion of the Riverdale Mill, for example, is in Georgia. Living near a state line was another factor that allowed residents a bit more independence than might have prevailed in other mill villages. A lot of couples got married in Georgia, either because the legal age was lower there, or because it was more convenient to get a license just across the river in West Point, Georgia, rather than traveling thirteen or fourteen miles to Lafayette, the county seat of Chambers County, Alabama. One enterprising store owner took advantage of lower cigarette taxes in Georgia by setting up a floating store on the river, permanently anchored ten feet off the west bank and connected by a gang plank to the sovereign state of Alabama. These are two examples of the expanded options available to border residents.[35]

West Point's mills were not built on the fringes of a sizable existing town with an established middle class. The first two mills were sited several miles downriver and on the opposite bank from West Point, Georgia, which had a population of less than one thousand in the 1860s.[36] Although the merchant and professional families in West Point often were snobbish toward the mill families, the white mill families in Chambers County felt less of a sense of inferiority and otherness than was common elsewhere in the South. Whether they were operatives, section hands, or supervisors, nearly everyone had come to these communities to work in a mill.

The paternalistic system lingered longer in the Chattahoochee Valley than in most southern company towns. West Point Manufacturing Company continued its community welfare activities following World War II, long after other mills had abandoned the field. West Point even built two dozen new worker houses in 1947 in Riverview, among the last company housing added to an established community anywhere in the country. The firm also contributed more than a million dollars to the George H. Lanier Memorial Hospital, which opened in 1950. One reason for paternalism's durability was the continued close involvement of the Lanier family in company operations. In the 1950s, the third generation of the family, represented by company president Joseph L. Lanier, was at the helm. Another reason was the valley's isolation. Although one-quarter to one-third of families had automobiles in the 1930s, car ownership was not the norm until the 1950s, providing workers with many more options for living and shopping. In the early 1950s, West Point began drawing back from its longstanding paternalistic role. The biggest change came in 1953, when the company sold off the village houses, granting ten-year no-interest sales contracts to those who needed them.[37]

When the mill houses entered private ownership, approximately 80 percent of the new home owners made changes and improvements to their properties. These changes reveal a deep-seated desire by owners to place their own stamp on their living spaces. Few have gone so far as to add a second story, but room additions are common. The most pervasive change was the placement of new siding materials over the original wood siding. Asbestos siding was the first option, with aluminum or vinyl now being the sheathing of choice. With the coming of air conditioning, many porches were enclosed. The transition from dirt yards to grass seems to have been a gradual thing, with most yards having turf by the 1950s. New houses have been added, both as infill and also on the outskirts of the mill villages. Many of these are brick ranch-style houses, which have changed the visual character of some streets. De facto residential segregation persists three decades after the passage of open housing laws. Two of the company's "Negro villages" have disappeared, but two (Fairfax and Morris Line, associated with Langdale Mill) remain exclusively African American neighborhoods. West Shawmut, another African American village, has disappeared, but there are few black residents in Shawmut itself.

Air conditioning allowed southerners to stay indoors in the hot weather, and front porch socializing in these towns has all but disappeared. James Hooks, born in Shawmut in 1910, marveled that on a drive through the village in the 1990s he saw nobody outside.[38] Desegregation, too, has had its effects. When the public swimming pools integrated, most whites stopped going, and the few who could afford it built backyard pools.[39] These changes have produced a more private, self-contained pattern of living for each family. Overall, the mill villages of the West Point Company today have many of the life-style characteristics of dozens of other lower-middle-class southern suburbs. Fast food emporia on U.S. 29 run right to the edge of Shawmut's old frame mill housing. In 1980, the citizens of Shawmut, Langdale, Fairfax, and Riverview (until then unincorporated portions of Chambers County) voted to incorporate as the City of Valley, Alabama. At least one resident feels that the reluctance of Valley voters to approve bond issues and tax increases is a lingering legacy of the decades when the company provided so many of the necessities of life.

During the fifty years that West Point Manufacturing Company maintained its paternalistic system, its mill villages slowly evolved, under the impact of the company's efforts to plan and organize community life and the residents' strong attachment to a rural southern way of life. The isolation of the West Point villages was already beginning to break down in the

1920s, with the advent of radio, motion pictures, and limited automobile ownership. As late as 1934, however, the company could set up just two roadblocks and effectively control all movement in and out of its communities.

Throughout the first half of the twentieth century, an unspoken paternalistic bond linked the workers and their families to the all-providing West Point Company. The terms of this compact included a sanction of rigid racial segregation in job assignments, housing, and recreation. The terms also prohibited efforts by workers to join forces to bargain collectively through labor unions. Unionism, with its insistence that all workers in a single job classification had the same rights, was anathema to paternalistic owners. The essence of paternalism was that each family had it own personal relationship with the company. The bond allowed workers a small degree of flexibility, but it was always a personal bond and one subject to unilateral revocation by the company. As long as a family was productive on the job and did not challenge corporate authority, it had some leeway in its off-the-clock activities. The river and the woods were close by for those who wanted to engage in traditional southern pastimes of hunting, fishing, or messing about in boats. The company tolerated the making and drinking of moonshine as long as its control over public space was not challenged by open displays of drunken or disorderly behavior.

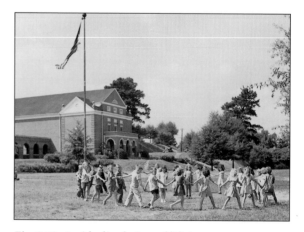

Fig. 9.10. An idealized view of life in a company town, Langdale, c. 1940. Courtesy of Cobb Memorial Archive.

The company extended certain privileges, like the recreation program, to all white employees. Other privileges were doled out more selectively. The paternalism of the Lanier family recognized hard work and ambition, and those who showed promise might be trained for more responsible jobs or invited to the Laniers' home for a social event. All of these privileges were offered on a personal basis; the mere possession of a job conferred limited rights. As the five towns in the Chattahoochee Valley became more connected to the rest of the country after World War II, paternalism was bound to decline. Good hard-surfaced roads and widespread automobile ownership opened up the mill towns, allowing mill workers to live farther away and more readily look for work elsewhere. Television brought a vision of consumer affluence and a glimpse of other ways of life. Today, the West Point Company's control of space beyond the mill door is long past. The impact of company paternalism survives most strongly in the basic organizational pattern of each community—its road systems and the often conspicuous clustering of community buildings. These are the last vestiges of a paternalism that once colored every aspect of mill village life.

Notes

This chapter grew out of research done for the tour book produced for the Vernacular Architecture Forum's Annual Meeting in Columbus, Georgia, in 1999. I owe a substantial debt to the work of, and lively interchange of ideas among, the team members who collaborated with me on the mill village chapter of the book: Steve A. Davis, Cari Goetcheus, Jennifer Brown Leynes, Kaye Lanning Minchew, Richard Sussman, Christine Trebellas, and Lisa Diane Vogel. Any errors of fact or interpretation in this chapter are my responsibility.

1. Broadus Mitchell's *Rise of the Cotton Mills in the South* (Baltimore: Johns Hopkins Univ. Press, 1921) emphasized the positive aspects of paternalism. Muckraking journalists and pioneering sociologists, especially those at the University of North Carolina, saw paternalism as stifling for workers. Harriet L. Herring's *Welfare Work in Mill Villages: The Story of Extra-Mill Activities in North Carolina* (Chapel Hill: Univ. of North Carolina Press, 1929) and Liston Pope's *Millhands and Preachers: A Study of Gastonia* (New Haven: Yale Univ. Press, 1942) are representative of this point of view, which was firmly cemented among opinion makers by Wilbur J. Cash's widely read *The Mind of the South* (New York: Alfred A. Knopf, 1941). Cash flatly asserted that the mill village was a plantation, where poor whites worked and lived in an environment wholly controlled by patrician whites. David L. Carlton's innovative work, *Mill and Town in South Carolina, 1880–1920* (Baton Rouge: Louisiana State Univ. Press, 1982), emphasized the symbolic and public relations aspects of the mill owners' paternalistic rhetoric and explained how building successful mills served the economic and prestige needs of the emerging merchant/professional town elites in the Piedmont South. The seminal work positing a robust and autonomous mill worker culture is *Like a Family: The Making of a Southern Cotton Mill World* (Chapel Hill: Univ. of North Carolina Press, 1987) by Jacquelyn Dowd Hall, James Leloudis, Robert Korstad, Mary Murphy, LuAnn Jones, and Christopher B. Daly. This view is further developed in Mary Letherd Wingerd's recent examination of labor relations at Erwin Mills in Cooleemee, North Carolina, "Rethinking Paternalism: Power and Parochialism in a Southern Mill Village," *Journal of American History* (Dec. 1996): 872–902. A fine overview of the historiography of southern mill paternalism can be found in David L. Carlton's essay, "Paternalism and Southern Textile Labor: A Historiographical Review," in *Race, Class, and Community in Southern Labor History,* ed. Gary M. Fink and Merl E. Reed (Tuscaloosa: Univ. of Alabama Press, 1994).

2. Margaret Crawford, *Building the Workingman's Paradise: The Design of American Company Towns* (London: Verso, 1995), 67.

3. Joseph L. Lanier, *The First Seventy-five Years of West Point Manufacturing Company, 1880–1955* (New York: Newcomen Society in North America, 1955), 8–17, 19, 21.

4. Lanier, *First Seventy-five Years,* 9–10.

5. Jean Crowder Williams, interview with author, Feb. 15, 1999, Valley, Alabama, tape and transcript in author's possession.

6. See Crawford, *Building the Workingman's Paradise,* 61–67, 77–81.

7. Janet Irons, *Testing the New Deal: The General Textile Strike of 1934 in the American South* (Urbana: Univ. of Illinois Press, 2000), 13–14.

8. Lanier, *First Seventy-five Years,* 19; Floyd Tillery, "Magnolias and Monarchs: An Historical Story of the West Point Manufacturing Company," 1948, unpublished typescript in the collection of the Cobb Memorial Archive, Valley, Alabama.

9. Olmsted Post-1949 Correspondence Collection, File no. 20-15, National Park Service, Olmsted National Historic Site. I am indebted to Dean Sinclair for supplying information on Marquis.

10. See plat, West Point Manufacturing Company, "Fairfax Village Property, Fairfax, Alabama," revised to 1-5-43, in collection of Cobb Memorial Archive, Valley, Alabama.

11. James Brooks Sr., interview with author, Mar. 3, 2000, Valley, Alabama, tape and transcript in author's possession.

12. Harry Shumway, *I Go South: An Unprejudiced Visit to a Group of Cotton Mills* (Boston: Houghton Mifflin, 1930); Eloise Echols Gray, *We Had It All* (n.p.: self-published, 1998); Ruth Royal Crump, *Fairfax: An English-Style Village on the Osanippa Creek* (n.p.: Craftmaster Printers, 1994), 20–23; Williams interview; Annie Hawkins, interview with author, Feb. 15, 1999; Carl Earnest and Mary Earnest, interview with author, Feb. 20, 1999; and Marshall Lane, interview with author, Feb. 20, 1999; tapes and transcripts in author's possession, all interviews conducted in Valley, Alabama.

13. Irons, *Testing the New Deal,* 15.

14. Crump, *Fairfax,* 12; Hawkins, Carl Earnest, and Lane, interviews.

15. See plat, "Fairfax Village Property."

16. Tillery, "Magnolias and Monarchs," 210–16, 251; Carl Earnest interview.

17. Shumway, *I Go South,* 22, 26–29, 60–63, quotation at 29; Carl Earnest interview.

18. West Point Manufacturing Company property books, Cobb Memorial Archive, Valley, Alabama; Shumway, *I Go South,* 49, 15–16; Gray, *We Had It All,* 7; Williams interview; Brooks interview; Irons, *Testing the New Deal,* 24.

19. Tillery, "Magnolias and Monarchs," 210, 216, 260, 265, 268.

20. Ibid., 206.

21. Brooks interview.

22. Williams interview; Brooks interview.

23. Hawkins interview.

24. Lane interview.

25. Lane interview; Joseph L. Reichler, ed., *Baseball Encyclopedia,* 6th ed. (New York: Macmillan, 1985), 1023.

26. Crump, *Fairfax,* 24–25, 163; Williams interview; Lane interview.

27. Lane interview; Hawkins interview.

28. Elizabeth Lyons, interview with author, Valley, Alabama, Apr. 2001.

29. Irons, *Testing the New Deal,* 4.

30. U.S. Congress, Senate, Committee on Education and Labor, *Violations of Free Speech and Rights of Labor,* 76th Cong., 1st. sess., 1939, Senate Report 6, 41–45; *Atlanta Constitution,* July 20, Sept. 9, 23, 1934.

31. Eloise Echols Gray, *Nine at the Table (and Then Some)* (n.p.: self-published, 1988), 141, 151; James Hooks interview, with Cari Goetcheus, Oct. 18, 1997, Valley, Alabama, transcript in author's possession.

32. Hawkins, Brooks, Williams, and Lane interviews; quotation is from Hawkins interview.

33. Lane interview; Hawkins interview; Williams interview; Brooks interview. See also Margaret Anne Barnes, *The Triumph and Tragedy of Phenix City, Alabama* (Macon, Ga.: Mercer Univ. Press, 1998).

34. Gray, *We Had It All,* 41; Hawkins interview; Williams interview.

35. Williams interview; Carl Earnest and Mary Earnest interview.

36. William H. Davidson, "West Point on the Chattahoochee—The First 100 Years," in *West Point on the Chattahoochee,* Bulletin 3, Chattahoochee Valley Historical Society, 1957, 30.

37. Lanier, *First Seventy-five Years,* 26; James R. Young, *Textile Leaders of the South* (Columbia, S.C.: R. L. Bryan, 1963), 363.

38. Hooks interview.

39. Hawkins interview.

10

IDENTITY AND ASSIMILATION IN SYNAGOGUE ARCHITECTURE IN GEORGIA, 1870–1920

STEVEN H. MOFFSON

During the nineteenth and early twentieth centuries, Jews prospered in cities and small towns throughout the South. Synagogues were central in the lives of most Jews, yet few scholars have explored the religious and social significance of synagogue architecture in the United States.[1] In Georgia, Jewish congregations viewed the building of synagogues not only as a step toward greater social and economic integration with the broader gentile community but also as an expression of religiosity and group identity among the state's ethnically diverse Jewish population. In adding synagogues to the existing array of religious institutions, Jews sought to enter the American mainstream even as they affirmed their Jewish identity.[2] The dichotomy between Jewish identity and cultural assimilation can be seen in the tradition of synagogue building: the exterior treatment reveals how congregations viewed their place in the community, and the organization of the interior space reflects how Judaism was practiced. This chapter explores the dramatic changes that occurred in synagogue architecture in Georgia between 1870 and 1920 as a result of increased Americanization and the rise of Reform Judaism. Some of the

state's first synagogues were designed to blend with existing religious buildings, but most featured Oriental revival–style architectural motifs that proclaimed the buildings' Jewish association. By the time these first synagogues were built in the 1870s, the role of the congregation in worship had begun to shift from participant to observer. Synagogues featured basilica plans to accommodate early manifestations of Reform Judaism. After 1900, Reform Jewish congregations embraced the neoclassical revival style, which they used to identify themselves as modern and American and to distinguish themselves from the newly arrived and unacculturated Russian Jews. As the exterior appearance of the synagogue evolved, Jewish congregations reorganized the sanctuary space in the form of auditorium plans, which were similar to the layout of many Protestant houses of worship.

Reform and Orthodox Judaism in America

Jewish religious practices and the space of worship remained virtually unchanged from the early Medieval period until the beginning of the nineteenth century.

Jews followed the laws, customs, and ceremonies described in the teachings of the Talmud. These laws pervaded every aspect of daily life and blurred distinctions between the religious and secular realms. Within the synagogue, the Torah remained the primary focus of worship (fig. 10.1).

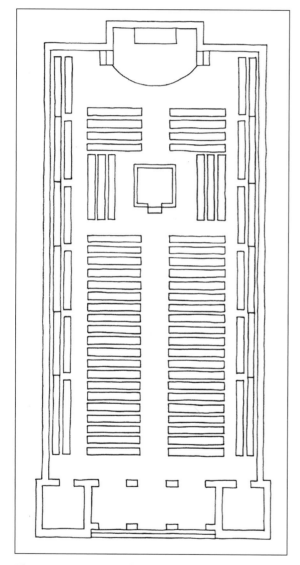

Fig. 10.1. Reconstructed Plan of Congregation Ahavath Achim, Atlanta, 1901. No scale. In this traditional plan, the bimah, or reading desk, was located near the center, opposite the pulpit and ark. Women worshiped from an upper gallery.

Customarily, the Torah scrolls were placed in an ark along the eastern wall. The Torah was read aloud from the bimah, an elevated reading desk located near the center of the sanctuary. Services were neither led nor conducted by a central figure, although a reader lead the congregation in prayer. Both the reader and congregation faced east toward the ark with some worshipers seated on benches along the side walls. The congregation read aloud and at its own pace, and services included chanting but no musical instruments. Women had no formal role in traditional Jewish worship. They could neither conduct religious services nor serve as witnesses in ritual matters. They were not included in a minyan, a quorum of ten required for public prayer, and when permitted to worship in a synagogue, women were seated apart from men in either a screened area to the rear of the sanctuary or an upper gallery.

For most of the nineteenth century, Judaism in the United States was dominated by Jewish immigrants from Germany, who arrived between 1820 and 1850. During the second half of the nineteenth century, these immigrants began to abandon liturgical practices that they believed were no longer relevant in modern society. These reforms, collectively known as Reform Judaism, began with modest changes in ritual that emphasized conformity with Protestant religious practices.[3] Reform Judaism was guided not by an established ideology but by separate compromises made by Jews who sought acculturation and integration with the gentile community. "For our own part, we are Jews in the synagogue and Americans everywhere," wrote Isaac Mayer Wise, a leader of the Jewish Reform movement.[4] Wise's vision of religious reform describes a Jewish self-image based on cultural similarities shared with the broader society. Eventually, the desire among Jews to be "Americans everywhere" resulted in changes in the way Judaism was practiced.

Reform congregations sought respectability and Americanization through decorum and propriety in the synagogue. Congregations discouraged chanting and praying aloud and instead sung hymns accompanied by an organ and robed choir, traditions long a part of Protestant worship. Worship services were shortened, second days of holidays were eliminated, and bar mitzvahs were replaced by confirmation services for boys and girls. Eventually, separate seating for women was discontinued and entire families worshiped together. German, which had been the language of worship for Reform Jews, gave way to English. Fewer congregations worshiped with talit (prayer shawls) and head coverings, visible distinctions between Jewish and Christian worship. The issue of head coverings during worship was never of primary significance in Jewish law, but its abrogation is symbolic of a desire to emphasize conformity with American behavior and discard rituals that were distinctly Jewish.[5] Reform came incrementally and was often contentious, but by 1870 nearly all congregations in Georgia had adopted some level of religious reform.

Rabbis, an outward symbol of reform, led few of Georgia's nascent Jewish congregations before 1860. Lay readers with sufficient knowledge of Hebrew conducted Orthodox religious services for congregations that spoke mostly German. Sometimes members of the congregation took turns leading services and on occasion delivered sermons. In the 1850s and 1860s, the state's largest congregations sought the services of a hazan (reader) who also served as a shochet (ritual slaughterer). Most congregations practiced the German Orthodox minhag (rite), and when sermons were delivered, they were often in the German vernacular.[6] Some congregations had begun to speak English during religious services. In 1859, Congregation Beth Israel in Macon advertised for a hazan who practiced according to the German rite but was also "capable of giving an English lecture every other Saturday."[7]

By the end of the nineteenth century, the role of the congregation in worship had shifted from participant to observer, and most congregations had become dependent on rabbis to lead religious services. The first rabbis arrived from Germany in the early 1840s, but it was not until the 1880s, when rabbis were ordained in the United States, that they were available to most congregations. Like their Protestant counterparts, rabbis provided religious leadership and conducted religious services, officiated at important events in the lives of constituents, and provided religious instruction. Matters of religious reform, however, were decided not by rabbis but by the membership

of the congregation. In Georgia, most congregations had difficulty attracting and maintaining qualified rabbis, and smaller congregations, including those that had built synagogues, were often led in worship by visiting rabbis. David Marx, rabbi at the Hebrew Benevolent Congregation in Atlanta, traveled to west Georgia to conduct services at Temple Beth El in West Point seven to eight times each year from 1895 to 1943.[8] Similarly, Rabbi Edmund Landau from Albany conducted services at Temple Beth El in Bainbridge on alternating Sundays from 1909 to 1945.

Reform congregations, which had enjoyed hegemony among American Jews and believed that they represented the future of Judaism in America, soon found themselves a minority in an ethnically diverse Jewish population. Beginning in 1881, massive numbers of East European Jews, mostly from Russia, emigrated to the United States to escape severe poverty and governmental anti-Semitism. The Jewish population in the United States increased from 230,000 in 1880 to 400,000 in 1888. By 1914, the estimated number of Jews in America had reached nearly 3 million.[9] Many of these immigrants, who often arrived in family groups and with little money, settled in Northeastern cities, where they formed ghetto districts. Hoping to avert a crisis, Reform Jewish leaders established relief organizations that resettled some the newly arrived immigrants in communities beyond the major port cities. The Industrial Removal Office (IRO) was among the most successful of these organizations. Between 1901 and 1916, the IRO sent 70,000 immigrants to 1,500 communities, including Atlanta and smaller cities throughout Georgia.[10]

The established Jewish communities remained ambivalent about the Russian Jews who had little in common with their Reform coreligionists. The East Europeans left a land in which they constituted a national group. Few had been affected by the Enlightenment and the vast majority followed Orthodox traditions that dictated much of their behavior. They formed close-knit, insular communities where Yiddish was the day-to-day language, and they had little contact with Reform Jews, whom they viewed as "scarcely better than gentiles."[11] For Reform Jews, the foreign appearance of the new immigrants conformed too closely to popular Jewish stereotypes and threatened their own status in the gentile community. Reform congregations responded by transforming their synagogues into bastions of Americanism to distinguish themselves from the new immigrants. However, the massive numbers of immigrants reduced the established Jewish community to small minority, and by 1900 the progressive face of Judaism that German Reform Jews had developed over half a century was in a few decades replaced by the image of Old World orthodoxy.[12]

The East European immigrants, mostly Russians, quickly established their own houses of worship, increasing sharply the number of synagogues in the United States. In 1880, there were 270 synagogues, most built by German Reform congregations. During the next ten years this number doubled, and by 1906 there were 1,769 synagogues in the United States.[13] In the 1910s and 1920s, Russian Jews built new synagogues in Georgia's largest cities. These new synagogues served as the center of communal Jewish life and became mainstays for preserving Orthodox Judaism.

First Synagogues in Georgia

In Georgia, Jews first settled in Savannah early in the eighteenth century, though it was not until the 1840s and 1850s that Jews ventured inland. Newly arrived German immigrants settled in small towns and larger cities at the Fall Line and throughout South Georgia. Jewish communities formed in larger cities but because the Jewish population was small and dispersed across the state, synagogue building was largely a post–Civil War phenomenon. Fledgling congregations first worshiped together in the parlors of one another's houses before leasing larger rooms downtown. The congregation of B'nai Israel in Thomasville worshiped above the library for nearly thirty years, and in Savannah, Congregation Agudath Achim worshiped above a block of commercial buildings and held High Holy Day services in the larger Eagles' Hall. Macon's first synagogue was a rented room twenty-eight feet by fifty feet and was located over Horn's Confectionary Shop on Cherry Street, a bustling downtown commercial

corridor. The walls were whitewashed, chandeliers were installed, and a member of the congregation provided "a very fine picture, a view of the City of Jerusalem."[14] Most congregations met in rented space for many years, and in Albany, Atlanta, and Columbus, for example, Jews worshiped in private homes and rented rooms for twenty years or more before building synagogues. These early places of worship convey little architectural meaning because of their impermanence and because the congregations could not easily modify borrowed spaces and rented rooms.

Reform Synagogues: Exterior Appearance

Reform congregations in Georgia built some of the first synagogue buildings in the 1870s and 1880s to establish their place in the broader community. Some congregations chose architectural styles that identified the buildings' Jewish affiliation while others emphasized assimilation, building synagogues in styles that had long been part of the state's architectural vocabulary. Mickve Israel in Savannah, the state's oldest Jewish congregation, built a small frame synagogue in 1820.[15] It was destroyed by fire eight years later and replaced by an equally small brick synagogue in 1834. In the decades before the Civil War, the congregation grew in self-confidence and wealth and believed that an impressive new synagogue would honor its members and distinguish Mickve Israel as one of the city's great religious institutions.[16] Completed in 1878, the new synagogue is a large Gothic revival–style building with an entrance tower and a cruciform plan (fig. 10.2). The nave and side aisles are supported by ribbed piers and vaulting.

The synagogue is striking for its complete appropriation of Christian forms, both stylistic details and the cruciform plan. Typically, Jewish congregations avoided designs that imitated other religions and, particularly, the cruciform plan because it was so closely associated with Christianity. Mickve Israel, however, wanted a Gothic synagogue. In 1875, the full congregation unanimously approved the plan for a Gothic sanctuary. Later, the building committee accompanied the architect to several local churches for inspection.[17]

Fig. 10.2. Congregation Mickve Israel, Savannah, 1878. The Gothic-style synagogue reflects the congregations desire for a building that would look like the city's existing churches.

The congregation likely sought a design that would be appropriate for its prominent Monterey Square location—a design that would stand alongside Savannah's churches without standing out as different. The gentile community responded positively to the new synagogue in newspaper articles and in a letter from a Pennsylvania women who wrote the president of the congregation: "You are the first Israelites I have ever heard of to build a church in the shape of the cross, the symbol of the Holy Trinity . . . the symbol of Him who is despised by so many of your people. . . . What a comfort to know you have taken this step to enter our fold. . . . Doubtless, you have had to overcome great perplexities before your people consented to have a church built so ultra-Christian in form."[18] Minutes of the congregation suggest it had neither experienced great perplexities in adopting the cruciform plan nor considered converting to Christianity. The

letter writer's mistake, while presumptuous, is understandable. In shedding virtually all Jewish symbolism in favor of Christian architectural forms, Mickve Israel removed visual distinctions between itself and the gentile community. The ambiguity resulted in misinterpretations by non-Jews. On the outside the congregation had become architecturally assimilated, but on the inside its Jewish beliefs remained unchanged.

Other synagogues built in the last decades of the nineteenth century also appeared churchlike but less ecclesiastical than Mickve Israel and more generically high Victorian Gothic. In 1884, Congregation Children of Israel in Athens built a Gothic-style brick synagogue, and in 1887 Congregation B'nai Israel in Columbus dedicated their new picturesque synagogue. In 1896, Congregation B'nai Israel in Albany completed a large, twin-towered brick synagogue with a semicircular apse.

Although four Reform congregations in Georgia built Gothic revival–style synagogues that emphasized assimilation with buildings that appeared similar to Christian houses of worship, three Reform and two Orthodox congregations built Oriental-style synagogues in the belief that they could enhance integration with the gentile community with synagogues that conspicuously identified the buildings' Jewish affiliation. The Oriental revival style, which included Turkish, Persian, Syrian, Indian, and Moorish architectural motifs, was among the most popular styles for synagogues in the late nineteenth century. The Oriental revival style was first embraced by Jews in Germany, who built large synagogues to confirm their place in modern European society. This style, with its onion domes and horseshoe arches, was not an archaeological revival style but an eclectic and romanticized vision of the golden era of Judaism in Spain. Although few Jews in Germany or the United States would have seen Moorish buildings in Spain, they used the Oriental style to set synagogues apart from churches and establish a distinctly Jewish identity that drew upon their Eastern origins.[19]

The Oriental-style synagogue is part of the broader Oriental revival that took hold in the United States at the beginning of the nineteenth century. In the South, however, the Oriental style was never widely adopted. Picturesque onion domes and other exotic elements most often were seen at fairs and expositions, such as the Cotton States and International Exposition held in Atlanta in 1895. In Georgia, the Oriental style became closely associated with Judaism because only Jews consistently employed the style for synagogues and other buildings. In Atlanta in 1888, for example, Reform Jews built the Hebrew Orphans Home, a sprawling Oriental-style building with horseshoe-arched loggias, interlacing terra-cotta ornament, ogee roofs and onion domes, and a clock tower in the form of a minaret. In 1893, Reform Jews in Atlanta built Concordia Hall, a three-story Jewish social club that was distinguished by an onion-domed oriel window.

The earliest Oriental-style synagogues in Georgia were built by first-generation German congregations who had adopted some elements of religious reform. In 1874, Congregation Beth Israel in Macon built an Oriental-style synagogue with a bulbous-domed corner tower. Minutes of the building committee declared that the building "will be a monument to ourselves, our race and our city."[20] This unusually personal sentiment expressed the belief that the new synagogue would elevate the status of its builders as it honors its city and Jews everywhere. After reviewing plans for the synagogue, the *Macon Telegraph and Messenger* agreed "the building will be a decided addition to our [city's] handsome buildings."[21]

In Atlanta in 1877, the Hebrew Benevolent Congregation completed an exuberant Oriental-style synagogue (fig. 10.3). In his speech at the cornerstone-laying ceremony, Rabbi Henry Gersoni alluded to the complexity that belies these buildings: "We [Jews] always build synagogues in the style of architecture most approved by our neighbors, and most suitable to the locality of the place."[22] The rabbi believed either that the exotic synagogue would not appear any different from the High Victorian Gothic buildings that lined the city's streets or that if the new synagogue did appear different its style would conform with gentile expectations for a synagogue, even though none had yet been built in Atlanta. In either case, the congregation placed a high value on the views of the broader community and was probably pleased when the *Atlanta Constitution* described the completed building as "an ornament to the city and a monument to the honor of the congregation." Its reaction to the paper's comment that "the exterior is decidedly unique and will attract attention at once" was probably less favorable.[23]

The Hebrew Benevolent Congregation and other congregations throughout Georgia used the construction of synagogues as opportunities to display their acculturation and to demonstrate their commitment to the community both as Jews and Americans. Congregations adopted the custom of public cornerstone-laying ceremonies, which had long been used to inaugurate the construction of public buildings and churches. The Hebrew Benevolent Congregation laid the cornerstone for their synagogue after a procession through downtown Atlanta that included the mayor and city council and officers of the city's fraternal lodges. Rabbi Gersoni lectured to the crowd about "the common brotherhood of man" and declared, "I

Fig. 10.3. Hebrew Benevolent Congregation, Atlanta, 1877. The synagogue's exuberant Oriental revival–style design proclaimed the building's Jewish identity. Courtesy of the Atlanta History Center.

have no prejudice whatsoever to call you my brothers and treat you as such. . . . Let this pile of stones be a witness between us that we shall not pass this place with evil intentions against each other, let it be a monument of virtue and true piety, of brotherly love, of peace and harmony between Jew and Christian."[24] In October 1901, Congregation Beth Israel in Macon laid the cornerstone for its second synagogue. The Masonic grandmaster of Georgia presided over the event, which included city officials and local and visiting clergy. The afternoon ceremony closed with the city's Second Regiment Band, a choir, and the two thousand citizens in attendance singing "America."[25]

Reform Synagogues: Interior Plan

Americanization of the synagogue transformed not only the building's exterior where congregations expressed their sense of place in the community but also the interior, which evolved as religious reform changed the way Judaism was practiced. Rifts in congregations sometimes formed over the planning of new synagogues because the interior arrangement of spaces dictated the presentation of the liturgy. This forced congregations in which Reform and Orthodox members had coexisted to choose how future worship would be conducted. In 1874, for example, Beth Israel in Macon was nearing completion of its first synagogue. The mostly Orthodox congregation had begun to adopt elements of liturgical religious reform, but some members resisted. Mark Isaacs, an Orthodox member of the congregation, rescinded his contribution toward construction of the new synagogue. The congregation filed suit for the money, and Isaacs petitioned the court to protect his personal possessions and his baking business.[26] To explain his motives and perhaps restore his reputation, Mark Isaacs placed an open letter in the *Macon Telegraph and Messenger:* "I subscribed twenty-four dollars . . . with the expressed understanding that innovations of the latter day reformers should never enter the portals of the Synagogue, and thereby destroy the ancient faith of our fathers. . . . While I am ever ready to give . . . support, not only of my own, but to the churches of my brethren . . . , I cannot and will not consent to give one farthing . . . to the so-called Synagogue."[27] Isaacs may have objected to any number of reform elements that were programmatically incorporated into the new synagogue. The Macon newspaper described the plans for the sanctuary as having a "gallery over the entrance suitable for a choir and organ."[28] In traditional Jewish worship, music, especially festive music, was viewed as inappropriate for a people mourning the loss of the Second Temple. Moreover, if the gallery accommodated the organ and choir and not women during worship, the new synagogue likely had family pews for mixed worship. Here, the construction of a new synagogue cast religious differences among members of the congregation in high relief. The Isaacs conflict intensified because the congregation's tentative steps toward reform were about to be realized in brick and stone.

Many Reform congregations accommodated changes in ritual with churchlike buildings that included basilica plans or sometimes just long naves without side aisles or transepts. Because the emphasis was placed on preaching, the bimah was moved from the center of the sanctuary to the east end, allowing more seating and fewer visual obstructions.[29] By the time Temple Beth Tefilloh in the coastal town of Brunswick built its synagogue in 1890, the congregation had embraced Reform Judaism (fig. 10.4). The temple features a basilica plan with the ark and bimah at the front of the sanctuary (fig. 10.5). Services included a choir and organ, and long rows of pews seated entire families. The gallery, a feature once reserved for women, accommodated overflow crowds on holidays.[30]

Orthodox Synagogues

Orthodox congregations in Atlanta and Savannah maintained traditional Jewish worship by building Oriental-style synagogues with traditional sanctuary plans. In Atlanta at the end of the nineteenth century, the late-arriving Russian Jews initially worshiped at the Reform Hebrew Benevolent Congregation, which they found "shockingly impious."[31] They established Congregation Ahavath Achim and in 1901 completed an Oriental-style synagogue (fig. 10.6).

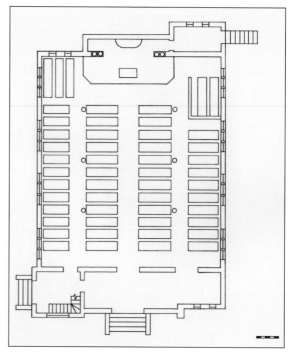

Fig. 10.5. Plan of Temple Beth Tefilloh, Brunswick, 1890. Typical of Reform congregations at the end of the nineteenth century, Temple Beth Tefilloh built a basilica-plan synagogue in which the bimah and ark were consolidated at the front of the sanctuary.

Fig. 10.4. Temple Beth Tefilloh, Brunswick, 1890. This Brunswick synagogue is a church-like building with elements of the Oriental revival style.

On the exterior the new synagogue appeared stylistically like the Reform synagogue but the interior remained Orthodox (fig. 10.1). The Torah was read from the center of the sanctuary, and women worshiped from an upper gallery in the traditional manner. In 1909, Congregation B'nai B'rith Jacob, whose membership swelled with East European immigrants, built a massive brick synagogue near Broughton Street, the commercial center of Savannah. Designed by Hyman W. Witcover, the architect of Savannah's city hall, the synagogue features a three-story facade relieved by horseshoe arches and richly patterned surfaces and surmounted by two hipped domes.[32] The square-shaped sanctuary is set above a full basement and rises two gallery levels, each dedicated to women's worship.

Emergence of Neoclassical-style Synagogues

At the beginning of the twentieth century, just as Ahavath Achim and other Orthodox congregations in Georgia were building their first synagogues, the Oriental revival style was losing favor as the preferred architectural style among Reform congregations. In 1908, Abram S. Isaacs wrote in *American Architect and Building News* that the Oriental style "undoubtedly strengthened the impression that the Jew was necessarily an alien, and did not wish to be regarded as an American. The delicate minarets, stately dome, the arabesque decoration, and the rest, were to be a protest against Yankee notions."[33] The Oriental-style buildings proclaimed the congregations' Jewish affiliation even as increased numbers of Reform Jews sought to minimize differences between themselves and mainstream American society.

For Reform Jews, nothing could be more disquieting than to be regarded by the gentile community as foreign. Where some earlier congregations had proudly asserted their Jewish identity, later, more Americanized Jews sought architectural forms that expressed their desire to assimilate with the broader community. The neoclassical style quickly supplanted the Oriental revival style as the preferred idiom for synagogue architecture. Scholars of synagogue architecture defended the choice of neoclassicism noting that recent archaeological investigations in Palestine

Fig. 10.6. Congregation Ahavath Achim, Atlanta, 1901. Built by newly arrived Russian Jews, Ahavath Achim appeared stylistically like the Reform synagogue of the established Hebrew Benevolent Congregation. From *Reform Advocate*, Nov. 4, 1911, 47.

had unearthed classical synagogues with "unmistakable columns and masonry."[34] However, it is unlikely that this argument proved persuasive or that most congregations were even aware of the neoclassical synagogue's architectural lineage. Reform Jewish congregations embraced neoclassicism not because of its connection to ancient Jewry but because it was part of the widely popular City Beautiful movement. Neoclassical synagogues were built in the first decades of the twentieth century as monuments displaying the affluence and taste of congregations without appearing any less American than the myriad churches and public institutions that had already adopted the style.

Moreover, within the neoclassical synagogue, the space of worship was reorganized to accommodate the continuing reform of American Judaism. Many congregations, increasingly dependent on rabbis to lead religious services, adopted auditorium plans. Preferred

Fig. 10.7. Congregation Beth Israel, Macon, 1902. Neoclassicism supplanted the Oriental revival style as the preferred idiom for synagogue design, especially among Jews who wished to assimilate with the broader community. A dome centered above the sanctuary and a classical portico were typical of neoclassical-style synagogues.

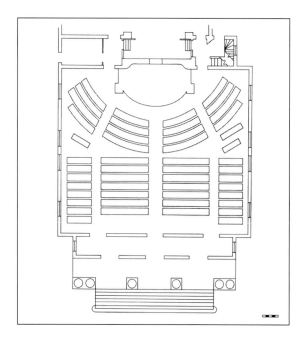

Fig. 10.8. Plan of Congregation Beth Israel, Macon, 1902. Rear additions built in 1919 and 1954 are not delineated. Neoclassical-style synagogues reflected the continuing reform of American Judaism with auditorium plans that emphasized the role of the rabbi in religious services. Beth Israel's square-shaped sanctuary provided more seats near the front than did the earlier basilica-plan synagogues.

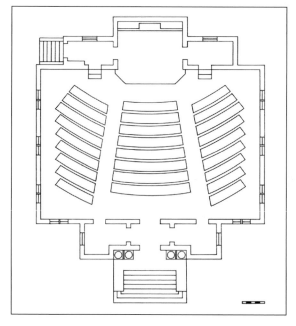

Fig. 10.9. Plan of Temple Beth El, Bainbridge, 1916. The importance of the rabbi to the Bainbridge congregation is seen in the synagogue's rectangular plan with the bimah centered on a long wall for unobstructed views from the back corners of the sanctuary.

by many Protestant denominations, auditorium plans provided more seats near the front than did the basilica-plan synagogues. Macon's Congregation Beth Israel, which had been divided over the construction of its Oriental-style synagogue in 1874, had fully adopted the tenets of Reform Judaism by the time it completed its neoclassical-style synagogue in 1902 (fig. 10.7). Typical of neoclassical synagogues of this period, it features a dome centered above the sanctuary and a two-story portico. Although pedimented porticoes are most common in neoclassical synagogues, a stepped parapet caps Beth Israel's hexastyle portico. The interior of the synagogue is nearly square in shape, and the pews are curved to provide better views of the front bimah (fig. 10.8). The organ and choir loft were incorporated into the design and placed prominently above the ark.

Reform at Congregation Beth Israel may also be gauged by the sanctuary art. Jewish law prohibits the making of figurative or representational art, so it is surprising to find above the choir loft at Beth Israel a series of stained-glass windows modeled after Sir Edward Burne-Jones's *Days of Creation,* which is dominated by the human form. Even more striking is an audacious stained-glass depiction in the dome of the omniscient Eye of God, which peers down on the congregation through a break in the clouds. In Judaism, God is incomprehensible to man and thus has no likeness that can be represented in art. The Macon "Eye," which may derive from Masonic imagery, contradicts traditional interpretations of the Second Commandment, which prohibits the making of graven images.

Reform Jews in Bainbridge built a neoclassical-style synagogue in 1916. When Temple Beth El was completed, visiting rabbis conducted religious services almost entirely in English as few members of the congregation could read Hebrew. The layout of the interior emphasizes the bimah at the front near the ark (fig. 10.9). The sanctuary is wider than it is long and features a sloped floor and curved pews that provide unobstructed views of the bimah from the back corners of the sanctuary. The organ, which had become a defining characteristic of the Reform synagogue, is treated as a central design element, filling the front niche and surrounding the ark.

Reform and Orthodox Congregations in Atlanta

The construction of synagogues in Atlanta at the beginning of the twentieth century illustrates the tense relationship between Reform and Orthodox congregations that existed in large cities and small towns throughout the United States. In Atlanta, the state's largest Jewish community was divided along ethnic lines. Jews of German ancestry represented the city's established Jewish community. Nearly all were native-born or had lived in the United States for several decades. They embraced American culture and shed traditions that might have appeared foreign. However, by 1900 Russian Jews accounted for nearly half of Atlanta's two thousand Jews, and by 1915 they represented the majority.[35] The newly arrived Russian Jews, for whom religion pervaded every aspect of daily life, viewed the German Jews as the "established burghers" who wanted an "undemanding Jewish church which would affirm their respectability without interfering with their life style."[36] For their part, the German Jews eased the plight of the new immigrants by providing them with kosher food, funds, and a place to worship. At the same time, many Germans sought to distance themselves from the Russians because, as historian Steven Hertzberg wrote, "their distinctive language, 'un-American' appearance, and 'backward' ways did not endear them to their Reform coreligionists. The uncouth foreignness of the Russians provided the prosperous Germans with a disquieting reminder of their own humble origins and, by conforming closely to the popular Jewish stereotype, threatened the status of the established community."[37]

The cultural divide among Atlanta's Jews was riven further by economics and geography. The newly arrived Russian Jews lived in a ghetto district along Decatur Street, a major commercial thoroughfare of attached, two-story, brick buildings that contained stores, pool halls, and saloons with dwelling space above. Apartment buildings and tightly spaced, frame houses lined the interior streets with two-dozen "negro tenements" in the alleys. Ahavath Achim was located on Piedmont Road in the center of the district. The Russian Jews, most of whom worked as proprietors, street vendors, and grocers, represented the largest minority in a neighborhood that included African Americans, Greeks, Chinese, Syrians, Italians, and Hungarians.[38]

The wealthier German Jews resided on tree-lined streets south of downtown. Many had begun their careers as peddlers but by the end of the nineteenth century had achieved a high level of economic status. By 1896, over half were either company officers, proprietors of factories and wholesale houses or white-collar workers. As Atlanta's business district expanded, the city's German Jews moved south of Fair Street to large, widely spaced houses on fashionable streets, such as Washington and South Pryor Streets and Capitol Avenue. By the end of the nineteenth century, 54 percent of the German Jews in Atlanta resided in the southside neighborhood.[39]

Both German and Russian congregations in Atlanta built synagogues that underscored social and religious distinctions that existed within the city's Jewish community. The Reform Hebrew Benevolent Congregation broke ground south of downtown on its second Atlanta synagogue in 1901 (fig. 10.10), just one month before Orthodox Ahavath Achim dedicated its Oriental-style synagogue in the Jewish ghetto district (fig. 10.6). The cruciform plan, hexastyle portico, and central dome of the new Reform synagogue provided an overt symbol that redefined the estab-

Fig. 10.10. Hebrew Benevolent Congregation, Atlanta, 1901. Atlanta's established Reform congregation built a neoclassical-style synagogue to appear current and fashionable and to distinguish it from the Oriental-style synagogue of the city's Orthodox Russian Jews.

lished German Jewish community as modern, while the onion domes of Ahavath Achim identified it with the Old World.

During this period, some of the more prosperous and Americanized members of Ahavath Achim joined or attempted to join the Hebrew Benevolent Congregation and were coolly received. In response they organized Congregation Beth Israel and in 1907 built a neoclassical synagogue with a two-story portico and central dome. The architectural firm that the congregation selected, Bruce and Everett, were well known in the Southeast for their designs for large public buildings in the neoclassical style. The completed synagogue appeared similar in plan and style to a number of Bruce and Everett churches designed in the early 1900s.[40]

Congregation Beth Israel expressed its social aspirations in both the architecture of its new synagogue and its choice of location, not among the East European Jews but in the neighborhood where most Jews belonged to the Reform temple. However, within ten years, the congregation had begun to disband. Several of its most affluent members had left to join the Hebrew Benevolent Congregation, and those that remained were under fire from the Orthodox congregations for "getting away from Judaism."[41]

By 1920, the membership of Ahavath Achim had more than tripled since the congregation built its first synagogue, and many in the congregation had already moved to the more fashionable southside neighborhood because commercial and industrial enterprises had overtaken the Decatur Street neighborhood. In 1921, Ahavath Achim replaced its Oriental-style synagogue with a neoclassical-style building located in the southside Jewish neighborhood (fig. 10.11).

Like the synagogues of the city's Reform Jews, Ahavath Achim featured the familiar classical portico and a low saucer dome. The sanctuary featured a gallery on three sides and the bimah remained in the center, just as it had been in the earlier Oriental-style synagogue (fig. 10.12). The schism between the progressive exterior appearance of the building and traditional interior plan reflects division among the congregation on the issue of assimilation. The steady stream of East European Jews arriving in Atlanta ensured that Orthodox practices remained, even as more

Fig. 10.11. Congregation Ahavath Achim, Atlanta, 1921. Ahavath Achim's second synagogue was in the neoclassical style with a classical portico and a saucer dome above the sanctuary. Courtesy of the Ida Pearle and Joseph Cuba Archives of The William Breman Jewish Heritage Museum.

Fig. 10.12. Interior of Congregation Ahavath Achim, Atlanta, 1921. Though its exterior appeared like the Reform synagogue, its interior layout was Orthodox, with a gallery on three sides for women's worship and the bimah in the center (*bottom*, with men standing), just as it had been in the earlier Oriental-style synagogue. Courtesy of the Ida Pearle and Joseph Cuba Archives of The William Breman Jewish Heritage Museum.

Americanized members of the congregation, through the exterior architectural treatment of the building, demonstrated a willingness to appear current and fashionable, if not acculturated and American.

Orthodox Congregations Elsewhere in Georgia

The massive immigration from Eastern Europe that brought increased numbers of Jews to Atlanta and Savannah also resulted in large Orthodox Jewish communities in the smaller Fall Line cities of Columbus, Macon, and Augusta.[42] These communities established congregations at the end of the nineteenth century and, after worshiping in the homes of congregation members for over a decade, built small, plain synagogues in the 1910s and 1920s. In 1915, Congregation Shearith Israel in Columbus built a plain, gable-front, wood-frame synagogue that was just slightly larger than the adjacent houses. The bimah was located near the center, and women worshiped from an upper gallery. In Macon, Congregation Sherah Israel completed its brick synagogue in 1922, and in Augusta in 1914, Congregation Adas Yeshuron purchased a neoclassical church for use as a synagogue. The high ceiling enabled the congregation to install a balcony for women's worship. In sharp contrast to the monumental synagogues of the established Reform Jews, these small, plain synagogues were built from the wages of newer and poorer immigrant communities. The emphasis on interior function over the exterior appearance of the buildings reflected the congregations' desire to preserve the practice of traditional Jewish worship.

In Georgia's smaller cities, the pressures of assimilation were strongest for Orthodox Jews, whose small, isolated communities faced many of the problems German Jews in larger cities had confronted decades earlier: increased interaction with gentiles, lack of religious leadership, and difficulty obtaining kosher foods. East European Jews, mostly from Russia, found they could not sustain their traditions in small isolated groups and eventually merged with existing Reform Jewish communities. In the south Georgia city of Thomasville, Jewish immigrants from Eastern Europe bolstered the small German Jewish community, which had struggled since the 1860s. In 1905, they formed Congregation B'nai Israel and in 1913 built a Romanesque-style synagogue. In an attempt to accommodate both Reform and Orthodox traditions, the bimah was located near the ark at the east end, yet the Torah was read in the Orthodox tradition with the reader facing the ark, his back to the congregation. Women worshiped from a rear balcony. In contrast to this attempted coexistence, the Brunswick Orthodox community by 1927 could no longer sustain itself and merged with Reform Temple Beth Tefilloh, ending the practice of Orthodox Judaism in the small coastal town.[43]

In Georgia between 1870 and 1920, dramatic changes occurred in synagogue architecture as a result of increased Americanization and the rise of Reform Judaism. The first synagogues built in Georgia were constructed as monuments or civic improvements that would move congregations toward greater social and economic integration with the gentile community. A few were designed to blend with existing religious buildings, but most featured Oriental architectural motifs which proclaimed the building's Jewish association. By the time these first synagogues were built in 1870s, the role of the congregation had begun to shift from participant to observer, and synagogues featured basilica plans to accommodate early manifestations of Reform Judaism. After 1900, Reform Jewish congregations embraced the neoclassical style to identify themselves as modern and American and also distinguish themselves from the newly arrived East European Jews. These neoclassical synagogues featured auditorium plans for congregations that had become dependent on rabbis to conduct religious services. By 1920, Reform and some Orthodox congregations in Georgia had made the transition from exotic synagogues that expressed Jewish identity to neoclassical monuments that emphasized assimilation with American mainstream culture.

Notes

1. Several of the most useful works on synagogue architecture include Rachel Wischnitzer, *Synagogue Architecture in the United States: History and Interpretation* (Philadelphia: Jewish Publication Society of America, 1955); Carol Herselle Krinsky, *Synagogue Architecture of Europe: Architecture, History, Meaning* (Mineola, N.Y.: Dover Publications, 1985); and Lee Shai Weissbach, *The Synagogues of Kentucky: Architecture and History* (Lexington: Univ. Press of Kentucky, 1995).

2. Leon A. Jick, *The Americanization of the Synagogue, 1820–1870* (Hanover, N.H.: Univ. Press of New England, 1976), 57.

3. "Orthodox" is a term first used at the beginning of the nineteenth century to describe the traditional Jewish way of life in contrast to the tenets of Reform Judaism.

4. Quoted in Jick, *Americanization of the Synagogue,* 173.

5. Ibid., 182.

6. Janice O. Rothschild, *As but a Day: The First Hundred Years, 1867–1967* (Atlanta: Hebrew Benevolent Congregation, 1967), 4–5. Congregation Mickve Israel in Savannah, a Sephardic congregation, practiced the Portuguese Minhag until 1895.

7. Newton J. Friedman, "A History of Temple Beth Israel of Macon, Georgia" (Th.D. diss., Burton College and Seminary), 28–29.

8. Temple Beth El included the Jewish communities in West Point, Georgia, and Lanett, Alabama, where the congregation built its synagogue in 1909.

9. Leon A. Jick, "The Reform Synagogue," in *The American Synagogue: A Sanctuary Transformed,* ed. Jack Wertheimer (Hanover, N.H.: Univ. Press of New England, 1987), 93.

10. Steven Hertzberg, *Strangers within the Gate City: The Jews of Atlanta, 1845–1915* (Philadelphia: Jewish Publication Society of America, 1978), 77.

11. Nathan Glazer, *American Judaism* (Chicago: Univ. of Chicago Press, 1957), 66.

12. Michael A. Meyer, *Response to Modernity: A History of the Reform Movement in Judaism* (New York: Oxford Univ. Press, 1988), 292.

13. Glazer, *American Judaism,* 62.

14. Minutes of the Trustees of Temple Beth Israel, Macon, Georgia (Jan. 1860), 17.

15. Mickve Israel is one of five colonial congregations founded by Spanish and Portuguese Jews. It remained the

only Sephardic congregation in Georgia until the early twentieth century.

16. Mark I. Greenberg, "Creating Ethnic, Class, and Southern Identity in Nineteenth-Century America: The Jews of Savannah, Georgia, 1830–1880" (Ph.D. diss., Univ. of Florida, 1997), 210. Jick, *Americanization of the Synagogue*, 181.

17. Saul Jacob Rubin, *Third to None: The Saga of Savannah Jewry, 1733–1983* (Savannah, Ga.: Saul Jacob Rubin, 1983), 170, 175.

18. Mary M. Chisolm to President of the Israelite Church, Apr. 8, 1876, Mickve Israel Collection, Savannah Jewish Archives, Savannah, Georgia.

19. Krinsky, *Synagogue Architecture of Europe*, 63, 83.

20. Minutes of the Trustees of Temple Beth Israel, Macon, Georgia, Mar. 29, 1874, 107.

21. *Macon Telegraph and Messenger*, July 21, 1872.

22. *Atlanta Constitution*, May 25, 1875.

23. *Atlanta Daily Constitution*, Sept. 1, 1877.

24. *Atlanta Constitution*, June 25, 1875.

25. *Macon Telegraph*, Oct. 31, 1901.

26. Homesteads and Personalties Exemptions, Bibb County (1875–1895), Microfilm Drawer 88, Box 71, pp. 40–41, Georgia Department of Archives and History, Atlanta, Georgia.

27. *Macon Telegraph and Messenger*, July 23, 1875. See Macon, Ga., Congregation Beth Israel, Box X-129, American Jewish Archives, Cincinnati, Ohio.

28. *Macon Telegraph and Messenger*, July 21, 1872.

29. Krinsky, *Synagogue Architecture of Europe*, 65–66.

30. "Seventy Fifth Anniversary: 1886–1961," Temple Beth Tefilloh, Brunswick, Georgia, n.p., Glynn County Library, Brunswick, Georgia.

31. Hertzberg, *Strangers within the Gate City*, 86.

32. Witcover, a member of Congregation Mickve Israel, was among the few Jewish architects practicing in Georgia before 1920. See Mary L. Morrison, ed., *Historic Savannah: Survey of Significant Buildings in the Historic and Victorian Districts of Savannah, Georgia*, 2d. ed. (Savannah: Historic Savannah Foundation, 1979), 6, 56, 124, 253, 265.

33. Abram S. Isaacs, "Recent American Synagogue Architecture," *American Architect and Building News* 94 (Sept. 2, 1908): 74.

34. Ibid., 74–75. Arnold W. Brunner, "Synagogue Architecture," *Brickbuilder* 16 (Mar. 1907): 37.

35. Hertzberg, *Strangers within the Gate City*, 77, 97, 232. Jacob Rader Marcus, *To Count a People: Jewish Population Data, 1585–1984* (Lanham, Md.: Univ. Press of America, 1990), 49–50.

36. Jeffrey S. Gurock, "The Orthodox Synagogue," in *The American Synagogue: A Sanctuary Transformed*, ed. Jack Wertheimer (Hanover, N.H.: Univ. Press of New England, 1987), 41.

37. Hertzberg, *Strangers within the Gate City*, 117.

38. Ibid., 110–13.

39. Ibid., 101–2, 110–11.

40. Untitled Bruce and Everett promotional catalogue, c. 1910, Architects file, Georgia Department of Natural Resources, Historic Preservation Division, Atlanta, Georgia.

41. Hertzberg, *Strangers within the Gate City*, 93–94.

42. Marcus, *To Count a People*, 50–51. Between 1905 and 1927, the Jewish population of Columbus increased from 335 to 700, Macon's increased from 500 to 650, and Augusta's increased from 125 to 970.

43. Most congregations in Georgia that practiced Orthodox ritual now practice Conservative Judaism; only congregations in Atlanta and Savannah continue to practice Orthodox Judaism.

11

ROOMFUL OF BLUES

JUKEJOINTS AND THE CULTURAL LANDSCAPE OF THE MISSISSIPPI DELTA

JENNIFER NARDONE

Segregation and its legacy have been indelibly linked to the Mississippi Delta since the turn of the twentieth century; while Reconstruction ended in the late 1870s, it was the pivotal 1896 ruling of *Plessy v. Ferguson* which ignited the spark of Jim Crow throughout the South. The word "segregation" describes both a political policy and the tangible evidence resulting from the implementation of those policies. The dissolution of Reconstruction in Mississippi during the 1870s gave way to the development of a network of small Delta towns, often deriving from former plantation railroad stops. These rural towns were literally built on the principles of racial segregation and therefore offer a highly complex system of sorting out the community spatially. This process, however, did not create a neatly delineated series of separate spaces falling down racial lines. Instead, the cultural landscape of the Delta developed an official landscape created and closely monitored by the dominant white culture as well as a more covert landscape, developed out of the defiance of the African American community toward this official landscape.[1]

Out of this manifold cultural landscape, the African American community developed often-abstruse spaces as refuges from the random harassment and unchallenged violence indistinguishable from the day-to-day life of southern blacks. In historian John Dollard's 1936 case study of a small Mississippi Delta town (Indianola) called *Caste and Class in a Southern Town*, he observed that "Negroes experience much less security in their own homes and pursuits than do whites. Physical invasion of Negro privacy is not taken too seriously." Within these volatile parameters African Americans developed a system of communicating and moving within the built environment with little or no detection by the ever-present white authority. The role of music, specifically blues, within the black community during this period offers a key example of how they constantly renegotiated and undermined the segregation within the cultural environment. Jukejoints are the spatial manifestation of blues culture, and are still a significant piece of the African American community today. The Delta remains a racialized landscape despite the official dismantling of segregation; in turn, jukejoints today continue to operate under the same principles incorporated during Jim Crow segregation.[2]

Jukejoints are not permanent structures in a traditional sense. They tend to inhabit buildings originally intended for other purposes, and as a result, no real physical or aesthetic commonality ties these buildings together. Rather, ways of thinking about the space by both the patrons and the owners create patterns reflecting how the African American community dealt with the imposition of segregation on the built environment, as well as how these patterns remain part of the cultural landscape of the Delta today. Of the five jukejoints discussed in this article, three began operating under Jim Crow—Poor Monkey's Lounge, Junior Kimbrough's jukejoint, and Smitty's Red Top Lounge—and offer an example of how the social patterns that developed under segregation remain ingrained in the landscape. J. J.'s Jukejoint and the Do Drop Inn, also considered here, illustrate how more contemporary jukejoints continue to function in the same tradition as their earlier counterparts.

In many ways, J. J.'s juke, located in Clarksdale, Mississippi, epitomizes how little the patterns of segregation still affect the Delta today. Clarksdale represents a typical rural Delta town, established as a railroad nexus of the cotton industry supported by the slave-turned-sharecropper plantations encompassing the town. The major building boom in Clarksdale occurred during segregation, and the complex separation of black and white culture was literally built into the town. In 1889, as Reconstruction came to a political close in the Deep South, a huge fire leveled the newly established town of Clarksdale, requiring a rebuilding phase coinciding with the rise of Jim Crow

segregation and several landscape elements present in Clarksdale directly relate to this period. Historian Leon Litwack noted that while the racism and segregation of the Jim Crow South was certainly not new to the early twentieth century, the formalization of segregation was. The appearance of official signs designating separate behavior and space for blacks and whites was a visual device used to codify longstanding racial differences.[3]

It was this generation of southern blacks that established blues music as a form of folk expression, and jukejoints served as the primary location where the music and culture of blues were experienced. Historian LeRoi Jones refers to blues as "functional music," created and "used" by the first generation of African Americans born out of slavery to articulate the pain and frustration of life under segregation. Blues historians often call Clarksdale, Mississippi, the home of the blues, and it remains today a town with more jukejoints than food stores or restaurants.[4]

In Clarksdale in the 1940s, the building now known as J. J.'s divided its space between a segregated café known as the Belmont and a store called the OK Grocery. Following the close of the Belmont, several segregated cafés operated in the building. The three front doors still present at J. J.'s are physical reminders of the former days of segregation (fig. 11.1): one door was used by whites for the OK Grocery (African Americans entered through a back door no longer extant), the second served as the "Whites Only" entrance to the café, and the third door was designated for "Negroes Only." J. J. closed the former "Negroes Only" door when he purchased the property in 1991.[5] Jukes are never built from scratch in the Delta. Instead, proprietors and patrons reappropriate almost any available building and transform the space to a jukejoint with complex yet subtle gestures. In a sense, the information offered in a floor plan fails to show the defining elements of a jukejoint. Historian Dell Upton wrote that much of the significance of a landscape derives from the unseen elements, and only by unraveling both the seen and unseen pieces of evidence can we begin to reassemble a complex and complete analysis of a space. Jukejoints exemplify the fusion of seen and unseen elements within the Delta landscape. While segregation left definite visual legacies along this landscape, such as the three front doors at J. J.'s, the space of that particular jukejoint is really defined by larger, unseen principles.[6]

J. J.'s bears no formal signage designating this building a jukejoint or, for that matter, any kind of public space. Instead, J. J.'s depends on word of mouth for patronage. The path leading to jukejoints is unconventional in this sense; it is a path of information about the jukejoint, not formal advertising or even visual evidence on the building, that leads people to the space. The word-of-mouth process probably derived from the practical circumstances of segregation in place when jukejoints first began appearing on the cultural landscape. Any public or communal gathering of African Americans during Jim Crow was a dangerous undertaking, and deflecting attention from that space was a method of protection. In fact, African American historian Katrina Hazzard Gordon connects the clandestine gatherings of slaves, when social activities were covert as protection from the slave master, to the development of the jukejoint during segregation, when

an equal amount of protection was necessary from the violence still inflicted upon the African American community. These veiled methods of communication defined the space of a jukejoint by filtering those with knowledge and subsequent entrance into the space. At J. J.'s, as with most jukejoints in the Delta, these covert methods continue to function as part of the space.[7]

The front entrance of J. J.'s demonstrates how the fusion of the seen and unseen elements necessary during Jim Crow remain part of jukejoints today. J. J.'s Jukejoint spills out to the sidewalk in front of the building, where patrons are almost always gathered during peak hours. In this sense, the entrance functions as much more than a simple threshold. Walking through the doorway begins a process of interactions with the patrons, and often with J. J. himself. This relatively ordinary detail becomes complicated by the absence of signage at jukejoints. A filtering process begins at J. J.'s with the dependence on word of mouth and the transaction of information among the clientele. A system that once functioned as a way of keeping the jukejoint protected under segregation has become one of the defining principles of the jukejoint. In an interesting twist, however, there is a lack of anonymity within the jukejoint itself.

This is not to say that the entrance of J. J.'s or any other jukejoint necessarily operates as a way of

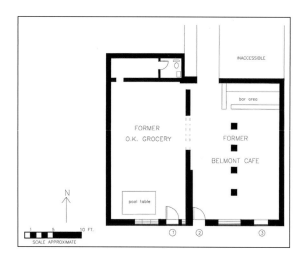

Fig. 11.1. Plan of J. J.'s Jukejoint, Clarksdale, Mississippi. 1: Former OK Grocery front door. 2: Former "Whites Only" door at the Belmont Café. 3: Former "Negroes Only" door at the Belmont Café (later permanently closed off). The wall that divided the café and grocery was partially knocked down by J. J.

Fig. 11.2. Patrons gathered in front of J. J.'s Jukejoint, Clarksdale, Mississippi.

turning people away; however, it does remove any anonymity among the patrons. The jukejoint literally offers a place where everybody knows your name. The quasi-privacy offered at other public gatherings does not work within the jukejoint. Entering a jukejoint without participating in this initial greeting process disrupts the entire social dynamic and would not be tolerated by fellow patrons. The community gathered within the jukejoint sorts itself out through the dialogue, interaction, and response occurring within the space.[8]

What happens within the jukejoint is not extraordinary by conventional standards. In Mississippi, a jukejoint license can be purchased at the town hall for fifty dollars, although a large number of jukejoints operate without these licenses. Proprietors such as J. J. purchase beer by the case at a local store or warehouse and then sell it to patrons by the can (Budweiser, Budweiser Lite, and Natural Lite are the only selections offered). Patrons freely bring hard liquor into jukejoints, particularly Crown Royal Canadian Whiskey, which is not legal but acceptable according to jukejoint standards. Drinking serves as a primary activity within a jukejoint, as important as the blues music playing either live or on a jukebox inside, but unlike in other drinking establishments, does not serve as a money-making endeavor for the proprietor. In fact, jukejoints never generate a significant amount of revenue for the proprietor; every proprietor discussed in this essay has a full-time job, and operates his jukejoint on his own time. In most cases, these are the social gathering spaces for his particular community, as well as a way of listening to blues and having a certain amount of freedom to drink, dance, smoke, and celebrate without real threat of being stifled or stopped. This directly relates to the earlier discussion of the path of information leading to the jukejoints and the subsequent lack of anonymity once inside.[9]

The proprietors maintain a very personal involvement with their jukejoints and their patrons. Although all the proprietors discussed in this article are men, jukejoints have always catered to both men and women; female proprietors are not uncommon, although they are less prevalent than their male counterparts. Like blues music, a certain sexual dynamic exists within the jukejoint (perhaps adding to a sense of celebration and even escapism), and both men and women participate. Again, a contained community exists within the walls of a jukejoint not dependent on turning people away but on the intimacy and absence of anonymity key to defining these spaces.

Poor Monkey's Lounge, located in Merigold, Mississippi, offers another example of how the defining principles of jukejoints function within a particular cultural landscape. Willie Seaberry, a sharecropper on the Hiter Farm located in Merigold and proprietor of Monkey's jukejoint, has gone by the moniker Monkey since he was a child. He moved to Hiter Farm in 1954, when he was thirteen, and began operating a jukejoint with his older brother in a former sharecropper shack located on the farm. In 1963, however, Monkey made an interesting choice about his jukejoint and his residence: he moved into his jukejoint. By 1963, overseeing the jukejoint had become the primary definition of Monkey's life. It figuratively, and subsequently literally, become his home. This fusion of the private home with the public jukejoint further blurs the line between these two realms.[10]

Despite the relatively little time this building serves as a jukejoint, Monkey still felt it made a better home for him than an actual house. Initially the building consisted of only the main room; after moving in, Monkey added the poolroom, stage area, kitchen, and bedroom. Like the former segregated café that now houses J. J.'s Jukejoint, the reuse of a 1940s sharecropper shack as a Monkey's jukejoint offers another link between the era of Jim Crow and the present.

Fig. 11.3. Poor Monkey's Lounge, Merigold, Mississippi.

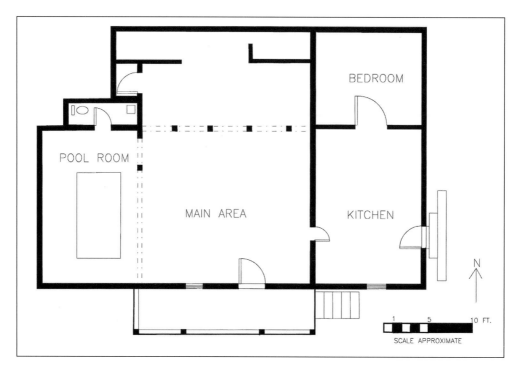

Fig. 11.4. Plan of Poor Monkey's Lounge, Merigold, Mississippi. The main area shows the original sharecropper shack.

The path into Monkey's, however, requires an even more intimate knowledge of the people and the place than J. J.'s. The fusion of home and jukejoint at Monkey's highlights the intimacy found among the patrons and proprietors of jukejoints. Entering Monkey's jukejoint strips patrons of individual anonymity, with Monkey himself stationed at the front door on nights he opens his jukejoint. Once again, Monkey does not turn people away, but instead uses the initial welcome into his jukejoint to personalize his relationship with every person who crosses inside. Getting to the greeting stage of Monkey's jukejoint follows a similar path of information seen at J. J.'s. Like J. J.'s, the crowd at Monkey's has been going to his jukejoint for many years; some of the patrons are fellow Hiter Farm employees who have known Monkey since he began running jukejoints in the 1950s. People outside the regular crowd—myself, for example—begin by talking to people who know of Monkey's jukejoint to find out when it will be open. In my case, lunch at Turner's Grille across Issaquena Street from J. J.'s (and owned by musician Ike Turner's family) was where I inquired about whether Monkey would open his jukejoint that week, and whether there would be room for out-of-town visitors. Asking the right questions of the right people was essential for attaining access to all the jukejoints discussed in this chapter. Many jukejoints rely solely on word of mouth and personalized knowledge of the place for business. There is no listing of Monkey's jukejoint in any directory, yellow pages, map, or other official guide.[11]

In this tradition, Monkey's has no formal sign designating the building as a public space. Monkey does, however, have a way of signaling the transformation of his home into his juke, one fitting with the intimate nature of his (and many other) jukejoints. A single string of Christmas lights, when turned on, alerts those who understand the sign that Monkey's is open for business that night. The lights function more as a gesture; since Monkey's is located so far off the main roads of Merigold, patrons must already know where they are headed to find it.

Junior Kimbrough's jukejoint in Holly Springs, Mississippi, offers a complicated example of the connection between the community and space within a juke. The now-deceased Kimbrough was a well-known blues musician who grew up sharecropping on a Delta plantation and later moved to the North Central Hill region of Mississippi. During his life, Junior operated his jukejoint in a variety of places throughout the Delta; he moved to Holly Springs in the early 1980s because of its proximity to Memphis, Tennessee, where he often performed. The move out of the Delta to Holly Springs brought a new element to this jukejoint not seen at any others considered in this essay: a truly racially and socially mixed patronage.[12]

Holly Springs lies about thirty miles northwest of the essentially middle-class white campus of the University of Mississippi in Oxford. Over the years, Junior's developed a following of students and other Oxford residents who traditionally frequent his juke on Sunday nights. Junior's son Kinny now primarily runs the jukejoint, and he referred to Sunday night as "white night." Kinny said Junior's runs on other nights during the week and is not open to general patronage (implying Ole Miss students). In this sense, Junior's complicates the absence of anonymity within the jukejoint in a new way.

Like the previous jukejoints considered in this essay, Junior's does not have any signs identifying it as a public space. The building itself is an old store located about eight miles away from the closest commercial business. The addition of a more racially mixed crowd on Sunday nights may change the scope of the juke temporarily, although the proprietor and patrons that constitute the regular crowd at Junior's maintain ultimate control through the dissemination of information.

Once inside Junior's, patrons are enveloped by colorful wall paintings, transforming the physical space into a metaphorical experience. The paintings range from abstract to portraiture; there are some that reestablish the definition of the space itself. The main walls inside Junior's are covered with floor-to-ceiling paintings of places: a house settled within a landscape filled with trees, clouds and water, a forest scene, a huge setting (or perhaps rising) sun framing the pool table, palm trees, and mountainscapes. The lintels within the main room have portraits of famous African Americans, although many bear only a vague resemblance to the real person, ranging from Oprah Winfrey to Little Richard, Magic Johnson to Martin Luther King Jr. These paintings were done by a local patron of Junior's shortly after he moved into the building, at the proprietor's request.

Similar to the unseen principles behind the path of information leading patrons into the jukes, the paintings or a vase of plastic flowers on a table can transform an old country store into a Delta tradition because they symbolize the ways the community sees the space. The people, the music, and the atmosphere of a jukejoint surpass the physical layout of the building or aesthetic details. The details may vary from place to place, but the intention remains the same. At Monkey's, Polaroid photos line the lintels, while shimmering batting, confetti, and party streamers hang throughout the juke (no decorations of any kind are found in his bedroom). Signs reading Happy Birthday and Merry Christmas hang around the pool table and stage area. J. J.'s also has interior decorations, although very different from Monkey's and Junior's. An old NAACP sign hangs over the jukebox, and each window has a curtain.

The sense of escapism associated with blues music in many ways manifests itself in the celebratory and figurative decor inside a jukejoint. Paul Oliver wrote

Fig. 11.5. Wall paintings inside Junior's, Holly Springs, Mississippi.

Fig. 11.6. Do Drop Inn, Shelby, Mississippi.

that blues music is a "rich storehouse of the fantasy production" of the lower-class African American communities in the South. Jukejoints "function" because of this collective understanding. Participation in the scene depends on a certain amount of knowledge and acceptance that the jukejoint amounts to more than meets the eye through the communal experience within its walls.[13]

The Do Drop Inn, located in Shelby, Mississippi, demonstrates these same principles. On most Friday and Saturday nights for the last twenty years, Earnest Walker, who goes by the name Big E., has operated the Do Drop out of an old lumberyard building. Big E., who grew up on a sharecropping farm in the Delta and for a time attended elementary school with Monkey, holds a day job as a maintenance worker for the town of Shelby. The present jukejoint is only the latest in a long line Big E. has run throughout his life. He rents the building, and he told me that most months he can just cover his rent check and liquor purchases with the money he makes running the juke. The town of Shelby spans about three blocks off of Highway 61, with no major grocery store or restaurant, yet has at least five jukes that run at various times. They remain an important, if not altogether visible, piece of the Delta landscape.[14]

Unlike the other jukejoints considered in this article, the Do Drop (which is referred to by patrons and local residents as Big E.'s) has a sign on the front of the building. Over the front door, DO DROP INN is painted directly on the shingles, below is spray-painted

Big E. Place [*sic*], and the same words are repeated to the right of the front door. Despite these visual signs, Big E. told me the real sign that he is operating the jukejoint depends on his truck, which is always parked in front of the Do Drop when open for business. Big E.'s truck functions as an Open sign at the Do Drop, but like the lights at Monkey's, patrons must know what they are looking for before they can find it.

Physically, Big E.'s has very little internal definition. Big E. renovated part of the existing space for the kitchen and bar area shortly after opening, but it is the stage and main area of the juke that occupies the large open space remaining from the former lumberyard building. This transformation from lumberyard to jukejoint however, depends primarily on the stories found on the walls. Similar to the paintings seen at Junior's, Big E. has framed the main area as well as the stage with scenes of celebration and, to a certain extent, escapism. The paintings here are less abstract than those at Junior's yet enclose the crowd and music in the same way. The paintings evoke another world within the Do Drop, particularly in the main painting. In this painting the Do Drop Inn, with Big E.'s truck parked right in front, floats in a fantasy world, surrounded by palm trees and a promise that this is where the good times are (fig. 11.7). Other paintings show couples dancing and huge, surreal champagne glasses clinking together, although champagne is never served at a juke.

Fig. 11.7. Wall painting at the Do Drop Inn, depicting the jukejoint and Big E.'s truck floating in a fantasy surrounded by palm trees and clouds.

Smitty's Red Top Lounge opened about 1950 on Yazoo Street, only two streets away from J. J.'s Jukejoint in Clarksdale. Despite the proximity of these two jukes, however, patrons of one rarely go to the other. While talking with patrons at J. J.'s, I was told by many people that Smitty's was not a good crowd and not a place they would feel welcome. A few days later while talking to patrons at Smitty's, I was told essentially the same thing about J. J.'s.

Like the Do Drop Inn, Smitty's consists of a large open area with the bar on one wall and a pool table stationed close to the front door. Smitty's also has a sign visible over the front door, as does the Do Drop. The sign here is a professional one, not the hand-painted and spray-painted indicators at Big E.'s. The sign simply reads Red Top Lounge, however, with no mention of Smitty.

Fig. 11.8. Smitty's Red Top Lounge, Clarksdale, Mississippi.

Since it opened in the early 1950s, three different men have operated the Red Top Lounge. James Alford has owned and run the jukejoint since 1993, when he made a decision reminiscent of Monkey's choice to move into his jukejoint. Interestingly, Alford began going by the name Smitty, as the previous proprietors had all done. Alford also runs a juke in West Helena, Arkansas, located about thirty minutes east of Clarksdale, where he does not use the name Smitty. "Smitty" belongs to Smitty's. It defines the space as well as the person. Just as historian Lawrence Levine wrote that no single person owned a blues song, no one person owns Smitty's or, in a broader sense, designs or defines a jukejoint.[15]

The basic happenings within a jukejoint are not extraordinary: people go to drink, smoke, dance, and listen to music. The covert nature of jukejoints can easily be disregarded as protection of the illegal activities such as prostitution, drug use, and gambling that often occur inside, concluding that patrons and proprietors deliberately seek a low profile for their jukejoints as a form of protection. Anonymity within the landscape, however, disintegrates once inside the jukejoint, where an intimate relationship with both the activities and the people redefines the space from an anonymous building or private residence into a communal experience.

To consider only the dialectic of anonymity and intimacy as a protective device of illegal activity misses the larger story of jukejoints. They are complicated buildings, not because they offer historians a new example of African American architecture but because they hold a key story in the evolution of the Mississippi Delta's cultural landscape. Jukejoints are not extraordinary buildings, and often the decisions and devices used by proprietors and patrons seem like simple common sense, unworthy of rigorous academic investigation. The Mississippi Delta, however, *is* an extraordinary landscape, a place considered even today as a Third World country on America's own soil. Initially, segregation dictated the look and layout of the Delta towns, but ultimately, the definitions roped around the African American community broke down under a process of redefinition. Jukejoints are an important piece of this redefinition because of their continued importance within the communities. Segregation left a racialized physical landscape in the Delta, one where people constantly renegotiate the definition of these spaces. Jukejoints are one site where this negotiation occurs in both tangible and non-visible ways.

The most important element of any jukejoint comes through the shared experience and sense of belonging within a group. Jukejoints are interactive spaces, between people and people, people and spaces, spaces and music, music and dancing, public and private, and individual and communal, constantly moving and blurring the lines between the tangible and the ephemeral. What occurs in the space relies heavily on how people see themselves within the space, represented by a detail as simple as the palm tree in Big E.'s wall drawing, or the overflow of J. J.'s Jukejoint onto the street as a means of controlling interaction with the interior space.

Visitors to these places must become willing participant observers within the landscape. In retrospect, I think I initially (and unknowingly) used the right tool: I simply talked to people, on the street, in the lunch grilles, and at the jukejoints. I have often considered whether I was able to see the "real" jukejoints, that perhaps my whole observation was a "white night." Even so, the processes and relationships I did observe within the communities and the jukejoints were significant to how the people I met viewed and understood these spaces, as well as their overall environment. Dismissing jukejoints as unimportant because they lack a template or a certain amount of physical uniqueness within the environment misses Upton's call that we as researchers and historians consider the unseen and intangible as well as the physical

Fig. 11.9. Sign at the Crossroads Jukejoint, Clarksdale, Mississippi.

evidence. Jukejoints are essential pieces of the cultural landscape because of the fusion of the physical and the metaphorical, offering a wider lens for understanding the Delta.

Notes

1. See Eric Foner, *Reconstruction: America's Unfinished Business* (New York Harper and Row, 1988), 603–12. See Linton Weeks, *Clarksdale and Cohoma County: A History* (Clarksdale, Miss.: Linton Weeks and the Clarksdale Carnegie Public Library, 1982) as well as James Cobb, *The Most Southern Place on Earth: The Mississippi Delta and the Roots of Regional Identity* (New York: Oxford Univ. Press, 1992). Both discuss the development of rural towns within the preexisting network of large cotton plantations during the post-Reconstruction period known as Redemption.

2. John Dollard, *Caste and Class in a Southern Town* (New Haven: Yale Univ. Press, for the Institute of Human Relations, 1937), 341. Michael Omi and Howard Winant, *Racial Formation in the United States* (New York: Routledge Press, 1994). Omi and Winant use the word "racialization" to describe the principles beyond ethnicity, class, and nation which create the fundamental principles inherent in racism. They argue that these principles are part of a larger "racial trajectory" encompassing all facets of life in the United States. In essence, a series of "racial projects" have created a complex racial dynamic within the United States leaving no element of political or cultural environment untouched by the concept of racialization. Jim Crow serves as an example of a successful racial project.

3. Weeks, *Clarksdale and Cohoma County*, chaps. 1 and 2. Leon Litwack, *Trouble in Mind: Black Southerners in the Age of Jim Crow* (New York: Alfred A. Knopf, 1998), 288.

4. LeRoi Jones, *Blues People: The Negro Expression in White America and the Music that Developed from It* (New York: Morrow Quill Paperbacks, 1963), 51–52. Also in chapter 7 Jones discusses the disjuncture of the freedom offered African American under Reconstruction and the subsequent reality found under Jim Crow. This disjuncture created a need to articulate emotions without disrupting the tenuous safety of the African American community. Blues functioned as one method of safe expression.

5. Clarksdale city directories list the café and grocer between 1939 and 1949.

6. Dell Upton, "Seen, Unseen, and the Scene," *Understanding Ordinary Landscapes,* ed. Paul Groth and Todd W. Bressi (New Haven: Yale Univ. Press, 1997), 176.

7. Katrina Hazzard Gordon, *Jookin': The Rise of Social Dance Formation in African American Culture* (Philadelphia: Temple Univ. Press, 1990), 77.

8. See Alan Dundes, *Mother Wit from the Laughing Barrel: Readings in the Interpretation of Afro-American Folklore* (Jackson: Univ. Press of Mississippi, 1981), for detailed discussions of the call-and-response tradition in blues music which becomes part of the African American dialect, serving as a method of communication outside of blues music.

9. John Rusky, former director of the Delta Blues Museum in Clarksdale, Mississippi, discussed the social dynamics of the jukejoints with me in an informal interview in May 1996 in Clarksdale.

10. All the information about Monkey's life and jukejoint came from an informal interview with him in May 1996 in Merigold, Mississippi.

11. From interviews with patrons at Monkey's jukejoint, May 1996, Merigold, Mississippi.

12. Junior Kimbrough's son, Kinny, told me this during an informal interview, May 1996, Holly Springs, Mississippi.

13. See Paul Oliver, *Blues Fell This Morning: Meaning in the Blues* (New York: Cambridge Univ. Press, 1990), Jones, *Blues People,* and James Baldwin's "Uses of the Blues," in *Voices of Concern: The* Playboy *College Reader,* ed. *Playboy Magazine* editors (New York: Harcourt Brace Jovanovich, 1971), for a discussion of how blues and the spaces of blues function within the black community.

14. This information was gathered from interviews with John Rusky, former curator of the Delta Blues Museum in Clarksdale, Mississippi, as well as Big E. in May 1996 in Shelby, Mississippi. Both mentioned about five other jukes within the town limits of Shelby, although I did not visit any Shelby jukes other than Big E.'s. The description of Shelby comes from my own observation during my three visits to the town during the past several years.

15. Information about Alford and Smitty's gathered in informal interviews with Alford and patrons, May 1996. Also, see Lawrence Levine, *Black Culture and Black Consciousness: Afro-American Thought from Slavery to Freedom* (New York: Oxford Univ. Press, 1977), 228–29.

PART III

PLACE

12

PREINDUSTRIAL FRAMING IN THE CHESAPEAKE

WILLIE GRAHAM

Cary Carson and his colleagues' 1981 landmark article, "Impermanent Architecture in the Southern Colonies," summarized what had been learned about building construction from a decade of recording archaeological remains of early Chesapeake buildings and studying the few extant frame structures that could possibly date to the end of the seventeenth and beginning of the eighteenth centuries. Carson's study and work by fellow colleagues Dell Upton, Garry Stone, and Fraser Neiman have described the unique character of the Tidewater framing system and the social forces that shaped it. Virtually all subsequent findings have been interpreted in light of their endeavors. Now, after a significant passage of time and since many additional buildings have been analyzed, it is worthwhile to reevaluate the nature of the framing systems employed in constructing these local buildings.[1]

Research over the intervening years allows for a more precise look at the evolutionary character of structural carpentry. Defining the sequence of changes Chesapeake buildings underwent requires the establishment of a more precise date when a recognizable system developed. That is, when in the experimentation process did a preferred framing tradition emerge that generally solved the particular economic, cultural and environmental problems of the region? Earlier scholarship acknowledged that a key component of the solution to local conditions was simplification of the structural system resulting from expenses associated with the lack of readily available labor (fig. 12.1). This body of work further suggested that the basic Chesapeake frame had developed by 1700, which coincided with a drop in mortality rates and a significant rise in social stability.[2] But documentary and empirical data indicate the form may have assumed its unique regional character much earlier and probably had coalesced by the middle of the seventeenth century. It has been understood that the streamlining of the frame, resulting from the need for economical use of labor, led to simplification of its joinery. It can also be theorized that this development produced a two-tiered structural system characterized by distinctions made between primary structural elements—or load-bearing members—and those considered secondary. The result was to establish a hierarchy of joints for each type of framing member ranked by the ease with which the joints could be fabricated and based on the nature of the load and load-bearing capacity of the members.

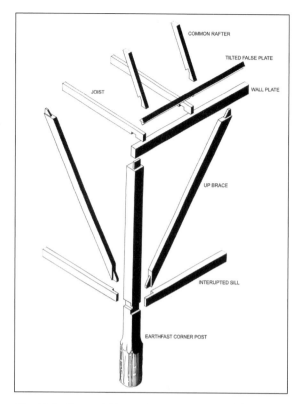

Fig. 12.1. Chaney Tobacco Barn, Anne Arundel County, Maryland.

efforts to reduce awareness of the building's structural components.[3] Thus, the standard frame of a late colonial structure, whether rural or urban, echoed that of its seventeenth-century counterpart, but how it functioned and the extent to which it was decorated had changed. Modifications continued so that by the time of the Civil War, many necessary elements were in place to ease the introduction of balloon framing to the region.

Local building practices in Tidewater Maryland and Virginia evolved in a very fundamental way out of an earthfast tradition that well suited the culture, economic conditions and climate of the region (fig. 12.2). Early years of settlement were affected by an anticipation of profiteering from speculation on tobacco and the boom-and-bust cycles of that market. The inability of colonists to tame their environment and the absence of a large number of women necessary to establish stable families and households aggravated the situation. Available money was largely spent on tending to tobacco production, with great sums used to stock a work force of indentured servants. After 1660, capital was

Not long after it developed into a recognizable form, Chesapeake carpentry was under renewed pressure to adapt to new constraints and did so by disguising its structural components and working parts. This trend is the direct result of the social stability that had been achieved, by aesthetic considerations brought about by a consumer revolution that was gaining momentum in the Chesapeake late in the seventeenth century, and by Georgian influences on American architecture in the century following. Rural areas were slow to abandon certain aspects of the seventeenth-century frame. Instead, builders sought to blend some of the newly introduced stylistic elements and a higher degree of finish with exposed, elaborated framing. Before the end of the colonial period, concealed frames and refined, Georgian finishes were commonly used in buildings found in both town and country.

This shift can also be attributed to the interaction between the simplification process and continued

Fig. 12.2. Archaeological excavation of an earthfast posthole at the Gray Farm Barn, Suffolk, Virginia. Note that the post was cut off above grade and a new sill and foundations were inserted below it in the early twentieth century.

increasingly expended on purchasing and housing African slaves. The combination of these conditions dissuaded most from attempting capital-intensive physical improvements of their property. Unlike circumstances in Britain, wood was abundant in the Chesapeake, but building tradesmen continued to be scarce. Therefore, wood could be used more freely, but its preparation had to be minimized. Combining English ideas of architectural expectations with New World realities on the riverbanks of the Chesapeake watershed, carpenters developed a specialized tradition that influenced building practices for the next three centuries.[4]

The essential features of the new system emphasized ease of assembly and the use of minimal labor to produce its various structural parts. Instead of the heavy frames used in New England, early Chesapeake craftsmen depended on a bay system with lighter structural infill, most often with posts spaced on an eight- or ten-foot module. Normal (or sidewall) assembly was used, permitting the long walls of a building to be raised as individual units that were then joined into a single, stable structure with large tie beams corresponding to the principal bays. For structures of greater widths, summer beams were connected perpendicularly to the tie beams, breaking the span of lighter joists that were in turn set on a twenty-four to thirty-inch interval. A false plate was lapped on top of the joist ends; it was designed to carry the common rafters and isolate the roof from the lower frame.[5]

Even in more elaborate buildings, the range of joint types in the frame was limited. Tenons were used for primary members in compression and lap joints for elements in tension. Non-load-bearing framing components were lapped, usually in the form of a bevel. In larger buildings, bays were defined by principal rafters aligned with the structural posts of the wall below. To carry the siding, flooring, and roof covering, less consequential and lighter structural members in the form of studs, common joists, and common rafters filled the gaps between the principal load-bearing parts. Riven clapboards (feather-lapped on their ends and lapped top and bottom like weatherboards) were favored for covering roofs, instead of the English preference of stones or clay tiles. Buildings whose roofs spanned relatively short distances could now rely on a lighter, common-rafter system. Collars, either nailed or lapped to the side of the rafter pairs, kept them from spreading. This system was altogether new for the Chesapeake and was made possible by this clapboard roofing that provided horizontal stability, thereby reducing dependence on the connection between rafters and joists.[6]

Carson's example of Cedar Park (1702) in Anne Arundel County, Maryland, well illustrates the structural arrangement of the Chesapeake frame as it had matured during the seventeenth century. Large, earthfast posts define a bay system of ten feet, while a "girt" or principal rafter roof covers the structure. The principal rafters align with the posts below. Lighter studs supported by interrupted sills fill the space between the posts, much as the common rafters, carried on purlins, are set between the principal rafter pairs. Likewise, tie beams, used to support the principal rafters, carry common joists whose main function is to receive the flooring. A thick board false plate laps over the joist ends and carries the feet of lightweight kick rafters. Cedar Park is more substantial and refined than most buildings of this period, yet it shares a similar ordering of its structure with the modest, joined frames of neighboring structures.[7]

Although alignment of the principal posts from front to back wall was technically unnecessary in the Chesapeake framing system due to a reliance on sidewall assembly, it was usually done for two reasons. First, laying out the postholes and joints in the plates was more easily accomplished. For example, every ten feet a hole could be excavated in the ground and a corresponding mortise cut into the plate for a post, regardless of where internal room divisions, doorways, and windows were intended. The joints for secondary infill could be cut ahead of time, but it was not necessary to install them until after the walls were raised. Second, the transfer of load from principal roof members directly to the posts avoids secondary framing of the lower wall. Therefore, the principal rafters are located directly over these posts, forcing their alignment one wall to the other. The increased load the main rafters assume by carrying the weight of the common rafters and roof covering (via the purlins) is transferred directly to the posts below them, not to the

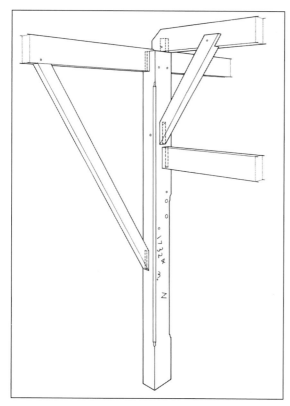

Fig. 12.3. Reconstructed view of framing associated with a reused post employed in the support of a sagging floor at the Mason House in Accomack County, Virginia. This post, with the date 1732 inscribed on its side, came from a bent-frame structure. Integral to this system of framing is the linking of front and rear posts by a tie beam and the raising of these three pieces as a unit, in contrast to sidewall assembly. Post measured by Cary Carson.

entirety of the lower wall. It should be noted that these conventions were not always strictly followed since experimentation continued well into the eighteenth century. Buildings can be found with posts that poorly aligned, various roof systems were attempted, and more complex joinery continued to be tested (fig. 12.3).[8] However, conformity was increasingly the tendency after the middle of the seventeenth century, indicating that a developed version of the Virginia frame had sufficiently evolved to become a generally accepted solution to the peculiarities of the region.

Evidence from archaeologically excavated sites of earthfast structures reinforces the notion that mid-century framing systems appeared much the same as the region's earliest surviving wooden structures that date to the last two decades of the seventeenth century. That is to say, alternative technologies such as puncheon construction (walls formed by small, closely spaced studs with sharpened ends driven into the ground or set in back-filled, shallow trenches), or structures raised in bents began to fade from common use. Prior to this time, the frame was characterized by a high percentage of uncarpentered work, including both puncheon buildings and unbayed ones with posts set in predug holes that are casually arranged. Likewise, a variety of technologies were used for buildings with joined frames. For instance, the so-called stone house at Flowerdew Hundred had paired earthfast posts, probably representing unevenly spaced bents set in an excavated trench, with silt-stone foundations between the bays to support a brick wall that in turn carried interrupted sills.[9] Occasionally sites are discovered in which elongated holes for posts are set transverse to the length of the building, a benefit when raising sidewall structures. Such was the case at the circa 1636 dwelling, Structure 1, at Nansemond Fort in Suffolk County, Virginia. However, elsewhere in this early fortified settlement are buildings more typical of the era: earthfast structures raised in bents, but without foundations between the posts. Some of the Nansemond buildings utilized earthfast studs, suggesting the lack of interrupted sills and the absence of flooring, while others had no stud evidence, thereby indicating a better treatment of its floor and framing (fig. 12.4).[10] The lack of uniformity applied to construction methods reflects the high degree of experimentation that was undertaken during the first half of the seventeenth century.

Archaeological sites reveal the tendency to apply more carpentry skill when building structures after 1650. Cabin construction (such as puncheon buildings) fades from common use in settled areas, while sidewall assembly replaces bent construction as the preferred raising method for joined structures.[11] Two notable examples from this new era are located in Calvert County, Maryland: Compton Structure 1 dating to about 1651 and Capt. John Odber's 1658 dwell-

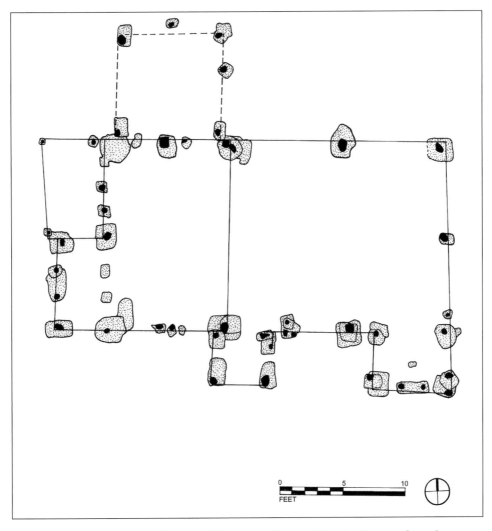

Fig. 12.4. House 2, Nansemond Fort, Suffolk County, Virginia. This dwelling was framed as a two-room unit with a front porch and a later rear shed. The main posts are paired from front to rear walls and were likely raised as tie-beam pairs. Earthfast studs were used in the west room, suggesting that this space had a dirt floor. The east room lacks evidence for studs and thus had interrupted sills, probably to create a raised floor. Note the frame chimney on the west wall of the smaller room and one on the south wall of the larger hall. Measured by Nicholas Luccketti.

ing at Patuxent Point. Both are clearly the product of normal assembly since each incorporates a new feature associated with sidewall raising—stepped holes for the main posts—which assisted in the raising of the wall and is an indicator of the direction in which the posts were raised. Plan flexibility provided by bent construc-

tion allowed for the creation of uneven bays at will. But variability in layout soon became less important since a two-room module with end chimneys emerged as a successful solution to organizing space. For that matter, conventions of this period did not preclude partitions from falling where they may, regardless of the position of the principal wall framing. By the third quarter of the century, then, buildings in the more-established areas of the Chesapeake were generally better built, more regularly framed, and more likely to be raised in sidewall units.[12]

Along with this new uniformity came a classification system that delineated carpentry work as either "English" or "Virginia" frame. Thomas Cornwaleys had hoped the English model would prevail in southern Maryland. Having to this point lived in an inferior framed dwelling, he wrote to Lord Baltimore in 1638, "I am building of A house toe put my head in, of sawn Timber framed A story and half hygh, with A sellar and Chimnies of brick, toe Encourage others toe follow my Example, for hithertoe wee liue in Cottages."[13] But nearly fifty years later, William Fitzhugh warned Nicholas Heyward against building:

> Either a great, or English framed house, for labour is so intolerably dear, & workmen so idle & negligent that the building of a good house, to you there will seem insupportable, for this I can assure you when I built my own house, & agreed as cheap as I could with workmen, & as carefully & as diligently took care that they followed their work[,] notwithstanding we have timber here for nothing, but felling and getting in place, the frame of my house stood me in more money in Tobo . . . than a frame of the same Dimensions Would cost in London, by a third at least where everything is bought, & near three times as long preparing, Your brother Joseph's building that Shell, of a house without Chimney or partition, & not one tittle of workmanship about it more than a Tobacco house work, carry'd him into those Arrears with your self, & his other Employers, as you found by his Accots. at his death.[14]

Only a small number of colonists during this first century were able—or chose—to build an English house with proper foundations, stout frame of sawn timbers, substantial braces, a preponderance of tenon joints, brick chimneys, and up-to-date finishes. What sufficed for most who built more than mere cabins was a modest structure that came to be known as the Virginia house.

Initially, the Virginia house referred to an earthfast building with simplified joinery, riven clapboard

covering, little sawn stock, a wooden chimney if heated, and a one- or two-room plan.[15] The Virginia legislature acknowledged that the Virginia house had emerged as a recognizable type by 1647, when they decreed that it should be a model for county prisons: "Whereas divers escapes have been made by prisoners, and more likely to be, for want of sufficient prisons in severall countyes, to which the poverty of the countrey and want of necessaries here will not admitt a possibillitie to erect other then [sic] such houses as we frequently inhabitt . . . Be it therefore enacted, That such houses provided for that purpose shall be accompted sufficient prisons as are built according to the forme of Virginia houses, from which noe escape can be made without breaking or forcing some part of the prison house."[16]

A set of specifications was drawn up in 1692 by justices in Middlesex County, Virginia, to build "one strong Substantiall Virga built house for a court house . . . Well Braced Above and below Studded double Joysts & Covered with four foot Boards."[17] Sotterley (c. 1717), in St. Mary's County, Maryland, for all its Virginia house traits—hewn and riven frame, predominately lapped joinery, earthfast posts, and clapboard roof sheathing and wall covering—was erected with the English frame characteristics of brick chimneys and plastered internal walls. Cedar Park further blurred the line between Virginia and English construction. Although its posts initially stood in the ground without benefit of masonry foundations, it does have a substantial sawn frame whose members are largely connected with tenon joints. Moreover, it was originally covered with round-butt shingles (over clapboard sheathing), it is solidly braced, and it has large brick chimneys. But whether English, Virginia, or a mixture of the two, the carpentry of these house types was unmistakably a product of the Chesapeake, and they drew on a similar set of rules for organizing and assembling their frames.

Central to the framing system was the near universal use of riven clapboards to cover walls and roofs. Four- or five-foot clapboards served as a module that assisted the simplification process by creating bays of either eight- or ten-foot intervals, with studs and common rafters set on two- or two-and-a-half-foot centers, thus allowing short clapboards to be used with little extra trimming.[18] In fact, so integral was the length of clapboards to the structural system that the expression "clapboard work" or "clapboard house" became synonymous with the term "Virginia house." A late example can be found in a 1727 Essex County, Virginia, order in which the justices "agree[d] with a workman to build a house to hold court in, of common clapboard work thirty foot long and twenty foot wide."[19] Reading between the lines, the carpenter was to build a structure using a ten-foot module, space the common structural members on two-and-a-half-foot centers, and cover the roof and walls with five-foot clapboards.[20]

A key component of the Chesapeake frame is the false plate. It shows up in documents as early as 1673, when a Middlesex County court ordered a house "to be jointed with false plate[s]."[21] In Charles County, Maryland, false plates are noted in court records for a house that is sufficiently old to need repair by 1678.[22] The date of introduction can be pushed back further by looking at the earliest surviving building in Virginia, Bacon's Castle in Surry County dating to 1665, which includes a square, board false plate used to carry the common rafters in its principal rafter roof. This plate looks much the same as those used on trussed and common rafter roofs seventy-five years

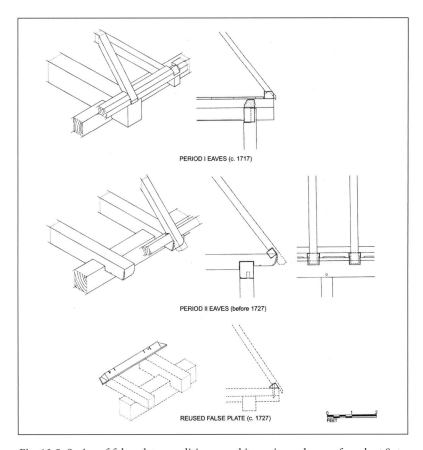

Fig. 12.5. Series of false plate conditions used in various phases of work at Sotterley, St. Mary's County, Maryland. The top drawing is the original eaves condition of the house and includes a heavy board false plate that was notched to catch the rafter feet. The center drawing is from a pre-1727 wing and includes chamfers and stops on the joist ends and on the bottom of the tilted false plate. The bottom image is a variation of the tilted false plate that sits directly on top of the joists. It was reused in the 1780s as a roof strut.

later and demonstrates their existence by the third quarter of the seventeenth century.[23]

The purpose of the false plate was to simplify the joinery between rafters and joists. Whereas New England builders typically relied on tenons to make the connection, Tidewater framers limited this time-consuming method to the principal bays. Initially, the common rafters sat in beveled notches in a heavy board false plate or bird-mouthed over them, with the false plate set on top of or lapped over the joist ends (fig. 12.5). A tilted variant of the false plate was introduced in the 1710s that had the advantage of shedding water better and did not easily twist from thrusts imposed on them by the rafters. The shape of tilted-false plates may have been inspired by purlins; in fact, they act much like a purlin that has simply been dropped to the level of the eaves. However, the predominant reason for introducing the tilted false plate was to serve as a decorative element in an era when exposed framing was desirable. In much the same way as ridge boards carried the peaks of common rafters on eighteenth-century king-post trusses, the false plate was intended as an efficient means to support non-load-bearing parts and eliminate joints between rafter feet and joists, thereby making this a significant labor- and

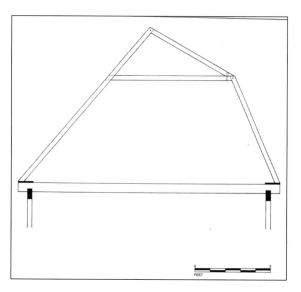

Fig. 12.7. Section through the roof frame of Marlborough, King and Queen County, Virginia, 1805. This odd roof has a gambrel form on the front and is gabled on the rear. A board false plate is used, simplifying the eaves condition to make installation of a classical cornice easier.

cost-savings measure. Eventually in later phases of the frame's development, this connection was reduced to a simple, nailed, butt joint on a thin board (figs. 12.6 and 12.7). As common rafter roofs became more universal, all tenon joints could be eliminated between rafters and joists.[24]

For these early buildings with their simplified structural system, distinctions were made between framing considered load bearing and those pieces simply designed to receive the building's skin. Few connections were more complicated than lap or tenon joints, and even those were reduced to lap joints wherever possible to engage available labor most efficiently. A lap rebate is made by two saw cuts with the intervening wood knocked away by a few well-aimed blows of a hammer and chisel. On the other hand, mortises were more time consuming to prepare, relying on precise and extensive chisel work. Likewise, the lap in a corresponding member is more easily produced and need not be as accurately fashioned as a tenon.

Lap joinery works for members primarily in tension—the joints help keep parts from spreading. But

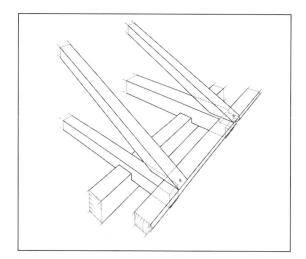

Fig. 12.6. Eaves detail of the Peyton Randolph House, Williamsburg, Virginia, 1715–18. As a transitional type, this false plate was beveled to accommodate a crown molding on a recently introduced feature, the classical cornice.

in compression, the tendency is for a lap joint to open and fail. Thus, builders of English frame structures used tenons to join *primary* structural elements loaded in compression while *secondary* members were treated more superficially. Posts were designed to take the weight of the roof, and as such, were tenoned top and bottom. Studs were intended simply to carry the siding and interior finishes, and therefore were bevel-lapped to plates and sills. Builders seemed uncertain how to categorize common rafters in both trussed and non-trussed roofs. To what extent are they load bearing and is the load in compression or tension? As a result, rafters are sometimes tenoned, and in other buildings, lapped at their peak. The lengths of common rafters in trussed roofs are supported midway by purlins, while their bases are carried on a thick board false plate. Common joists are bevel-lapped to summers or tie beams, with the structural load they assumed limited to carrying the flooring and the more

superficial common rafters. For the Virginia house, all joints were reduced to laps despite being a more unstable solution, making these frames that much easier and cheaper to fabricate.

The earliest surviving testament to a fully developed early Chesapeake frame is the Third Haven Meetinghouse in Talbot County, Maryland, for which specifications were drawn up in 1682. Like Cedar Park, it was erected on a bay system with large posts, smaller infill studs, simple joinery, and false plates. It has a common rafter roof with rafters spaced on two-and-a-half-foot centers. However, it is boxed framed; that is, it is fully silled, with wood blocks for underpinnings. Significantly, nothing about the form of the meetinghouse frame is foreign to the wooden buildings erected in the region over the next quarter century.[25] Thus, by 1647 documentary reference is made to a recognizable local arrangement, archaeological excavations indicate a preference for sidewall assembly

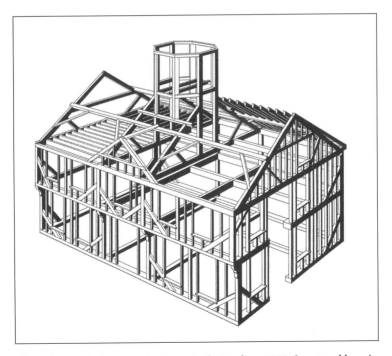

Fig. 12.8. Cupola House, Edenton, North Carolina, 1758. Structural bays in this late colonial house are related to the plan and are not set on regular intervals as before. Note the unusual use of a jettied second floor. Measured by Cary Carson, Carl Lounsbury, and the author.

after 1650, and the area's earliest surviving buildings employ components essential to this Chesapeake framing system. Moreover, the region's oldest extant frame dwellings dating to a few years before and after the turn of the eighteenth century not only express this developed model but also frequently show signs of advancement toward new structural forms.[26] The process of refining and simplifying the structural system proceeded into the industrial era. Continued efforts to simplify and conceal the frame in eighteenth-century structures gradually altered the way carpenters understood the engineering problem they had to solve. Little by little they came to view a timber frame, not as a series of separate bays, but as a fully integrated construction sequence that bore the weight of the house very differently than buildings had in the seventeenth century (fig. 12.8).

The first step toward concealment and refined finishes affected homes of both town and country folks, but in varied ways. Certainly attention to well-finished and regularized treatments of buildings had long been the prerogative of some members of the gentry; one need look no further than Arthur Allen's Bacon's Castle to see extensive brickwork, plastered walls, and molded framing. But for most, including the gentry, it was not until the end of the century that buildings became more than a container of domestic functions or a means of protection from the weather. Architecture was rapidly becoming a means to express class-bound distinctions with one's neighbors.[27] What was desired of buildings in both town and country was a more refined appearance. How they differed was in the nature of their finishes, and this difference affected the framing system of each.[28]

By the 1690s, the notion that the frame should be exposed, consciously expressed, and even decorated extended to all structural and mechanical parts of the building—take brickwork, for example. The ever-more-apparent construction of chimneys on the outside of houses was in part to reflect the owner's status. That a masonry chimney could be built may have been accomplishment enough, yet increasingly it was the focus of elaboration for many houses throughout the region. Brickwork was often decorative, calling attention to its structural makeup by selected glazed headers used to emphasize the bonding pattern. Another obvious illustration of construction expression is the manner in which hardware was finished and displayed. Late-seventeenth- and early-eighteenth-century buildings of a refined nature tended to use highly decorated hinges and locks, thereby accentuating these rather functional items. Foliated H hinges were filed to a bright polish and decorated with chamfered edges and stops. Decoration in this era highlighted the functional nature of the constituent elements, and this decoration extended to the frame.[29]

In rural areas, building frames continued to be articulated and this treatment was used to great advantage in defining the architectural embellishment of these early dwellings. The interior of the frame was prominently displayed and often molded, thereby attesting to the building's solidity. Furthermore, the structure was used to indicate the level of importance of the space it enframed. For instance, the Matthew Jones House was built as a hall-and-chamber earthfast dwelling with posts set on ten-foot bays (fig. 12.9). The posts, plates, and joists were decorated, with plaster filling the space in between the principal uprights on lighter, bevel-lapped studs. The ceiling joists in the

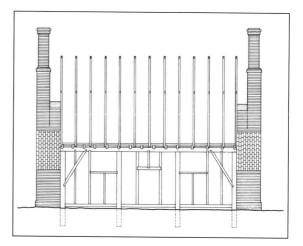

Fig. 12.9. Reconstructed view of the Matthew Jones House, Newport News, Virginia, c. 1720. Except for brick chimneys, this dwelling has all the characteristics of the Virginia house—earthfast posts, heavy false plate, common rafter roof—and it was covered in riven clapboards.

smallest room were planed, chamfered, and set on two-and-a-half-foot centers. In contrast, those in the hall were more tightly arranged and molded with cymas and lamb's tongue stops, reflecting the more important nature of this room.[30] On the outside, the frame was covered in clapboards, except the eaves. Although the roof frame was largely hidden on the exterior, on close inspection its structural system was still evident. A view of the eaves revealed that a common rafter roof was carried on a tilted false plate with oversailing rafter feet, while accompanying curved joist ends articulated the wall at cornice level.[31] An extraordinary example of a similar eaves condition survives in a pre-1727 wing at Sotterley in which the bottom edges of its tilted false plate and rounded joist ends have been chamfered and given beveled stops, again highlighting these structural components.

Country builders were slower to accept all aspects of the second phase of framing development that featured a concealed frame and Georgian detailing. Articulated frames remained common in the countryside as can be seen at Pear Valley and Belle Air (c. 1725–50) in Virginia and Portland Manor (1754–55) and the farmhouse at Hampton (1746) in Maryland.[32] Yet none of these buildings could be mistaken for their seventeenth-century counterparts. Since all have sills and proper masonry foundations, placement of posts could break the prescribed eight- or ten-foot module and did so. At Pear Valley and Hampton they are used for corners and doorways, but nowhere else. The builder of Belle Air employed them to decoratively flank all openings (fig. 12.10). Posts are spaced at Portland Manor so as to be hidden in closets or nestled against partitions to reduce their visibility and it is simply the principal roof and summer beams that remain consciously exposed. Georgian features were accepted to varying degrees. All four structures received sash windows, and some, like Portland Manor and Hampton, even utilized a boxed cornice. At Hampton, the frame was decorated, not with integral moldings as before, but with superficially applied trim, another concession to Georgian sensibilities. Many of these structures included tilted false plates as a decorative device, further indicating that expression of structural components was still a desirable alternative as late as

mid-century outside the region's few towns. It is this blending of more traditional elements with classical components that characterizes rural structures early in this second phase.

Georgian detailing affected all parts of the building; however, it did take nearly fifty years for typical dwellings of the gentry to appropriate most elements commonly associated with this new style. Locally, these factors include beaded weatherboard siding, boxed eaves, shingled roofs, wainscoted interiors with plaster walls and ceilings, raised-panel doors, sash windows with wood muntins, brickwork unified in color, less-decorative hardware intended to be largely hidden from view, and a completely concealed frame. After 1750 the constructional aspect of raised paneling was also seen as antiquated and was therefore often omitted in favor of "modern wainscot" (flush-board paneling) or plaster walls covered in wallpaper.[33]

With growing frequency after 1700, those who aspired to a new house expected the same as was directed for a glebe house near Williamsburg in which "all ye: fframe to be sawn & fframed flush, as ye new way of Building is."[34] Although occasionally used in rural houses, this new penchant for diminishing the

Fig. 12.10. Interior view of Belle Air, Charles City County, Virginia, during its restoration. Posts and plates are exposed in the room, but unlike seventeenth-century framing, the articulated posts flank openings instead of being set on regular eight- or ten-foot intervals. Colonial Williamsburg Foundation photograph, 1954.

visibility of the frame was at first largely an urban phenomenon. Now the building's frame was not intended to be celebrated; it simply became the skeleton on which modern finishes were to hang (fig. 12.11). In 1694–95, the builder of the Nelson-Galt House in Williamsburg worked out a framing plan in a sophisticated manner considering its early date, that is, with braced corner and door posts, but without structural bays defined by articulated posts. Moreover, the posts that did remain have been made to fit within the plane of the wall, being reduced from, say, ten inches square to five inches thick, and the studs were increased to the same depth. Plaster was intended to hide the first-story wall frame, and by the 1710s, both the walls and ceiling were so treated. Not all aspects of the new refinements were included in the initial design. The building used a heavy board false plate with rafters set flat, wall plates still projected into the rooms, and the ceiling joists may have been intended to be exposed, as indicated by their roughly chamfered corners and planed bottom surfaces. Riven clapboards, ranging from three to fifteen inches in exposure, protected the exterior of the house, while the rafters, collars, and clapboard roof sheathing remained open to view on the interior until the 1710s remodeling. This building had not taken on the full array of refinements that characterized the coming Georgian period, yet

Fig. 12.11. Second phase of the John Blair House, Williamsburg, Virginia, 1722. All framing has been hidden within a skin of plaster as was typical for urban buildings early in the eighteenth century.

significant progress had been made by containing the frame within the plane of the interior wall finish.[35] Other builders wrestled with similar compromises since they, too, had to erect a competent frame while attempting to hide the structural parts within a skin of plaster and paneling. A group of buildings from Annapolis and Williamsburg dating from the 1710s and 1720s reflect this new desire to accommodate their posts and ceiling frame within a plaster surface, but the plates were still large and projected into the room, since builders did not yet trust the dimensions of a slimmed-down plate the width of wall framing to carry the weight of the roof. In addition to concealing the frame, these buildings were covered with more classical finish elements and began to look like standard dwellings of the late colonial period.[36]

An early, successful attempt to conceal the frame was accomplished in William Robertson's 1715–18 dwelling in Williamsburg, today known as the Peyton Randolph House. Robertson resolved problems associated with hiding the frame of his new dwelling by accepting a lighter plate and, like the builder of the Nelson-Galt House (which Robertson also owned), fabricating its studs and posts to an unusual depth of five inches. Here, posts were not omitted; three structural bays defined each wall of the square-plan house. The posts simply were not intended to be visible and bore no relationship to internal partitioning. Once plaster and paneling were applied to the walls and ceilings, the frame was completely hidden. A shingle roof, sash windows, modillion cornice and beaded weatherboard siding made this truly a building of the modern era.[37]

This second phase in the Chesapeake framing sequence had three major components: the standardization of parts, the reduction in the size of structural members, and the elimination of structural bays (fig. 12.12). In place of bays, reliance was made on the entirety of the walls below eaves level for load-bearing purposes. Since studs were no longer structurally superficial but had assumed a load-bearing role, tenons replaced the simpler bevel-lap connections used in early frame buildings. As such, bevel-lap joints for vertical members were relegated to residual status and were only used in upper gables where studs were not load-bearing (roof trusses not needing studs for support), for crippled studs over openings, and for secondary partitions. The subtle shift from bearing on posts to placing whole walls under load had the added advantage of streamlining the process of laying out the joints. Tenons were precut for posts and studs alike at regular intervals, by this time placed every two feet, regardless of the building's fenestration pattern or location of internal partitions. Given the acceptance of the concealed frame, carpenters eventually concluded that the thickness of all members within the wall—studs, posts, braces, and plates—could be standardized to about four inches. In the battle between which bay module would predominate-two or two and a half feet—it ultimately did not matter. Whereas four- and five-foot clapboards required a specific spacing, houses covered in shingles using sawn boards for sheathing, and weatherboards that could be cut to any desired length had no such constraint. The two-foot stud interval won out as a standard and provided for a more solid frame. Occasionally a mortise was left empty because the pre-established spacing was inconvenient (for instance, a window might be installed that did not correspond to the prescribed interval), but this lost effort was offset by the ease with which the joints could be laid out and precut. Paired tenons in the sills and plates were easily marked and fashioned without having to think of all consequences in advance. Thus, the more developed eighteenth-century structure was characterized by lighter framing, a common thickness for framing members in a given plane, regularity to spacing of all structural elements, and similar joinery for studs, braces and posts. Posts were limited to corners, doorways, and occasionally to the intersection of partitions or the midpoint of a long wall. By the third quarter of the eighteenth century, well-built structures in and out of town had adopted most of these traits.[38]

As the eighteenth century progressed, the frame underwent several other improvements. In 1799, corner posts for the John Steele House in Rowan County, North Carolina were specified "to be hewed nine Inches Square guttored."[39] Guttered corner posts (ones cut to an L-shaped profile) were introduced in the 1750s, were commonly found in the 1780s, and were

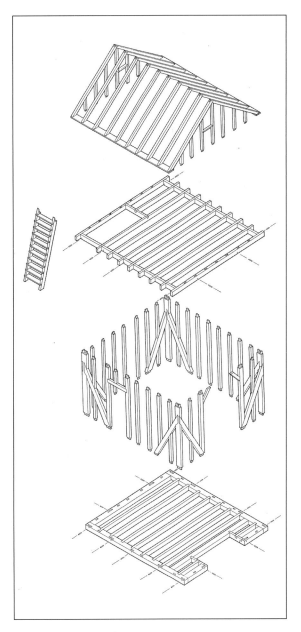

Fig. 12.12. Cibula Slave House, Prince George County, Virginia, c. 1820. The structure of this building has all the features of the traditional Chesapeake frame as it had matured in the nineteenth century. The frame has been streamlined, bay posts have been omitted, and studs act as load-bearing members. Members in compression are joined with tenon joints. A board false plate remains the predominant method for carrying the rafter feet. Measured by Edward Chappell, Jeffery Bostetter, and the author. Drawing by Jeffery Bostetter.

used in some well-built structures into the early nine-teenth century. They not only helped contain the frame within plaster walls—plaster lath could neatly fit in the corner of the L without a nailer scabbed onto the side of the post—but they were also a recognition that the end walls were now under load.[40] Time took a toll on many traditional framing elements, though. Tilted false plates with over-sailing rafter feet and rounded joist ends did not easily accommodate classi-cal cornices and thus thin, flat board plates became universal in common-rafter construction.[41] Guttered posts were labor-intensive to produce and their use waned in the early nineteenth century. Board false plates, however, were an inexpensive and successful solution to structuring eaves conditions. They re-mained popular into the third quarter of the nine-teenth century and were used in more traditional structures well into the twentieth century.[42]

The final phase of the traditional Chesapeake frame's development is characterized by a reduction in complexity of many connections and the wide accep-tance of milled lumber. Traditional pit sawing of tim-bers held on in the Chesapeake much longer than in the North, but could not keep up with the fast-paced growth of towns. Thus, by 1800 sawmills played a major role supplying stock for the ever-growing fall-line cities, and by 1820, it had become the standard method for material production in the countryside as well. For carpenters, mill-sawn timbers added a level of precision that made production of building parts eas-ier. As cross-sectional dimensions of framing members were regularized, joinery could be more efficiently pro-duced. No special adjustment was needed for applica-tion of trim and finishes, with the greatest benefit seen in fitting of floorboards. Gauging and undercutting of flooring (a time consuming method of laying boards

with a flat top surface) was no longer necessary since the thickness was easier to regulate when mill cut. Mortises had by this time long been the standard for studs, but still had been relatively labor intensive to fabricate. With the wide acceptance of the screw-tip bit after 1800, mortises were no longer cut only with chis-els. Instead, large amounts of wood were removed by the use of this bit, thereby minimizing production time for such joints. Increasingly, butt joinery was em-ployed in superficial locations such as partitions, studs over openings, and for closet framing. Carpenters in the second quarter of the nineteenth century realized that ridge boards could replace bridle joints at the peak of common rafter roofs, a lesson learned from late colonial trusses in which such a system was routinely accepted for common pairs between the principals. By the middle of the century, even the ridge board was often eliminated and the rafter pairs were simply butted and nailed to each other.[43]

On the eve of the Civil War—and for those in the Chesapeake, the eve of acceptance of mass-produced building parts—the joined frame had been stripped to its essential components. An efficient system resulted that treated virtually all structural members as pri-mary elements, but with the frame entirely hidden within the finished wall surfaces. By standardizing member sizes and minimizing joinery, many funda-mental features of balloon frame construction were adopted that formed the basis for the system that came to dominate the region in the latter half of the nineteenth century. Thus, this antebellum model of load-bearing walls and hidden structure contrasted dramatically with the articulated frame and its two-tiered structural ordering of the seventeenth century that Carson and his colleagues recognized as quintes-sentially Chesapeake in inspiration.

Notes

1. For a broader understanding of the prevailing litera-ture on early Chesapeake framing technology, see Fraser D. Neiman, "Domestic Architecture at the Clifts Plantation: The Social Context of Virginia Building," *Northern Neck Historical Magazine* 28, no. 1 (1978): 3096–3128; Cary Carson, Norman F. Barka, William M. Kelso, Garry Wheeler Stone, and Dell Upton, "Impermanent Architecture in the Southern Colonies," *Winterthur Portfolio* 16, nos. 2/3 (Summer/Autumn 1981): 135–96; Dell Upton, "Tradition-al Timber Framing," in *Material Culture of the Wooden Age,* ed. Brooke Hindle (Tarrytown, N.Y.: Sleepy Hollow Press, 1981), 35–61; Gary Wheeler Stone, "Society, Housing, and Architecture in Early Maryland: John Lewger's St. John's" (Ph.D. diss., Univ. of Pennsylvania, 1982). Note that

Herman J. Heikkenen of Dendrochronology, Inc., has derived all dendrochronological dates in this essay. I am indebted to my colleagues Mark R. Wenger, Orlando Ridout V, Carl Lounsbury, Cary Carson, Edward Chappell, Gary Stanton, and Garry Stone for their insights into this essay. To Lawrence McLaughlin I owe my gratitude for editorial assistance.

2. Dell Upton, *Holy Things and Profane: Anglican Parish Churches in Colonial Virginia* (Cambridge: MIT Press, 1986), 60. Although Upton suggests 1700 as the date by which a local framing tradition had developed, Stone has broken down the evolution into four stages that he calls substitution and selection (c. 1607–50), evolution (c. 1650–75), refinement (c. 1675–1725), and readjustment (c. 1725–50). He argues that a specialized form developed during the evolutionary stage. See Stone, "Society, Housing, and Architecture," 231–32.

3. Upton, "Traditional Timber Framing," 59–61.

4. Dennis B. Blanton, "The Weather Is Fine, Wish You Were Here, Because I Am the Last One Alive: 'Learning' the Environment in the English New World Colonies" (paper presented at the Society for American Archaeology, Philadelphia, Apr. 9, 2000); Cary Carson and Lorena S. Walsh, "The Material Life of the Early American Housewife" (paper presented at the Conference on Women in Early America, Williamsburg, Va., Nov. 5–7, 1981); Allan Kulikoff, *Tobacco and Slaves: The Development of Southern Cultures in the Chesapeake, 1680–1800* (Chapel Hill: Univ. of North Carolina Press, 1986), 4–10, 31–37; Upton, "Traditional Timber Framing," 38–44, 51–61.

5. For a description of elements that make up traditional Chesapeake frames, see Dell Upton, "Early Vernacular Architecture in Southeastern Virginia" (Ph.D. diss., Brown Univ., 1979), 65–113.

6. Cary Carson, "The 'Virginia House' in Maryland," *Maryland Historical Magazine* 69, no. 2 (1974): 185–96; Upton, "Traditional Timber Framing," 64–65.

7. A more thorough description of Cedar Park can be found in Carson et al., "Impermanent Architecture in the Southern Colonies," 145, 187–89. Trees were felled for construction of Cedar Park at the end of the growing season of 1702. This date was derived by dendrochronology.

8. For example, a reused timber fashioned to support sagging joists in the Mason House, Accomack County, Virginia, is inscribed with the date 1732. It was first fabricated for a building that had been raised using bent construction

and one with more complex joinery than is typical for this region. A few attempts were made in the eighteenth century to construct clasp-purlin roofs, the known examples being an attached dependency at Westover (early eighteenth century), Charles City County, Virginia, Sudley (c. 1725–50), Anne Arundel County, Maryland, and Pear Valley (dendro date 1740–41), Northampton County, Virginia. Kneed principals are another minor variant roof form and were used at Bruton Parish Church (dendro date 1709–14), Williamsburg, Merchant's Hope Church (c. 1720), Prince George County, Virginia, Cloverfields (c. 1730), Queen Anne County, Maryland, and Sweet Hall (c. 1730), King William County, Virginia. Morgan Hill, an early-eighteenth-century frame house in Calvert County, Maryland, was built with a common rafter roof but without a false plate. Instead, the rafters are tenoned and pinned to the joists.

9. James Deetz, *Flowerdew Hundred: The Archaeology of a Virginia Plantation, 1619–1864* (Charlottesville: Univ. Press of Virginia, 1993), 35–38. Norman Barka excavated this building in Prince George County in 1972–78 for Southside Historical Sites.

10. Nicholas Luccketti, "The Road to James Fort," in *Jamestown Rediscovery V*, ed. William M. Kelso, Nicholas M. Luccketti, and Beverly A. Straube (Richmond: Association for the Preservation of Virginia Antiquities, 1999), 21–33.

11. Terminology of the period makes distinctions between various levels of building practices, cabins being the meanest of the group. This term refers to unjoined and uncarpentered structures. Puncheon construction is a type of cabin construction. The other levels in ascending order of refinement include the Virginia house (or Virginia frame), English frame, and brick.

12. Alain Outlaw and Amy Friedlander excavated Compton for Louis Berger and Associates in 1988. See Cultural Resource Group, "The Compton Site circa 1651–1684 Calvert County, Maryland 18CV279," MS report, Louis Berger and Associates, East Orange, N.J., 1989. Patuxent Point was excavated by Julia King for the Jefferson Patterson Park and Museum in 1989–90. See Julia A. King and Douglas H. Ubelaker, eds., *Living and Dying on the 17th Century Frontier* (Crownsville: Maryland Historical Trust, 1996), 15–27.

13. Thomas Cornwaleys to Lord Baltimore, 16 Apr. 1638, *The Calvert Papers, Number One,* Fund Publication No. 28 (Baltimore: Maryland Historical Society, 1889), 1:174, quoted in Stone, "Society, Housing and Architecture," 153.

14. Richard Beale Davis, ed., *William Fitzhugh and His Chesapeake World, 1676–1701* (Chapel Hill: Univ. of North Carolina Press, 1963), 202.

15. Upton, "Early Vernacular Architecture," 113; Stone, "Society, Housing and Architecture," 230–99.

16. *Statutes at Large, Being a Collection of All Laws of Virginia, from the First Session of the Legislature in the Year 1619,* ed. William Waller Hening (New York: for the editor, 1819–23), 1:340. Several counties did not comply with this order, and thus in 1662 it was again enacted that "a good strong prison built after the forme of Virginia houses be built within eight months." *Statutes at Large* 2:76–77.

17. Middlesex County, Virginia, Deed Book 1687–1750.

18. Stone, "Society, Housing and Architecture," 230–33.

19. Essex County, Virginia, Court Order Book 1726–1729.

20. Stone and others have argued that creation of a bay system and employment of a false plate resulted from an outgrowth of tobacco barn construction. Certainly there is an association between the two: the four- or five-foot "rooms" in a tobacco barn are linked both to the length of riven sticks on which the tobacco hung and to clapboards that covered the buildings. However, creation of the Virginia house framing system may have developed before substantial tobacco barns became commonplace. Most likely the two systems developed simultaneously, the Virginia house becoming an efficient solution for all types of framing needs in the region. See Stone, "Society, Housing and Architecture," 233–36.

21. Middlesex County, Virginia, Court Records, 1673.

22. Charles County Court and Land Records H, no. 1, folio 139, Maryland Hall of Records, Annapolis. Another early example is described in a 1684 promotional pamphlet encouraging settlement in Pennsylvania in which instructions were given on how to build what was clearly a Virginia house, specifying "two false Plates of thirty foot long" in its fabrication. "Information and Direction to Such Persons as Are Inclined to America, More Especially Those Related to the Province of Pennsylvania," *Pennsylvania Magazine of History and Biography* 4 (1880): 334, quoted in Upton, "Traditional Timber Framing," 52.

23. The date for Bacon's Castle was derived by dendrochronology.

24. Thick, board false plates are used in the earliest buildings of the region, including Bacon's Castle; the Third Haven Meetinghouse (1682) in Talbot County, Maryland;

the Nelson-Galt House (dendro date 1694–95); Cedar Park; and the first period at Sotterley. This latter example utilizes a particularly thick plate with beveled cuts on the top face to receive the foot of rafters and foreshadows the tilted false plate. The first recorded tilted false plate is used at Sarum in Charles County, Maryland (dendro date 1717). Tilted false plates are also found at Lynhaven House in Virginia Beach (dendro date 1724–25) and phase II at Sotterley (c. 1725). See Garry Wheeler Stone and Herman J. Heikkenen, "A Horizon in Chesapeake Architecture: The Evidence of Dendrochronology and the Tilted False Plate" (paper presented at the annual meeting of the Society for Historical Archaeology, Savannah, Ga., Jan. 10, 1987).

25. Orlando Ridout V, "An Architectural History of Third Haven Meetinghouse," in *Three-Hundred Years of Third Haven Quakerism,* ed. Kenneth L. Carroll (Easten, Md.: Queen Anne Press, 1984), 67–87. Although specifications call for "strong, substantial framed work with good white oak ground sills and posts, double studded and well braced, with girders and summers and small joists, the roof to be double raftered and good principal rafters," the instructions were not entirely followed. It has been debated as to whether the present common rafter roof is original. Observations made by Ridout suggest that the roof exhibits signs of having been altered where it had to be infilled in the eighteenth century, when its original rear wing was demolished. Thus, what remains is likely largely from initial construction. Third Haven Meetinghouse Minute Book, 1676–1746, Maryland State Archives, Annapolis.

26. The Nelson-Galt House, as an example, has a hidden frame, representing this next phase of development.

27. Cary Carson, "The Consumer Revolution in Colonial British America: Why Demand?" in *Of Consuming Interests: The Styles of Life in the Eighteenth Century,* ed. Cary Carson, Ronald Hoffman, and Peter J. Albert (Charlottesville: Univ. Press of Virginia, 1994), 483–697.

28. Upton, "Traditional Timber Framing," 60.

29. Constructional elements of these early buildings are molded instead of finished with applied trim. Likewise, hardware from this period is decorated on functional surfaces, in contrast to brass HL hinges of the late colonial period, for instance, in which *artificial* brass legs snap onto functional iron hinges and simply exist for decoration.

30. See Edward Chappell, "Looking at Buildings," in *Fresh Advises* (Williamsburg, Va.: Colonial Williamsburg

Foundation, 1984), i–vi, for discussion of trim and moldings used to create hierarchical room distinctions in Tidewater houses.

31. Portions of the original frame of the Matthew Jones House are buried within the present brick walls, a remodeling that has been dated by dendrochronology to 1729. Colonial Williamsburg archaeologists Merideth Moodey and Jennifer Jones revealed that the original building had earthfast posts. Scarring on the ends of the few remaining attic joists indicates that the roof originally consisted of common rafters carried by a false plate. The false plates had been pinned in place, limiting the member type to a heavy board or tilted plate. Rounded joist ends—usually associated with tilted false plates—suggests it was used here. Willie Graham, William J. Davis, Donald W. Linebaugh, Leslie McFaden, and Vanessa Patrick, "A Preservation Plan for the Matthew Jones House, Fort Eustis, Virginia," MS report, William and Mary Center for Archaeological Research, Williamsburg, Va., 1991.

32. The dates for Portland Manor and Hampton Farmhouse were derived by dendrochronology. A few examples of decorated wall framing and molded collars can be found in the early nineteenth century. The c. 1805 secondary dwelling at Fairfield, Hanover County, Virginia, was built with posts projecting from plaster walls. The Maynard-Burgess House (dendro date 1793) on Duke of Gloucester Street, Annapolis, is another late example, but seems initially to have served as a storehouse, and as such, a more conservative framing system could be expected. In Surry County, Virginia, the James House (1811) and the c. 1825 remodeling of the Enos House both display exposed, beaded collars covered with planed flooring. More common to see in rural nineteenth-century houses are beaded ceiling joists without other exposed framing, as can be found at the Bryant DeLoatche House (c. 1810) in Southampton County, Virginia, and the 1810s wing of the Coke-Garret House in Williamsburg. Once the capitol moved to Richmond and the intensity of urban development shifted to the fall-line towns, Williamsburg took on a more conservative, rural character, as expressed by this framing detail.

33. Margaret Beck Pritchard and Willie Graham, "Rethinking Two Houses at Colonial Williamsburg," *Magazine Antiques* 149 (Jan. 1996): 166–75.

34. C. G. Chamberlayne, ed., *Vestry Book and Register of St. Peter's Parish New Kent and James City Counties, Virginia*

1684–1786 (Richmond: Division of Purchase and Printing, 1937), 129 [1708], quoted in Upton, "Traditional Timber Framing," 60.

35. Mark R. Wenger, "Nelson-Galt House," memo to files, Colonial Williamsburg Foundation, Williamsburg, Va., Apr. 20, 1998.

36. Dwellings with plates projecting beyond the plane of the wall include the Brush-Everard House (dendro-date 1718) and the Timson House (dendro date 1714–15), both in Williamsburg, Virginia, and the Sands House (c. 1725) and Charles Carroll, Barrister House (c. 1725) in Annapolis. Note that a few posts in both Annapolis houses also break the plane of the plaster walls.

37. Although it took more than thirty years for finishes to be applied to all interior surfaces, the Peyton Randolph House was set up from the start to receive wall and ceiling finishes. Houses are frequently left in a partially finished state for years, as is evident in many extant Williamsburg dwellings built during the first decades of the town's founding. Willie Graham and Mark R. Wenger, "A House Befitting Mr. Attorney," *Colonial Williamsburg Interpreter* 20, no. 3 (Special Edition 1999): 19–24. The dates for various periods of construction for the Peyton Randolph House have been derived by dendrochronology.

38. Often empty mortises are found on top of sills with corresponding ones on the undersides of plates that have never been utilized, indicating that they are simply cut as part of a routine. They are abandoned when original features such as windows or stairs get in the way of these mortises. A good example is the c. 1840 granary at Sabine Hall in Richmond County, Virginia.

39. John Steele Papers, Southern Historical Collection, Chapel Hill, North Carolina.

40. The earliest known use of guttered corner posts are in the 1754–55 (dendro date) extension of the Peyton Randolph House where the leg of the L is modest, projecting a slight 1½". George Washington employed them in his two-story library extension at Mount Vernon in 1775. By the 1780s they became commonplace in the region, the member by this time usually containing a tenon at the ends of each leg of the L to join it to the gable and sidewall sills, plates, and upper joists. Guttered posts are rarely seen in the Chesapeake after the 1810s.

41. As with many eighteenth-century advancements in framing, adopting thin, board false plates seemed to take

place first in towns. Contemporary with the introduction of tilted false plates, builders of Williamsburg structures were experimenting with false plates that would easily accommodate classical cornices. William Robertson's new dwelling, the Peyton Randolph House, still used a thick board plate, but beveled its outer face and cantilevered it sufficiently to seat the crown molding of its exterior, modillion cornice. Bruton Parish Church is the earliest structure known to have used a conventional, thin board false plate. Integrated with a principal rafter roof with kneed principals at each gable end, the board was simply used to carry the feet of the common rafters, the weight of the main roof having been transferred to principal rafters by the purlins. The Timson House is the first structure recorded using a thin false plate in conjunction with a common rafter roof. By the time John Brush built his house in 1718, flat board false plates were ubiquitous in Williamsburg. Based on surviving buildings, after this date there is little evidence in Williamsburg save one reused tilted false plate in the 1769–70 tower of Bruton Church for anything other than thin board plates.

42. The J. O. James House in Petersburg, Virginia, dating to 1893, is largely a balloon framed structure that incorporates a false plate in its common rafter roof. Nearby at 303 West Washington Street is a framed garage dating to 1915 that is made with similar roof details.

43. Ridge boards are commonly found in late colonial roofs, extending between king or queen post trusses to carry common rafters and for the roofs of secondary pediments. Ridge boards were included in the trussed roofs of Ridout Row in Annapolis (1774–75) and Fielding Lewis's house, Kenmore, in Fredericksburg, Virginia (dendro date 1772). Blandfield (1769–73) in Essex County, Virginia, utilized a ridge board for its front pediment. The earliest recorded use of a ridge board in a common rafter roof is the John Brice III House on Prince George Street, Annapolis, dating to about 1770. However, it is not until the second quarter of the nineteenth century that its use in nontrussed roofs is widespread. Marcia Miller and Orlando Ridout V, eds., *Architecture in Annapolis: A Field Guide* (Crownsville: Maryland Historical Trust Press, 1998), 47–49.

13

IMPERMANENT ARCHITECTURE IN A LESS PERMANENT TOWN

THE MID-SEVENTEENTH-CENTURY ARCHITECTURE OF PROVIDENCE, MARYLAND

JASON D. MOSER, AL LUCKENBACH, SHERRI M. MARSH, AND DONNA WARE

Introduction

During the seventeenth and eighteenth centuries, a number of town sites developed in the Chesapeake Tidewater of Maryland and Virginia only to ultimately disappear from the landscape. They are "lost towns," not in the sense that people have forgotten where they were, but because little if any of the architecture that defined them survives above ground. Much of what might have been learned about building traditions, town planning, and town life disappeared with their physical structures.

On the Western Shore of the Chesapeake Bay, a long list of once-familiar names, like Calverton, Herrington, Providence, and London Town, have not only now been forgotten but also have left little trace in the documentary records. Those Maryland town sites for which plat maps survive are few and lie principally along the Eastern Shore.[1] Virtually nothing survived of the early housing stock that once defined these port towns.

Over the last decade, Anne Arundel County's Lost Towns Project, an archaeological and historical research program in Anne Arundel County, Maryland, has uncovered the remains of impermanent, or earthfast, buildings in the "lost town" of Providence (1649– c. 1680s) (map 13.1). Neither "impermanent" nor "earthfast" hints at the variability exhibited by this once-common technology. This chapter presents a number of architectural findings from Providence, examining the archaeological evidence within the contexts of current understandings of earthfast buildings and the town of which they were a part. Analysis of historic documents, archaeological floor plans and architectural artifacts suggest urban ambitions, as well

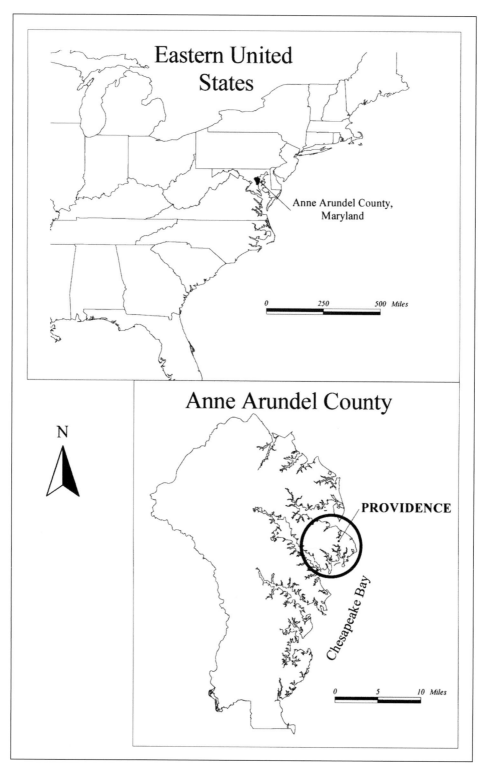

Map 13.1. Providence, Anne Arundel County, Maryland, USA. Courtesy of Anne Arundel County, Maryland, the Lost Towns Project.

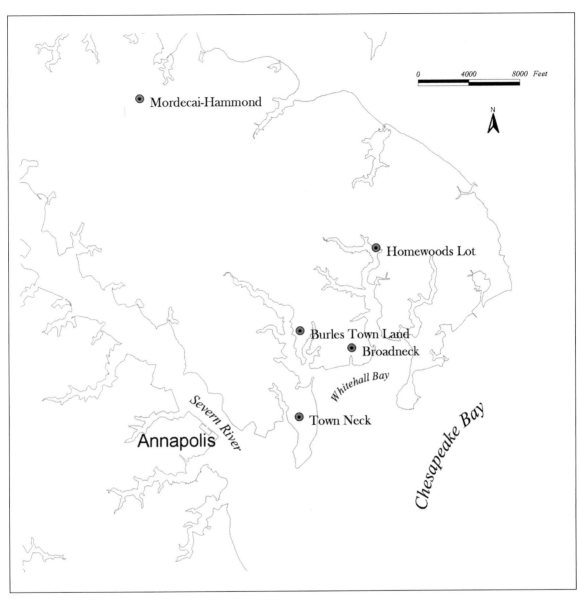

Map 13.2. General archaeological site locations for portions of Providence. Courtesy of Anne Arundel County, Maryland, the Lost Towns Project.

as local solutions to the technical and aesthetic considerations of housing in towns, real or envisioned.

Excavations conducted at four sites within the town of Providence provide the data for this analysis. Additional, supporting data will be drawn from a fifth house site located within the original bounds of Providence but postdating the primary occupation of the town by nearly forty years (map 13.2). This site not only provides additional information but also demonstrates the possible persistence of local seventeenth-century vernacular building traditions into the first decades of the eighteenth century.

Methods in Earthfast Construction

Earthfast construction refers to a variety of related building techniques in which the lower framing members lie directly on the ground or are supported by earth-set wooden posts.[2] In the seventeenth century these construction techniques arrived on the shores of the southern colonies, most likely adapted from a much earlier English building tradition.[3] Used throughout the colonial period, the popularity, or desirability, of earthfast construction started to wane in the eighteenth century. Chesapeake carpenters continued building earthfast structures until the end of the Civil War, but later examples are limited almost exclusively to barns and outbuildings.[4]

Architectural study of colonial buildings in the Chesapeake has shown that more expensive traditional frame and brick buildings were not erected in significant numbers until the second quarter of the eighteenth century,[5] although at least two late-seventeenth-century traditionally framed buildings, the Sands House and Holly Hill, still survive in Anne Arundel County, Maryland.[6] Historians explain this late appearance of conventional framed buildings in the Chesapeake as a result of labor-intensive tobacco farming combined with the short life expectancy of early Chesapeake immigrants.[7] Agricultural diversification by planters in the 1720s and 1730s and shifts in the composition of the Chesapeake population resulted in the formation of a demographically stable society. With increased social stability also came a higher standard of living, and with this, more durable construction methods and materials.[8]

Many earthfast buildings employed a false-plate roofing system structurally independent of the wall frame. This separation of roof and wall systems accommodated differential settling and wracking common in earthfast structures.[9] Other research has shown that riven clapboards covered the exteriors, and interior walls often bore plastered lathing. Fenestration included leaded casement windows, although other types of windows undoubtedly were used. Brick chimneys were a rarity: wattle-and-daub exterior end chimneys with brick hearths generally served the purpose. Floors were earth, wood, or—in a few instances—tile, with partial earthen cellars typically constructed beneath the wooden floors.

Compared with traditional English box framing and masonry, earthfast construction used a light, simplified structural system, requiring less-skilled labor and coarser materials. Consequently, earthfast construction was more economical than other construction techniques. The resulting product, however, was considerably inferior and less permanent than other construction methods used at the time. Generally, the average life-span of an earthfast building was about twenty-five years, barring extraordinary maintenance.[10] "Earthfast" applies to a variety of coexistent building methods more related in purpose (ease and economy of construction) than in structural similarity. Post-in-the-ground, or framed hole-set, buildings dominated this building tradition and consisted of three subtypes defined by how and in what order the posts were erected.

Most earthfast structures uncovered by archaeologists are framed hole-set, where posts were set two to four feet into the ground. Builders raised hole-set buildings as preconstructed sidewall units, as paired posts, or bents, and as individual posts. Each of these methods leaves a distinctive archaeological footprint. Sidewall construction employed parallel lines of two or more postholes, the long axes of the holes perpendicular to the long axis of the building and the molds from the timber posts set against the inside edges of the holes. In profile, the postholes ordinarily are stepped, the deepest part of the hole located closest to the building. The long axes of postholes for bent-raised structures parallel the building's long axis, and the deepest parts of the stepped holes tend to be located at the same end of each hole, suggesting bent-raising from one direction. In "Impermanent Architecture in the Southern Colonies," Carson et al. have suggested that independent post construction was the least sound and least common building technique. Such structures are readily identified by irregular, nonstepped postholes that may vary in shape and orientation within a single building. Postmold placement within the posthole varies as well.

Sill-on-ground construction constitutes another form of impermanent architecture. Builders rested continuous sills directly on the ground or embedded them in shallow trenches, tenoning the principal members and intermediate studs into the sills.[11] Although vulnerable to decay, sill-on-ground structures repaired easily, particularly by using the third earthfast technique: frame-on-block. This method elevated a continuous-sill structure on hole-set blocks. Frame-on-block structures share many similarities with sill-on-ground type buildings, and some frame-on-block buildings may have been attempts to salvage sill-on-ground structures.[12]

Architectural historians have documented only three extant colonial earthfast houses in the Chesapeake region: Cedar Park and Sotterley, both post-in-ground buildings, in southern Maryland, and the Matthew Jones House in Virginia. Each of these structures survived as a result of extensive alteration. Each represents multiple phases of construction and repair that show the adaptability and ironically, the sometimes permanence of impermanent architecture. These three buildings represent only a small fraction of the earthfast buildings that once dominated the Chesapeake region. Most of the colonial Chesapeake's housing stock survives only as patterned stains in the subsoil and scatters of architectural artifacts. Archaeologists commonly encounter these structures on rural sites and, increasingly, on town sites such as Providence, Maryland.[13]

The "Lost Town" of Providence

A small group of Puritans from Virginia founded Providence, or Severn, in 1649, invited to Maryland by Governor William Stone. They settled along the Severn River, near present-day Annapolis. In a context of religious and political strife in the English world, and unsure of their future under the rule of the Catholic proprietor, the Puritans occupied relatively small tracts in close proximity to one another for defense. They initially envisioned Providence as a center for the fur trade and signed treaties to that end with the Susquehannock tribe in 1652.[14] Fur trading proved unsuccessful, however, and the Puritans soon turned to the economic mainstay of the Chesapeake, tobacco production.

Never a town in the modern colloquial sense of the word, Providence nevertheless provided at least some of the social, political, and economic functions of a town.[15] That the Puritans regarded Providence as a town, or at least as a town in the making, is clearly evidenced by their designation of a "Town Path" and "Town Creek" and references to certain properties as "Town Lands."[16] In reality, Providence was little more than what anthropologists would call a "hamlet." A grouping of homes, in this case, arranged around a public center or structure. This form of dispersed settlement is not unique and sounds similar to Lord Baltimore's 1668 description of St. Mary's City, which also used a "town land" system. Writing over three decades after its initial settlement in 1634, Lord Baltimore described St. Mary's City: "The principal place or towne is called St. Maries where the General Assemblies and Provincial court are kept . . . but it can hardly be called a towne, it being in length by the water about five miles and in breadth upward toward the land not above six miles, in all which space, excepting my own house and buildings where in the said courts and public offices are kept, there are not above 30 houses and those at considerable distances from each other. . . ." Providence probably had a somewhat similar, dispersed appearance. A small hamlet comprised of a meetinghouse and several dozen widely dispersed houselots on small plantations, averaging from five to fifty acres.

Relations between the Protestant Providence settlers and the Catholic proprietor soured quickly, and open hostilities culminated in the Battle of the Severn on March 25, 1655. The resulting battle was an overwhelming victory by the Providence forces, wresting power from Lord Baltimore's Maryland government. The Puritans maintained control of the government until 1657, when power was returned to Lord Baltimore. The perceived threat from Lord Baltimore abated; the Puritans rapidly expanded their holdings in Anne Arundel County or moved to new lands in Baltimore County and on the Eastern Shore of the Chesapeake. Providence, town or hamlet, ceased to exist, or, more accurately, a portion of its extent developed into a new locus called "Arundelton" (eventually Anne Arundel Town, and finally Annapolis) on the western bank of the Severn River. By the 1680s the settlement's core on the Broadneck Peninsula began consolidating into large rural tobacco plantations.

Archaeology of Providence

Significant architectural data assembled from test excavations is available for four Providence sites: Broadneck (18AN818), Burle's Town Land (18AN826), Town Neck (18AN944), and Homewood's Lot (18AN871).[17] This chapter discusses these sites, as well as Mordecai Hammond's Addition (18AN943), an early-eighteenth-century site, within Providence proper but postdating the primary occupation (map 13.2).

Broadneck

Excavations in 1991, prior to the construction of a residential subdivision, led to the discovery of the Broadneck site (18AN818), the earliest definitive evidence of European occupation within Anne Arundel County. Located in an abandoned agricultural field, the site occupied a slope at the head of a small cove on Whitehall Bay, an embayment of the Chesapeake. Temporally diagnostic artifacts indicate that the site was occupied for a limited time, beginning around 1650, demonstrably among the earliest Providence sites settled. Few documents from this period of early settlement in the county survive, and intensive archival research has yet to identify the occupant.[18]

Archaeological excavations at the site revealed a cellar, a pit feature, several postholes, puncheon-set posts, and the possible evidence of sills.[19] The most prominent remains, the cellar and the pit feature, were located thirty feet apart, and measured ten by six feet and six by three feet, respectively (fig. 13.1). A group of small puncheon set posts farther up-slope may

demarcate the location of a small outbuilding.[20] Two small, shallow features, devoid of artifacts, were discovered in a line running perpendicular to the main cellar and exactly five feet away from the side of the main cellar. These features were interpreted as evidence for a sill-on-ground constructed building. The location of the pit features within the footprint of the building implies the presence of a wooden floor. Ash and burned daub from the cellar deposits suggests a single wattle-and-daub chimney on the west gable-end of the building. Additionally, large quantities of daub recovered from across the site suggest that the principal building at the Broadneck site may have possessed wattle-and-daub walls or may have been a log structure sealed with clay chinking.

Excavations at the Broadneck site reveal evidence of a number of architectural features used in one of the earliest buildings in the county. However, more illuminating is the lack of certain architectural details. Neither window leads nor window quarrel fragments were recovered, suggesting shuttered windows.[21] In addition, the low numbers of hand-wrought nails recovered supports the theory that the building was of a wattle-and-daub wall construction, possibly with a thatched roof. Evidence of thatched roofs in the Chesapeake is sparse, but examples have been documented.[22] Pegged shingle roofs are also known. The Broadneck site appears to have been a two- or three-room

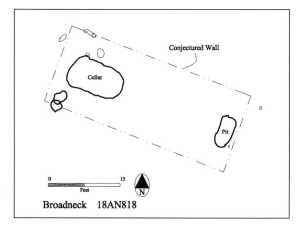

Fig. 13.1. Plan view of features at Broadneck site (18AN818). Courtesy of Anne Arundel County, Maryland, the Lost Towns Project.

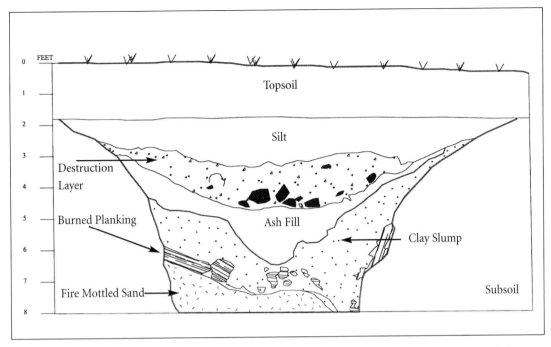

Fig. 13.2. Profile of cellar at Town Neck site (18AN944). Courtesy of Anne Arundel County, Maryland, the Lost Towns Project.

building approximately thirty-six to forty feet in length and sixteen feet in width. Given the evidence of a single gable-end chimney, only one room was heated.

The artifact assemblage from Broadneck indicates that the site was occupied for only a short duration. This structure may relate to the first generation of building activity at Providence. A 1684 pamphlet promoting colonization of Pennsylvania describes a house "30 feet long and 18 feet wide, with one partition near the middle and another to divide one end into two smaller rooms," and one which usually lasted ten years without repair.[23] Referencing to the same pamphlet, Carson et al. (1981) noted that "it is perhaps more likely that the pamphleteer was remembering houses in which the studs, too, were buried in holes or trenches or were fastened to unframed lengths of sill beam laid in slots in the ground." The description approximates the interpretation of the principal structure at Broadneck.[24] The short length of occupation and the relatively crude construction suggest that the Broadneck site buildings date to the ini-

tial phase of settlement at Providence. Structures uncovered at other Providence sites contrast markedly with the architecture at Broadneck.

Town Neck

The Town Neck site (18AN944) was located during sediment trap excavations associated with construction of athletic facilities at the Naval Radio Transmitter Facility on Greenbury Point. Further investigation revealed that the Navy construction crew had cut through a seventeenth-century cellar (fig. 13.2). The site is located on peninsula near the mouth of Carr Creek, a tidal tributary of the Severn River. Salvage excavations were conducted by the Anne Arundel County archaeology program and by KCI Technologies, a private firm under contract to the Department of the Navy.

Richard Bennett and eight other individuals settled portions of this peninsula "for their Mutual Security" between 1649 and 1658.[25] In 1658, Bennett, by this time the sole owner the entire tract deeded the property to Nathaniel Utie, secretary to Governor

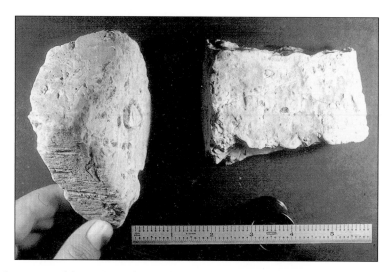

Fig. 13.3. *Dodekop* staining from yellow brick header recovered at Town Neck site (18AN944). Courtesy of Anne Arundel County, Maryland, the Lost Towns Project.

Stone, who patented it as Towne Neck. In November 1661, Utie sold the property to William Pennington, who sold it a month later to Ralph Williams, a Bristol merchant and a magistrate of Anne Arundel County. Williams held the 250-acre Town Neck tract until his death in 1673, after which the property was conveyed to his heirs, then to Edwin Perrin in 1685, and finally transferred to Nicholas Greenbury, who named the property Greenberry's Point. Temporally diagnostic artifacts recovered from the site indicate the property was occupied from at least about 1660 until the 1680s, when the structure was destroyed by fire.

Excavations were limited in scope but provided a great deal of architectural evidence. The most notable feature was a timber-lined cellar or half-cellar (Feature 1), probably twelve by fifteen feet in plan and eight feet in depth (fig. 13.2). In addition to the cellar, several other architectural features were documented, including three postholes and a large refuse pit, interpreted by the excavators as a trash-filled borrow pit.[26] Because of the limited scope of these excavations, the floor plan of the Town Neck structure remains unknown; however, significant information can be derived about the finishing and appurtenances of this building.

Excavators observed more brick at Town Neck than at any other Providence site. Recovered samples included an English-standard sized red brick and three varieties of yellow brick. Quantities of quartzite foundation stones were also noted. Typical seventeenth-century yellow bricks are hard *klinker* varieties imported from the Netherlands. Because of their resistance to high temperature, these bricks typically were used for fireboxes. The three varieties of yellow brick recovered from the Town Neck site also included softer Dutch *moppen* construction brick, and a third, larger type of unknown derivation. A number of examples exhibited evidence of *dodekop* staining, an iron oxide stain applied for decorative effect (fig. 13.3). Joseph Sopko identified similar staining at the Fort Orange site Albany, New York.[27] Sopko suggests that *dodekop* stained brick was used to create decorative brickwork patterns typical of Dutch brickwork or, alternatively, as an attempt to blend yellow bricks with red.[28]

At Town Neck, the combination of red and yellow brick with the building stones probably represents the remains of a substantial and notably decorative brick chimney stack seated on a stone base. The quantity of brick observed during excavations may even have been sufficient to represent the remains of decorative brick gable ends.[29]

Other artifacts recovered from the excavations at Town Neck indicate the use of leaded casemate windows. Two window lead fragments bear the name of the English glazier Frances Good and are dated 1661.[30] Also recovered were a number of yellow and green lead-glazed *estrikken* floor tiles, discussed in more detail below (fig. 13.4). These architectural artifacts suggest that the building displayed a high degree of finished and decorative detail not typically found on most mid-seventeenth-century Chesapeake sites. The builders imported the windows, yellow bricks, and floor tiles from Europe. Based on form and materials, the bricks and the floor tiles are Dutch. As will be discussed, excavations of Robert Burle's residence (c. 1649), another nearby Providence site, Homewood's Lot, and Mordecai Hammond's Addition also reveal the existence of Chesapeake earthfast framing utilizing Dutch imported finishing materials, a housing standard atypical of the Chesapeake building tradition.

Burle's Town Land

Robert Burle, county surveyor, patented one hundred acres called Burle's Town Land in 1663. Although patented late, artifacts recovered from the site support an earlier construction date possibly as early as 1650. He lived there until his death in 1676, leaving the plantation to his youngest daughter, Rebecca. Rebecca

Burle married Humphrey Boone in 1680, and the couple seems to have moved their household to Boone's land in the northern part of Anne Arundel County, effectively abandoning the Burle homelot.

The nature of the archaeological excavations at the Burle site was quite different than that seen at Broadneck and Town Neck. The latter were both limited salvage investigations designed to collect as much information as possible within a narrow time frame. Excavations at the Burle's Town Land site, however, were extensive and systematic, consisting of over 225 five-by-five-foot excavation units conducted over a period of years (fig. 13.5). This sample size provides a context that neither the materials from Broadneck nor Town Neck are capable of providing.

Situated at the head of a small drainage on a terrace overlooking Mill Creek, Burle's Town Land lies partly within a plowed field and partly within an eighteenth- to nineteenth-century family cemetery. Graveshafts have disturbed seventeenth-century deposits, damaging some portions of the principal dwelling.

Fig. 13.4. *Estrikken* tiles recovered at the Town Neck site (18AN944). Courtesy of Anne Arundel County, Maryland, the Lost Towns Project.

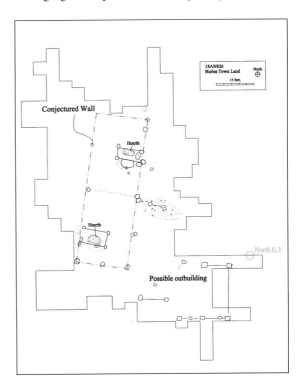

Fig. 13.5. Plan view of excavations at the Burle's Town Land site (18AN826). Courtesy of Anne Arundel County, Maryland, the Lost Towns Project.

However, because the core of the site lies within this cemetery, large areas have escaped plowing. A second building or enclosure, found in the plowed field, escaped damage from grave digging but remains only partially delineated by excavation.

The principal dwelling measured roughly sixty by twenty feet and had three rooms, or possibly six, depending on the interpretation. The structure appears to have consisted of two sections, each an inverted mirror image of the other (fig. 13.5). Both were constructed simultaneously during period one. Each section had an interior wattle-and-daub chimney located along the west and east walls. Gable-end wattle-and-daub chimneys would have been more typical of seventeenth-century Chesapeake architecture. Dutch yellow *klinker* bricks were used to complete the firebox. The vertical support posts were likely raised in pairs using bent construction, and tied into an interrupted sill. The exterior most likely was riven clapboard, while burned daub impressions and lath nails indicate interior split lathing. Other areas of the building incorporate more unconventional materials.

Large quantities of red clay "pantiles," or roofing tiles, apparently of Dutch origin, were found across the site. Computer simulation mapping of the tile fragment distributions demonstrate that at least the northern half of this "duplex" was roofed with pantiles. However, lower amounts recovered in the southern portion may only be the result of plowing in this area. Pantiles have been found at few seventeenth-century Chesapeake sites, and these were predominately brick public buildings.[31]

Like at the Town Neck site, fragments of *estrikken* tiles—red bodied earthenware floor tiles with white slip under green or yellow glaze—were also recovered at Burle.[32] Equal numbers of green and yellow tile fragments were excavated, suggesting alternating colors of either a "checkerboard "or a "striped" pattern arrangement. Paintings by Vermeer and De Hooch, and other seventeenth-century Dutch genre painters, illustrate the use of such tiles in scenes of Dutch domestic life. Several paintings in particular show checkerboard patterns (fig. 13.6). The exact placement of the tiles is open to speculation, but they seem to be located directly in front of the hearths.

Fig. 13.6. Nicolaes Maes, *Interior with a Sleeping Maid and Her Mistress (The Idle Servant)* illustrating the green and yellow *estrikken* floor tiles, c. 1655. Courtesy of the National Gallery, London, England.

Robert Burle's house also utilized blue and white Dutch tin-glaze earthenware, or "delft" tiles, as either fireplace surrounds or, less likely, baseboards or chair rails. The one identifiable fragment found at the Burle site depicts a portion of a soldier, modeled after the engravings from De Gheyns's *Exercise of Armes* (1609), an important and influential early-seventeenth-century military manual (fig. 13.7).[33] Similar Dutch tiles have been recovered from a number of other seventeenth-century sites. Examples include St. John's, van Sweringen's "Council Chamber," the Country House, and Smith's Town Land at St. Mary's City, Maryland, Jamestown, Virginia, Dutch Manhattan, and Fort Orange, New York.[34]

Two marked window cames were recovered from the Burle site, as well as a nearly intact quarrel with

Fig. 13.7. Portion of tin-glazed earthenware tile recovered at the Burle site. Courtesy of Anne Arundel County, Maryland, the Lost Towns Project.

glazing, indicating the presence of leaded casement windows. One marked window lead bears the letters RICHAR—. Hanna, Knight, and Egan (1992), suggest that these letters are possibly the mark of Richard Holland, an English glazier.[35] The second mark contains the fragmentary inscription "—SON OF BRIS—." This is the mark of John Mason of Bristol, England, for which the only known associated date is 1647.[36] This approximates the circa 1650 assumed construction date for the Burle's Town Land site.

The extensive use of Dutch materials (including a variety of lead-glazed earthenware floor tiles, tin-glazed earthen decorative tiles, pantiles, and yellow bricks) and glazed casement windows suggest a well-appointed dwelling unrivaled in Providence, and perhaps on a par with anything else in Maryland. The relatively small quantities of these materials actually recovered from the Burle site, and the paucity of architectural hardware, probably indicate an extensive salvage of building materials following the abandonment of the building.

Homewood's Lot

Homewood's Lot (18AN871), also called Belfield Farms, is the location of the fourth Providence archaeological site for which substantial clues about the original architecture currently exists. Evidence from the seventeenth-century component of the site further refines the chronology of settlement, occupation, and vernacular architectural forms relating to the town of Providence.

This complex site located overlooking Whitehall Creek was occupied almost continuously from the mid-seventeenth century through the present. In 1650, the first property owner James Homewood had the property surveyed into a 210-acre tract called Homewood's Lot. The property remained within the family for the next eighty-one years until it was resurveyed in 1731, incorporating additional tracts totaling 1,392 acres.

Excavation of forty-one five-by-five-foot test units revealed a diversity of architectural features from as many as six distinct buildings, many of which can be associated with seventeenth- and eighteenth-century occupations. These overlapping chronological and spatial sequences generated significant difficulties in site interpretation. As a result of these difficulties, discussion of the site within the context of this chapter is largely limited to the structure incorporating Feature 30, one of the earliest site components.

Feature 30 is a ten-by-six-foot cellar/pit approximately two and a half feet in depth. Paralleling the cellar was the remains of a linear feature containing ironstone debris (a naturally occurring ferrous rock). Although clearly linear in plan, the surviving portion of the trench was irregular and in some cases indistinct from surrounding subsoil. At one end of the cellar was a dark U-shaped stain (Feature 33) enclosing the burn area of the hearth. A cross-section of one portion the hearth feature revealed a clear half-round profile that extended approximately .3 feet into the subsoil. Though ambiguous, this trench is interpreted as the remains of the bottom half of a sill-on-ground earthfast chimney base.

The dimensions of the structure itself would have been approximately eight by twelve feet, with a single gable chimney projecting from the north end.

Diagnostic artifacts from the cellar include ceramics and tobacco pipe fragments that indicate that it was filled beginning in the 1660s and probably abandoned well before 1670. The cellar was filled relatively rapidly with large quantities of active fireplace ash deposits, and a remarkable quantity of faunal material, especially fish bone. A single leaded window came dated 1661 was recovered at the base of the cellar/pit and provides a *terminus post quem* for the filling of the cellar but not for its construction.

The dated window came is interpreted as construction debris from a nearby, unexcavated building. Other materials recovered from the Feature 30 cellar supporting the existence of a clearly more elaborate building include *moppen* yellow brick, a single frag-

ment of green *estrikken* floor tile, a large unglazed floor tile, and large quantities of hand wrought nails. The plowzone also produced large quantities of Dutch pantile fragments that may relate to another unexcavated building.

The building encompassing Feature 30 is considered one of the earliest structures yet found in Providence. Interestingly, it most closely resembles the Broadneck site in that it possessed a sill that was either ground laid or supported by a crude ironstone base.

The presence of another mid-seventeenth-century structure at Homewood's is clearly indicated by the construction debris encountered. It clearly contained the same Dutch trait bundle seen with the finishings at Burle's Town Land.

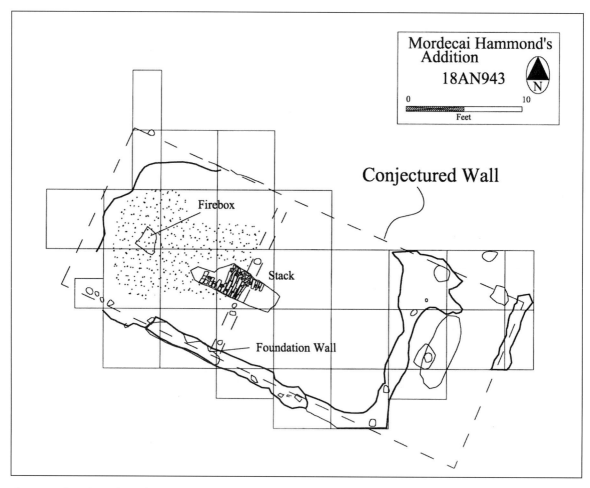

Fig. 13.8. Plan View of Mordecai Hammond's Addition site (18AN943). Courtesy of Anne Arundel County, Maryland, the Lost Towns Project.

Mordecai Hammond's Addition

In the spring of 1993, construction activity led to the discovery and salvage of the Mordecai Hammond's Addition site (18AN943). Unlike the sites discussed above, Hammond's Addition is not considered a part of the initial settlement at Providence, although it was located in the Providence locale. Hammond's Addition probably was constructed about 1719, almost forty years after the disappearance of the town. Temporally diagnostic artifacts indicate that the structure was occupied between about 1720 and the 1780s. After its abandonment, the chimney toppled, falling

into the interior of the building. Plowing destroyed only the uppermost exterior face of the chimney, while much of the articulated lower exterior of the chimney survived. Interestingly, the firebox and chimney stack combined red and yellow bricks in a manner not only functional but also decorative, with alternating bands of yellow and red.

The structure itself measured sixteen by twenty-four feet, with sills laid on native ironstone foundations (fig. 13.8). The firebox and chimney were the most interesting architectural elements at Hammond's Addition (fig. 13.9). The firebox was constructed with

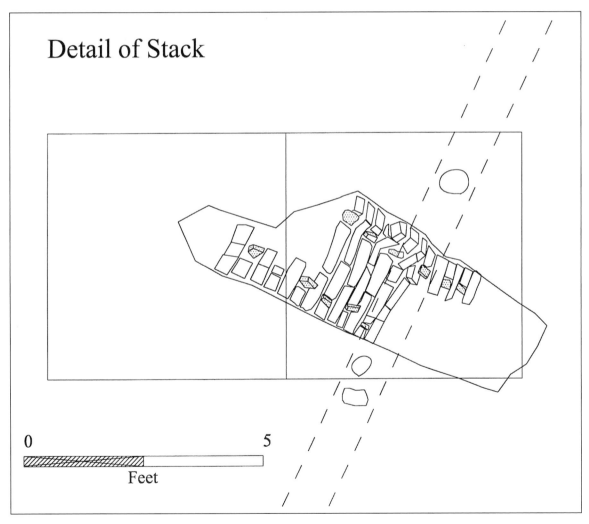

Fig. 13.9. Detail of the chimney stack at Mordecai Hammond's Addition site (18AN943). Courtesy of Anne Arundel County, Maryland, the Lost Towns Project.

courses of large red brick stretchers alternating with courses of Dutch yellow *klinker* bricks laid on edge in rowlock fashion.[37] The remaining length of yellow rowlock bricks projected into the interior of the firebox. Yellow bricks were then mortared into the interior rowlock bricks on their stretcher edges, forming an interior entirely faced with yellow brick, and an exterior of horizontal red and yellow stripes.

Twenty-six courses of articulated brick from the chimney stack were also excavated. In this case, two red brick stretchers and a half-yellow brick on edge, as a "queen closer," formed each course. Bricks in the adjacent courses were laid in the reverse pattern, forming a square stack approximately twenty-four by twenty-four inches. There is no indication that the building materials used at Hammond's Addition were salvaged from another site.

This uncommon use of brick fulfilled both functional and aesthetic considerations. The only other examples of horizontal red and yellow striped masonry

of which the authors are aware occur in Christiana, Norway. One building built in 1714, and located at building number 213, in Dronningenst 15, is the oldest example of its use within the town.[38] Builders in the city attempted to emulate this style, even painting timber buildings to achieve the same effect. Many of the builders of Christiana were reputed to be workers imported from Denmark or Germany. Whether this includes Dutch workers is unknown.

At least one Dutch painting entitled *The Courtyard of a House in Delft,* painted in 1658 by De Hooch, depicts an archway with alternating bands of red brick and blocks of white stone, or mortar (fig. 13.10). This painting, while not the same as the buildings in Christiana, Norway, or at Mordecai Hammond's Addition, creates a similar visual effect.[39]

Summary and Conclusions

The structures located through archaeological investigations at Burle's Town Land and Town Neck represent variations of hole-set earthfast architecture differing in terms of plan, construction technique, building materials, and comprehensiveness of finish. Architectural evidence from Broadneck and Homewood's Lot indicate the presence of further variations, presumably of earthfast "ground laid sill" construction. Finally, the Mordecai Hammond site evidences continued emphasis on unusual, decorative brickwork that may relate to Dutch influences first seen at Providence with sites like Town Neck.

Despite their close temporal and spatial relationships, these buildings exhibit considerable distinctiveness. The principal dwelling at Burle's Town Land, however, is extraordinary. Although earthfast in construction, the plan and the Dutch "trait bundle" of roof pantiles, *estrikken* floor tiles, yellow bricks, and blue and white Delft fireplace tiles set it apart from every other building in seventeenth-century Maryland (fig. 13.11), except perhaps the unexcavated structure at Homewood's Lot. Robert Burle's substantial and unusual building may have its closest parallel in Structure 115 in Jamestown, Virginia, a five-part townhouse block similar to "townhouses" in England.[40] Robert Burle may have built a townhouse on his "town land."

Fig. 13.10. Pieter de Hooch, *The Courtyard of a House in Delft,* illustrating decorative archway, 1658. Courtesy of the National Gallery, London, England.

Fig. 13.11. Artist's reconstruction of Robert Burle house based on archaeological evidence. Courtesy of animators Tracy Corder and Carl Gehrman.

The architectural materials recovered from Town Neck also suggest sophisticated finishing detail. While Town Neck did not possess a tiled roof, it had a potentially elaborate brick chimney, or possibly a brick gable end, and a substantial wood-lined cellar.

Such finds from the excavations at Providence are clear evidence that Chesapeake, and presumably English, architectural traditions were hybridized with extensive Dutch finishings. This is perhaps attributable to Puritan/Protestant connections with the Netherlands during this period.[41] The artifacts recovered from Providence indicate extensive Dutch trade connections. This is supported by documentary evidence from the Dutch Notarial Acts, which indicate Chesapeake planters engaged in a substantial trade with Amsterdam and Rotterdam, between 1620 and 1653.[42] In 1648, over 35 percent of the vessels trading to the Chesapeake were from the Netherlands.[43] In addition

to Dutch building materials, excavations at Providence have recovered numerous examples of Dutch utilitarian goods such as tobacco pipes and ceramics. The presence of refined Dutch building materials and a Chesapeake earthfast framing tradition suggest a unique blend of architectural styles forming a distinct vernacular tradition at Providence.

Portions of this "Providence" building tradition may have persisted locally into the early eighteenth century. Evidence supporting this is inconclusive; however, excavations at Mordecai Hammond's Addition document an unusual type of decorative brickwork that may have origins in earlier Dutch masonry styles. This brickwork may also relate to similar examples found in Christiana, Norway, the earliest of which dates to about 1714, predating the construction of Hammond's Addition by approximately six years. Red brick and several varieties of yellow brick recovered from Town Neck (including some with *dodekop* staining) suggest some form of masonry patterning on chimneys in the same region nearly seventy years before.

Not surprisingly, the architectural survey of standing structures in the Providence area has failed to locate any extant examples of buildings dating to the seventeenth or even to the first half of the eighteenth centuries. Intensive archival research, although successful in reconstructing the general layout of Providence, has been able to yield few details about domestic, commercial, or industrial architecture. Archaeological excavation and analyses have proven to be the only means of studying early Providence architecture which, to date, has all been earthfast. The results, however, do not fully conform to the paradigms concerning this construction type that have developed over the past twenty years.

Given the known conventions of earthfast construction, Providence households appear to express far more variability than might be expected. Such finishing materials as roofing and floor tiles, and even decorative fireplace surround tiles, seem to belie the interpretation of earthfast buildings as impermanent structures intended to last no more than a generation in a swidden-based agricultural system. Archaeological investigations of the dwelling houses of Robert Burle, and Ralph Williams beg the question: why were their dwellings so elegantly finished while those of most other Chesapeake inhabitants, including members of the planter elite, were not? Perhaps Robert Burle and Ralph Williams envisioned a town reminiscent of those in Great Britain. The very names of their lands convey an optimism for urbanity. Burle's household on Burle's Town Land and Ralph Williams's Town Neck both imply if not the presence of town, then at least aspirations for a formal town. Perhaps they thought their "town lands" would eventually stand in the middle of a densely populated urban center.

The architectural variability of Providence suggests its inhabitants achieved some of their urban ambitions, though perhaps not the cosmopolitan prospects they initially imagined. Providence, at least the portion of Providence north of the Severn River, never developed into more than a dispersed hamlet. After the 1680s, as the population of town core declined, the focus of urban settlement shifted to the south side of the Severn River. The general assembly designated as an official port of entry in 1669, that part of Providence south of the Severn River. Named Arundelton, and later Anne Arundel Town, this area was the direct predecessor of the town of Annapolis. It was here the spatial organization, specialization, commercial prominence, craft-specialization, and administrative importance first envisioned by the original Providence settlers were achieved.

Notes

1. Dennis J. Pogue, "Calverton, Calvert County, Maryland: 1668–1725," *Maryland Historical Magazine* 80 (1985): 271–76; John W. Reps, *Tidewater Towns: City Planning in Colonial Virginia and Maryland* (Williamsburg, Va.: Colonial Williamsburg Foundation, 1972); Joseph B. Thomas, *Settlement, Community, and Economy: The Development of Towns on Maryland's Lower Eastern Shore, 1660–1775*, Volumes in Historical Archaeology 38, ed. Stanley South, South Carolina Institute of Archaeology and Anthropology (Columbia: University of South Carolina, 1997).

2. Carl R. Lounsbury, ed., *A Glossary of Early Southern Architecture and Landscape* (New York: Oxford Univ. Press, 1993), 126.

3. Cary Carson, Norman F. Barka, William M. Kelso, Garry Wheeler Stone, and Dell Upton, "Impermanent Architecture in Southern American Colonies," *Winterthur Portfolio* 16 (Summer/Autumn 1981): 138.

4. Lounsbury, *Glossary*, 126; Carson et al., "Impermanent Architecture," 174–75.

5. H. J. Heikkenen and Mark R. Edwards, "The Key-Year Dendrochronology Technique and Its Application in Dating Historic Structures in Maryland," *Bulletin of the Association for Preservation Technology* 25(3): 3–25.

6. Donna M. Ware, *Anne Arundel's Legacy: The Historic Properties of Anne Arundel County* (Annapolis, Md.: Anne Arundel County Office of Planning and Zoning, 1990).

7. Lorena Walsh, "'Till Death Us Do Part': Marriage and Family in Seventeenth-Century Maryland," in *The Chesapeake in the Seventeenth Century: Essays on Anglo-American Society* (New York: Norton, 1979), 128.

8. Carson et al., "Impermanent Architecture," 171.

9. Dell Upton, "Early Vernacular Architecture in Southeastern Virginia" (Ph.D. diss., Brown Univ.), 1981.

10. Carson et al., "Impermanent Architecture," 141.

11. Upton, "Early Vernacular Architecture."

12. Carson et al., "Impermanent Architecture," 153.

13. Carson et al., "Impermanent Architecture"; Henry M. Miller, *Discovering Maryland's First City: A Summary Report on the 1981–1984 Archaeological Excavations at St. Mary's City,* St. Mary's City Archaeology Series No. 2 (St. Mary's City, Md.: St. Mary's City Commission, 1986); Fraser D. Neiman, "An Evolutionary Approach to Archaeological Inference: Aspects of Architectural Variation in the 17th-Century Chesapeake" (Ph.D. diss., Yale Univ., 1990).

14. Al Luckenbach, *Providence 1649: The History and Archaeology of Anne Arundel County Maryland's First European Settlement* (Annapolis: Maryland State Archives and the Maryland Historical Trust, 1995).

15. See Pogue, "Calverton, Calvert County, Maryland," on defining towns in terms of function, rather than population density.

16. See Luckenbach, *Providence 1649.*

17. Registered archaeological sites are number based on the U.S. National Museum system. In the trinomial designation system, 18 is for Maryland, AN stands for Anne Arundel County, and 826 refers to the specific site number.

18. Most surviving documents postdate the restoration of power to Lord Baltimore.

19. The postholes are interpreted as associated with a nearby mid-eighteenth-century site.

20. Puncheon set posts, or a series of closely placed posts driven directly into the ground, are uncommon in the Chesapeake region. For further description of puncheon set posts, see Carson et al., "Impermanent Architecture," 148.

21. This may also partially be the result of the deflated nature of the archaeological deposits.

22. Orlando Ridout V, personal communication with author, Mar. 11, 1999. The use of thatched roofs in the Chesapeake is documented as early as the journals of Capt. John Smith and could be found on Virginia's eastern shore in 1640, Kent County in 1656, and Somerset County in 1682.

Some examples of thatched roofs have been documented as late as the twentieth century.

23. Carson et al., "Impermanent Architecture," 141.

24. Ibid.

25. Alan D. Beauregard, Al Luckenbach, Anthony Lindauer, and James Kodlick, *Phase II Archaeological Evaluation: The Ralph Williams Site (18AN944), Athletic Facilities Construction Project Naval Radio Transmitter Facility Annapolis, Anne Arundel County, Maryland,* Report to the United States Naval Academy, Annapolis, Md. (Mechanicsburg, Pa.: KCI Technologies, 1994), 32.

26. Beauregard et al., *Phase II Archaeological Evaluation,* 55.

27. M. J. Becker, "'Swedish' Colonial Yellow Bricks: Notes on Their Uses and Possible Origins in 17th Century America," *Historical Archaeology* 11 (1977): 114; and Joseph S. Sopko, *An Analysis of Dutch Bricks from a 17th Century Structure within the Site of Fort Orange at Albany, New York* (Waterford: New York State Parks, Recreation and Historic Preservation Bureau of Historic Sites, 1982), 37.

28. Sopko, *Analysis of Dutch Bricks,* 37.

29. The presence of large quantities of brick probably indicate that building materials were not salvaged from the site following its destruction.

30. Beauregard et al., *Phase II Archaeological Evaluation,* 69.

31. Silas D. Hurry, *Masonry Roof Tile from the St. John's Site (18ST1-23) in St. Mary's City, Maryland,* unpublished manuscript, St. Mary's City Commission (1980), 5–10. Fragments of pantile roofs have been recovered from excavations at Jamestown, Virginia, and St. Mary's City, Maryland, including the State House, St. Johns site, and the Mattapony-Sewell site. All were occupied by prominent individuals, including the Calvert family.

32. Paul R. Huey, *Archaeological Testing at Philipse Manor Hall, Yonkers, N.Y.* (Waterford: New York State Office of Parks, Recreation and Historic Preservation Research Unit, Bureau of Historic Sites, 1996), 9. Two Friesland archives documents dated 1614 and 1662 describe floors paved with yellow and green glazed tiles called *estrikken.* These tiles were more common in Friesland and less common in North Holland.

33. J. B. Kist, *Jacob De Gheyn: The Exercise of Armes* (New York: McGraw-Hill, 1971).

34. Gary Wheeler Stone, *Seventeenth-Century Wall Tile from the St. Mary's City Excavations, 1971–1985,* St. Mary's

City Research Series No. 3 (St. Mary's City: Historic St. Mary's City, St. Mary's County, Maryland, 1987), 1–2.

35. Susan Hanna, Barry Knight, and Geoff Egan, "Marked Window Leads from North America and Europe," unpublished manuscript, Historic St. Mary's City, Maryland, 1992.

36. Al Luckenbach and James G. Gibb, "Dated Window Leads from Colonial Sites in Anne Arundel County, Maryland," *Maryland Archeology* 30, no. 2 (Sept. 1994): 23–28.

37. Al Luckenbach, "The Excavation of an 18th-Century Dutch Yellow Brick Firebox and Chimney Stack in Anne Arundel County, Maryland," *Maryland Archeology* 30, no. 2 (Sept. 1994): 9–22.

38. Letter and photographs from Patricia Reynolds, July 11, 1995.

39. Donna R. Barnes and the Hofstra Museum, *The Butcher, the Baker, the Candlestick Maker: Jan Luyken's Mirrors of 17th-Century Dutch Daily Life* (Hempstead, N.Y.: Hofstra Museum, Hofstra University, 1995), catalog for an exhibition of drawings and prints at the Emily Lowe Gallery, 17 September–31 October 1995, curated by Donna R. Barnes, Ed.E., reports on p. 37 that Bentheim sandstone from Germany and Italian marble were also used for facade ornamentation.

40. John L. Cotter, *Archeological Excavations at Jamestown, Virginia,* rev. ed. (Richmond, Va.: Archaeological Society of Virginia, 1994), 121–29; and Edward Chappell, Colonial Williamsburg Foundation, personal communication with author, 1998.

41. James G. Gibb and Al Luckenbach, *Ceramic and Tobacco Pipe Seriations of Five 17th Century Domestic Sites in Anne Arundel County, Maryland.* Anne Arundel County's Lost Towns Project, Annapolis, Maryland. Submitted to the Maryland State Highway Administration, Baltimore, Maryland, 1997, 19.

42. Jan Kupp, "Dutch Notarial Acts Relating to the Tobacco Trade of Virginia, 1608–1653," *William and Mary Quarterly* 30(4): 653–55.

43. Sopko, *Analysis of Dutch Bricks;* Jan Kupp, "Dutch Notarial Acts Relating to the Tobacco Trade of Virginia; Karina Paape, "From Nansemond to Providence: The Quest for Piety and Profit in the Seventeenth-Century Chesapeake" (master's thesis, Univ. of Maryland–Baltimore County, 1997), 8–9; Sopko reports that most Dutch sailing vessels used "Dutch" yellow brick as ballast, which could be sold with the cargo. He suggests that the frequent Dutch trade vessels arriving in the settlement may have supplied a sufficient quantity of yellow brick for use in construction during the early years (*Analysis of Dutch Bricks,* 46–48).

14

FROM TICKET BOOTH TO SCREEN TOWER

AN ARCHITECTURAL STUDY OF DRIVE-IN THEATERS IN THE BALTIMORE–WASHINGTON, D.C.–RICHMOND CORRIDOR

SHANNON BELL

"Fiery meteors guided by evil monsters of another world gone mad," a free 1950 Packard, Patsy Cline, monkey cages, and a one-thousand-dollar insurance policy from Lloyds of London against "death by fright" constituted just a portion of the entertainment once offered by drive-in theaters.[1] Drive-in theaters emerged in the 1930s, multiplied during the post–World War II era, then ceased to be built as quickly as they had appeared. Not simply an unusual form to emerge and then all but disappear from the American landscape, drive-in theaters are indicative of the society and economy that created and later abandoned them. Americans of the postwar era had a passion for their cars and the movies alike. The drive-in theater was the successful marriage of the two. It provided Americans with a novel and entertaining activity that could be done with their automobile. A family or couple could drive to the theater, pass the ticket booth, find a perfect spot to enjoy the show, and arrive back home again without ever leaving the spacious comfort of their car. An industry reporter from *Boxoffice* was far from the mark when he doubtfully commented, "It remains to be seen whether the American people after their first initiation will care to further mix their motoring pleasures with their movies."[2] When the novelty had worn off, the "fiery meteors," free cars, and Patsy enticed them to return again and again, at least until changes in suburban growth, technology, and American society hastened the drive-in's decline.

Often overlooked is the impact this institution had on our built environment. While many works, scholarly and anecdotal, discuss the social and theatrical aspects of drive-in theaters, there are few serious architectural studies.[3] In part, the drive-ins' physical disappearance contributes to this absence. The drive-in theater is a distinctly American building type; very few were built outside the United States. They were spectacular roadside attractions and created an unusual imprint on the American vernacular land scape. In a short period of time, their design was standardized, uniformly comprised of several basic architectural elements. Overall this design was a hallmark of efficiency. These theaters were basically utilitarian structures designed to swiftly accommodate the movement of numerous automobiles and patrons throughout the theater. When ornament was applied it too was done efficiently, for the purpose of generating income. When closely examined, the physical structures also reflect broader social and economic issues. Specific examples drawn from a larger case study illustrate the design of the drive-in theater, and how and by whom this building type was used.[4]

Drive-in theaters were but one of several early-twentieth-century building types whose designs were inspired by the automobile. Like gas stations, drive-in restaurants, and motels, the drive-in theater belongs to a family of structures known as roadside architecture.[5] Found along American highways, roadside architecture encompasses the array of buildings erected to serve the automobile and motorist. As a whole, roadside architecture has had a tremendous impact on the American landscape, especially evident in the array of forms, images, and colors that comprise the panoramic view from our windshields.

The first drive-in appeared in Camden, New Jersey, in 1933. The number of theaters grew slowly, to just under one hundred in twenty-six states by 1942, at the time of America's entrance into the war. Wartime building restrictions, as well as gas and tire rationing, halted drive-in construction. Following the war, drive-ins experienced their greatest growth, with one thousand built by 1949, peaking to just over four thousand by the mid-1950s.[6] Gas and tire rationing were a thing of the past, new modern automobiles were readily available, and drivers took to the road in ever-increasing numbers. The rise in automobile ownership concurrent with postwar prosperity, our love of the movies, and the relatively cheap land still available

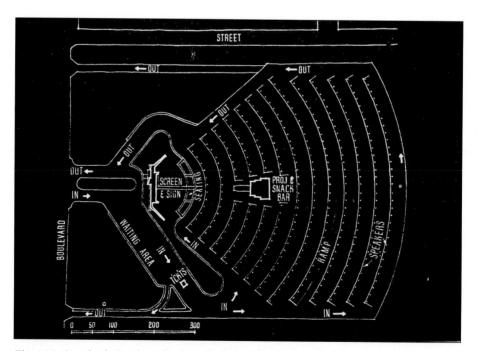

Fig. 14.1. Standard site plan of a drive-in theater by the late 1940s, illustrating the typical location of the screen, ticket booth, operations building, and layout of lanes and ramps. Courtesy of *Architectural Record,* a publication of McGraw-Hill, Inc.

on the outskirts of population centers made mid-twentieth-century America the perfect social and economic environment for this business to flourish.

At first glance, the design of the drive-in theater is deceptively simple: an empty lot with minimal construction. In actuality, it is a series of complicated design solutions based upon the concept of efficiency. At the same time, established features of the indoor theater (the screen, theater rows, and entrance) were drawn upon and adapted by drive-in theater designers for the automobile and the roadside. With the natural atmosphere of the starry night sky and rural location, drive-in theaters did not have to provide the luxurious, sometimes exotic, surroundings of indoor theaters. These elaborate interiors helped transport the viewer into the fantasy world of the film and became part of the moviegoing experience.[7]

Several key architectural elements common to all drive-in theaters can be identified and, as such, distinguish the drive-in as a building type. The salient architectural features of the drive-in theater are the screen and its encompassing tower; attraction board; ticket booth; operations building (housing concessions, projection and rest rooms); the entrance and exit lanes; the ramps; and the site plan. These elements were experimented with slightly in the 1930s and early 1940s, but by the postwar boom they became fairly standardized.

The screen tower is the most significant feature of the building type. In form, scale, and decoration, it embodies the vocabulary of the roadside. Prescribed by its function, the tall, flat, yet angular form of the screen at first called attention to the uniqueness of the theater, but with time became a symbol for the drive-in, instantly recognized and understood by patrons. Situated close to the highway, the screen piqued the curiosity of passing motorists, an essential factor in roadside design. While the form was prescribed by function, the decoration it received was purely ornamental, a design decision motivated by economics. In fact, the screen tower usually received the greatest degree of ornament of all the architectural elements of the drive-in. The back of the screen provided the perfect advertisement space and was frequently decorated with large-scale lettering, enormous figures or

murals, and bright neon signs and lights that illuminated the tower during the evening hours of operation. Walls or fencing often extended angularly from the body of the screen tower, serving multiple purposes. In addition to partially defining the space of the theater, fencing also directed access to the theater past the ticket booth, shielded the audience from highway lights, and provided extended advertisement space. The most extravagant screen towers combined the traditional form with elaborate additions, such as a southern plantation house, man-made clouds, or waterfalls. The screen tower advertised what the operator was selling, the fantasy world of cinema.

The attraction board at the drive-in theater was typically placed at the side of the road and often identified the entrance. Early drive-in operators used billboard-like signs to announce what was playing, while others attached their attraction board to the screen tower, but the latter quickly realized that the roadside was a more advantageous location. The attraction board was appropriately named because in addition to listing "coming attractions," its greater function was to help attract the eyes of the driver. Like the screen tower, the typically rectangular form of the attraction board was adorned with lights and bright colors. Like all roadside signs, the lettering used was larger than that on urban signage.

The ticket booth was the final architectural feature that constituted the exterior of the drive-in. It too exhibited a moderate degree of ornament, most frequently in the form of lights. The functional requirements and the precedent of ticket booths at indoor theaters dictated the form of the building, usually a small rectangular booth with the top half of the walls glazed on at least three sides. This amount of glazing was functional but also in line with Modern design principles and suggested materials. Like many other roadside structures, ticket booths of postwar drive-ins were frequently constructed with stainless steel and plate glass or glass block, and they exhibited rounded streamlined corners or exaggerated angles.

The interior of the drive-in theater consisted of the operations building, lanes, and ramps. At the earliest drive-ins, the operations building was a completely utilitarian boxy structure facilitating the projection of the films and sometimes providing restrooms and office space. Its location differed from one drive-in to the next. However, in the postwar boom, when drive-in theaters were no longer just a novelty, concessions proved to be a tremendous boost to profits; in fact, concessions often outweighed the profits from ticket sales by a greater margin than with indoor theaters.[8] Adding concessions to the functions of the operations building led to its standard location in the center of the lot where it was easily accessible to the greatest number of patrons, while still providing the best location for the projection room. Operations buildings varied in floor plans and the concession services they provided but usually included cafeteria-like counter service and some patio seating.

The operations building adapted well to popular forms of modernism. Most were rectangular structures built with modern construction materials such as steel, concrete, and glass. Designers were inspired by the forms, angles, and materials of the automobile in their creation of structural environments for it. Like other roadside buildings, the adaptation of machine-inspired design to drive-in theaters helped instill confidence in their patrons as to the efficiency and cleanliness of the concessions operation. Especially appealing at the height of drive-in construction in the 1950s was the Exaggerated Modern, which suggested the use of oversized roofs and unusual angles, V-shaped columns and glazed fronts of buildings with the glass canted inward.[9] Above all, these functional yet aesthetic elements of modern design could be applied to the drive-in, the operations building specifically, and still be relatively inexpensive to construct.

The system of lanes and ramps comprising the lot of the drive-in theater was an essential element of its design. Entrance and exit lanes, parking ramps, and traffic lanes on the exterior of the theater were created to provide the most direct and least congested flow of automobiles in and out of the theater. Entrance and exit lanes usually extended along and defined the sides of a drive-in. Parking ramps were graded to ensure the best sight lines from each parking space. Their layout was standardized early on as a series of semi-circular graded ramps, each slightly longer than the next and radiating from the front of the screen, a pattern derived from the indoor theater's rows of seats.

Different manners of grading these parking ramps were executed. The most popular was called the single drive-over type, which was graded upward but provided a gentle slope on the far side of the ramp so the driver could pull forward to exit. Another popular system was the double drive-over type, which had two adjacent ramps with driving lanes spaced between each set. The drawback of this type was that sometimes a driver had to back up to exit, which operators saw as potentially dangerous. An Ohio architect named W. S. Ferguson patented his "Drive Over and Drop in System," which used level parking ramps with concrete troughs at the rear that effectively lowered the back of the car as its rear wheels dropped into the trough.[10]

Encompassing all of the drive-in theater's architectural elements was the site plan, which revolved around the movement of the automobiles from their route off the highway, into the pattern of ramps, and out again. The triangular site plan—bordered by parking lanes, filled in with semicircular ramps radiating from the screen tower, featuring a support building in the center and ticket booth adjacent to the screen—became fairly standard by the late 1940s and is perhaps the most uniform feature of drive-in theaters.[11] The unique pattern of the site plan imprinted upon the landscape differentiates the drive-in from its surroundings and sets it apart from any other building type. In fact, many aerial photographers today still use the distinct pattern of the drive-in site plan as a landmark when interpreting aerial photographs.

Drive-in theaters once located in the mid-Atlantic metropolitan areas of Baltimore, Maryland, Washington, D.C., and Richmond, Virginia, offer a good cross section of this building type. While geographically close, these three cities are sufficiently different in economic base, demographics, and tradition, providing an excellent cross-section of cities nationwide. As a case study, the drive-ins once located within this tri-city corridor reflect the scope of development nationally and underscore how little regional variation occurred. An examination of these drive-ins, especially in comparison to theaters in other regions of the country, reveals no variation in the architectural elements, form, siting, plan, scale, or materials as a result of regional factors. Rather, patterns or trends in drive-in design appear to be based on successful, nationally executed design solutions. Variations occurred only in the regional imagery adopted by the theater (cactus and cowboys ornamenting drive-ins in the Southwest versus colonial plantations attached to screen towers on the East Coast) and, more important, in issues of theater segregation.[12] These theaters also clearly illustrate the efficiency of drive-in theater design and their attraction as novelties, as well as class and racial differences of the era.

In the area of the case study, only two drive-ins opened before the outbreak of World War II. In the immediate postwar boom, their numbers grew to nine. The biggest period of local growth was the early 1950s, when sixteen more were built around the three cities. At their peak, around forty drive-in theaters provided entertainment to the residents of Baltimore, Washington, and Richmond. The Mt. Vernon Open-Air Theater in Virginia and the Governor Ritchie in Maryland were the first to open in these two states and set the local standard.[13] The architectural features that proved successful at these theaters very likely

influenced designers of local postwar drive-ins. Both were built by E. M. Loew's theater chain, which operated three other drive-ins on the East Coast by the late 1930s. As a chain operator, Loew had the funds to construct large well-designed drive-ins in comparison to less expensive independently owned drive-ins of the prewar period, but it was theaters such as his that set the standard in the boom to come. Opening on August 15, 1938, the Mt. Vernon drive-in was the first in the Washington, D.C., area, located three miles south of Alexandria, Virginia, along Route 1. An essential aspect of roadside architecture was its location. Reflecting what became the national trend, the Mt. Vernon was located right on the edge of a heavily traveled highway and on the outskirts of town where land was cheap.

The Mt. Vernon screen tower was a typical massive rectangular form, with stepped back wing walls encompassing the front of the theater. Typically the back faced the highway and was decorated with two large circles topped with small images of theater masks. The circles read "See and hear movies in your car, Only 50¢" and "On every program, 2 Major Features." In between the circles hung a vertical sign displaying the name of the theater, outlined in neon. The screen

Fig. 14.2. Screen tower of the Mt. Vernon Open-Air Theater, Alexandria, Virginia, c. 1947. Courtesy of Don King.

Fig. 14.3. Interior space of the Mt. Vernon, c. 1947, illustrating the stationary birdhouse speakers that were briefly used at the theater after World War II. Courtesy of Don King.

tower, a new and unusual sight for this area, would certainly have caught the eye of local drivers. Typical of other early drive-ins, the attraction board at the Mt. Vernon was attached to one of the wing walls of the screen tower and, like the screen tower, only minimally decorated, using words as a method of advertisement, more than pictures. The ticket booth was a typical freestanding rectangular building with a pitched roof and three windows across the front. Inside the theater, the Mt. Vernon held five hundred cars on its nine drive-over semicircular ramps, which were covered in gravel and graded so that every car was elevated to view the screen without obstruction.[14]

A small building at the back of the lot housed the projection equipment, rest rooms, and vending machines. Operations buildings such as these were a precursor of the large concession buildings to come. In the late 1940s, a small refreshment stand with one counter was built partially sunken in the center of the lot, where popcorn, pizza, and fried clams could be purchased. Patrons were excited about this improvement, as previously only locally bottled soda and hot dogs had been available.[15]

As with many early drive-in theaters, sound was the most difficult technical problem at the Mt. Vernon. When the theater opened it was equipped with the latest in drive-in sound for 1938, the "Magic Voice of the Screen," in which speakers behind the screen produced sound that was to flow through and around

the screen.[16] Don King, the manager of the Mt. Vernon from 1946 to 1953, recalls that when he arrived that first spring, sound came from three speakers on top of the screen. By 1947, Loew's company had installed stationary speakers on poles that looked like birdhouses, according to Mr. King. These birdhouse speakers were quickly replaced in 1948 by in-car speakers, the eventual standard in drive-in theater sound. First developed by RCA in 1941, the war years prevented the in-car speaker from being widely adopted until the end of the decade.

E. M. Loew was also responsible for the Governor Ritchie Open-Air Theater, which opened almost a year later on May 14, 1939. That theater was located three miles southeast of Baltimore on Annapolis Boulevard, the principal route to the state capital. In comparison to the Mt. Vernon, the Governor Ritchie was erected in a less-elaborate vein, reflecting, perhaps, its less affluent surroundings. Unlike the Mt. Vernon, the Governor Ritchie was located in a fairly rural area, drawing patrons from the city as much as from the numerous small communities near, but not adjacent to, the theater. The screen tower, which housed a smaller screen, was built in a similar form, framed by a decorative rim of metal with the attraction board and the name of the theater displayed in red, blue, and green on the back.[17] The opening ad in the *Baltimore Sun* was not alone in falsely claiming that the drive-in had the "World's Largest Screen."

Although just a year had passed since the Mt. Vernon's opening, Loew's designers had already made

Fig. 14.4. Opening advertisement for the Governor Ritchie Open-Air Auto Theater, in Glen Burnie, Maryland, from May 14, 1939.

some changes to their drive-in design, which they implemented at the Governor Ritchie. From the beginning, sound was produced with a series of five speakers fit into a long rectangular space above the screen, similar to the second sound system installed at the Mt. Vernon. The Governor Ritchie had a larger capacity, 786 cars, and a series of ten drive-over gravel ramps. This increase in initial size reflects the ever-expanding capacity of the drive-in theater, motivated by economic desires of the operators. The brick dugout projection room was unusually placed in front of the first ramp and built partially underground to maintain proper sightlines for the audience. At a later date, when concessions became integral, a new operations building was built in the standard location at the center of the lot. The site plan of the Governor Ritchie was similar to that of the Mt. Vernon in its placement of the screen, attraction board, lanes, and ramps. However, the varied locations of these early operations buildings speak to an era prior to the dependence upon concessions profits, when Loew was still experimenting with the best location for this building.

For both these early drive-ins there was much excitement and fanfare surrounding their openings, generated by the operators, the press, and the people who showed up in droves opening night. The *Alexandria Gazette* dedicated two full pages to the opening of the Mt. Vernon "automobile drive-in emporium." Corsages were given to all the ladies, and a forty-piece band played as a floodlight aimed at the highway announced the opening. One reporter accurately captured the building of the Governor Ritchie, calling it "a startling growth on the peaceful Anne Arundel countryside."[18] Thirty uniformed ushers directed cars to their places to hear the dedication speeches by Baltimore mayor Howard W. Jackson and Maryland governor Herbert O'Conor. The theater was dedicated to four-term Maryland governor Albert C. Ritchie, and newsreels covering his career were shown prior to the feature film, *Gunga Din.*

America's involvement in World War II turned attention away from the burgeoning drive-in industry, nationally and locally. Both the Governor Ritchie and Mt. Vernon closed for a period during the war but reopened to continued success in 1946. A couple of

hours south, construction of several drive-in theaters was underway for the first time near the city of Richmond, Virginia, which caused one reporter to comment, "it is inevitable that drive-in motion picture houses should begin their encirclement of the city."[19] The first to open was the Midlothian Drive-in (later named the Sunset) on June 6, 1947, followed closely by the Broadway on June 25. A third, the Autoview Drive-in, opened later that summer of 1947 but closed soon after it opened. Other operators continued to believe the Richmond area was prime for more drive-in theater business, and Memorial Day of 1948 was the celebrated opening of the Bellwood Drive-in. The Bellwood claimed to be the largest drive-in in the South, with space for over one thousand cars, double the size of the earlier Richmond drive-ins. Typically, the Bellwood was located several miles from town along busy Route 1, known locally as Petersburg Pike, the same interstate highway on which the Mt. Vernon was located.

An architect's rendering was published in the local paper to build anticipation. That rendering illustrates the layout of the Bellwood—a standard triangular site plan, bordered with white fencing and exhibiting all the essential architectural features in their typical locations. The back of the screen tower, which faced the

Fig. 14.5. Architect's rendering of Bellwood Drive-in Theater, Richmond, Virginia, published in the local paper in 1947 prior to its construction. Courtesy of *Richmond-Times Dispatch.*

highway, displayed the name of the theater in neon, and an attraction board was located along the roadside, directing patrons with neon arrows. Once passing through the ticket booth to the right of the screen and choosing a spot, patrons could proceed to the operations building, complete with concessions, located at the center of the lot for greatest accessibility.

At first, it was the novelty of the marriage of celluloid and chrome that attracted patrons to these and other drive-in theaters. Advertisements for all these early theaters described the way they functioned. The opening advertisements for the Mt. Vernon and Governor Ritchie suggested that patrons could "dress as you please, smoke, laugh, talk." These same luxuries were not acceptable at indoor theaters, nor could you bring the children for free. Free admission for children under twelve was the policy from the beginning at both these theaters. The casual attire that was acceptable was a departure from dressing for the indoor theaters in the area, attractive to both families and the working class, who proved to be the greatest supporters of drive-ins, nationally and within the case study. Drive-ins were less expensive than indoor houses, es-

pecially when indoor theaters were running only a single show in contrast to the drive-in's double and sometimes triple feature. Added attractions, such as the Mt. Vernon's "Miracle Fairyland," which had a large playground, a stage for bands, pony rides, and cages of monkeys, were an investment to entice even more families.[20] After the novelty had worn off, it was the continuing appeal of this type of theater to families that cemented its success.

Drive-ins further became known as places where couples could go to be alone-together. The drive-in offered a place where you could watch a movie from the comfort of your car, when cars were large and comfortable. Patrons could essentially do whatever they pleased in the semiprivate space of their cars. At a time when there were few socially acceptable places where couples could channel their passions, the back of the drive-in lot was a safer place to "park" than anywhere else. In 1944 an indoor operator commented to *Boxoffice* that "the Drive-in should be encouraged as the most effective way to rid our legitimate motion picture theaters of the rowdyism, vandalism, necking parties and perversive nuisances that now prevail to

Fig. 14.6. Advertisement for the Bellwood Drive-in from 1948, indicating the segregated spaces at this theater.

the consternation of indoor theatre management."[21] The "passion pit" was one of the most popular nicknames for the drive-in.[22] In part, this was due to the unwritten understanding between operators and patrons that the realm of the car was private, as long as you were not disturbing other guests. Most operators silently condoned the type of behavior that earned drive-ins their reputation. Over time this reputation has overshadowed the equally significant presence of the family. While operators tried to project a wholesome image to make families feel comfortable attending their theaters, they certainly were not turning away the other half of their customers. This dual patronage of family and couples established its own spatial separation within the site plan of the drive-in theater, with the back of the theater for the passionate and the front for the wholesome.

Drive-ins also drew patronage from the rural, often lower-class, neighborhoods nearby, such as the residents of the trailer park located next to the Mt. Vernon. The class distinction evident at local drive-ins was strengthened by the popularity of "hillbilly" bands performing there and the Bathing Beauty Contest held in 1954, certainly not amusements that would have drawn the upper classes.[23] This class distinction was noted by a reporter describing the Bellwood clientele. He implied that it would be lower- to middle-class patrons who would be happy not to have to "exchange house dress and overalls for something more conventional [and once they arrived could] settle themselves with smokes," as well as families with "rambunctious youngsters" and the elderly or semi-invalid who "are fearful of the semidark aisles [of indoor houses], or hesitate to creep to their seats across the feet of other patrons."[24]

While the Bellwood did draw these typical drive-in patrons, it was unlike any of the other local drive-ins in that it admitted blacks. It was completely segregated with different entrances, rest rooms, concessions and parking area for its black patrons, separated by a wall dividing the back of the theater. Articles and advertisements promoted the Bellwood's "Separate Section Reserved for Colored Patrons."[25] The site plan of the Bellwood is a physical manifestation of the strict segregation policies of Virginia. The segregated spaces comprising this more complicated site plan are a good illustration of the ways in which society affects architecture.

Many drive-in theaters within the case study denied admission to blacks. For example, Don King remembers that legally he was not permitted to admit blacks to the Mt. Vernon during his employment there from 1946 to 1953. There was in fact a neighboring black community, Gum Springs, whose residents watched the films from the back of the theater, a brushy area accessible by a side road. King chose to wire a few speakers at the back of the lot to provide them with sound. Although he could not charge them admission, he did send ushers to sell them refreshments.

Overall, drive-in theaters varied in their policies on admitting black patrons depending on the general segregation practices of the regions in which they were located. The separate facilities of the Bellwood and the additional speakers wired at the back of the Mt. Vernon are physical features reflecting the ways in which racial segregation was manifested regionally. At least eighty-five black-only drive-ins were constructed in the southern half of the country, including Florida and Texas. Drive-ins in western cities, such as Los Angeles, admitted blacks by the early 1950s.[26] The few known examples of fully segregated drive-ins were also built in the South, in Virginia and Arkansas, states along the northern boundaries of the southern region.

Most indoor theaters of the tri-city corridor were white or black only, rather than segregated within the theater. Washington, D.C., first integrated in 1953, but denial of admission to blacks continued in some suburbs for at least another decade. The northern city of Baltimore integrated its theaters by 1958, but the rest of Virginia including Richmond was much slower to do so, not requiring theaters to legally desegregate until 1963.[27] It is uncertain when drive-in theaters within the case study also began to integrate, but likely they followed the desegregation patterns of neighboring indoor houses. Following the precedent set by other drive-ins in Prince George's County, Maryland, on the east side of Washington, D.C., blacks were not admitted to the Palmer Drive-in when it opened in July 1954. However, shortly after its opening, two black communities surrounding the Palmer protested their restriction from the drive-in, likely bolstered by the successful desegregation of all indoor theaters in Washington the previous year. Further north, east of Baltimore, the Bengies Drive-in began as a white-only drive-in, due to pressure from surrounding indoor houses when it opened in the summer of 1956, but became integrated a few months after its opening.[28]

Despite their popularity, drive-ins were not always embraced by the communities where they were located. Prince George's County citizens' groups opposed the increased traffic problems and noise anticipated by the Kentland Drive-in, designed by Jack Vogel for Sydney Lust, but never built. In addition to unwanted traffic pile-ups, drive-ins were often associated with low-end rural areas. Residents of Montgomery County, among the most affluent counties in the Washington, D.C., area, opposed the construction of drive-in theaters on several occasions. When Lust applied for a building permit there in the early 1950s, he encountered strong community opposition. Local citizens felt that drive-ins were "a demoralizing influence leading to promiscuous relationships" and that the "invasion of such amusement into the county will increase juvenile delinquency."[29] The county passed a regulatory ordinance that placed a one-thousand-dollar annual license fee for all drive-in theaters, prohibiting any drive-in from operating past 11:00 P.M., and a number of other stipulations that made it clear that Montgomery County was not a practical place to build. As a result, only one drive-in was built in Montgomery County, the Rockville Drive-in Theater, which opened on March 18, 1954. The Rockville included a playground from the outset and established itself firmly as a family drive-in. During the first years of operation, the Rockville showed one feature, in contrast to most drive-in theaters with double or triple features, in order to comply with the 11:00 P.M. curfew. Another Washington, D.C., area chain operator, Fred Wineland, admitted that while Montgomery County's restrictions were a "negative to expansion," he understood that the more rural, working-class population of Prince George's County was a better audience for his expanding chain.[30] Eventually, that county had a total of nine drive-ins, five of which were Wineland's. The comparison of the number of drive-ins within these

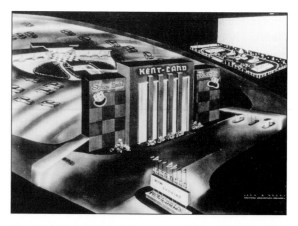

Fig. 14.7. Rendering of the proposed Kentland Drive-in, typical of theaters designed by Jack Vogel, which was not built because of objections from local residents. Courtesy of Jack K. Vogel.

two counties is a reflection of their differing class structures as well as strong evidence that reaffirms the popularity of drive-ins within rural working-class communities.

The early 1950s was a period of intense growth for drive-in theaters, nationally and in the mid-Atlantic region. They continued to draw upon the principles established in 1940s roadside design-efficiency, showmanship, and marketing to families and to the lower middle classes. Their architecture was patterned on the successful designs of their predecessors, consisting of the same elements, virtually unchanged. By 1950, designers had created a more minimalist aesthetic for the roadside while incorporating eye-catching exaggerations of specific building features. It was at the end of the 1940s that drive-ins began to adopt design aspects Chester Liebs identifies in his book *Main Street to Miracle Mile* as the Exaggerated Modern. He interprets this change in roadside imagery as a delayed response in the design community to the end of World War II and the several years needed to discontinue the prewar streamline curves and zigzags and create a simpler modern aesthetic focusing on utilitarian, boxy forms. At the height of drive-in construction this stripped-down functional form was adopted, but in concert with glazed visual fronts, oversized roofs, and V-shaped columns, considered to be structural exaggerations appropriate for roadside buildings.[31]

Throughout the country several architects became known for their specialization in drive-in theaters, creating high-end examples. Their theaters bore strong resemblance to inexpensive drive-ins at the other end of the scale but exhibited a greater degree of attention to their design quality. One such architect was Ohio-based Jack Vogel, who designed over three hundred drive-ins during his career, including a few internationally. The son of a theater architect, Vogel studied architecture and engineering at Ohio University and the École des Beaux-Arts. He began his career designing indoor theaters, like his father, but turned to drive-ins in 1948. In recent interviews, Vogel recalled meeting with his first client, trying to pass himself off as an expert. He claimed, "You could pretend you knew something about it because no one knew what they were doing to begin with." Vogel felt his clients gave him great latitude in his design choices, as they were less concerned with aesthetics than cost. Vogel was interested in designing drive-ins that were not, as he put it, "cow pastures." Where budgets permitted, he incorporated a great deal of landscaping and

improved upon the dramatic effect of the screen tower. He applied what he referred to as Art Deco details to the entrance of his theaters, specifically the screen tower, attraction board, and ticket office to entice patrons. In designing other elements of the drive-in theater, including the access lanes, ramps, and concessions building, Vogel stated that their functional aspects were more important than their aesthetics.

At the height of the drive-in boom in 1956, Vogel designed the Bengies Drive-in Theater east of Baltimore. Still operated by the same family, Bengies has changed little since the 1950s. although its immediate future remains uncertain. Bengies is a typical Vogel drive-in, except for the utterly utilitarian screen, never visible from the highway and a sharp contrast to Vogel's generally elaborate screen towers. The ticket booth is a modern box form with extended flat roof constructed of California redwood to tie the site to its wooded surroundings. Vogel's application of chaser lights to the roof line and the attraction board was not only to enhance the entrance but to do so in a way that was suggestive of the energy and movement of the

Fig. 14.8. A typical Vogel operations building at Bengies Drive-in Theater in Middle River, Maryland, 1956. Courtesy of Jack K. Vogel.

automobile. Vogel repeatedly designed his concession buildings with the same materials and forms he used at Bengies, such as the flat roof, canted glazed front, exposed brick or concrete walls, and indoor auditoriums, where patrons could sit in theater seats and outdoor screen from inside the building. One of the intentions of these climate-controlled auditoriums was to entice patrons to the theater even when the weather was bad. Bengies' projection booth was located in a penthouse configuration on top of the operations building, effectively decreasing physical interruption of the projection of the film. The center of the building contained the concessions area, carefully designed to serve the greatest number of patrons during the short intermission period. Patrons could be lured in during the movie as the glazed front allowed full visibility of the screen and interior speakers ensured not a word was missed. Canting the glass, while seen as a typical aesthetic detail associated with Vogel and many roadside structures of this period, had a functional purpose as it reduced glare. Vogel was so concerned with efficiency that he even designed the women's rest rooms with ladies' urinals, which are still functioning, although the state of Maryland outlawed further installation of these fixtures after 1958.[32]

The appearance and disappearance of the American drive-in theater speaks to our rapidly changing society, economy, and technology throughout the twentieth century and into the twenty-first. Greater commercial development along major highways and expanding suburbs over the past several decades have led to rising land values in the areas where drive-ins originally located. In addition, these theaters faced many obstacles to their continued financial viability, such as their limited adaptation to other uses; seasonal operation; the growth of the in-home entertainment industry (including affordable color televisions, cable and the VCR); the oil crisis in the 1970s; compact cars and our changing attitudes as a society toward the automobile; and inexpensive and poor-quality construction materials that rarely received maintenance. The drive-in theater emerged in a country that embraced the automobile and the cinema like none other. A uniquely American building type that encapsulated an era, the drive-in was a model of efficiency in design, an interwoven group of architectural elements responding to a variety of commercial, social, and aesthetic demands. The widespread construction of drive-ins enabled most every American the luxury of watching a picture several stories high in the comfort of their beloved car all within an atmospheric setting. Today, with less than six hundred remaining, many think fondly of the drive-in theater, symbolically linking it to a simpler past. Like these memories, the physical structures of the drive-in have become fleeting and intangible. While examples of this building type are disappearing, their impact on the American landscape is still clear. Design principles of early-twentieth-century roadside architecture, perfected and exemplified in the drive-in theater, continue to be practiced in modern American roadside design.

Notes

1. Opening advertisement for Super 29 Drive-in, *Washington, D.C., Evening Star,* Sept. 14, 1956. Advertisement for Broadway Drive-in Theater, *Richmond Times Dispatch,* Mar. 1950. Douglas Gomery, professor of journalism, Univ. of Maryland–College Park, telephone interview with author, Sept. 1997. Don King, former operator of Mt. Vernon and Branch Drive-ins, telephone interview with author, Mar. 28, 1998. "Advertisement for Queens Chapel Drive-in," *Washington, D.C., Evening Star,* May 15, 1958.

2. "The Doubtful Aspects of the Drive-in Theatre Project," *Boxoffice,* 20 May 1944, 17.

3. Scholarly studies include Kerry Seagrave, *Drive-in Theaters: A History from Their Inception in 1933* (Jefferson, N.C.: McFarland, 1992); Don Sanders and Susan Sanders, *The American Drive-in Movie Theater* (Osceola, Wisc.: Motorbooks International Publishers, 1997); Wil Anderson, *Mid-Atlantic Roadside Delights: Roadside Architecture of Yesterday and Today in New York, New Jersey and Pennsylvania*

(Portland, Maine: Anderson and Sons Publishing, 1991); and John Margolies and Emily Gwathmey, *Ticket to Paradise: American Movie Theaters and How We Had Fun* (Boston: Little, Brown, 1991). Architectural studies include Chester H. Leibs, *Main Street to Miracle Mile* (Baltimore: Johns Hopkins Univ. Press, 1995), Maggie Valentine, *The Show Starts at the Sidewalk* (New Haven: Yale Univ. Press, 1994), Harold D. Hauf, "Drive-ins: Banks, Theaters, and Restaurants," *Architectural Record,* Aug. 1950, 130–53.

4. This chapter is based on a larger study of the forty-three drive-in theaters that were built in the Baltimore, Maryland, Washington, D.C., and Richmond, Virginia, metropolitan areas, constructed between 1938 and 1967, used as a case-study for a building type analysis.

5. The most significant architectural history defining roadside architecture is Chester H. Leibs, *Main Street to Miracle Mile*. His landmark work discusses fully the architectural styles and tenants of roadside architecture and features a chapter on the drive-in theater.

6. Seagrave, *Drive-in Theaters,* 234.

7. See David Naylor, *American Picture Palaces: The Architecture of Fantasy* (New York: Van Nostrand Reinhold, 1981), and Valentine, *Show Starts on the Sidewalk.*

8. Seagrave, *Drive-in Theaters,* 89.

9. Liebs, *Main Street to Miracle Mile,* 61.

10. "The New 'Drive Over and Drop In' Theatre," *Theatre Catalog,* 1945, 105.

11. See featured articles on the drive-in theater in *Theatre Catalog* and *Boxoffice* in the 1940s.

12. Liebs, *Main Street to Miracle Mile,* 50–53. and Margolies, *Ticket to Paradise,* 113–39.

13. The Governor Ritchie is definitely the first drive-in theater in Maryland, supported by *Film Daily Yearbook* and several articles, notably "Outdoors Movie to Open Sunday," *Baltimore Sun,* May 12, 1939. Most of my sources indicate that the Mt. Vernon was the first drive-in theater in Virginia. The opening-day article for the Mt. Vernon states that it is the first to open in "this section of the country"—see "Open Air Theater Opening Monday," *Alexandria Gazette,* Aug. 10, 1938. The earliest available list of drive-ins, published in *Film Daily Yearbook* (1942, 854), indicates a few other drive-ins had been constructed in southern Virginia, in Bowling Green, Del Mar, Norfolk, and Williamsburg by 1942, but I found no evidence to suggest they opened prior to the Mt. Vernon.

14. "Open-Air Theatre Opening Monday," *Alexandria Gazette,* Aug. 10, 1938, and "Drive-in Theatre Opens Monday Night," *Alexandria Gazette,* Aug. 13, 1938.

15. King interview.

16. "Drive-in Theatre Opens Monday Night," *Alexandria Gazette,* Aug. 13, 1938, 6.

17. "Outdoors Movie to Open Sunday," *Baltimore Sun,* May 12, 1939.

18. "State's First Drive-in Movie Opens in Anne Arundel County," *Baltimore Sun,* 15 May 1939.

19. "Local Drive-in Boast's South's Biggest Screen," *Richmond Times Dispatch,* 14 June 1947.

20. King interview.

21. *Boxoffice,* May 20, 1944, 17.

22. Seagrave, *Drive-in Theaters,* 20.

23. King interview, and "Washington News," *Boxoffice,* July 1949 and July 1954.

24. "New Bellwood Drive-in Movie Sets Opening for Friday Night," *Richmond Times Dispatch,* May 26, 1948, 13.

25. Advertisement for Bellwood Drive-in Theater, *Richmond Times Dispatch,* May 29, 1948, 12.

26. Sanders and Sanders, *American Drive-in Movie Theater,* 55.

27. Douglas Gomery, "A Movie-Going Capital: Washington, DC, in the History of Movie Presentation," *Washington History,* Spring/Summer 1997, 4–23.

28. Jack Vogel to the author, Mar. 26, 1998.

29. "Drive-ins Labeled Only 'Licensed Petting Places,' So $1000 Fee, Curfew Set," *Variety,* 17 Dec. 1947, 1.

30. Fred Wineland, former Washington, D.C., drive-in theater chain owner, telephone interview with author, Mar. 29, 1998.

31. Liebs, *Main Street to Miracle Mile,* 60.

32. D. Edward Vogel, stepson of Jack Vogel and operator of Bengies Drive-in Theater, interview with author, Sept. 11, 1997, Middle River, Maryland.

15

"A Pleasant Illusion of Unspoiled Countryside"

The American Parkway and the Problematics of an Institutionalized Vernacular

TIMOTHY DAVIS

The history of the American parkway provides an ideal avenue for exploring the complex relationships between vernacular and official landscapes. The fundamental paradox of parkway development was that it employed sophisticated design strategies and aggressive governmental intervention to produce institutionally sanctioned substitutes for traditional roadside landscapes that were rapidly disappearing in the wake of urbanization and commercial development. Despite the dominant role played by professional designers, parkways embodied vernacular precedents and were embraced by broad segments of the public. This commingling of elite and popular influences produced provocative tensions, unheralded and often ironic convergences, and continuously evolving permutations of built form and social function. Initially conceived as elite retreats from disorderly urban streets, parkways shed their allegiance to cultivated European prototypes and began to embrace native

forms and desires. Allusively, at first, but with an increasing literalness that eventually verged on caricature, they evolved into idealized simulations of classic country roads. By the time this transformation was complete, middle-class motorists had become the primary audience, as elite nature-lovers retreated to remote wildernesses and a new generation of cultural tourists searched out charismatic relics of the early automobile-oriented commercial landscapes that parkway promoters had sought to suppress. While nostalgic baby boomers and ironic Gen-Xers celebrated unregulated roadside architecture as a more authentic and relevant "vernacular" than the landscape architects' romantic reconstructions, preservationists and historians cast parkways as embodiments of broad-based social and technological trends. The term "parkway" itself escaped the strictures of institutional control, as developers and a diverse array of civic groups applied it to mundane roadways that bore little resemblance to the rarified compositions of elite designers.

The parkway's multifaceted history would seem to present a provocative topic for students of the built environment, but the complex and sometimes contradictory nature of this quintessentially American space has mediated against a comprehensive analysis of its origins and evolution. The strictures of traditional academic disciplines have also hampered a more holistic historical treatment. The most prominent narratives of American parkway development have been written by art historians and historians of technology. The latter highlight the parkway's technological evolution as a precursor of modern freeways, while the former tend to construct chronologies of stylistic innovation and attribute them to a handful of heroic individuals. Both

approaches privilege the role of European antecedents, noted designers, and prestigious park commissions at the expense of local precedents, anonymous actors, and popular currents. Historians of vernacular architecture, who would seem to be interested in such influences, appear to have been deterred by the prominence of professional designers and institutional decision makers. A closer look at the historical record reveals that vernacular preferences and popular social practices had much more impact on American parkway development than has previously been acknowledged. By focusing on the complex relationship between elite and vernacular influences, moreover, this essay underscores the problems that can arise where rigid and artificial academic constructs are applied to the analysis of actual artifacts and social practices.[1]

Fig. 15.1. Blue Ridge Parkway, 1997. Courtesy of David Haas/Historic American Engineering Record.

At first glance, parkways would seem to be the antithesis of vernacular landscapes. They were developed by governmental authorities as explicit reactions to rapidly evolving vernacular environments that struck conservative observers as ugly, dangerous, and dominated by disturbing evidence of social and technological change. This was true both in the nineteenth century, when the first waves of urban sprawl spread out from America's major cities, and in the mid-twentieth century, when the rapid increase in automobile ownership created an explosion of commercial development along America's highways and byways. The parkway-building booms that arose in response to these developments epitomized J. B. Jackson's conception of an official landscape produced by institutionally empowered designers intent on imposing order, stability, and traditional notions of social and aesthetic propriety on unruly vernacular environments that struck refined observers as unsightly and undesirable.[2] Parkway developers sought to replace the physical deficiencies, visual dissonance, and vulgar commercialism of unrestricted roadsides with comprehensively designed and tightly controlled environments that accorded with elite ideals of landscape beauty, civic virtue, and tastefully regulated consumption. European models clearly played a prominent role in this process, but parkway promoters also worked within well-established native traditions of roadside improvement and landscape appreciation. They combined European design precedents with entrenched American beliefs in the virtues of rural life and the uplifting influence of nature. While historical accounts have emphasized the parkway's European heritage and sophisticated design attributes, parkways appealed to both elite and popular audiences and drew on a wide variety of reformist impulses, both urban and rural. The stylistic diversity and geographic distribution of American parkway development has also been underappreciated. A few prominent eastern prototypes dominate the scholarly discourse, but parkways of myriad shapes and sizes can be found throughout the American landscape, where they reflect local aims and aspirations regardless of their affiliation with "significant" designers or prestigious park commissions.

This complex and occasionally contradictory amalgam of elite and popular influences was present from the start of the parkway movement. The invention of the word "parkway" was in itself a striking demonstration of the shifting status of urban spaces and topographical terminology. Frederick Law Olmsted and his partner Calvert Vaux introduced the word "parkway" to describe the impressive boulevards they proposed in their 1868 report to the Brooklyn park commissioners. This neologism evoked agreeable associations and encapsulated the underlying concept of a landscaped recreational road that functioned simultaneously as both park and way. The new coinage also reflected contemporary concern about the vernacularization of formerly elite terms and spaces. By the 1860s, real estate boosters were invoking the traditional European appellations "boulevard" and "avenue" to enhance the prestige of dubious developments. Olmsted observed that one so-called avenue on Staten Island was nothing but "a narrow lane leading to a stable." The word "boulevard," he declaimed, was being "applied all around New York to wretched dirt roads fifty feet wide." The degradation of the term "avenue" so irked Olmsted that he refused to use it, exclaiming, "All association of dignity and wealth which once belonged to the word are lost and it henceforth suggests nothing but clap-trap."[3] Olmsted's new term brimmed with novelty and refinement, yet it tapped into a rich vein of American landscape symbolism. Not only did the concept of a parkway seem less formal and autocratic than its European precursors, but the word's pastoral associations accorded with the prevailing ideology that celebrated rural virtues and equated the suburban lifestyle with moral welfare and material progress. The owner of an ostentatious townhouse on a grand avenue could be criticized for forsaking homespun values in favor of Eurocentric affectation, but the inhabitants of a parkway district embraced the American dream of a middle landscape that united the best of city and country, nature and culture, virtuous yeomanry and social and economic advancement.[4]

From a pragmatic perspective, nineteenth-century parkways were designed to serve as safe and attractive approaches to suburban parks. The first of the genre,

Brooklyn's Eastern and Ocean Parkways, offered pleasant routes for carriage owners to drive to and from Prospect Park without subjecting themselves to the dangers and disruptions of crowded and poorly maintained city streets.[5] Other major metropolises such as Buffalo, Chicago, and Boston soon followed, creating impressive networks of parkways linking residential districts and urban centers with sprawling suburban reservations (fig. 15.2). For Olmsted and his contemporaries, these parks and parkways were not so much mirrors of English estates as substitutes for the traditional rural and suburban scenery that was fast disappearing from the metropolitan landscape. Throughout the first half of the nineteenth century, it had been a relatively easy matter to escape tightly packed urban areas for relaxing drives surrounded by soothing rural scenery. As urban sprawl, industrial development, and rising traffic began to diminish the appeal of suburban pleasure driving, however, it became necessary to create artificial landscapes to simulate the appeal of traditional vernacular roadways. Underscoring this motivation in their 1871 report to the Brooklyn park commissioners, Olmsted and Vaux observed, "It was from the rapid destruction of all charm in the suburban roads, and the constantly increasing difficulty of finding any place near the city in which natural landscapes or a rural ramble could be quietly enjoyed, that the want of a public park was

Fig. 15.2. Boston's Riverway, or Emerald Necklace, c. 1900. Courtesy of National Commission of Fine Arts.

experimentally known." They acknowledged that vernacular country lanes still offered the most appealing venues for scenic driving, in the lucky instances that they were still readily available.[6]

The carriage occupants that thronged the smoothly paved driveways of nineteenth-century parks and parkways were clearly more privileged than most Americans, but it is important to note that this form of pleasure driving represented a significant democratization of its European antecedents. In Europe, pleasure driving had long been the preserve of the landed gentry who could afford both expensive, handmade carriages and the carefully manicured driveways necessitated by primitive suspension systems. By the middle of the nineteenth century, improvements in carriage production combined with the development of cheap, smooth, and durable paving methods to make recreational driving both more appealing and more affordable. While the cost of maintaining horses and carriages kept this pastime beyond the reach of most citizens, the rapid growth of a metropolitan bourgeoisie created a burgeoning market for elegant coaches and attractively landscaped roadways.[7] The enjoyment of these pleasure drives was not restricted to the Astors, Vanderbilts, and Silas Laphams of the world, however.[8] Less-favored citizens, rural Americans, and residents of smaller towns and cities could enjoy park drives and country roads. Horse-ownership was more common outside of major cities and many small towns had their own parks and parkways along with locally renowned scenic drives and Lover's Lanes, where landscape appreciation mixed with other amusements. The parkways that Olmsted and his prominent colleagues designed for major American cities dominate the art historical record, but dozens, if not hundreds, of more modest parkways were developed by local civic improvement associations, municipal engineers, park departments, and real estate speculators.[9]

While the major urban parkways catered to the carriage trade, they were also intended to serve as local parks for the neighborhoods through which they passed. It has become fashionable to chastise nineteenth-century park designers for developing large pleasure grounds far from working-class populations, but

Olmsted and his contemporaries were well-aware of this shortcoming and saw parkways as the most effective means of extending the benefits of nature throughout the urban fabric.[10] Lower-class parkway neighbors may not have been able to afford carriages, but they could stroll along the footpaths and enjoy fresh air, sunlight, cooling shade, and soothing greenery.[11] Following the development of the electric trolley in the 1880s, moreover, many parkway proposals included provisions for electric car lines to accommodate ordinary urbanites.[12] The bicycle craze of the 1890s further expanded the audience for parks roads and parkways.[13] Some elite parkgoers objected to the increasingly populist impact of parkway development. Henry James blamed Boston's new parkways for the fact that the "rustle of petticoats" and the "eternal American note of . . . gregariousness" had "desecrated" formerly isolated suburban reservations where he once strolled in contemplative solitude with kindred spirits such as William Dean Howells and James Russell Lowell.[14]

Stylistically, the first parkways resembled conventional European boulevards. Olmsted and Vaux explicitly cited Paris' Avenue de l'Imperatrice and Berlin's Unter den Linden as precedents for their Brooklyn parkways. While Olmsted and Vaux were personally familiar with these prestigious prototypes, they were also aware of wide-ranging American efforts at roadside beautification.[15] Towns and cities throughout the colonial era and early republic promoted roadside tree planting and related improvements. Provincial capitals developed impressive ornamental streets, small towns passed laws protecting roadside trees, and George Washington and other members of the gentry attended to the appearance of roadways on their country estates.[16] Ordinary farmers and villagers occasionally embellished rural roadsides, as well, though most vernacular roads bore a more utilitarian appearance.[17] During the second half of the nineteenth century, the widespread Village Improvement movement promoted roadside tree planting as an essential component of its campaign to beautify America's small towns and rural landscapes. Directed more toward embellishing existing roadways than creating new pleasure drives, Village Improvement efforts transformed American roadsides and provided a

fertile environment for more ambitious parkway projects by promoting broad-based concern for roadside aesthetics.[18] Olmsted and Vaux's vaunted Brooklyn parkways were directly preceded by a number of impressive formal boulevards ranging from Boston's highly acclaimed Commonwealth Avenue to Manchester, New Hampshire's modestly named Elm Street, a company-built ornamental boulevard that some historians credit as the first divided roadway in America. While the Amoskeag Manufacturing Company's designers may have looked to European precedents as well, this overlooked project underscores the complex nature of the parkway's genealogy.[19]

Vernacular sensibilities played an increasingly prominent role toward the end of nineteenth century, as parkway developers forsook the traditional boulevard model in favor of a more informal aesthetic. Beginning in the 1880s with Boston's Emerald Necklace project, parkway designers increasingly sought to enfold visitors in a mixture of naturalistic and pastoral scenery. While the lingering impact of the English landscape gardening school undeniably influenced parkway designers, the similarities to traditional country lanes were undoubtedly more resonant with mainstream American audiences than highbrow allusions to John Ruskin, William Gilpin, and Humphry Repton. Even Olmsted, who was well versed in European landscape theories, credited his youthful experience touring New England byways as a major influence on his design approach, which prized broad pastoral effects over the more intricate arrangements of European gardens.[20] Leading American sources celebrated vernacular country roads as repositories of scenic beauty and symbolic values (fig. 15.3). During the 1890s, the short-lived but influential journal *Garden and Forest* vigorously promoted the appreciation and preservation of vernacular roadsides, praising their physical appearance and sentimental associations.[21] Charles Mulford Robinson, the City Beautiful movement's most ebullient popularizer, also extolled vernacular precedents, advising parkway designers to "have in mind—as the ideal—a country lane with its tangled flower-decked border, or a wood road with its dark vistas and twinkling sunlight."[22] Frank Waugh, an early-twentieth-century proselytizer for scenic

Fig. 15.3. Illustration of country road scenery. From Waugh, *Landscape Beautiful.*

improvement, similarly championed traditional vernacular roadsides, asserting, "Every man knows that the most attractive scenery in the world clings naturally to the country road."[23]

The ascendance of informal aesthetics enabled park commissions to substitute actual country roads for their highly stylized artificial counterparts, further blurring the distinction between vernacular and official landscapes. This approach was appealing for practical as well as aesthetic reasons. Major projects like Boston's Emerald Necklace consumed large amounts of time and money to construct new roadways and reproduce picturesque scenery in areas that had already lost their historic charm. Cities that had not yet succumbed to urban sprawl could often avoid these expenses by extending their authority over existing country lanes. A significant component of Minneapolis's acclaimed parkway system was cobbled together in this manner and many smaller municipalities pursued similar policies.[24] Where development pressures were minimal, vernacular landscapes continued to afford idyllic opportunities for pleasure driving. Leisurely Sunday driving along unimproved country roads was a widely popular pursuit, both before and after the invention of the automobile. Lengthier coaching expeditions were also prized, though long-distance excursions were generally the privilege of well-to-do excursionists who could afford to take extended vacations.[25] These rural rambles

offered a pleasing variety of scenery ranging from dense forests and sun-dappled clearings to working agricultural landscapes and quaint old farmsteads—the same scenes, in fact, that later parkway developers would attempt to reproduce for twentieth-century motorists.

The visual culture of the day provides ample evidence of the widespread appeal of vernacular roadside scenery. Sentimental country road imagery was enormously popular during the early decades of the twentieth century, appearing in myriad forms from advertisements and magazine illustrations to postcards and more expensive hand-tinted photographs. The preeminent popularizer of picturesque roadside scenes was the photographer Wallace Nutting. While primarily remembered for his colonial revival confections, Nutting produced an abundance of similarly saccharine country road imagery. Just as a great many Americans relished Nutting's romanticized images of colonial domesticity, they took solace in his sentimental scenes of dirt roads winding through bucolic landscapes untainted by signs of modern commerce and industry. His immensely popular "States Beautiful" book series was full of nostalgic views of charming country lanes, quaint covered bridges, and birch-lined forest roads. The Vermont volume began with a disquisition on driving conditions, while the Virginia edition abounded with roadside pastorals that presaged the design scheme of Blue Ridge Parkway, right down to the picturesque rail fences, rugged mountain pastures, and dilapidated log dwellings.[26]

Nutting's photographs reached their zenith of popularity in the 1920s and 1930s, just as the automobile and related commercial forces were radically transforming America's highways and byways.[27] Nineteenth-century suburban lanes may have struck refined citizens as ugly and undesirable, but the new automobile-related roadside elicited widespread condemnation as a menace to public safety, an affront to established norms of beauty and good taste, and an indication that America had lost its way in the pursuit of technological progress and unbridled commerce (fig. 15.4). Merchants defiled the countryside with garish billboards and decimated traditional roadside landscapes with mile after mile of tawdry businesses designed to capitalize on the burgeoning market of travelers in need of food, fuel, and lodging. Gas stations, cabin courts, and quick-lunch stands sprouted along previously undeveloped roads and employed all manner of architectural excess to capture the attention of passing motorists. The unregulated entrances to these establishments disrupted traffic, while the eye-catching gimmickry offended the sensibilities of excursionists in search of picturesque scenery. Popular and professional periodicals roundly decried the status of America's roadsides, not just on aesthetic grounds but as threats to the public welfare, obstacles to economic development, and infringements on the increasingly popular pastime of motor touring.[28] As highway conditions continued to deteriorate and automobiles worked their way down the social ladder, people with little knowledge of European landscape theory or Olmstedian park design began to look to parkway development as a means of rescuing America's roadsides and restoring beauty, safety, order, and comforting sense of propriety to the driving experience.

A key reason for the parkway's increasingly broad appeal was the widespread recognition that the new automobile-oriented parkways were not just more attractive than ordinary roadways, but safer and more efficient as well. The same development strategies that enabled parkway designers to keep roadside merchants at bay also helped alleviate the dangers and deficiencies of traditional roads, which were overburdened by rising traffic demands and poorly designed for high-speed auto travel. Since parkways were recreational facilities rather than public highways, it was technically easier and culturally more permissible to prohibit roadside development and restrict access from neighboring streets and properties. Limiting access and carrying intersecting roadways above or below the parkway drive greatly improved safety and efficiency, which was further enhanced by the fact that the parkway's broad right-of-way enabled designers to employ longer, more gracefully flowing curves that did away with the sharp turns and poor sightlines of roadways designed for horse-and-buggy speeds. Since parkway authorities owned the roadsides, billboards could be banished and the merchandising of gasoline and other travel-related supplies confined to a small number of carefully regulated and tastefully designed service plazas.

The principal models for this new type of parkway were the Bronx River Parkway and related developments constructed by New York's Westchester County Park Commission in the 1920s.[29] New York City's transportation czar Robert Moses borrowed Westchester County's design techniques to develop a similar parkway network affording access to the parks and beaches of Long Island. Though these parkways were initially intended as modernized versions of traditional pleasure drives, their practical appeal soon became apparent. Commuters flocked to take advantage of the clutter- and congestion-free roadways, causing consternation to traditionalists who fretted that recreational values would be diminished by utilitarian traffic. Many greeted the parkway's increasing popularization as a positive development, however, concurring with Philadelphia civic leader Andrew Crawford's contention that "the idea that a park or parkway is somewhat of an old-fashioned parlor—only to be used on Sunday when the parson comes to dinner after church—is one that should be completely discarded."[30] While traditional recreational motives continued to dominate parkway development throughout the 1930s, more broad-based transportation planners began to appropriate the basic design strategies for utilitarian purposes, sometimes employing the conventional term "parkway" but also coining new words, such as "freeway" and "expressway." Characterizing

Fig. 15.4. 1920s Roadside improvement cartoon. For *Nature Magazine,* reprinted in *American Civic Annual,* 1929. Courtesy of *Nature Magazine.*

high-speed limited-access motorways as "vernacular landscapes" would seem to stretch the limits of this increasingly elastic term, but freeways and interstates changed the face of America and have become quotidian backdrops to everyday life throughout the developed world; the fact that they are direct descendants of Olmsted and Vaux's nineteenth-century parkways underscores just how prosaic and ubiquitous formerly elite landscapes can become.

Stylistically, the first generation of motor parkways occupied a middle ground between the refined aesthetics of late-nineteenth-century developments and the overtly "vernacular" landscapes of later National Park Service (NPS) projects. While the bridges and service buildings occasionally evoked local vernacular traditions, classically composed naturalistic scenery dominated the landscape in accordance with the traditional Olmstedian goal of providing relief from the modern man-made environment (fig. 15.5). The Westchester parkways might remind motorists of the fast-disappearing country lanes of their real or imagined youth, but the relationship to traditional rural roads remained more allusive than literal and the development process and intended audience was less than democratic. The idealized landscape park rather than the historic country road remained the designers' overt model. In order to transform busy transportation routes and long-settled suburban areas into pristine linear parks, parkway developers did more than simply sweep aside offending billboards and uproot objectionable roadside stands. In keeping with a tradition of landscape "improvement" that dated back centuries, from the displacement of English tenant farmers to Olmsted's eviction of Central Park communities, existing vernacular landscapes were depopulated and radically reconfigured to produce picturesque environments devoted to leisure and aesthetic contemplation. Parkway commissions uprooted lower-class residents, tore down houses by the score—many of the sort that would soon be cherished as quaint, historic, and "vernacular"—and banished all signs of production and toil. Vegetable gardens, small businesses, and working farms were eradicated to produce lifeless pastoral illusions composed of placid meadows, winding streams, and artfully located plantings.[31]

Fig. 15.5. Bronx River Parkway, c. 1922. From *Report of the Bronx Parkway Commission,* 1925.

Despite this inherently inequitable process, the parkway landscape was moving further away from elite European prototypes. By the 1920s, designers found it necessary to simplify and exaggerate traditional aesthetic strategies, not simply because motorists were moving too fast to appreciate complex visual effects but because the majority of people were no longer concerned with the finer points of landscape appreciation. While some traditionalists viewed this situation with alarm, others interpreted the parkway's broadening popularity in a positive light. Prominent planner J. Horace McFarland applauded the democratizing influence of increasingly affordable automobiles. The traditional park had its "good roads for the barouche or victoria and its saddle-paths for the trotting-horses of the rich," McFarland observed, but it "did mighty little to make life worth living for the tired worker who occasionally walked the restricted paths." Thanks to the growing availability of cheap cars and the proliferation park and parkway systems, McFarland maintained, a broad spectrum of Americans could enjoy the benefits of pleasure driving and outdoor recreation.[32] Boston landscape architect Arthur Shurtleff similarly urged his colleagues to accommodate changing tastes, insisting that modern recreationalists had neither the time nor the inclination to "dwell in a lingering fashion upon the loveliness of these park landscapes and pause to contemplate them in the fashion of the Schools of Landscape Painters three-quarters of a century ago."[33] Further evidence of the parkways' transitional status could be seen in the appearance of rugged light poles, substantial log guardrails, and increasingly rustic bridges and service buildings. While nineteenth-century landscape architects also employed rustic design details, these twentieth-century artifacts were simpler, more robust, and somewhat more contextual than their elaborate Victorian predecessors, hinting at the more literal and emphatically "American" vernacular aesthetics that would soon dominate the parkway landscape.

Mount Vernon Memorial Highway, which linked Washington and Mount Vernon and was the first parkway completed by the federal government, carried the self-conscious invocation of vernacular motifs to another level. Along with the standard timber guard rails and light poles, parkway designers employed pseudo-vernacular colonial revival–style sign boards and engaged Edward Donn Jr., the architect of the National Park Service's fanciful recreation of Washington's birthplace, to design a colonial revival concession stand for the parkway's terminus (fig. 15.6). While previous parkway developers had ignored or eradicated the human history along their routes, Mount Vernon Memorial Highway was promoted as a cultural landscape steeped in historical associations that would theoretically inform and inspire motorists, turning them into more patriotic citizens as they drove along. These conspicuous historical references were intended to underscore the project's unique commemorative function, but they also reflected the pervasiveness of the contemporary colonial revival

Fig. 15.6. Terminus of Mount Vernon Memorial Highway, 1932. Bureau of Public Roads Collection, National Archives.

movement, which helped Americans adapt to modern times by infusing the rapidly changing landscape with comforting reminders of traditional values. While parkway promoters routinely condemned the kitsch sensibilities of contemporary roadside development, Donn's quaint concession stand was not far removed from the pseudo-colonial gas stations and neo–Mount Vernon motels motorists encountered along unregulated roadsides.[34]

The 1932 bicentennial of George Washington's birth provided the ostensible impetus for the memorial parkway, but the increasing emphasis on cultural tourism reflected broader social trends, as government authorities, local boosters, and commercial interests eagerly marketed the historic charms to be found along America's highways and byways. The National Park Service extended the historical parkway concept with the development of Colonial Parkway, linking Yorktown, Williamsburg, and Jamestown, Virginia. Not only did Colonial Parkway emanate from the cultural hearth of colonial revivalism, its designers attempted to evoke vernacular precedents by facing modern concrete bridges with colonial-style brick and going to great lengths to produce a rough-textured road surface intended to mimic local roads of the colonial era.[35] Despite the explicit invocation of historical figures, events, and building practices, the landscapes of both the Mount Vernon and Colonial Parkways retained a strong emphasis on traditional picturesque aesthetics in which man-made structures were held to a minimum and signs of industry and toil were replaced by carefully composed naturalistic scenery.

With the next generation of parkways, begun in the mid- to late 1930s, the NPS literally went to greater lengths to combine the growing interest in heritage tourism with the traditional emphasis on scenic appreciation. The Blue Ridge and Natchez Trace Parkways, each approximately five hundred miles long, were explicitly intended to recapture the experience of bygone country roads and encourage motorists to immerse themselves for days at a time in constantly changing panoramas of natural scenery, fertile fields, rustic log cabins, and placidly grazing livestock (fig. 15.7). A variety of practical, aesthetic, and symbolic influences fostered this newfound

Fig. 15.7. Blue Ridge Parkway, c. 1954. National Park Service.

embrace of cultural landscapes. From an aesthetic perspective, designers realized that most motorists would find hundred-mile-long stretches of unrelieved natural scenery to be deathly boring. In pragmatic terms, they knew it would be impossible to isolate motorists from surrounding cultural developments over such long distances. The NPS also realized it could reduce development costs by appropriating existing rural scenery, either physically, through fee-simple purchase, or visually, by securing scenic easements. On the symbolic level, the NPS recognized that many Americans were turning to scenes associated with the nation's pioneer past for the same sort of relaxation, inspiration, and cultural reassurance that earlier generations sought in the natural scenery of traditional landscape parks. According to NPS landscape architect Stanley Abbott, the Blue Ridge Parkway's emphasis on traditional cultural landscapes was intended to educate, soothe, and inspire overurbanized Americans by allowing them to experience "the look of homespun in an east that is chiefly silk and rayons."[36]

Abbott's terminology reflected a significant change in the parkway landscape: the explicit embrace of vernacular environments that earlier generations would have considered vulgarly utilitarian and ripe for reinterpretation through more refined pastoral allusions. Even the Colonial and Mount Vernon Parkways extolled the history of "great men and events" with little concern for the portrayal of everyday life. Condemning the elitist tendency of traditional preservation efforts

bent on securing "yet another George Washington's teacup," Abbott cast the new style of parkway development as a more democratic and socially beneficial means of addressing the needs of modern Americans. Automobile tourism had the potential to reconnect Americans with their storied past, Abbot believed, but he was worried that commercial development along unprotected roadsides eliminated contact with edifying traditional landscapes. "Only as we save some of the beauty of the countryside and some of the homespun folklore and the rural arts as part of our culture," Abbott advised, "will this favorite American pastime of touring be the salutary recreation that it might."[37]

While the iconography had become more egalitarian, the "vernacular landscape" of the Blue Ridge Parkway was as carefully composed and selectively edited as its predecessors. The NPS engaged in a comprehensive campaign to restore, improve, maintain, and—where it was deemed necessary—invent an idealized Appalachian landscape that combined seemingly unspoiled naturalistic scenery with engaging vignettes of traditional mountain culture. Designers went to great lengths to devise carefully crafted "vernacular" parkways that invoked an idealized national memory of rural bliss, replete with split-rail fences, hardy pioneer cabins, and carefully orchestrated displays of traditional agricultural practices. Detailed landscape plans complemented elaborate historic preservation and reconstruction efforts to create a carefully choreographed succession of scenic effects and symbolic messages. The meticulously orchestrated compositions were intended to allow modern Americans to experience the physical beauty and social harmony purportedly enjoyed by previous generations.

In many cases, the NPS's conception of an appropriate symbolic landscape contrasted sharply with existing vernacular environments as well as with the desires of the putative folk. To the park service's dismay, local residents were not always eager to participate in the noble project of helping urbanized Americans rediscover their mytical roots by touring landscapes frozen in a mythical past. Families that had lived within the proposed parkway reservations for generations frequently resisted relocation. Some had to be forcibly removed to make way for parkway development, though the NPS occasionally granted lifetime leases for aged mountaineers to occupy dwellings on parkway land, where they helped enliven and authenticate the park service's ode to rural America. The federal acquisition of thousands of acre of loosely regulated back country also conflicted with such traditional vernacular practices as moonshining, hunting, and the gathering of marketable forest commodities—activities that could not be countenanced within the boundaries of a national park.

Not only was there considerable opposition from displaced residents, but those who remained nearby frequently failed to play their assigned roles as blissfully uncontaminated American folk. Abbott complained that increasing prosperity and heightened self-consciousness prompted parkway neighbors to improve their buildings in ways that detracted from the desired "homespun" quality of the parkway landscape. "Hand-split shake roofs are replaced by tin, more utilitarian than attractive," he lamented. "Barns, heretofore a comfortable weathered gray get a coat of red paint; and board fences, the whitewash." Faced with the local population's reluctance to play the part of stolid, unchanging American folk, Abbott insisted the park service had an "obligation to save by other means the interest of the pioneer mountain architecture."[38] To make up for the locals' failure to adequately express their vernacular heritage, the NPS designed entrance stations and gas stations to emulate local building types, erected endless miles of rustic rail fence, restored historic buildings and grouped them together in themed developments, and celebrated romantic local figures and regional crafts in wayside exhibits. Structures that did not fit appropriate stereotypes were modified or removed. The most notable example of this revisionist landscaping occurred at the Mabry Mill site, where a photogenic millpond was created, the long-abandoned waterwheel was restored, and the owner's early-twentieth-century clapboard house was replaced with a more folksy log cabin transplanted from elsewhere in the park.[39]

The borderline between vernacular and official landscapes was further elided by the use of scenic easements and agricultural leases that encouraged local residents to continue farming on parkway land or nearby fields according to carefully prescribed policies designed to maintain an appropriately bucolic visual character. While NPS officials privately joked that an authentic presentation of traditional Appalachian agriculture would require replicating the region's dramatically eroded hillsides, the agency employed agronomists to instruct residents in more sustainable farming techniques.[40] With typical hubris, parkway landscape architects cast local residents as archaic simpletons who had unwittingly inherited a scenic and cultural treasure but had little idea of their good fortune and threatened to destroy it through ignorance and sloth. Describing an encounter with one of these local bumpkins, Abbott recalled, "I remember one day approaching a lean and lanky mountain man hoeing corn behind a yoke of oxen, in a steep and eroding field across which we had projected the Blue Ridge Parkway. He stood a long time after we told him that we wanted to buy his land. At last, he turned, slapped his thigh, and said, 'Ah bin livin' on this hyar mount'n well nigh on to 80 yars, and I never knew what this mount'n wuz fer—and now I know it's fer to put a road on it.'"[41]

Abbot's condescending anecdote underscored the differing perceptions that local citizens and federal officials held of the intended form and function of the Blue Ridge and Natchez Trace Parkways. Despite the NPS's rhetorical celebration of regional culture and its conspicuous invocation of vernacular motifs, the new parkways were intended to serve national rather than local interests. Many parkway neighbors complained that they had expected the heavily promoted motorways to serve as replacements for outdated local roads. They felt betrayed when the parkways turned out to be limited-access recreational routes that forbade trucks and commercial vehicles, cut across farms and homesteads, and generally complicated local travel by closing or diverting existing roads so that local traffic would not disrupt parkway motorists. Tensions were exacerbated by the fact that parkways were often the first paved roads in the areas they traversed. The focus on long-distance recreational travel drove home the message that the new parkways were intended primarily for urban tourists with ample incomes and leisure time. For local residents struggling to make do with

substandard country roads, the vision of affluent va-
cationists motoring smoothly along immaculately
maintained parkways epitomized the literal and symbolic marginalization of the rural South from mainstream America. Such disparities were especially galling
when school buses and emergency vehicles were
forced to make their way along narrow, unpaved, and
circuitous country roads that paralleled the safer and
more efficient parkways. Local residents were also dis-
mayed to learn that they were precluded from reaping
the benefits of increased tourist traffic due to pro-
scriptions against billboards and roadside stands.

Even when local residents embraced the new parkways, conflicts arose over aesthetic issues and social
values. Some Natchez Trace Parkway neighbors complained that the heavily wooded landscape was boring
and unattractive, urging the NPS to cut down more
trees to produce a manicured lawnlike appearance
that would distinguish the parkway from ordinary
local roads and present a more dignified impression of
local culture. Others called for the creation of facilities
for organized sports, which the NPS also dismissed as
inappropriate—though it was eager to provide camping facilities for long-distance motorists. One couple
living along the parkway requested that the trees buf-
fering the right-of-way be cut down so that they could
enjoy the parade of new cars displaying license plates
from across the country. The NPS denied all requests
deemed incompatible with the agency's goal of creating an idealized southern countryside.[42]

Natchez Trace Parkway development policies generally mirrored those applied on the Blue Ridge,
though the hillbilly theme park angle was toned down
somewhat and the NPS went to greater lengths to accommodate modern agricultural practices. Parkway
forces celebrated selected examples of local agriculture, recreating a traditional tobacco-growing operation at one wayside pullout and constructing an
elaborate scenic outlook designed to showcase a quin-
tessential family farm, which was reverently explicat-
ed with interpretive panels. The NPS built overpasses
to enable farmers to move stock and machinery underneath the parkway drive and endorsed large-scale
mechanized farming practices, particularly in the
blackland belt, where enormous fields were devoted to

soybeans and other major cash crops. As with Blue
Ridge Parkway, engaging historic structures and local
legends were celebrated with quaint signs and wayside
parks. While many functional local roads were severed
or abandoned, Natchez Trace Parkway designers carried the institutional embrace of vernacular roadways
to its apotheosis by preserving representative sections
of the historic Natchez Trace alongside the main motor-
way so that visitors could savor the experience of a
classic country road in all its embalmed glory.

The highly contrived nature of mid-twentieth-
century parkway landscapes might strike latter-day
observers as not only anti-vernacular, but superficial,
ahistorical, and politically or ecologically untenable.
Parkway designers were not beholden to later notions
of environmentalism or authenticity, however. NPS
designers prized the visual and associational qualities
of parkway landscapes and made no apologies for
their aesthetic biases and romanticizing intent. Abbott
and his colleagues repeatedly asserted the primacy of
the "roadside picture" and openly admitted that their
goal was to produce a "pleasant illusion of unspoiled
countryside."[43] Underscoring the preeminence of visual concerns and punctuating the parallels between
parkway development and contemporary regionalist
painting, Abbott suggested that a proposed Mississippi River parkway should be designed to present
motorists with a succession of "Grant Wood landscapes."[44] Since the NPS was not known to endorse the
iconoclastic irony that infused Wood's seemingly celebratory paintings with subversive undercurrents,
Abbott's assertion epitomized the naïve sincerity that
informed contemporary parkway development.

While it is easy to criticize the National Park Service's policy of constructing highly sentimentalized set-
pieces, the long-distance parkways proved enormously
popular with the American public. In fact, Blue Ridge
Parkway has long been the most heavily visited national park (fig. 15.8). Most tourists seem to accept the
NPS's reinterpretation of the Appalachian vernacular at
face value, or at to least welcome it as soothing respite
from the increasingly commercialized landscape outside the parkway boundaries, where modern building
practices and unconstrained development confound cultural expectations of what an Appalachian vernacular

Fig. 15.8. Blue Ridge Parkway, c. 1968. National Park Service.

landscape should be. Compared to nearby Dollywood or the tourist strips at Gatlinburg, Pigeon Forge and other gateways to the southern Appalachian parks, Blue Ridge Parkway presents a comforting illusion of cultural continuity and environmental harmony.

Despite their popularity with middle-brow motorists, the park service's paeans to primitive America provoked occasional criticism from the cultural elite. Presaging complaints that would soon be leveled against interstate highways, detractors asserted that parkways were sterile and monotonous, objecting that the rigidly controlled environments prevented motorists from experiencing authentic vernacular landscapes. While the NPS maintained it was preserving hallowed relics of the nation's cultural heritage, critics insisted that parkways isolated motorists within superficial displays of soporific sentimentalism. "Parkways are so perfect they're inhuman," complained a *New York Times* correspondent. "Miles and miles of scenery—trees, fences, walls, bridges—and never a town, never a house by the side of the road, friendly to man, never a lively billboard to relieve the dreary monotony."[45] Asserting that parkways were "deadly dull to drive on," a 1950 *Harper's Magazine* column concurred that parkway designers had gone too far in their efforts to constrain the inroads of consumer culture. Promoting the messy vitality of contemporary roadsides over the sterile serenity of the parkway's institutionalized vernacular, the magazine declared, "If this tame and empty post-card panorama is as good as we have, then no honor would be lost in opening it up immediately to a few enterprising merchants of pottery, salt-water taffy, and hooked rugs." Long before John Steinbeck and William Least Heat Moon turned such transgressive behavior into best-selling travelogues, *Harper's* urged motorists to escape the homogenized and pasteurized parkway landscape in order to discover the "real America" that lay along the unconstrained byways where vernacular cultures were allowed to flourish.[46] Applauding the chaotic heterogeneity that parkway designers had long labored to eliminate, the magazine enthused, "You can never tell what will appear around the next curve in an unfamiliar route. This is another way of saying that the roadside is still under the firm control of thousands of individualists who live along it."[47]

This embrace of unadulterated roadside entrepeneuralism remained muted, however, at least until the flames of baby-boomer nostalgia fueled an explosion of interest in mid-twentieth-century commercial architecture during the final decades of the twentieth century. Attempting to recapture the vanishing romance of its own mythical Golden Age, a new generation of sentimental excursionists set out in search of exotic roadside relics bypassed by the Interstate Highway System's legacy of calculated conformity. Casting the parkway purist's bete noire as the authentic vernacular landscape of the motor age, roadside architecture aficionados set about sanctifying, codifying, and commodifying gas stations, motels, and cabin courts in picture books, academic treatises, and National Register of Historic Places Nominations, and entrepreneurs attempted to capitalize on the retro-roadside architecture craze by building fanciful reproductions that rivaled the Blue Ridge Parkway's rustic follies. This increasingly organized enterprise began to bring the vernacular status of the mid-twentieth-century commercial roadside into question, however, as preservationists labored to save select specimens from evolving social processes. State and federal governments further clouded the relationship between vernacular and institutional landscapes by lending their imprimatur to heritage tourism programs that certified classic commercialized roadways such as Route 66 as official "Scenic Byways" and "All-American Roads."

Ironically, the institutional embrace of roadside kitsch coincided with what might be called the vernacularization of the parkway concept. Public officials and private developers appropriated the word as a stylish signifier to confer status on projects that shared little or nothing with the aesthetic concerns or social goals of parkway planners. In similar fashion, state and local authorities sought to elevate the stature of ordinary arterials through ostentatious "Memorial Parkway" designations, honoring such luminaries as guitarist Chet Atkins (Atlanta) and comedian Minnie Pearl (Tennessee). Replicating the process that inspired Olmsted to invent the term in the first place, tawdry speculative developments and run-of-the-mill subdivisions boasted nominal parkways adorned by paltry plantings or no embellishments at all. Even more mundane "industrial parkways" afforded access to equally oxymoronic "industrial parks." At the opposite end of the spectrum, "real" parkways garnered renewed acclaim as authentic touchstones of American culture. With the broadening of the historic preservation movement to include large-scale cultural landscapes and relics of the recent past, parkways were heralded as embodiments of important stages in the nation's social, artistic, and environmental development. Many parkways were nominated to the National Register of Historic Places, while the Blue Ridge and Natchez Trace Parkways made the Federal Highway Administration's inaugural list of "All-American Roads." Academics and governmental agencies also paid increasing attention to the history of American parkway development, generating reports, articles, books, and extensive collections of documentary photographs and drawings. The general public, meanwhile, continued to embrace parkways for their intended roles as scenic corridors, recreational retreats, and historic theme parks.

Tracing the evolution of the American parkway offers revealing insights into the complex and continually shifting relationships between vernacular and official landscapes. Elite and popular influences intermingled throughout the parkway's development and became increasingly difficult to differentiate as the automobile's impact on personal mobility elided distinctions between class-specific landscape experiences. While the irony of employing institutionally backed professional designers to preserve or reproduce "vernacular" landscapes is readily apparent—and authentic vernacular landscapes were undeniably compromised to create idealized scenic displays that conformed to romanticized and essentially conservative ideologies of aesthetic beauty and social harmony—the widespread popularity of parkways renders it difficult to dismiss them as hollow aesthetic constructs or elitist artifacts of cultural exclusion. The distinctions between varying degrees of institutionalized and unadulterated vernacular roadsides have become increasingly blurred, moreover, and to most observers, largely irrelevant. Not only have parkways performed the role of the traditional country road so convincingly that many observers view them as unproblematic survivals of authentic vernacular landscapes, but they have come to be regarded as significant cultural landscapes in their own right. In classic postmodern fashion, the simulacrum is now celebrated as much as its ostensible antecedent, and both the parkway and its commercialized counterparts are venerated as charismatic alternatives to the perceived banality of modern highway development. While it would be specious to declare that the parkway's heterogeneous origins and broad-based popularity qualify it as a vernacular landscape in the conventional sense of the term, the history of American parkway development underscores the difficulty of assigning complex and continuously evolving landscapes to static and inherently artificial academic categories.

Notes

1. Classic treatments of American parkway development appear in Norman T. Newton, *Design on the Land: The Development of Landscape Architecture* (Cambridge: Harvard Univ. Press, 1971); Christopher Tunnard and Boris Pushkarev, *Man-made America; Chaos or Control?* (New Haven: Yale Univ. Press, 1963); Carl Condit, *American Building Art: The Twentieth Century* (New York: Oxford Univ. Press, 1961), and David Schuyler, *The New Urban Landscape: The Redefinition of City Form in Nineteenth-Century America* (Baltimore: Johns Hopkins Univ. Press, 1986). Cynthia Zaitsevsky provides a detailed review of Olmsted's Boston parkway projects in *Frederick Law Olmsted and the Boston Park System* (Cambridge: Harvard Univ. Press, 1982). The important Buffalo park and parkway system is discussed in Francis Kowski, ed., *The Best Planned City: The Olmsted Legacy in Buffalo* (Buffalo, N.Y.: Burchfield Art Center, 1991). Clay McShane offers numerous insights into parkway development in his *Down the Asphalt Path: The Automobile and the American City* (New York: Columbia Univ. Press, 1994). Parkways are presented as emblems of modern design in Richard Guy Wilson, Diane Wilson, and Dickran Tashjian, *The Machine Age in America, 1918–1941* (New York: Brooklyn Museum/Abrams: 1986). Bruce Radde's paean to Connecticut's Merrit Parkway (*The Merrit Parkway* [New Haven: Yale Univ. Press, 1993]) and Sara Amy Leach's overview of parkway development in Washington, D.C. ("Fifty Years of Parkway Construction in and around the Nation's Capital," in *Roadside America: The Automobile in Design and Culture,* ed. Jan Jennings [Ames:

Iowa Univ. Press, 1990], 185–97) also provide brief summaries of the genre. My dissertation provides a comprehensive overview of American parkway development (Timothy Davis, "Mount Vernon Memorial Highway and the Evolution of the American Parkway" [Ph.D. diss., Univ. of Texas at Austin, 1997]). Important contemporary accounts of American parkway development include Sylvester Baxter's three-part series, "Parkways and Boulevards in American Cities" in *American Architect and Building News* 62 (Oct. 8, 1898): 11–12; (Oct. 22, 1898): 27–28; and (Oct. 29, 1898): 35–36; John C. Olmsted, "Classes of Parkways," *Landscape Architecture* 6 (Oct. 1915): 38–48; John Nolen and Henry Hubbard, *Parkways and Land Values* (Cambridge: Harvard Univ. Press, 1937); Stanley Abbott, "Parkways—Past, Present, and Future," *Parks and Recreation* 31 (Dec. 1948): 681–91; and Gilmore Clarke's "The Parkway Idea," in *The Highway and the Landscape,* ed. W. Brewster Snow (New Brunswick, N.J.: Rutgers Univ. Press, 1959), 32–55. Sigfried Giedion offered an insightful analysis of parkway aesthetics in *Space, Time and Architecture: the Growth of A New Tradition* (Cambridge: Harvard Univ. Press, 1941).

2. John Brinckerhoff Jackson, *Discovering the Vernacular Landscape* (New Haven: Yale Univ. Press, 1984), xii, 148–51.

3. Frederick Law Olmsted, "Report to the Staten Island Improvement Commission of a Preliminary Scheme of Improvement, 1871," in *Landscape into Cityscape: Frederick Law Olmsted's Plans for a Greater New York City,* ed. Albert Fein (Ithaca, N.Y.: Cornell Univ. Press, 1967), 254.

4. For the classic exposition of the cultural resonance of this idealized middle landscape, see Leo Marx, *The Machine in the Garden: Technology and the Pastoral Ideal in America* (New York: Oxford Univ. Press, 1964).

5. The parkway's value in compensating for the short-comings of contemporary roadways is discussed in Olmsted, Vaux and Company, "Report of the Landscape Architects and Superintendents to the President of the Board of Commissioners of Prospect Park, Brooklyn, January 1, 1868," in *Papers of Frederick Law Olmsted: Writings on Parks, Parkways, and Park Systems*, Supplementary Series, ed. Charles Beveridge and Carolyn Hoffman (Baltimore: Johns Hopkins Univ. Press, 1997), 1:112–46.

6. Olmsted, Vaux and Company, "Report of the Landscape Architects and Superintendents to the Brooklyn Park Commissioners, January 1871," in *Papers of Frederick Law Olmsted: The Years of Olmsted, Vaux & Company, 1865–1874*, ed. David Schuyler and Jane Turner Censer (Baltimore: Johns Hopkins Univ. Press, 1992), 6:399.

7. Carriage driving figured prominently in popular illustrations of park culture and played a significant role in such early journalistic accounts of Central Park as T. Addison Richards, "The Central Park," *Harper's New Monthly Magazine* 23 (Aug. 1861): 289–306, and [Henry W. Bellows], "Cities and Parks; With Special reference to the New York Central Park," *Atlantic Monthly*, Apr. 1861, 416–29. The mid-nineteenth-century carriage craze is discussed at greater length in Roy Rosenzweig and Elizabeth Blackmar, *The Park and the People: A History of Central Park* (Ithaca, N.Y.: Cornell Univ. Press, 1992), 211–25; and in McShane, *Down the Asphalt Path*, 30–40.

8. Silas Lapham, the fictional Vermont paint merchant employed by William Dean Howells to exemplify the newly arrived metropolitan bourgeoisie, would vent his frustrations with urban society by taking his trotter out for spirited drives on Boston's Mill Dam, which was a popular vernacular driving course before the development of the Emerald Necklace (William Dean Howells, *The Rise of Silas Lapham* [Boston: Ticknor, 1885]).

9. The proliferation of parkways in smaller cities and towns can be traced in municipal directories and, more emphatically for the visually oriented, by the abundance of postcard imagery celebrating local parkways that vary considerably in physical extent and formal development.

10. Olmsted critics love to point out that Central Park was located prohibitively far from New York's population center when it was built in the 1860s; Olmsted acknowledged this and presented parkways as a means of spreading park amenities throughout the urban landscape (Olmsted, *Public Parks and the Enlargement of Towns* [Cambridge, Mass.: Riverside Press, 1870; reprint, New York: Arno Press, 1970], 22–31). Promoting his parkway proposals for Minneapolis and St. Paul, H. W. S. Cleveland remonstrated, "It is well to provide parks for the rich, appropriate to the wealth and grandeur of the city, but remember the poor who cannot provide for themselves." (Cleveland, *Public Parks, Radial Avenues, and Boulevard: Outline Plan of a Park System for the City of St. Paul* [St. Paul: Globe Job Office, 1885], 14.)

11. Despite these efforts to accommodate less-fortunate citizens, parkways were not designed as lower-class recreational facilities in the same spirit as later neighborhood playgrounds and community centers. The emphasis on pleasure driving and aesthetic contemplation reflected both elite conceptions of appropriate park behavior and the conviction that parkways would upgrade the socioeconomic status of their surroundings. Though they were often located in marginal areas occupied by lower-class populations, parkways were usually built with the expectation they would promote the development of attractive districts inhabited by more substantial citizens. Parkway neighborhoods did not always develop as rapidly or as comprehensively as their promoters predicted, however, so lower-class residents were often able to enjoy parkway amenities alongside the more prosperous citizens who dominated the central carriageways. The socioeconomic status of many parkway neighborhoods rose and fell over time, moreover, so that lower class citizens were occasionally able to appropriate environments abandoned by upwardly mobile residents in search of more exclusive suburban enclaves.

12. The merits of incorporating trolley lines in parkways are discussed in F. L. and J. C. Olmsted, "The Projected Park and Parkways on the South Side of Buffalo" [1888], in *Civilizing American Cities: A Selection of Frederick Law Olmsted's Writings on City Landscapes*, ed. S. B. Sutton (Cambridge: MIT Press, 1971), 148; Essex County, N.J., Department of Parks, *Second Annual Report of the Board of Commissioners, 1897* (Newark, N.J.: W. H. Shurts, 1897),

14–15; Charles W. Eliot, *Charles Eliot, Landscape Architect* (Boston: Houghton Mifflin, 1903), 509–10, 605; Charles Mulford Robinson, *Modern Civic Art; Or the City Made Beautiful* (New York: G. P. Putnam's Sons, 1903), 312–13, 342–43; and John C. Olmsted, "Classes of Parkways," *Landscape Architecture* 6 (Oct. 1915): 43–46.

13. Charles Mulford Robinson acknowledged that contemporary "speedways" and parkways were designed to "cater to wealth," but observed that "of late the ubiquitous bicycle, and the provision for it, has given a touch of democracy to the latter." (Robinson, *The Improvement of Towns and Cities; Or the Practical Basis of Civic Aesthetics* [New York: G. P. Putnam's Sons, 1901], 166.)

14. Henry James, *The American Scene* (New York: Harper & Brothers, 1907; edited, with an introduction by W. H. Auden, New York: Charles Scribner's Sons, 1946), 71.

15. Olmsted and Vaux cited these precedents in "Report of the Landscape Architects and Superintendents to the President of the Board of Commissioners of Prospect Park, Brooklyn, January 1, 1868," 134.

16. John Reps covers various aspects of early urban street improvement in *The Making of Urban America: A History of City Planning in the United States* (Princeton, N.J.: 1965). Watertown, Massachusetts, enacted legislation to protect shade trees along town highways as early as 1647 (Watertown Historical Society, *Watertown Records* [Watertown, Mass.: Press of Fred G. Barker, 1894], 14).

17. John Stilgoe, *Common Landscape of America, 1588–1845* (New Haven: Yale Univ. Press, 1982), 111–15, 128–32.

18. John Brinckerhoff Jackson, *American Space, the Centennial Years: 1865–1876* (New York: W. W. Norton, 1972), 37, 102–3; Nathaniel H. Egleston, *Villages and Village Life with Hints for Their Improvement* (New York: Harper and Brothers, 1878); Burton Willis Potter, *The Road and the Roadside*, 2d ed. (Boston: Little, Brown, 1887).

19. Condit, *American Building Art*, 277.

20. For Olmsted's acknowledgment of the influence of rural scenery, see Laura Wood Roper, *FLO: A Biography of Frederick Law Olmsted* (Baltimore: Johns Hopkins Univ. Press, 1983), 1–18, 92, and Mariana Griswold van Rensselaer, "Frederick Law Olmsted," *Century Illustrated Magazine* 46 (Oct. 1893): 860–61.

21. "Wayside Beauty," *Garden and Forest*, Mar. 21, 1888; Charles Garfield, "Roadside Beauty," *Garden and Forest*, 23

May 1888, 147; "Country Roads," *Garden and Forest*, 24 Dec. 1890, 617–18; "The Value of Rural Beauty," *Garden and Forest*, 8 July 1891, 313; "A Fine Road," *Garden and Forest*, Sept. 16, 1891, 435; "Foes to Country Road-sides," *Garden and Forest*, Aug. 3, 1892, 361; "Country Roads and Roadsides," *Garden and Forest*, July 10, 1895, 271–72; "Road-side Shrubberies," *Garden and Forest*, Dec. 28, 1892, 613; W. J. Beall, "Village Streets and Country Roads," *Garden and Forest*, Jan. 1, 1896, 2; "Roadside Trees," *Garden and Forest*, Mar. 24, 1897, 111–12.

22. Robinson, *Modern Civic Art*, 315.

23. Frank Waugh, *The Landscape Beautiful* (New York: Orange Judd, 1912), 212–15, quoted, 215; Frank Waugh, *Rural Improvement: The Principles of Civic Art Applied to Rural Conditions, including Village Improvement and the Betterment of the Open Country* (New York: Orange Judd Publishing, 1914), 59–61, 109.

24. H. W. S. Cleveland, *Suggestions for a System of Parkways for the City of Minneapolis* (Minneapolis: Johnson, Smith, and Harrison, 1883), 6–12; Cleveland, *Public Parks, Radial Avenues, and Boulevards*. Essex County, New Jersey, embarked on an ambitious campaign to preserve the renowned beauty of its country lanes, see Baxter, "Parkways and Boulevards in American Cities," pt. 1, p. 12; Essex County, N.J. Department of Parks, *Second Annual Report of the Board of Commissioners, 1897*, 14–15; Olmsted Brothers, "Report of the Olmsted Brothers on a Proposed Parkway System for Essex County, N.J. 4 June 1915," reprinted in *Landscape Architecture* 6 (Oct. 1945): 37–48.

25. W. C. Prime's *Along New England Roads* (New York Harper and Brothers, 1892) described this practice in detail. Prime made extended excursions throughout rural New England during the second half of the nineteenth century. He and his companions explored the New England countryside for weeks on end, traveling in a carriage driven by a coachmen and staying in wayside inns.

26. Wallace Nutting's *Vermont Beautiful* (Framingham, Mass.: Old America Company, 1922), *New Hampshire Beautiful* (Framingham, Mass.: Old America, 1923), and *Virginia Beautiful* (Framingham, Mass.: Old America Company, 1930). Nutting produced books on numerous other states as well. For an insightful assessment of Nutting's oeuvre and its relationship to contemporary cultural concerns, see Thomas A. Denenberg, "Consumed by the Past: Wallace

Nutting and the Invention of Old America" (Ph.D. diss., Boston Univ., 2002).

27. Nationwide auto registrations exploded from eight thousand in 1900 to over eight million by 1920. Increased production, the institution of installment sales programs, and the growing availability of used vehicles combined with the general prosperity of the 1920s to cause American automobile registrations to surpass twenty-two million by 1930 (John Rae, *The Road and the Car in American Life* [Cambridge: MIT Press, 1971], 50, 57).

28. Notable examples of this genre include: Gilmore Clarke, "Our Highway Problem," *American Magazine of Art* 25 (Nov. 1932): 287–90; Gilmore Clarke, "Modern Motor Ways," *Architectural Record,* Dec. 1933, 430–37; Benton Mackaye, "The Townless Highway," *New Republic* 62 (Mar. 12, 1930): 93–95; Benton Mackaye and Lewis Mumford, "Townless Highways for the Motorist: A Proposal for the Automobile Age," *Harper's Monthly* 163 (Aug. 1931): 347–56; "Unfit for Modern Motor Traffic," *Fortune* 14 (Aug. 1936): 85–99; and J. M. Bennett, *Roadsides: The Front Yard of the Nation* (Boston: Stratford, 1936). Daniel Bluestone summarizes contemporary roadside beautification concerns in "Roadside Blight and the Reform of Commercial Architecture," in *Roadside America: The Automobile in Design and Culture,* ed. Jan Jennings (Ames: Iowa Univ. Press, 1990), 170–81. In terms of fatal accidents per passenger mile, the 1920s and 1930s were the most dangerous decades in the history of American roads (Department of Transportation, *America's Highways 1776–1976: A History of the Federal-Aid Program* [Washington, D.C.: GPO, 1976], 115; W. A. Bugge and W. Brewster Snow, "The Complete Highway," in *The Highway and the Landscape,* ed. W. Brewster Snow (New Brunswick, N.J.: Rutgers Univ. Press, 1959), 11.

29. Westchester County parkway design principles were discussed in numerous contemporary publications, including Stanley Abbott's "Ten Years of the Westchester County Park System," *Parks and Recreation* 16 (Mar. 1933): 305–14; Jay Downer, "County Parks and Roadside Development in Westchester County, N.Y.," in *Roadside Development,* ed. J. M. Bennett (New York: Macmillan, 1929), 173–82; Gilmore Clarke, "Westchester Parkways: An American Development in Landscape Architecture," *Landscape Architecture* 28 (Oct. 1937): 40–41; and E. W. James, "Parkway Features of Interest to the Highway Engineer," *Public Roads* 10 (Apr. 1929): 21–28.

30. Andrew W. Crawford, "Cultural Opportunities in Regional Planning," *Transactions of the American Society of Civil Engineers* 92 (1938): 1122.

31. Criticism of the coarsening effect on motoring on parkway and park road design was expressed in Charles Eliot, 2nd, "The Influence of the Automobile on the Design of Park Roads," *Landscape Architecture* 13 (Oct. 1922): 37, and Phelps Wyman, "New Tendencies in Park Design," *Parks and Recreation* 11 (Mar.–Apr. 1928): 253–55.

32. Horace McFarland, "Parks and the Public," *Parks and Recreation* 6 (Sept.–Oct. 1922): 12.

33. Arthur Shurtleff, *Future Parks, Playgrounds and Parkways* (Boston: Boston Park Department, 1925), 9, 20.

34. For more comprehensive accounts of the development of Mount Vernon Memorial Highway, see Timothy Davis, "Mount Vernon Memorial Highway and the Evolution of the American Parkway" (Ph.D. diss., Univ. of Texas at Austin, 1997); and Timothy Davis, "Mount Vernon Memorial Highway: Changing Conceptions of an American Commemorative Landscape," in *Places of Commemoration, Search for Identity and Landscape Design,* ed. Joachim Wolschke-Bulmahn (Washington, D.C.: Dumbarton Oaks, 2000), 123–77.

35. For more on Colonial Parkway, see Michael Bennett, "Addendum to HAER Report No. VA-48: Colonial Parkway," Historic American Engineering Record, National Park Service, U.S. Department of the Interior, 1995 (file copy in Library of Congress Prints and Photographs Division). NPS officials limited the colonial road-reproduction strategy to superficial elements that did not interfere with the primary goal of moving motorists safely and efficiently between designated historic sites. A proposal to mimic the layout of the original roads was shot down, since the sharp curves, steep hills, and inconvenient alignments would be dangerous, confusing, and inefficient.

36. Abbott, "Parkways," 684.

37. Stanley Abbott, "Historic Preservation: Perpetuation of Scenes Where History Becomes Real," *Landscape Architecture* 40 (July 1950): 157.

38. Abbott, "Parkways," 687.

39. For a detailed account of the NPS's romantic reinterpretation of the Mabry Mill site, see Barry M. Buxton, "Mabry Mill Historic Resource Study," U.S. Department of the Interior, National Park Service, 1987; for a summary of

other NPS efforts to produce a carefully tailored cultural landscape that reified contemporary stereotypes of Appalachian culture, see Phil Noblitt, "The Blue Ridge Parkway and the Myths of the Pioneer," *Appalachian Journal* 21 (Summer 1994): 394–409.

40. The "authentic erosion" prospect was mentioned in the "Land Management Practices," section of Granville Liles, "Book Draft," unpaginated manuscript in Blue Ridge Parkway Library, Asheville, North Carolina.

41. Abbott, "Parkways," 690.

42. Local reactions to Natchez Trace Parkway are recounted in Jean Fulton, "Natchez Trace Parkway," HAER Report No. MS-15, 1998 draft copy in Historic American Engineering Record office files, National Park Service, U.S. Department of Interior, 36–40, 95–102.

43. Abbott, "Parkways," 686, 681.

44. Abbott invoked Grant Wood's painting as a precedent for the proposed Mississippi River Parkway in "Parkways—A New Philosophy," *American Planning and Civic Annual, 1951,* ed. Harlean James (Washington, D.C.: American Planning and Civic Association, 1951), 44.

45. Letter to the editor, *New York Times,* reprinted in *Landscape Architecture* 35 (Oct. 1944): 15.

46. John Steinbeck's *Travels with Charley, In Search of America* (New York: Viking Press, 1962) and William Least Heat Moon's *Blue Highways: A Journey into America* (Boston: Houghton Mifflin, 1982) are two of the most prominent examples of the popular genre of biographical travelogues urging motorists to discover the "real America" by forsaking main-traveled highways.

47. Originally appearing as "America Landscape" in the January 1950 issue of *Harper's Monthly,* this article was reprinted in *Landscape Architecture* 40 (July 1950): 182–83. Published under the nom de plume "Mr. Harper," the witty and insightful piece was probably written by contributing editor John Kouwenhoven. Echoing his fellow patrician Henry James, Lewis Mumford condemned NPS developments as "perversions of the cult of nature and the principals of democracy" that transformed formerly remote environments into vulgar spectacles for mass (Lewis Mumford, *The Culture of Cities* [New York: Harcourt, Brace, 1938], 334–35).

16

REAL AND IDEAL LANDSCAPES ALONG THE TACONIC STATE PARKWAY

KATHLEEN LAFRANK

The automobile has brought the country to the door of the city dweller.

Gov. Alfred E. Smith, 1923

In this message to the legislature, New York's governor articulated both the cause and effect of the Empire State's early twentieth-century public recreation programs.[1] Smith was seeking legislative approval for *A State Park Plan for New York,* a 1922 proposal for a comprehensive statewide system of parks and parkways. Embodying a recreation philosophy for the twentieth century, the new plan was entirely premised on connecting city to country via the automobile. The plan was part of a large-scale early-twentieth-century effort to reorganize New York state government. Under the leadership of Alfred E. Smith and the aegis of the New York State Association, a statewide civic group devoted to formulating and advocating government policy, a number of significant changes to state government were proposed during the 1920s that were intended to simplify its unwieldy administrative structure and implement a Progressive Era reform program.[2]

Like the larger reform agenda, *A State Park Plan* was contemporary in structure and program. Within the New York State Association, the Committee for the State Park Plan, which included such noted park planners as George Perkins Jr., Madison Grant, William Welch, Jay Downer, and Frederick Law Olmsted Jr., had worked to develop a park planning document that legitimized recreational planning as a function of state government and a program that addressed the specific needs of twentieth-century New Yorkers.[3] The park system thus conceived was premised on trends that had significantly changed contemporary American life, including urbanization, demographic shifts, increased leisure time and the proliferation of the automobile. Centrally planned but regionally administered, the system was to include a dispersed collection of parks and recreational facilities that took advantage of scenic and underused land areas, were located near the state's major population centers and were connected by a statewide system of parkways, boulevards and improved highways, all intended to provide New York's middle-class urban citizens with easy access to the state's abundant scenic and recreational attractions. Significantly, the idea of movement—the act and method of traveling from city to country, park to park, region to region—was the plan's central organizing concept.[4]

In the Hudson Valley, connections between city and country had always played an important role in regional history. The early juxtaposition of a great urban society with a great rural one and their link via the Hudson River, the state's earliest and most important transportation corridor, had helped to keep the relationship between urban and rural society at the forefront of economic and social history. But by the twentieth century, the extraordinary growth of metropolitan New York had generated enormous physical and social demands that exaggerated both differences and dependencies. Open space and natural resources were depleted. Extremes of wealth and poverty caused social imbalances. And the density of development within such a small area demanded physical and social outlets, especially for the swelling middle- and working-class populations. But as the needy looked north for relief, vast tracts of rural and scenic land in the Hudson Valley remained in private hands and much of it was not easily accessible. Although tantalizingly close to the city—and long a destination for tourists traveling by boat and railroad—this area did not offer an immediate solution to the complex recreational needs of the burgeoning urban population. This was soon to change, however, as the rapid increase in automobile ownership in the first decades of the twentieth century began to make it possible for the middle class to leave for the country. And as the automobile became the instrument of inexpensive and independent travel, scenic highways—modern, pleasant thoroughfares that carried urbanites ever further from the city—emerged as key elements in New York State's plan to provide restorative recreational opportunities for its citizens.

The parkways proposed under the 1922 state park plan were inspired by and modeled after the Bronx River Parkway (BRP), the first limited-access automobile parkway in America. Built between 1916 and 1925, this fifteen-mile scenic drive between New York City and northern Westchester County provided city residents with the opportunity to enjoy a new kind of recreational activity—the pleasure drive. Not only was the parkway an immediate success with the public, it was also credited with promoting regional planning and economic development, earning unequivocal endorsement from leading planners.[5] Moreover, the BRP helped to define the act of riding through the landscape by car as a recreational activity and set the design standard for thousands of miles of scenic roads laid across New York State and the nation over the next few decades.

By 1964, more than three hundred miles of parkways had been constructed in the Hudson Valley. Building on the success of the BRP, the Westchester County Park Commission (WCPC) had developed an extensive countywide network of parks and parkways, and state agencies in New York and New Jersey had worked separately and together to construct an integrated system of scenic roads on both sides of the Hudson River, affording access to parks and recreational attractions in New York State and connections to scenic highways extending south to the New Jersey shore and east into Connecticut. Together, the Hudson Valley parkways formed the nucleus of a regional transportation network linking thousands of acres of parkland and hundreds of scenic, recreational and historic places. But as these modern, limited-access highways brought motorists to specifically designated recreational spots outside the city, their design and character also allowed visitors a new freedom to move independently through the older, long-settled regions of the state. As parkways extended into the rural environs of the northern Hudson Valley, the kind of recreational travel that they made possible had the effect of conceptually reinterpreting an immense private landscape as a public benefit park.

The Taconic State Parkway (TSP) follows a north-south route up the east side of the Hudson River from northern Westchester County through Putnam, Dutchess, and Columbia Counties. Although its southernmost section opened in 1931, construction of the Taconic worked its way north slowly, not reaching

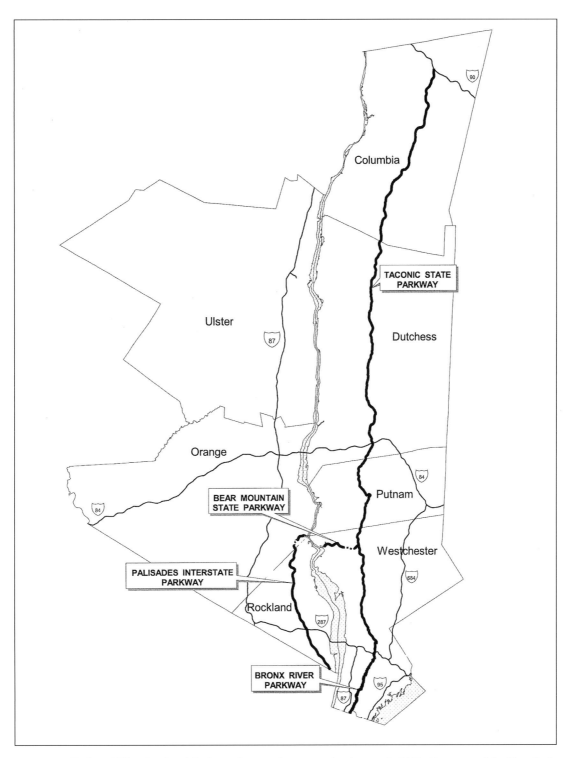

Map 16.1. Hudson Valley Regional Parkway System. Lawrence Scarborough, 2002. Courtesy of the New York State Department of Transportation.

northern Columbia County until the early 1960s. Like the cars that traveled it, the parkway's design changed over time, keeping pace with new ideas about engineering, landscape design and recreation. While the earliest section, a narrow, tightly curving roadway set within a parklike corridor, was planned to give motorists in Model Ts a taste of the country, the design of the northern end, with its broad curves, widely separated roadways, substantial right-of-way and enormous view shed, catered to a contemporary clientele, giving travelers in T-Birds the opportunity to go faster and farther.

An automobile trip up the east side of the Hudson might begin with a short hop from New York City to Valhalla on the Bronx River Parkway and continue north on the Taconic from its origin near the Kensico Dam. During the ensuing 105-mile drive to the end of the parkway near Chatham, the traveler would pass through a diverse cultural landscape shaped by centuries of human activity. The route took in a wide range of landforms and land uses. Landscapes reflected distinctive methods of land division and settlement, and built features and designed spaces embodied the social, economic and ethnic diversity of the population. Features abounded that provided

Fig. 16.1. Aerial view of the southern Taconic as it cuts a new path through the Putnam County landscape. Looking northwest near Barger Pond during parkway construction, 1934. Courtesy of the New York State Office of Parks, Recreation and Historic Preservation–Taconic Region.

evidence of the region's long history: buildings, transportation features, field patterns and vegetation, settlements and cemeteries—even place names helped to reveal the story of natural and human history over a long period of time. Following the Taconic, the traveler could glimpse many pieces of the complex puzzle of nature, time and activity that defined the history of the Hudson Valley. But, for the most part, the motorist's view was one that had never been seen before. Tracing a new path through an old landscape, the parkway made it possible to see new scenes from new vantage points at new speeds, and these fundamental changes to the order and pace of viewing engendered entirely new kinds of experiences.

Like the Bronx River Parkway, the first automobile parkways were controlled spaces, designed landscapes experienced from a moving vehicle. They followed carefully chosen routes with designated access points, regular rest stops, designed views and planned recreational facilities. Travel was intended to flow at optimum speeds along uniform roadways and, despite continuous movement, the motorist's relationship to the landscape remained relatively consistent. In creating experiences for such captive audiences, designers focused on the treatment of the linear park itself. Roads followed serpentine paths through narrow, carefully landscaped corridors, with plantings augmenting tightly framed views. These were naturalistic landscapes: "gardens" for the auto, created by modifying and enhancing nature.

As products of twentieth-century progressivism, these parkways also engendered social improvement. The Bronx River Parkway grew out of a conservation project (c. 1906) to reclaim a polluted river, while the Palisades Interstate Parkway was conceived in the 1920s (although not built until the 1940s) to prevent development atop the dramatic escarpment that defines the southwest bank of the Hudson River.[6] By acquiring endangered lands and laying parkways through them, public agencies could provide recreational access to scenic areas while strictly controlling their use. Citizens could enjoy these preserves; however, encouraged to keep moving, they were not given the opportunity to engage in the kind of intensive use that might damage fragile environments.

Fig. 16.2. The earliest sections of the Taconic were designed with a narrow right-of-way and enclosed views, similar to those on the Bronx River Parkway. Looking north on the Taconic State Parkway near Roaring Brook State Park, Putnam County, 1936. Courtesy of the New York State Office of Parks, Recreation and Historic Preservation—Taconic Region.

The first thirty-three miles of the Taconic continued to reflect these planning traditions and social goals. This section, which extended the Bronx River Parkway north to the Putnam County line, was designed and constructed in two parts, generally referred to as the Bronx Parkway Extension (BPE), by the Westchester County Park Commission in cooperation with New York State.[7] With implementation of the state park plan in 1924, the WCPC was incorporated into the state park system, affording it representation on the new State Council of Parks (SCP), the statewide park planning agency, and access to state funding. Although the WCPC continued to develop other county projects independently, the SCP was closely involved in planning the Bronx Parkway Extension and financed its construction. Its design, however, was the work of WCPC staff, notably, Jay Downer, Gilmore Clarke, Leslie Holleran, Herman Merkel, and Arthur Hayden, all of whom had contributed to the design of the Bronx River Parkway. The BPE was an important component of the state parkway system, facilitating connections between metropolitan New York and the northern Hudson Valley and between parks and parkways on the east and west sides of the river. It also functioned within the Westchester County Park and

Parkway System, a tightly constructed recreational network that catered to the specific needs of nearby urban and suburban populations. In the latter context, the BPE had a role in encouraging suburban growth while preserving limited open spaces as development spread north. Because the Westchester parkways followed the county's north-south river valleys, they protected streams from pollution, proved less challenging for road builders and facilitated movement of traffic through the county. While the efficient new transportation system and corresponding recreational amenities encouraged development, the WCPC's foresight in planning the road system and acquiring land for parks ahead of development also had a role in determining its location and density.[8]

However, as the parkway left the metropolitan region and traveled north through Putnam, Dutchess, and Columbia Counties under the guidance of the new Taconic State Park Commission (TSPC), the purpose and experience of the road began to shift. Moving away from the tightly enclosed Westchester County corridor, the road traversed rugged, sparsely settled Putnam County and then emerged into the broad open agricultural landscape of the mid–Hudson Valley. The upper Taconic was a collaborative effort, planned by the TSPC and designed and constructed by the commission and the New York State Department of Public Works (with oversight and funding from the SCP). Although layout, engineering, and landscaping were done by a number of different individuals (and consulting firms) from both agencies, the TSPC maintained firm control over planning and design throughout the parkway's forty-year construction period, thus ensuring that the northern Taconic was completed substantially as it was originally conceived. The park commissioners, citizen appointees with varying experience in park and parkway development, brought a different perspective to parkway planning, focusing less on planning and environmental goals and more on recreational and social ones. Although construction of the upper Taconic involved public acquisition of land, conservation was not its primary purpose. And although intended to augment regional and interstate highway systems, the Taconic was not a major component of transportation planning initiatives. Rather, this

Fig. 16.3. As construction moved north, new sections of the parkway were designed to take in expansive views of the eastern Hudson Valley. Looking northwest from the northbound lane of the parkway, near the overlook south of CR 8, Columbia County, 1960. Courtesy of the New York State Office of Parks, Recreation and Historic Preservation—Taconic Region.

Fig. 16.4. The parkway's landscape designers juxtaposed near and distant views, cultivated and natural landscapes. As the road curves northwest in Columbia County, a middle view of cultivated farmland is set against a distant view of the Catskill Mountains on the west side of the river.

road was dedicated to encouraging and enhancing the experience of pleasure driving. And although the parkway connected a system of seven state parks and other public use areas, the planned recreational experience extended far beyond the bounds of public parkland.

More radical on the northern Taconic was the redefinition of the designed landscape. As the recreational purpose of the road expanded, the narrow visual frame of the earlier parkways fell away. Instead of small scenic pictures carefully arranged to frame the right-of-way, travelers were presented with seemingly unrestricted views of the expansive agricultural landscape of the eastern Hudson Valley. Rather than idealized naturalistic designs, viewers took in the dramatic scenery of the Catskill and Berkshire Mountains. Parkway enhancements (buildings, bridges, etc.) designed as "picturesque" references to the local building tradition were augmented by the "real" artifacts of everyday life that defined the landscape outside the right-of-way. And as the viewer's gaze expanded beyond the controlled environment of the parkway, the rural vernacular landscape itself took on the qualities of a park. But although travelers may have thought they were enjoying the uncensored rural ambiance, the pleasure drive was a foreign object in the working landscape, and its location and design were as purposeful as they had been on other parkways. Instead of creating new landscape pictures, these planners had adapted old ones.

In appropriating a vernacular landscape as a park, what had those who planned this parkway intended? Perhaps views of a traditional rural landscape that appeared unchanged were intended to suggest a way of life unchanged. Just as the ancient natural landscape could symbolize an enduring spiritual order, a centuries-old cultural landscape could suggest an enduring social order, conveying a sense of civic well being and stability to Americans in rapidly changing times. As motorists traveled north on the Taconic, they were presented with a complex juxtaposition of images: modest nineteenth-century farms adjacent to the parkway, glimpses of rolling pastoral scenes beyond, and dramatic natural scenery in the far distance. These images seemed to juggle past, present, and future: the family farm was an icon of self-sufficiency, the pastoral landscape implied a stable rural order, and the

wilderness hinted at the restorative power of nature and the opportunities of space.

In a sense, this was a landscape of possibility. To understand the social agenda, we might consider some of the subtle changes to the regional landscape during the early twentieth century. Although the upper Hudson Valley remained a locally based rural society, its agricultural economy had declined considerably and land uses were rapidly changing. During the first third of the century, 30 percent of Dutchess County's farmland went out of agricultural use. Most towns witnessed an increase in overall population and in nonfarming rural dwellers, while the number of farmers and agricultural prosperity decreased. Some farms near urban areas were absorbed into cities; others were taken over by newcomers. While some of the better land in the valley towns was acquired by the wealthy, some of whom established hobby farms, the interior hill towns saw a large increase in foreign born and needy urban refugees seeking subsistence. These towns showed the greatest decrease in farm value and increase in poverty. Milan, which had the poorest soil in the county, also had the lowest population density and the lowest valued farms. Much of its hilly land, which had once supported dairy farms, was now virtually bare. The inexpensive land attracted some of New York City's Depression-era poor, who replaced cash crops with poultry and vegetables to feed their families.[9] There were similar land-use changes in Columbia County. By 1930, the town of Gallatin had lost 34 percent of its farms, Ghent 39 percent, and Taghkanic 60 percent.[10] But as rural society changed, the traditional values associated with agrarian life were internalized and preserved by Americans who had been raised to revere them.[11] For urbanites, many of whom had personal, familial, or cultural ties to rural society, a weekend trip to the country could help to restore these values. One could always return to the land—if only as a visitor. Connections with the past and opportunities for the future could be discovered in the ancient landforms and enduring land uses framed in the windshield, while the contemporary difficulties of farm life could be left along the roadside. Despite significant economic and social changes, in 1936 the Dutchess County landscape was still perceived as creating "an atmosphere of rural stability disassociated from the city roar of twentieth century life."[12]

This historicist view is personified in Franklin D. Roosevelt (1882–1945), who played a major role in placing the eastern Hudson Valley landscape in the public domain. Roosevelt was a member of an old Hudson Valley Dutch family. Growing up on his family's estate in the small hamlet of Hyde Park, Roosevelt acquired an intimate knowledge of the regional landscape, a deep concern for conservation and agriculture, and a lifelong interest in local history. Although he fancied himself a product of rural America, Roosevelt was far from the eighteenth-century farm. Nevertheless, he sustained a deep spiritual bond with his ancestors, and he believed that the artifacts they left behind could provide contemporary Americans with tangible connections to the noble and enduring way of life that he believed their forbears had established. Writing the foreword to Helen Wilkinson Reynolds's *Dutch Houses in the Hudson Valley Before 1776* in 1928, Roosevelt expressed his concern with the rapid pace of twentieth-century development and the threat it posed to the spiritual and material culture of the region. As he rose to national prominence during the Depression, Roosevelt embraced a duty to present the image of a stable, prosperous rural America to its citizens, while he tried to preserve the way of life on which it was based.[13]

Between the mid-1920s and the end of his life, Roosevelt was actively involved in a wide range of efforts to revive interest in regional history and architecture. He served as Hyde Park town historian, and he was instrumental in publishing books documenting the region's settlement-period architecture (including *Dutch Houses*). He built cottages for family members based on Dutch colonial–era architecture, and he designed five regional post offices modeled on local vernacular buildings. In these and other projects, Roosevelt drew upon the history and building traditions of Dutchess County's first settlers in order to inspire and enhance the lives of its contemporary residents.

When the New York State Council of Parks expanded the new state park system in 1925, the Taconic State Park Commission was created to oversee recreational development in the eastern Hudson Valley.

Appointed to the commission by Governor Alfred E. Smith, Roosevelt was elected its first chair. As he led the commission during its formative years (1925–28), FDR played a crucial role in establishing the parkway as the principal state park initiative in the Taconic region and securing the SCP's commitment to the project.[14] More important, evidence suggests that Roosevelt was the person most responsible for establishing the route of the Taconic and the character of its view.

Roosevelt himself attested to his early ideas for a scenic highway in the eastern Hudson Valley, asserting that he had only accepted the request to chair the TSPC because he had been assured that he would be allowed to build the parkway as he intended.[15] At the commission's third meeting (28 June 1925), Roosevelt proposed a specific route, commencing at the northern terminus of the Bronx River Parkway and extending north through the centers (what he termed the "wild country") of Putnam, Dutchess, Columbia, and Rensselaer Counties.[16] Although the Taconic did not reach northern Columbia County until 1963, nearly twenty years after Roosevelt's death, the completed parkway generally follows the route that he described in 1925. Although there were several changes to his scheme, particularly in northern Dutchess County, they were made to accommodate difficulties in acquisition, engineering and/or politics, rather than to redefine the program goals.[17] The character of the Taconic, as it made its way over an elevated mid-county route juxtaposing views of the pastoral and scenic landscapes, remained faithful to FDR's original conception of the scenic drive.

Although Roosevelt's ideas were not the only considerations in locating and designing the parkway, his commanding presence during the commission's formative years, his very specific ideas about the route of the parkway, his active role in land acquisition and design, and his personal interaction with state and local officials, county highway commissions and the press had a significant effect on the outcome of the project.[18] In addition, as a Hudson Valley native, FDR's own life was divided between city and country environments. Throughout his public life, Roosevelt treasured opportunities to return to the Hudson Valley for restorative purposes.[19] He also had an avid personal interest in automobile tourism and was known to enjoy long drives during his sojourns in the valley.[20] Thus, he was well aware of the potential value a drive in the country might hold for urban residents.

The parkway project provided Roosevelt with an opportunity to share his beloved Hudson Valley with untold numbers of citizens. But although Roosevelt was intimately familiar with the Hudson Valley from years of exploration and study, the historic landscape he wished to present was one that he could only imagine. He was far from the settlement era in time, further in context. As he knew from his own observation and study, evidence of the old rural society that he revered was disappearing. In a historicist sense, the only way to stabilize these fading images was to "squint," abstracting the essence of the past from the complex and conflicting landscape of change, ennobling its associations and reusing them in the design and construction of new cultural icons for the present.

Part of Roosevelt's process of abstraction was revealed in his interest in the materials and workmanship that defined the regional vernacular, as if these details themselves embodied the values he sought to preserve. He insisted on reusing stone from old buildings and walls in his construction projects, and he called parkway engineers to task when he thought they were using overly finished stone on parkway bridges.[21] In a similar way, he drew on abstractions of location or siting for cultural content. For example, Roosevelt suggested that the "cozy places back from the highway . . . far from a neighbor" where he discovered eighteenth-century farmhouses were chosen by builders to assert their independence and self-sufficiency.[22] He seemed unaware or unconcerned that his reading of the twentieth-century landscape might not reveal the visual and social context of the settlement era.

Similarly, as the parkway cut a completely new path through the more sparsely settled, less accessible interior of the eastern Hudson Valley, views of both the immediate and distant rural landscapes that were new, untraditional, and temporary (i.e., as seen from the car) could be endowed with restorative contemporary cultural connotations. Roosevelt seemed to prefer long views of the Hudson Valley from the eastern hills of Dutchess County. He frequently took visitors to his Hyde Park home on automobile drives to enjoy these spectacular prospects, and he chose the location for Top Cottage, his own private retreat, for the expansive view it commanded west across the Hudson Valley to the Catskills, south to the Hudson Highlands and east to the Berkshires.[23] The elevated, inland route that FDR advocated for the parkway took advantage of similar views, suggesting that he intended to share the source of his own inspiration with the public. Today, long views east and west over valley lands framed by distant mountains are the most dramatic and the most characteristic landscape elements on the Taconic.

It was relatively easy for the Taconic State Park Commission to acquire land along these interior hilltops in the 1920s and 1930s. By 1930, the commission had already acquired more than 75 percent of the right-of-way, much of it at low cost and nearly three-quarters by gift.[24] Although not everyone was happy when the parkway arrived, the generally low prices and the substantial amount of donated land in Dutchess and Columbia Counties suggest that many of these farmers were not overly concerned about the loss of some of their acreage.[25] This region had always had poorer farmland and less affluent farmers, and its smaller, less improved farms contrasted with the larger scale, prosperous agricultural enterprises in the Hudson and Harlem valleys, east and west of the parkway. Further, by the twentieth century, many fields at these upper elevations had already reverted to an earlier, more wooded appearance. A number of farms that survive adjacent to the right-of-way today illustrate these small operations, with modest, early- to mid-nineteenth-century farmhouses and one or two agricultural buildings; and, whether still farmed or not, much of this landscape retains the pattern of small fields and woodlots established in the early nineteenth century. It is easy to see why FDR may have found this an appealing location for the parkway: its spectacular natural setting and potential for dramatic views, less intensive land use, and scattered, small family farms may have created scenes that were closer to his idea of the settlement-era landscape.

Ironically, agricultural decline and poverty had helped to preserve an image of farm life in a more optimistic period. This image could now be recycled to renew belief in a contemporary agrarian ideal.

But because those who planned this parkway were so intent on presenting a vision for the twentieth century, they could never convey an authentic view of the past. Although the components were real, they were gathered into scenes that were unfamiliar. Parkway travel was different from local travel in purpose and experience; views from the parkway were foreign to the local population, and while the parkway traveled through places with long histories, it did not fit easily into the established patterns of local life. Always the place from which to see the view, the parkway remained aloof from the place being viewed. In fact, almost no one returned the gaze. Beyond immediately adjacent properties, it is extremely difficult to get even a glimpse of the parkway, and there are few views of the road from afar. The parkway experience even suggested a time lag: the image of the road itself was "the latest," while the view from the road was intended to be "old-fashioned." Thus the Taconic created a paradox: it went nowhere, was part of no place, and formed no relationship with the local population, yet it purported to hold the soul of rural America in its view shed. By virtue of its location and design, the parkway created contradictions of time, place, and perspective and changed what it sought to protect.

Fig. 16.5. Old road. Dutchess County landscape just west of the parkway.

Fig. 16.6. New road. Looking north at the parkway from the underpass bridge at NY 23, Columbia County.

The contemporary character of the road made the historic landscape less accessible. Old roads were small and irregular. Nineteenth-century roads were perhaps sixteen-feet wide, providing a lane and a half for two-way travel. They followed paths determined by economic and social activity and they were inconsistently constructed and maintained. These roads not only passed things, they became part of them. They functioned within the layout of the farms through which they traveled, wove through communities and found the easiest accommodation around geographic obstacles. They provided a sequence of unexpected experiences, requiring travelers to acknowledge diversity as they adapted to changing local conditions.

The parkway was designed for uninterrupted high-speed travel. This experience was made possible by eliminating variations. The parkway took a fairly direct route determined by scenic, environmental and economic considerations. It order to maintain speed and minimize interruption, the parkway avoided cities, villages and local roads. Isolated within a wide, landscaped right-of-way, the parkway maintained an objective distance from more diverse local vegetation and land uses. A consistently precise, crisply defined roadway, uniform modern materials, grade separations, and controlled access all ensured a comfortable ride and a neat roadside, while obstructing perception of the changing local landscape. Where old and new roads intersected, conflicts in design and function accentuated their differences. There was no graceful way for the modern parkway and the old east-west farm roads to meet: the new road either obliterated the old crossings or bypassed them with grade separations. And when, despite the intentions of designers, these small-scale roads survived, the TSP interrupted them, creating dangerous conflicts of vehicle types and speeds at crossings.

While the parkway's route aimed to showcase the historic region, the road didn't really go there. For centuries the Hudson River had linked riverfront communities to each other and to the outside world; later it provided access to east-west turnpikes, canals and railroads and established the pattern for the ma-jor highway routes. But although the parkway mimicked the river's route, its isolated inland location had the opposite effect. In the early years, the Taconic north of Westchester County was generally a self-contained system that simply allowed movement north and south through a relatively undeveloped region. Initially, the parkway created its own reason for being, drawing recreational travelers from the south. But this was essentially a one-way system: metropolitan New Yorkers escaping crowds, heat, noise, and twentieth-century angst had plenty of reasons to venture up the parkway, but their rural counterparts had fewer to travel down. Later, of course, the parkway precipitated a new north-south pattern, encouraging people within commuting range to live upstate and work in the city; however, the commercial and residential development that followed was often in conflict with established settlement patterns.

As the Taconic journeyed into some of New York's oldest settlement areas, it purposely avoided them. The parkway followed no existing routes, incorporated no existing roads and avoided villages and ham-lets. On nineteenth-century maps of thesetowns, the links between activity and transportation are clear: creeks, railroads, and roads run east-west or northeast-southwest, linking domestic, economic and social components and facilitating regional connections to riverfront cities and ports. Despite twentieth-century changes, this pattern essentially survives today. But although the Taconic goes *through* these towns, it doesn't really go *to* them. Instead, the parkway snakes through the least-developed areas, avoiding settle-

Fig. 16.7. Farmhouse, road, and barn. Travelers pass through this traditional landscape. View of farmhouse, mature tree line, local road, and barn just west of the parkway in Dutchess County.

ments, separating regional centers and interrupting local transportation patterns. Although the parkway may have had a role in the development of regional transportation systems and later became a desirable or convenient alternative for local residents, it was not laid out to serve the familiar routines of daily life.

As the parkway forged a new path through the region, its layout contradicted the historic character of its own location. The Taconic followed an inland ridge dividing communities oriented either to the Hudson Valley and New York (to the west) or to the Harlem Valley and New England (to the east). Seemingly part of neither, the region at the center was most notable for its lack of definition. It had some of the least desirable land and attracted less-affluent settlers (sometimes tenants, migrants, or squatters) with weaker physical, economic, or social ties to the more established communities in the valleys. But if the road took command of its location and defined its place by asserting a strong visual relationship with distant landforms—the Catskill and Berkshire Mountains and the intermediate, rolling valley farmlands—few of the inhabitants of this ridge appropriated similarly dramatic views. Instead, farms along the right-of-way were tucked into a more intimate local landscape and oriented to the elements that defined their own social spheres: climate, animals, fields, and each other, and the route to market, church, school, or railroad.

Spaces outside the right-of-way that were different and disorderly were unified by consistent speed, distance, and point of view. The view from the parkway was always the passing glance of the sightseer. As travelers sped along, a sense of place was captured in the frame of the window. Scenes were frozen in time, their detail erased by speed and distance. Roadside elements that carried information about local history lost their ability to convey it: farm fields were severed; some built features were screened out and traditional organizational patterns were unrecognizable; an old cemetery encompassed by the right-of-way was left inaccessible and anonymous; and sections of the extensive network of stone walls that once mapped ownership and land use lost their function, deteriorated and were redefined as scenery.[26]

Although traditional activities outside the right-of-way continued, the parkway offered an unfamiliar view of them. Following a path never before used for transportation, the Taconic brought what had previously been background—fields, pastures or woodlots—into the foreground. Aerial photographs taken in the 1930s reveal the new road's relationship to the existing landscape of southern Dutchess County. Most adjacent farms were oriented to the east-west roads that cross the parkway. Generally, the TSPC acquired small interior strips of these farms; thus, the parkway passed along the rear or side elevations of buildings and farmyards and through cultivated farmland or woods. Field divisions, boundary markers and sometimes vegetation were left largely undisturbed; in some cases, they continued across the parkway. The informal, "private" views of these farms now possible from the parkway—glimpses of ongoing agricultural processes—differ significantly from the farm views captured in nineteenth-century prints. The latter are often characterized by hierarchical compositions of buildings and lands arranged to present a neat and well-ordered public image to the road. Although those scenes were themselves idealizations, they reflect ideas about space held by those who commissioned and executed them. Although the farmsteads we see from the parkway may appear to occupy the "cozy place[s] . . . back from the highway" that FDR described, our view may not capture their builders' intent or experience of location.

Fig. 16.8. Farmhouse, road, barn, and parkway. Parkway travelers are observers, traveling near to but outside of traditional cultural landscapes. View of a farm at Rigor Hill Road, Columbia County, from the northbound lane of the Taconic.

Fig. 16.9. Aerial view of the Taconic looking north in the town of East Fishkill, 1943. As the parkway took a serpentine path through southern Dutchess County, it bisected farms and cut across the eastern Hudson Valley's traditional east-west transportation system. Courtesy of the New York State Office of Parks, Recreation and Historic Preservation—Taconic Region.

Rolling across the rural landscape, the Taconic imposed its own orderly framework over the sequence of disorderly spaces along its route. Large-scale and unvarying, the parkway brought adjacent areas into a single visual and organizational pattern in which distinction and transition were not apparent. Names that were local and descriptive were announced on identical signs. Speeding up the parkway, we cross Near Road and North Road but remain ignorant of what we are near to or north of. At Peekskill Hollow Road, a bridge preserves the consistent vertical alignment of the parkway but distracts us from the deep hollow below. Nine Partners Road marks mileage but fails to identify the eighteenth-century proprietors so influential in establishing Dutchess County's spatial organization. Plaques at scenic overviews refer to broad historical themes without explaining what the viewer can see from these locations.

And as regional building types became design sources, functional and social content were left behind. Gas stations were designed using the forms and materials of the region's eighteenth-century domestic architecture. Although they provided attractive, picturesque enclosures to meet practical needs, these twentieth-century buildings offered only vague references to the region's historic building traditions.

While remaining outside the local order, the parkway nevertheless changed local experience. The Taconic interrupted numerous historic patterns of activity and association. It left some farmers without access to fields, orchards, or barns. It laid a wide swath of concrete through a small-scale agricultural landscape and imposed movement, speed, noise, and exhaust on the organic order of farm life. It severed long-established routes, forcing those who relied on them to find new east-west connections. And it bisected nearly three dozen school districts in Dutchess and Columbia Counties, leaving a number of old schoolhouses stranded along the right-of-way. Although these small buildings may have been outdated when the parkway was built, the relationships between home and school that they represented were not. Even today, decades after the parkway was completed, local school district patterns continue to reveal the conflict between the order of the road and that of the region, as school busses forced to cross the busy parkway at grade become sources of concern and controversy.

In addition to altering historic land uses, the parkway precipitated new ones. The scenic road introduced a new kind of tourist economy to this previously isolated region, and new groupings, which were not communities, of commercial features began to form around exits. Gas stations, diners, and motels were sited to serve parkway traffic. Buildings near the right-of-way acquired new functions: residences became restaurants; gas pumps were installed at old inns. And as the parkway borrowed local names, new local enterprises borrowed the parkway's. Scattered along the parkway corridor are the Chief Taconic Diner, the Taconic and Parkway Motels, Camp Taconic, Taconic Market, Taconic Convenience Store, Taconic Auto Parts, and even Taconic Sculpture, a gallery that orients massive sculptural figures to passing motorists.

In some cases, the persistence of historic patterns challenged the designers' ability to control them and altered the intended recreational experience. Defying one of the most important goals of parkway design, the Taconic is interrupted by a significant number of at-grade crossings. These narrow east-west roads, many unpaved, some private, preserve age-old transportation and land-use patterns, continuing to link east and west valley areas and draw residents of the interior toward the river. As local and long-distance travelers are forced to acknowledge each other, these are places where the real and ideal landscapes meet literally and symbolically.

In redefining a vernacular landscape as a park, designers created an unconflicted image of rural America whose meaning could be processed in the imagination. The view from the parkway was not about the past but the present. The story it told was not about the places viewed but those who viewed them. The living landscape painting combined myths about the past and the future: the pastoral vision of the cultivated landscape and the romantic notion of an undeveloped American continent ripe with possibility. That this vision did not convey the complexity of the historic landscape was no secret—many of its creators and patrons were refugees from a more complicated contemporary America. Although they knew, as do we, that the view from the parkway recast the real as the ideal, the vision still served as a powerful image of stability. If the goal was to preserve an image of rural life that tied America's past to its future, then the mythic view helped to sustain the kind of illusions about possibility and permanence that help us to live hopeful lives.

Notes

1. Alfred E. Smith, "First Message from Governor Alfred E. Smith to the Legislature Relative to the Development of State Parks," Apr. 18, 1923, New York State Archives, Albany, N.Y.

2. For a discussion of New York state government reform 1915–28, see Robert A. Caro, *The Power Broker: Robert Moses and the Fall of New York* (New York: Knopf, 1974), 92–135. Caro argues that the *Report of the Reconstruction Commission to Governor Alfred E. Smith on Retrenchment and Reorganization in the State Government* (Albany, N.Y.: J. B. Lyon Co., 1919) was an influential document, embodying the essence of progressive philosophy. As chief of staff to the commission and secretary to the New York State Association, Robert Moses had a powerful role in the reorganization, particularly in drafting legislation to implement most of the reform proposals. For information about the New York State Association, see its newsletter, *State Bulletin,* 1921–26.

3. Although Moses is often credited with the state park plan, committee members attribute its genesis to an idea of George W. Perkins Sr. See New York State Association, Committee on the State Plan, *A State Park Plan for New York* (1922; rev. ed., Albany: State Council of Parks, 1922), 2. Given the commission's professional expertise and Moses's legendary political skills, it seems more likely that his role was to synthesize ideas into a compelling document and assemble the political and legal mechanisms to implement them.

4. See New York State Association, *A State Park Plan for New York;* see also State Council of Parks, "The Principles of State Park Planning as Applied to New York," *First Annual Report* (n.p., 1925), 10–13.

5. In 1924, even before its completion, the Bronx River Parkway was already accommodating more than twenty thousand cars on Sundays and holidays. Jay Downer, *Public Parks in Westchester County* (n.p., n.d.), 13. For a contemporary assessment, see "Regional Plan of New York and Its Environs," in *The Graphic Regional Plan* (1929; reprint, New York: Arno, 1974), 1:269–72.

6. For Bronx River Parkway, see Downer, *Public Parks,* 1. For Palisades Interstate Parkway, see "Consider Parkway to Save Palisades . . . Regional Planners Study the Future of the River Cliffs as Building Wave Nears," *New York Times,* May 21, 1928; Palisades Interstate Park Commission (New Jersey Commission) Minutes, Nov. 1929, Palisades Interstate Park Commission, Bear Mountain, N.Y.; Thomas Adams, *Regional Plan of New York and Its Environs* (1931; reprint, New York: Arno, 1974), 2:556–63.

7. The two Westchester sections were originally known as the Bronx Parkway Extension and the "state parkway." In Putnam, Dutchess, and Columbia Counties, the parkway, built in nine sections, was originally known as the Eastern State Parkway. The entire 105-mile road from Kensico Dam through Columbia County was not officially named Taconic State Parkway and administered as a single entity until 1941.

8. Downer noted, "The great program must be regarded as having a much broader scope than the primary and designated purpose of providing public parks." Downer, *Public Parks,* 22–24.

9. Edith Adelaide Roberts and Helen Wilkinson Reynolds, *The Role of Plant Life in the History of Dutchess County* (n.p., 1938), 25–28; Martha Collins Bayne, *The Dutchess County Farmer* (Poughkeepsie, N.Y.: Women's City and County Club, 1936), 7–14, 22–29, 32. Bayne's book, based on a detailed study of eight towns, includes a substantial amount of data and offers an especially thoughtful analysis of Dutchess County's changing landscape, population and society.

10. Peter H. Stott, "Industrial Archeology in Columbia County, New York," 1990, Columbia County Historical Society, Kinderhook, N.Y.

11. Kenneth S. Davis, *FDR: The Beckoning of Destiny, 1882–1928* (New York: Putnam, 1971), 632–34.

12. Bayne, *Dutchess County Farmer,* 8.

13. Davis, *FDR,* 632–34.

14. FDR was assertive in pressing for support and funding, particularly as political disagreements (especially with long-time SCP chair Robert Moses) and competition among park regions threatened the state's commitment to the parkway. He insisted that "unlike many of the other state park Commissions, our principal function is the acquisition of the parkway." FDR to Alfred E. Smith, Dec. 20, 1927; see also FDR to Frances R. Masters, commissioner, Taconic State Park Commission, Oct. 22, 1925; FDR to Smith, Dec. 3, 1926; and FDR to Alexander MacDonald, commissioner, New York State Conservation Department, Feb. 3, 1927, all in Franklin D. Roosevelt Library, Hyde Park, N.Y. (hereafter cited as FDRL). When funding cuts stymied the commission's work in 1927, FDR led the other commissioners in confronting the governor, stating that without funding for its entire program, the commission "sees no reason for its continued existence." See FDR to Smith, Dec. 14, 1927, and Taconic State Park Commission Minutes, 16 Feb. 1927, both in Taconic State Park Commission, Staatsburg, N.Y. (hereafter cited as TSPC Minutes).

15. FDR to Smith, Dec. 3, 1926, FDRL; FDR to Smith, telegram, Dec. 14, 1927. Reproduced in TSPC Minutes, Dec. 16, 1927.

16. For a more detailed description of FDR's route, see TSPC Minutes, June 28, 1925; for maps of FDR's route, see *Poughkeepsie Sunday Courier,* May 6, 1928, and *Chatham Courier,* Mar. 7, 1929; "wild country," FDR to Smith, Dec. 3, 1926, FDRL.

17. In mid–Dutchess County, FDR's original route veered northeast toward Stissing Mountain, where he envisioned a scenic drive to a recreational area at the top. However, in 1928 the parkway was rerouted two and a half miles west after owners along the proposed route expressed opposition and a group of farmers in nearby Lafayetteville offered to donate eight miles of right-of-way. FDR agreed to the change, stating that his objectives could be met so long as the new location was no more than two and a half miles away. TSPC Minutes, Dec. 3, 1928.

18. FDR was appointed liaison to the WCPC and the SCP; see TSPC Minutes, June 28, 1925. Among other achievements, he persuaded Robert Moses to support his proposed route, rather than the one that Moses himself had suggested (which started north along the riverfront). FDR to Robert Moses, June 9, 1925; Moses to FDR, June 12, 1925, FDRL. FDR was also designated to act for the commission to make park purchases in Dutchess County. TSPC Minutes, Mar. 3, 1927. For FDR and materials, see note 9. For FDR and design, see Caro, *Power Broker,* 288. Caro reported that FDR drew sketches for picnic tables and fireplaces. FDR pressed county highway officials to refrain from building mid-county highways parallel to the Taconic and suggested options for mitigating the potential effect of new county roads on the parkway. See FDR to Vernon Rockefeller, chair, Dutchess County Board of Supervisors, Jan. 7, 1926; FDR to Lester J. Bashford, Columbia County Superintendent of Highways, Jan. 7, 1926; FDR to Benson Frost, Jan. 28, 1926; FDR to E. J. Howe, engineer, Taconic State Park Commission, Aug. 6, 1926, all in FDRL. FDR was also frequently in the local press, promoting the parkway and soliciting public support; see Press Clipping Scrapbooks, 1920s–1930s, TSPC.

19. Davis, *Davis,* 636; 759.

20. Geoffrey C. Ward, foreword to *Franklin D. Roosevelt's Top Cottage: Historic Structure Report,* by John G. Waite Associates, Architects (Albany: Waite Associates, 1997); Olin Dows, *Franklin Roosevelt at Hyde Park* (New York: American Artists Group, 1949), 167–69, 180.

21. On the use of stone, see William B. Rhodes, "Franklin D. Roosevelt and Dutch Colonial Architecture," *New York History* 59 (Oct. 1978): 446, 448. For FDR and bridges, see TSPC Minutes, July 21, 1931.

22. Franklin D. Roosevelt, introduction to *Dutch Houses in the Hudson Valley Before 1776,* by Helen Wilkinson Reynolds (1928; reprint, New York: Dover, 1965).

23. Ibid.

24. In 1928, the commission resolved to pay no more than ten to fifteen dollars an acre. TSPC Minutes, Jan. 11, 1928. These estimates proved somewhat low; the commission's minutes for 1925–30 suggest that land was acquired for approximately fifty to one hundred dollars per acre in the southern sections and less farther north. For acquisition data, see New York State Conservation Department, *Annual Report,* 1929, 414. See also subsequent annual reports for yearly acquisitions summaries.

25. Although a detailed analysis of the acquisition history has not yet been undertaken, a reading of the Taconic State Park Commission's minutes for 1925–70 suggests that there were relatively few large-scale controversies (at least in comparison to the battles between Robert Moses and Long Island property owners that Caro reports in *The Power Broker*). The commission's stated policy was to attempt to reach a satisfactory agreement with owners before resorting to appropriation. Paul T. Winslow to Ronald F. Bogle, July 3, 1947, TSPC.

26. For a similar analysis of the effect of railroad travel on the perception of space, see Wolfgang Schivelbusch, *The Railway Journey* (New York: Urizen, 1977), 41–50, 57–72.

17

DESIGNING "COMMUNITY" IN THE CHERRY HILL MALL

THE SOCIAL PRODUCTION OF A CONSUMER SPACE

STEPHANIE DYER

Following in the footsteps of John Brinckerhoff Jackson, writing on the vernacular landscape has sought to bring a critical and scholarly eye to the common structures of everyday life. Though much of the field has traditionally focused on the historic creations of nonprofessional builders, scholars of the recent vernacular past are showing increasing interest in the work of "professional" builders: the real estate developers who created the commercial buildings and housings tracts that constitute the everyday landscape of the twentieth-first-century United States. The study of such structures complicate a simplistic understanding of vernacular landscapes as representations of the cultural lives of their inhabitants. The professionalization of real estate development, a long process that accelerated over the course of the past century, largely removed the shaping of the common landscapes of ordinary Americans in metropolitan areas from their direct control. This makes it incredibly difficult for scholars to "read" popular social meanings and uses from the stylistics of the built environment of the recent past.

But if the American built environment no longer represents the vernacular, that is, the product of the folk, they nonetheless remain thick with social meaning. Henri LeFebvre suggests that the production of contemporary landscapes, which entail the mobilization of immense economic and political resources, are one of the most visible signs of power relations in contemporary society. Instead of the product of the folk, such areas are the contested product of many actors—architects, real estate developers, retailers and tenants, politicians, citizens, and consumers. The social meaning of such spaces are not fixed at the moment of their physical creation, but are continually renegotiated through the management and popular use of the space throughout its commercial life-span. Such an approach to the everyday modern landscape captures the dynamic lived environment of these spaces in the modern American marketplace.[1]

The balance of this chapter will attempt to recover the social meaning of a popular space of the mid-twentieth century: the Cherry Hill Mall, which opened in Delaware Township, New Jersey in 1961. Cherry Hill Mall is a historically significant example of a classic postwar shopping center, being the first enclosed regional mall in the northeastern United States. Designed by renowned shopping center architect Victor Gruen, it was developed and operated by James Rouse's Community Research and Development Corporation (hereafter called CRD). Though Rouse is best known as the force behind new town developments like Columbia, Maryland, and urban "festival marketplaces" of the 1970s and 1980s, he was a respected shopping center developer during the postwar period, one whose formula for tenant mix and community relations was widely imitated during the 1950s and 1960s. Cherry Hill's design and management pedigree preclude it from being considered vernacular in origin; nonetheless, its creators were obsessed with the role of the shopping center in the "community," and endeavored to render their professional creation adaptable to the local vernacular culture.

The "Community" Ideal in Professional Shopping Center Design

In terms of their creation, shopping centers can hardly be described as the product of an American vernacular building tradition. Many shopping centers of the postwar period were created by well-respected architects who also worked on more esteemed forms of commercial building, such as office buildings and hotels.[2] As Richard Longstreth has noted, their exclusion from canons of professional architecture can only derive from the current denigration of the aesthetic and social value of shopping centers and other popular commercial spaces of the recent past.[3] Cherry Hill's design was the product of long and careful analysis by experienced professionals based on current trends in design theory and management. Both Victor Gruen and James Rouse theorized extensively about the social effects of urban design and articulated complex

notions of how shopping centers could transform the suburban spatial environment. Both used Cherry Hill Mall as a vehicle to implement their theories.

Like many social critics of the mid-twentieth century, Gruen thought the rampant suburbanization of the postwar period destroyed a sense of community among its inhabitants because it lacked the diversity of people and functions present in cities. He wrote, "Suburbia had become an arid land inhabited during the day almost entirely by women and children and strictly compartmentalized by family income, social, religious, and racial background." Gruen saw this "Feminine World" as one breading conformity and limited life experiences—and one potentially rife with "mental health hazards." Strange as it may sound to us, Gruen viewed shopping centers as a panacea for suburban anomie. He saw the shopping center as an attempt to create a town square for suburban residential districts lacking any identifiable geographic center: a singular, dominant commercial and civic center to impose a healthy social order onto sprawling subdivisions. For Gruen, planned shopping centers simultaneously alleviated the problems of commercial strip development and served as a corrective to the feminized "psychological climate peculiar to suburbia": "By affording opportunities for social life and recreation in a protected pedestrian environment, by incorporating civic and educational facilities, shopping centers can fill an existing void. They can provide the needed place and opportunity for participation in modern community life that the ancient Greek Agora, the Medieval Market Place and our own Town Squares provided in the past."[4]

Gruen invented the peculiar introverted architectural design that became the basis for the classic regional shopping center in order to foster healthy and appropriate forms of community socialization in the suburbs. Early versions of this form consisted of stores with open fronts lining an enclosed, temperature- and lighting-controlled mall walkway that terminated at either end with larger anchor stores. His design for Cherry Hill was a single-story, L-shaped structure, with more than one million square feet of retail space on two mall legs connecting three anchors: two department stores (Strawbridge and Clothier and Bambergers) and

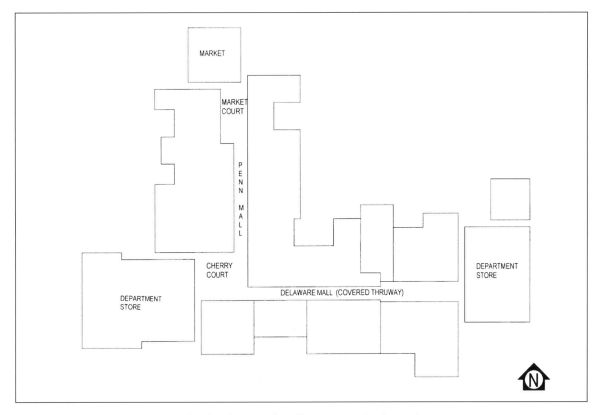

MARKET

MARKET
COURT

P
E
N
N

M
A
L
L

CHERRY
COURT

DEPARTMENT
STORE

DELAWARE MALL (COVERED THRUWAY)

DEPARTMENT
STORE

Fig. 17.1. Victor Gruen's blueprint for the Cherry Hill Mall, 1961. Drawing by Paul Dyer.

a supermarket (fig. 17.1). For Gruen, introversion and enclosure were essential features in order for suburban commercial spaces to overcome the "vulgarity" of sprawling highway strips and in order to have greater utility as community space. As an added bonus, it gave retailers a captive consumer base. "Once in, [consumers'] buying nerves are ripe for a subtle attack by tasteful presentation of merchandise in attractive open store fronts," he noted.[5]

"Among Gruen's strengths," according to Longstreth, "was his ability to translate theory into practice—to adapt the radical notions of form and space nurtured by the avant-garde to the pragmatic needs of the merchant and the investor, while making the ideas seem as if they originated with retail concerns."[6] Yet Gruen's understanding of shopping centers was clearly not limited to building aesthetics. He coauthored *Shopping Towns, USA*, his 1960 treatise on shopping centers, with Larry Smith, a well-known retail market analyst. Even though *Shopping Towns, USA* opened

with Gruen's shopping center design theory, the balance of the tome was dedicated to the more mundane task of outlining the business of building a successful shopping center through consumer research, tenant selection, advertising and public relations, and land economics. Designing a shopping center had as much to do with managing capital, employees, and consumers over the course of its existence as constructing the perfect building.

Unlike architects, real estate developers whose relationships with buildings continued over their useable life-span view good design as not merely an architectural concern, but a managerial one: it is an issue of controlling the social use of the space over time in order to maximize its profitability. Cherry Hill Mall's developer, James Rouse, equated a shopping center's value for its community with the profitability of its stores. This does not mean that Rouse denigrated the importance of fostering a sense of community among his shopping center patrons; on the contrary,

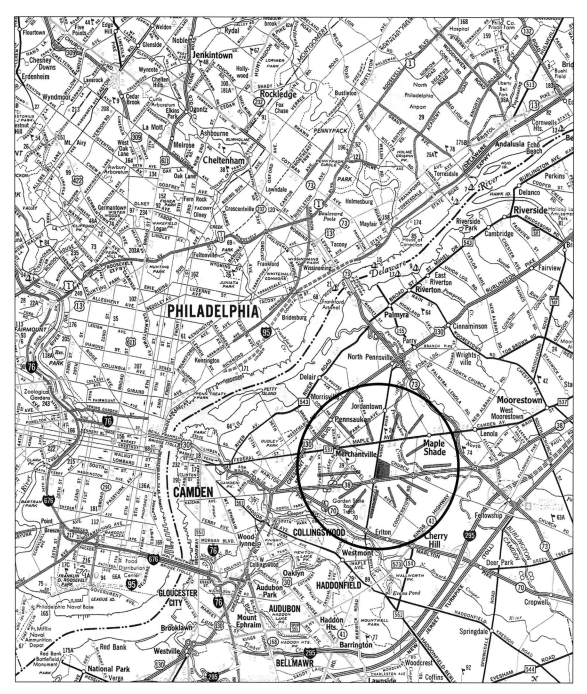

Map 17.1. Map pinpointing the location of Cherry Hill Mall in the Philadelphia metropolitan area, c. 1960. Courtesy of Columbia Archives, Columbia, Maryland.

he saw communal value as an increasingly important aspect of shopping center design by the 1960s. The rapid proliferation of suburban shopping centers brought increasing competition and a shortened life cycle of popularity and profitability. Under such market conditions, Rouse believed that shopping centers needed to serve increasingly variegated and complex functions in their communities in order to maintain a stable market base. "In today's centers," he noted, "design is of paramount importance to create an environment, an atmosphere, a physical condition in which resourceful and creative management can work to discover all sorts of ways in which that environment can be used to serve the community—to become central to the community, so that the community will adopt it as its center and develop deep feelings of pride, enthusiasm and concern for it, and for its shops."[7]

Producing the Cherry Hill Mall

Gruen and Rouse viewed the Cherry Hill Mall as the embodiment of their community-building design theories. But for several years financial investors held up construction of the shopping center due to concerns that there was no community for it to serve. The original plans for the center were inaugurated in 1952 by Eugene Mori, a real estate developer who sought to transform Delaware Township, New Jersey—twenty-four square miles of farmland located a mere seven miles outside Philadelphia—into a prosperous suburban community (map 17.1). Mori's Garden State Race Track, which opened in 1942, drew thousands of visitors from throughout New Jersey and metropolitan Philadelphia to the township to wager on horses. After the war, he funneled his track profits into residential construction in an area of the township he called Cherry Hill. By the early 1950s, Mori's Cherry Hill Enterprises built the Cherry Valley and Cherry Hill Estates residential subdivisions and two high-rise towers of a planned twelve-tower Cherry Hill Apartments complex. Other developers followed suit, snapping up township farms for residential developments. But Mori did not foresee his Cherry Hill as merely a bedroom suburb for Camden and Philadelphia. He wanted Cherry Hill to be a destination in its own right, and so he added commercial and industrial sections to his planned community. In 1952, he negotiated with RCA to move its electronics division from Camden to a site on his Cherry Hill tract; next to their headquarters he placed a hotel and conference center, and planned to add a large regional shopping center across from it along highway route 38.[8]

Mori's shopping center plans intersected those of Philadelphia retailers, who were furiously competing to colonize the Philadelphia suburbs with branch department stores. Mori approached John Wanamaker's about joining his shopping center, but store executives showed little interest in the site due to its distance from Camden, the principal South Jersey population center. Mori next approached Wanamaker archival Strawbridge and Clothier (hereafter S&C), who, after similar hesitation, agreed to join Cherry Hill. Cherry Hill Enterprises and S&C publicly announced plans for the shopping center in 1954 and signed on Welton Becket Associates of Los Angeles as architects for the center. Becket drew up plans for what was to be among the ten largest shopping centers in the world at that time: 766,000 square feet of retail space, including a 216,000-square-foot department store, two restaurants, a supermarket, furniture and appliance stores, and a medical building centered on an outdoor mall and surrounded by parking for five thousand cars.[9]

Yet Mori ran into difficulties financing his center. Insurance companies, the main source of financing for the incredibly capital-intensive shopping center projects, remained skeptical about the market potential of the location. Unlike housing and industrial facilities which could be economically placed on low-cost, undeveloped land, regional shopping centers needed to draw on vast populations at close distances; market analysts such as Larry Smith agreed that four hundred thousand persons within a twenty-minute driving range was a good consumer base for a regional center. Mori insisted that consumers would drive to his center from Camden and its suburbs; however, investors noted that other shopping centers were cropping up in locations closer to Camden. By 1957, Mori tabled his plans due to a lack of financing.[10]

Rather than give up on Cherry Hill and have to find another location, S&C took over Mori's entire shopping center and brought in Rouse's Community Research and Development as developer in 1960. CRD had already developed several shopping centers including Mondawmin, a pioneering pedestrian mall located in Baltimore, which was designed by Victor Gruen. CRD recommended to S&C that Gruen revise Welton Becket's plans for Cherry Hill, which were already several years old in a fast-changing industry. S&C experienced little trouble finding investors for their collaboration with Gruen and Rouse at Cherry Hill, thus speeding construction for a fall 1961 opening.[11]

After nearly ten years in the making, CRD opened the Cherry Hill Mall on October 12, 1961 (fig. 17.2). Opening ceremonies manifested Rouse's concern for engendering communal bonds with his shopping center. More than three thousand people attended ribbon-cutting ceremonies hosted by New Jersey governor Robert Meyner. Rouse proudly announced that the shopping center "would enrich the lives of the people of the Cherry Hill area." "This is something more than a shopping center," S&C president G. Stockton Strawbridge promised the crowd. "We have brought a community feature to New Jersey." Cherry Hill Mall's interiors showed Rouse's attention to fostering a distinctive atmosphere. The mall area itself replicated an island paradise, with tropical birds such as parrots, mynas, and toucans in a twenty-foot-high aviary, fourteen thousand different kinds of tropical plants, fountains, and a humidified climate (figs. 17.3 and

Fig. 17.3. Cherry Hill Mall's tropical splendor, 1963. From "Cherry Hill: Retailing's Lush Greenhouse," *Greater Philadelphia,* Apr. 1963.

17.4). *Women's Wear Daily* estimated that one hundred thousand people perused its malls the first day alone. One man recollected that when he was ten years old, he and his mother took a bus trip from northern New Jersey to see the Cherry Hill Mall shortly after its opening. "We were told there was no shopping experience like it," he said. "People were calling it the Disneyland of shopping. The first sensation when I walked in was that I was dazzled by the fact that there were growing plants and trees inside. I was fascinated by that. I thought it was one of the prettiest places in the world."

Rouse sought to make sure that a festive atmosphere permeated the daily experience of mall

Fig. 17.2. Cherry Hill Mall on opening day, 1961. Courtesy of Columbia Archives, Columbia, Maryland.

Fig. 17.4. Father and child take in the tropical fauna, 1971. *Philadelphia Bulletin* Collection, Urban Archives, Temple University, Philadelphia, Pennsylvania.

Fig. 17.5. Entertaining the masses in Cherry Hill Mall, 1964. *Philadelphia Bulletin* Collection, Urban Archives, Temple University, Philadelphia.

shoppers and routinely presented art exhibits, boat shows, and skiing demonstrations in its common spaces. The center's first three anniversaries brought a touch of exotica to South Jersey, consisting of a luau, an "Oriental festival," and a Mexican fiesta, each offering food served by costumed salesgirls; music, dancing, and theatrical entertainment (fig. 17.5); and prizes such as vacation packages and automobiles. The mall's ambiance was magical enough to induce Cherry Hill High School students to use it for their junior prom for several years during the 1960s.[12] In all these ways, mall space was marked as extraordinary—a fundamental break from the everyday landscapes of the township.

Included among the mall's "community features" were those associated with normative civic activities. A community hall and four-hundred-seat auditorium— "destined to become a focal point for the life of the community," according to one promotional article— were available for the use of civic organizations at a nominal charge. Women's groups, political meetings, and church events all regularly occurred in these

spaces. Civic uses did not take place only in recessed spaces of the shopping center; throughout the 1960s and into the 1970s, the Rouse Company let various groups leaflet and solicit signatures along its central pedestrian malls. Rouse attempted to hold a free market of ideas in his center: during 1964, the Cherry Hill Mall hosted a civil rights forum in its community hall and allowed Goldwater campaign supporters to hand out pamphlets in the mall. During the height of the Vietnam War, the mall held events from both peace demonstrators and law enforcement officials.[13]

The Value of Cherry Hill Mall to its Township

In 1962, a focus group study conducted by CRD suggested that township residents had embraced the mall within their community. Company representatives interviewed eight architects, eight merchants from the center, and eight local residents, including the local newspaper editor, a township commissioner, a convalescent home director, the local high school principal, and high school students. "The people who lived and worked there knew better than we did what Cherry Hill [Mall] was," Rouse reported. "Delaware Township had been galvanized. The principal noted that students were dressing better at school. The woman from the mental health society reported that the shopping center had become the favorite place for old folk to go to sit and enjoy themselves. A high school girl said that until Cherry Hill was built, there was no sense of community in the area. Everybody lived in a development. Now everybody had a sense of belonging to the same thing."[14] The assistant superintendent of schools corroborated the focus group findings. "We were just another series of housing developments until the mall was built," this township official stated. "Now we have a sense of community—Cherry Hill Mall is the only main street in south Jersey" (fig. 17.5). The importance of the mall to the township was seemingly confirmed when local residents voted to change the name of their town to Cherry Hill in November 1961, one month after the mall's opening.[15]

But what exactly was the "sense of community" the mall engendered in the township? Minus the three teenagers, Rouse's focus group subjects consisted of local retailers and municipal officials who had an interest in promoting economic growth in the township. Indeed, the history of Delaware Township in the postwar period was one of tremendous real estate speculation and an obsession with local growth. During the 1950s, the rapid pace of suburban development transformed Delaware Township from a farm community into a landscape of sprawl. In the single decade between 1950 and 1960, the township's population tripled, from under eleven thousand residents to over thirty-two thousand. In the midst of the building boom, housing developers paid little attention to how their subdivisions held together within the municipality as a whole, and commercial strips spread along the length of state highways running through the township. There was no visible town center with a clustering of public buildings and businesses. Delaware Township officials feared the area's lack of spatial cohesion would result in "an identity crisis." Yet the imperative for finding a distinctive identity for Delaware Township seemed to be based more on promotional purposes than a response to any kind of social

malaise. As evidence of the township's identity crisis, in 1954 Mayor Christian Weber suggested to the township council that a new, "less mundane" name be chosen for Delaware Township after discovering fifteen "Delawares" in his atlas.[16]

With the release of Delaware Township's first comprehensive plan in 1957, boosters again picked up the rallying cry of identity crisis. The report scorned the township for what it described as its "lack of community consciousness." "People living in large scale residential developments become interested only in their own rather limited surroundings," it noted. "Interest in the development of the town as a whole is lacking." If planning for future growth was to be successful, the report concluded that "some sort of community consciousness should be developed." The planning board felt that the best way to achieve this would be through the creation of town center. "The township has no recognizable 'center' at present. A township center would do much to identify the township in the region and would foster the feeling of 'association' and a sense of civic pride in township residents," the report stated. Ideally, a center would combine civic, cultural and commercial facilities in one location.[17]

The Cherry Hill Mall would seem to provide the perfect solution to the town's problematic public image; the name change seems to confirm its importance to the local community. Yet the name change actually had little to do with the mall's opening. The movement to change the township's name to Cherry Hill began in 1958, when the shopping center's development seemed most remote. Boosters chose the name in order to identify the township with its most developed section. The local newspaper editor noted that "Cherry Hill is the obvious name that immediately obviates the need for any such period of 'building up' the name. . . . It's a name that's known across the nation."[18] Cherry Hill was a name that signified the importance of development to township officials, businesses, and interested citizens, chosen because it was well known in real estate circles and would allow the township as a whole to capitalize on the Cherry Hill section's publicity.

This does not mean that Delaware Township's civic boosters failed to appreciate the important role the Cherry Hill Mall came to play in putting the township on the map. But boosters appreciated the center less for its role within the community than its role in bringing investment from outside the community. As with the Garden State Racetrack, the Cherry Hill Mall quickly became a tourist destination that attracted patronage from far beyond its municipal borders. Busloads of visitors from as far as New York and Virginia arrived daily to view the splendor of the Mall's interior walkways and controlled climate, to partake of its numerous entertainments, as well as to shop. The mall's function as a magnet for tourism significantly enhanced the township's growing reputation as a center of housing and commercial development in South Jersey. In recognition of the value shopping center publicity held for the township, officials honored Rouse in 1965 for the "very large contribution which we know [the Cherry Hill Mall] has made in the attraction of other worthwhile development to the community." Hoping to cash in on the national publicity the mall generated, civic boosters had begun circulating an apocryphal tale relating to the town name change. In 1962, Mayor Christian Weber told a *New York Times* reporter, "We changed the name of Delaware Township to Cherry Hill because of the shopping center. . . . Cherry Hill Shopping Center has become our community center." The tale of the town's name change circulated across several media outlets over a number of years, including architectural historian Margaret Crawford's 1993 article on shopping centers.[19] The myth has been so often repeated that both Cherry Hill Township's boosters and critics seem to have forgotten that the story was a promotional device designed to sell the township as a safe real estate investment itself by giving its spaces a social value which assured financial permanence in the flux of real estate speculation.

Locating Communal Value in the Commercial Marketplace

If, as Rouse suggested, communal value was what moored a shopping center's economic success, then the Cherry Hill Mall's declining fortunes were a sure sign of the lack of communal value placed in it. As early as 1966, net profits from the mall stagnated and began to decline, dropping from a high of $3.4 million

in the first quarter of 1966 to $2.5 million by 1970. The proximate cause of its decline was the continuing proliferation of regional shopping centers in the South Jersey and Philadelphia areas. The Moorestown Mall, which became home to S&C's competitors John Wanamaker and Gimbel Brothers, opened in 1963 one mile away from Cherry Hill Mall and immediately began siphoning off Cherry Hill's consumer base. The 1965 opening of the first phase of the "super-regional" shopping center at King of Prussia, Pennsylvania, which would eventually consist of a pair of two-story, four-anchor enclosed malls, eclipsed consumer interest in Cherry Hill as a tourist destination in the Philadelphia region. With the construction of Echelon, a multi-use commercial and residential center in Vorhees Township beginning in 1969, Cherry Hill was no longer even the premiere Rouse Company project in South Jersey. By the early 1970s vacant store fronts in the Cherry Hill Mall bespoke the center's increasingly moribund status. A 1973 letter of complaint from one mall tenant illustrates the declining fortunes of the Cherry Hill Mall. "When we leased the store in Cherry Hill," he wrote, "WE WERE TOLD-

1. Cherry Hill Mall is reventilating itself and cleaning up.
2. A new tenant was being looked for and you would replace Firestone.
3. The area where Kiddie Park Land was . . . a Children Shop, a Card Shop, and a Toy Store were going into that area. As of the first of May, none of them have opened.
4. They were negotiating on some large concern to take over the balance of the Food Market that we had taken part of.
5. They were negotiating and closer now than ever, with a Department Store to be tailed on to our end of the Mall.

WE WERE NOT TOLD-

1. That Kresge's was going out and this left a very big hole at that end of the Mall. . . .
2. The Hobby Shop was going out.
3. The Ladies Shop has not paid their rent for almost one year, and were going bankrupt.

He went on to note that his firm's store in a strip shopping center elsewhere in South Jersey was "doing much more business than Cherry Hill," despite being half its size.[20]

A 1972 Rouse Company report confirmed the mall's declining fortunes, bleakly stating that "Cherry Hill Mall is threatened with economic, competitive, physical and social deterioration." The report noted that despite having provided in its early years "a sense of community and a sense of place strong enough to function as a town center," patronage of the center had declined for all social groups except the elderly. The Rouse Company believed that the solution to the mall's problems lay in diversifying its uses in order to enhance its communal value. By the 1970s, Rouse had abandoned the creation of regional suburban shopping centers to concentrate on building "new towns" and dense, mixed-use centers like Echelon, which combined shopping with residences, professional offices, cultural events, tourism, and civic functions in a holistic entity. The company now proposed creating

"the concept of Cherry Hill Town Center as a dynamic and compact center with a strong urban character [that] will make the economic value of Cherry Hill, as well as the social and environmental value, greater than the sum of its parts." The report concluded that Cherry Hill's new town makeover was ideally suited to capitalizing on Cherry Hill's "unique reputation as the shopping center which named a town."

To expand Cherry Hill Mall's appeal to consumers, the Rouse Company planned to add another leg to the shopping center and another department store for an additional three hundred thousand square feet of retail space. They also proposed adding an office building, a medical complex, three hundred apartment units, a hotel, a restaurant and "Gourmet Food Fair," movie theaters, a playhouse, an ice rink, a swim club, space for community groups and local artists, and a township information and transportation center (fig. 17.6). By undertaking such a development, the Rouse Company hoped to halt Cherry Hill Mall's rapid decline in market share and allow it to maintain a steady

Fig. 17.6. Rouse Company plan for Cherry Hill Center, 1972. *Philadelphia Bulletin* Collection, Urban Archives, Temple University, Philadelphia.

rate of growth for the next decade. However, in 1973 the Rouse Company's ambitious expansion plan was stopped dead in its tracks by widespread complaints from neighboring residents who feared the impact such a dense, urban, mixed-use development would have on their low-density, single-use zoned suburban landscape. By 1970, Cherry Hill Township's population had doubled, topping sixty-four thousand residents. The focus among boosters has shifted from maximizing growth to maximizing quality of life in the township. Creating a dense urban center for the township was out of step with local's desires to preserve the existing Cherry Hill Township as is. Responding to residents' complaints, the Cherry Hill Planning Commissioners refused to approve the Rouse Company plans, causing the firm to scale back to a rudimentary addition of retail space. The expanded mall, which opened in 1978, did little to stop Cherry Hill's market position in South Jersey from continuing to slide along with its importance as a destination in the region.[21]

My evidence suggests that the social value of Cherry Hill Mall for those who built, managed, and consumed its spaces was largely a factor of its perceived prestige in the commercial marketplace. For designers and developers like Gruen and Rouse, Cherry Hill was a prestige product whose social value was confirmed by its embodiment of their design theories and its initially high sales. For Cherry Hill Township boosters, the mall's notoriety and commercial success became a vehicle through which to attract business and development to the township. For consumers, the uniqueness of the mall in the suburban landscape of early 1960s southern New Jersey lent it a spectacular appearance and convivial social atmosphere, yet one that faded with the proliferation of production of similar centers across the suburban landscape by the late 1960s. This suggests that to look for vernacular meanings in the productions of the modern real estate industry is to find shifting value that can be as ephemeral as fashion, though made of concrete and steel.

Notes

1. See Henri Lefebvre, *The Social Production of Space* (London: Blackwell, 1991). Delores Hayden, *The Power of Place: Urban Landscapes as Public History* (Cambridge, Mass.: MIT Press, 1995), and Paul Groth's introduction to Paul Groth and Todd W. Bressi, eds., *Understanding Ordinary Landscapes* (New Haven: Yale Univ. Press, 1997); both discuss the applicability of Lefebvre's writing to vernacular landscape studies. Neil Harris, *Building Lives: Constructing Rites and Passages* (Chicago: Univ. of Chicago Press, 1999), also examines the social uses of buildings over the course of their lives in order to interpret their social meaning.

2. See M. Jeffrey Hardwick, "A Downtown Utopia? Suburbanization, Urban Renewal, and Consumption in New Haven," *Planning History Studies,* Spring 1997. Richard W. Longstreth, *City Center to Regional Mall: Architecture, the Automobile, and Retailing in Los Angeles, 1920–1950* (Cambridge, Mass.: MIT Press, 1997), also details the broad-ranging commercial design backgrounds of important architects of Los Angeles' postwar regional centers.

3. See Richard Longstreth, *History on the Line: Testimony in the Cause of Preservation* (Washington, D.C.: National Council for Preservation Education and National Park Service, 1998).

4. Victor Gruen and Larry Smith, *Shopping Towns USA* (Rheinhold Publishing, 1960), 23–24. Gruen's basic argument about the communal value of shopping centers can be traced over time in articles and essays dating back to the late 1940s, the earliest published source being "What to Look for in Shopping Centers," (1948), which was reprinted in *Chain Store Age,* July 1948, 22, 63–66.

5. Gruen's remarks summarized in "Growth Planning: A Basic Problem," *Shopping Center Age,* Jan. 1962.

6. *From City Center to Regional Mall,* 323.

7. James Rouse, "The Regional Shopping Center: Its Role in the Community It Serves" (paper presented at Seventh Urban Design Conference, Harvard Univ., Apr. 26, 1963), 4, Box 201, Columbia Association Archives, Columbia, Md.

8. See Anne Marie Cammarota, "Changing Pattern: The Suburbanization of South Jersey Adjacent to the City of Philadelphia" (Ph.D. diss., Temple Univ., 1996). "Delaware Township for Community," *Courier-Post,* July 26, 1955;

"New Suburb Rises at Philadelphia," *New York Times*, Oct. 7, 1956.

9. On John Wanamaker: Eugene Mori to John Raasch, Oct. 20, 1952; John R. Wanamaker, internal memorandum, Oct. 27, 1952; Jane A. Stretch, *Camden Courier-Post*, promotional report on Cherry Hill shopping center project, Nov. 1952, Box 26, Folder 8, John Wanamaker Papers, Historical Society of Pennsylvania; John E. Raasch to Eugene Mori, May 6, 1954, Box 43, Folder 33, John Wanamaker Papers. On S&C: Alfred Lief, *Family Business: A Century in the Life and Times of Strawbridge & Clothier, 1868–1968* (New York: McGraw Hill, 1968), 264–65. G. Stockton Strawbridge to Eugene Mori, May 21, 1954; Branch Store Committee meeting, May 28, 1954; Dwight Perkins to Eugene Mori, Jan. 6, 1955, Box 8, Strawbridge & Clothier Papers, Hagley Museum and Library, Wilmington, Delaware. "Strawbridge & Clothier Plans Cherry Hill Store," *Courier-Post*, Jan. 11, 1955; "Strawbridge & Clothier Plans to Open Branch Store as Part of Tremendous Shopping Center," *Delaware Township News*, Jan. 13, 1955; "A Glimpse into the Future: The Cherry Hill Shopping Center," *Delaware Township News*, Apr. 25, 1956.

10. Reilly's law of retail gravitation, the industry standard, stated that consumers will patronize the most convenient centers, though this can be affected by merchandise selection. In no case will consumers routinely patronize centers more than twenty minutes distance by car, unless other options are lacking. Cf. Gruen and Smith, *Shopping Towns USA*, 30–37. On Cherry Hill Shopping Center difficulties: S&C Executive Committee meeting minutes, June 6, 11, 17, July 9, Aug. 9, Oct. 3 and 29, 1957; "Meeting to discuss branch store development," internal memorandum, July 17, 1957, Box 8, Strawbridge & Clothier Papers.

11. Lief, *Family Business*, 280–82. Executive Committee meeting minutes, Dec. 17, 1957, S&C Box 8; "Shopping Center Dead? Strawbridge Says 'No!'" *Delaware Township News*, Jan. 2, 1958; Board of Directors meeting minutes, Feb. 21, 1958, S&C Box 3. "Strawbridge Has Option on Cherry Hill Center," *Delaware Township News*, Aug. 14, 1958; G. Stockton Strawbridge to James W. Rouse, Sept. 17, 1958, S&C Box 3; Operating Committee meeting minutes, Mar. 2, 6, 27, 1959, S&C Box 9; Board of Directors meeting minutes, Apr. 6, 1959, S&C Box 3; James Rouse to T. A. Sedam, Mar. 17, 1960; Report to Directors, June 6, 1960, Box 421, James Rouse Papers, Columbia Archives, Columbia, Md.

12. "Giant Shopping Mall Opens," *Philadelphia Inquirer*, Oct. 12, 1961; "Cherry Hill Center Opening Crowd Is Put at 100,000," *Women's Wear Daily*, Oct. 12, 1961; "Aloha!" (advertisement for Cherry Hill Mall first anniversary), *Cherry Hill News*, Oct. 11, 1962; "Mall Celebrates Second Year with Oriental Ornamentation," *Cherry Hill News*, Oct. 10, 1963; "Mall Marks Third Year with 10-day Mexican Fiesta," *Cherry Hill News*, Oct. 8, 1964; "For One Night, Mall Becomes Wonderland!" *Cherry Hill News*, June 7, 1962; "Cherry Hill Mall Hosts Prom," *Cherry Hill News*, May 21, 1964.

13. "Community Hall Will Seat 400," *Courier-Post*, Oct. 10, 1961; "Civil Rights Forum Next Week in the Township," *Cherry Hill News*, Aug. 6, 1964; "No Backlash Seen in Camden . . . ," *Cherry Hill News*, Sept. 17, 1964; "Two Rouse Company Shopping Centers . . . ," *Shopping Center Newsletter*, June 1969; "Air War Slides to be Shown," *Burlington County Times*, Sept. 13, 1972; "Peace Petitions Going to Washington," *Burlington County Times*, Sept. 18, 1972. Admittedly, Rouse was uniquely liberal and public-minded of mall developers; nonetheless, most regional shopping centers included some civic activity, usually reflecting the developer's own political leanings and those of the desired market. There was typically no tolerance of marginal perspectives, nor any legal obligation to represent them. By the 1980s, Cherry Hill Mall also became less tolerant of groups using the center to express politically controversial ideas. Cherry Hill Mall was among the shopping centers named in *New Jersey Coalition Against War in the Middle East v. J.M.B. Realty* (1994), a case in which the New Jersey Supreme Court ruled that regional shopping centers could not prohibit freedom of expression on their property.

14. Quoted in Gurney Breckenfeld, *Columbia and the New Cities* (New York: I. Washburn, 1971), 215. Rouse's 1963 speech at the Seventh Urban Design Conference at Harvard seems to be the origin of this anecdote. An article on Cherry Hill in the *Ellicott City (Md.) Times*, Oct. 14, 1964, repeats the anecdote about the high school girl.

15. "'Meet Me at the Mall': Big Shopping Centers Are Becoming the Focus of Life in the Suburbs," *New York Times*, Feb. 20, 1969.

16. Robert Strauss, "Cherry Hill, Pits & All," *Philadelphia Inquirer*, Dec. 15, 1991; "For a Better Name . . . ," *Delaware Township News*, Apr. 3, 1958.

17. Delaware Township Planning Board and Community Planning Associates, *Comprehensive Plan for the Future Development of Delaware Township* (Camden County, N.J., 1957).

18. "What Delaware Township Needs," *Delaware Township News*, Feb. 27, 1958; "Cherry Hill, USA," *Delaware Township News*, Nov. 19, 1959.

19. Breckenfeld, *Columbia and the New Cities,* 214: "Delaware Township was so captivated by Rouse's center that it officially changed its name to Cherry Hill." Mayor Weber quotation: Arthur Herzog, "Shops, Culture, Centers—and More," *New York Times,* Nov. 18, 1962; other sources citing the mall as the cause of the name change include *Elliott City (Md.) Times,* Oct. 14, 1964; Charles Melchior to James Rouse, May 11, 1965, Box 421, Rouse Papers; "Fortunes on the Mall," *Time,* Mar. 1, 1968, 81; Laura Quinn, "From Novelty to a Fixture of Americana," *Philadelphia Inquirer,* Jan. 8, 1986.

20. Statistics: Cherry Hill Development Council, *Cherry Hill Center Development Program,* Box 421, Rouse Papers; Marvin Polakoff to James Rouse, May 1, 1973, Box 421, Rouse Papers.

21. *Cherry Hill Center Development Program;* "Zoners Delay Decision on Mall Expansion," *Cherry Hill News,* Nov. 29, 1973; "Rouse Withdraws Request for Mall Expansion OK," *Cherry Hill News,* Feb. 28, 1974; "Zoning Board Slates Hearing Tuesday on Mall Expansion," *Cherry Hill News,* Nov. 7, 1974; "OK Mall Expansion . . . ," *Cherry Hill News,* July 22, 1976.

SELECT BIBLIOGRAPHY

Abelson, Elaine S. *When Ladies Go A-Thieving: Middle-Class Shoplifters in the Victorian Department Store.* Oxford: Oxford Univ. Press, 1989.

Agee, James, and Walker Evans. *Let Us Now Praise Famous Men.* Boston: Houghton Mifflin, 1941.

Baxandall, Rosalyn Fraad, and Elizabeth Ewen. *Picture Windows: How the Suburbs Happened.* New York: Basic Books, 2000.

Bayne, Martha Collins. *The Dutchess County Farmer.* Poughkeepsie, N.Y.: Women's City and Country Club, 1936.

Benson, Susan Porter. *Counter Cultures: Saleswomen, Managers, and Customers in American Department Stores, 1890–1940.* Urbana: Univ. of Illinois Press, 1986.

Bowden, Martyn John. "The Dynamics of City Growth: An Historical Geography of the San Francisco Central District, 1850–1931." Ph.D. diss., Dept. of Geography, Univ. of California, Berkeley, 1967.

Breen, T. H. "Horses and Gentlemen: The Cultural Significance of Gambling among the Gentry of Virginia." *William and Mary Quarterly,* 3d ser., 34 (1977): 239–57.

Butler, Jon. *Awash in a Sea of Faith: Christianizing the American People.* Cambridge: Harvard Univ. Press, 1990.

Caro, Robert A. *The Power Broker: Robert Moses and the Fall of New York.* New York: Knopf, 1974.

Carson, Barbara G. "Early American Tourists and the Commercialization of Leisure." In *Of Consuming Interests: The Style of Life in the Eighteenth Century,* edited by Cary Carson, et al., 373–405. Charlottesville: Univ. Press of Virginia, 1994.

Carson, Cary, Norman F. Barka, William M. Kelso, Garry Wheeler Stone, and Dell Upton. "Impermanent Architecture in the Southern Colonies." *Winterthur Portfolio* 2/3 (1981): 135–96.

Clinton, Catherine, and Nina Silber, eds. *Divided Houses: Gender and the Civil War.* New York: Oxford Univ. Press, 1992.

Cobb, James. *The Most Southern Place on Earth: The Mississippi Delta and the Roots of Regional Identity.* New York: Oxford Univ. Press, 1992.

Coclanis, Peter A. *The Shadow of a Dream: Economic Life and Death in the South Carolina Low Country, 1670–1920.* New York: Oxford Univ. Press, 1989.

Cohen, Lizabeth. "From Town Center to Shopping Center: The Reconfiguration of Community Marketplaces in Postwar America." *American Historical Review* 101, no. 4 (1996): 1051–80.

Conroy, David W. *In Public Houses: Drink and the Revolution of Authority in Colonial Massachusetts.* Chapel Hill: Univ. of North Carolina Press, 1992.

Cotter, John L. *Archeological Excavations at Jamestown, Virginia.* Courtland, Va.: Archaeological Society of Virginia, 1994.

Crawford, Margaret. *Building the Workingman's Paradise: The Design of American Company Towns.* London: Verso, 1995.

Davis, Kenneth S. *FDR: The Beckoning of Destiny, 1882–1928.* New York: Random House, 1971.

Downer, Jay, and James Owen. *Public Parks in Westchester County.* N.p., n.d. Reprinted from *History of Westchester County, New York,* edited by Alvah P. French. New York: Lewis, 1925.

Ewen, Stuart. *Captains of Consciousness: Advertising and the Social Roots of the Consumer Culture.* New York: McGraw-Hill, 1976.

Ewing, George. "Forked Stick Folkcraft." In *Corners of Texas,* edited by Francis Edward Abernethy, 105–13. Publications of the Texas Folklore Society, 52. Denton: Univ. of North Texas Press, 1993.

Finnegan, Margaret. *Selling Suffrage: Consumer Culture and Votes for Women.* New York: Columbia Univ. Press, 1999.

Geier, Clarence R., and Susan E. Winters, eds. *Look to the Earth: Historical Archaeology and the American Civil War.* Knoxville: Univ. of Tennessee Press, 1995.

Green, Barbara. *Spectacular Confessions: Autobiography, Performative Activism, and the Sites of Suffrage, 1905–1938.* New York: St. Martin's Press, 1997.

Groth, Paul. *Living Downtown: The History of Residential Hotels in the United States.* Berkeley and Los Angeles: Univ. of California Press, 1994.

Hall, Jacquelyn Dowd, James Leloudis, Robert Korstad, Mary Murphy, Lu Ann Jones, and Christopher B. Daly. *Like a Family: The Making of a Southern Cotton Mill World.* Chapel Hill: Univ. of North Carolina Press, 1987.

Hanchett, Thomas W. "U.S. Tax Policy and the Shopping-Center Boom of the 1950s and 1960s." *American Historical Review* 101, no. 4 (1996): 1082–1110.

Harris, Neil. *Building Lives: Constructing Rites and Passages.* Chicago: Univ. of Chicago Press, 1999.

Hauf, Harold D. "Drive-ins: Banks, Theaters, and Restaurants." *Architectural Record,* Aug. 1950, 130–53.

Hertzberg, Steven. *Strangers within the Gate City: The Jews of Atlanta, 1845–1915.* Philadelphia: Jewish Publication Society of America, 1978.

Hurston, Zora Neale. *The Sanctified Church.* Berkeley, Calif.: Turtle Island Press, 1981.

Irons, Janet. *Testing the New Deal: The General Textile Strike of 1934 in the American South.* Urbana: Univ. of Illinois Press, 2000.

Isaac, Rhys. "Communication and Control: Authority Metaphors and Power Contests on Colonel Landon Carter's Virginia Plantation, 1752–1778." In *Rites of Power: Symbolism, Ritual, and Politics since the Middle Ages,* edited by Sean Wilentz, 275–302. Philadelphia: Univ. of Pennsylvania Press, 1985.

Jackson, John Brinckerhoff. *Discovering the Vernacular Landscape.* New Haven: Yale Univ. Press, 1984.

Jackson, Kenneth T. *Crabgrass Frontier: The Suburbanization of the United States.* New York: Oxford Univ. Press, 1985.

Jeffrey, Paul. *The City Churches of Sir Christopher Wren.* London: Hambledon Press, 1996.

Jennings, Jan, ed. *Roadside America: The Automobile in Design and Culture.* Ames: Iowa Univ. Press, 1990.

Jick, Leon A. *The Americanization of the Synagogue, 1820–1870.* Hanover, N.H.: Univ. Press of New England, 1976.

Jones, LeRoi. *Blues People: The Negro Expression in White America and the Music that Developed from It.* New York: Morrow Quill Paperbacks, 1963.

Kaplan, Wendy, ed. *Designing Modernity: The Arts of Reform and Persuasion. Selections from the Wolfsonian.* London: Thames and Hudson, 1995.

Kirby, Jack Temple. *Rural Worlds Lost: The American South, 1920–1960.* Baton Rouge: Louisiana State Univ. Press, 1987.

Krinsky, Carol Herselle. *Synagogue Architecture of Europe: Architecture, History, Meaning.* Mineola, N.Y.: Dover Publications, 1985.

Lanier, Joseph L. *The First Seventy-five Years of West Point Manufacturing Company, 1880–1955.* New York: Newcomen Society in North America, 1955.

Leach, William. "Transformations in a Culture of Consumption: Women and Department Stores, 1890–1925." *Journal of American History* 71, no. 2 (1984): 319–42.

Lefebvre, Henri. *Writings on Cities.* Translated and edited by Eleonore Kofman and Elizabeth Lebas. Malden, Mass.: Blackwell, 1996.

Leibs, Chester H. *Main Street to Miracle Mile.* Baltimore: Johns Hopkins Univ. Press, 1995.

Levine, Lawrence. *Black Culture and Black Consciousness: Afro-American Thought from Slavery to Freedom.* New York: Oxford Univ. Press, 1977.

Longstreth, Richard. *City Center to Regional Mall: Architecture, the Automobile, and Retailing in Los Angeles, 1920–1950.* Cambridge, Mass.: MIT Press, 1997.

Lounsbury, Carl R., ed. *A Glossary of Early Southern Architecture and Landscape.* New York: Oxford Univ. Press, 1993.

Luckenbach, Al. *Providence 1649: The History and Archaeology of Anne Arundel County Maryland's First European Settlement.* Annapolis: Maryland State Archives and Maryland Historical Trust, 1995.

MacCannell, Dean. *The Tourist: A New Theory of the Leisure Class.* New York: Schocken Books, 1976.

Marchand, Roland. *Creating the Corporate Soul: The Rise of Public Relations and Corporate Imagery in American Big Business.* Berkeley and Los Angeles: Univ. of California Press, 1998.

Margolies, John, and Emily Gwathme. *Ticket to Paradise: American Movie Theaters and How We Had Fun.* Boston: Little, Brown, 1991.

McClelland, Linda. *Building the National Parks: Historic Landscape Design and Construction.* Baltimore: Johns Hopkins Univ. Press, 1998.

McDaniel, George. *Hearth and Home: Preserving a People's Culture.* Philadelphia: Temple Univ. Press, 1982.

McInnis, Maurie D., et al. *In Pursuit of Refinement: Charlestonians Abroad, 1740–1860.* Columbia: Univ. of South Carolina Press, 1999.

McShane, Clay. *Down the Asphalt Path: The Automobile and the American City.* New York: Columbia Univ. Press, 1994.

Mitchell, Reid. *Civil War Soldiers.* New York: Viking, 1988.

———. *The Vacant Chair: The Northern Soldier Leaves Home.* New York: Oxford Univ. Press, 1993.

Nagel, Paul C. *Lees of Virginia: Seven Generations of an American Family.* New York: Oxford Univ. Press, 1990.

Neiman, Fraser D. "Domestic Architecture at the Clifts Plantation: The Social Context of Virginia Building." *Northern Neck Historical Magazine* 28, no. 1 (1978): 3096–3128.

Nelson, Dean E. "'Right Nice Little House(s)': Impermanent Camp Architecture of the American Civil War." In *Perspectives in Vernacular Architecture,* edited by Camille Wells, 79–93. Annapolis, Md.: Vernacular Architecture Forum, 1982.

New York State Association. Committee on the State Park Plan. *A State Park Plan for New York.* 1922. Rev. ed., Albany: State Council of Parks, 1924.

New York State Council of Parks. *First Annual Report to the Governor and the Legislature of the State of New York.* N.p.: n.p., 1925.

Nye, David. *American Technological Sublime.* Cambridge: MIT Press, 1994.

Olmsted, Frederick Law. *The Papers of Frederick Law Olmsted: Writings on Parks, Parkways, and Park Systems.* Edited by Charles Beveridge and Carolyn Hoffman. Supplementary Series Vol. 1. Baltimore: Johns Hopkins Univ. Press, 1997.

Oshinsky, David. *Worse than Slavery: Parchman Farm and the Ordeal of Jim Crow Justice.* New York: Free Press Paperbacks, 1996.

Pease, William H., and Jane H. Pease. *The Web of Progress: Private Values and Public Styles in Boston and Charleston, 1828–1843.* Athens: Univ. of Georgia Press, 1985.

Perry, William, ed. *Historical Collections Relating to the American Colonial Church.* 5 vols. New York: AMS Press, 1969.

Pezzoni, J. Daniel. "Brush Arbors in the American South." *PAST: Pioneer America Society Transactions* 20 (1997): 25–34.

Prunty, Merle, Jr. "The Renaissance of the Southern Plantation." *Geographical Review* 45, no. 4 (Oct. 1955): 459–91.

Raper, Arthur. *Preface to Peasantry: A Tale of Two Black Belt Counties.* Chapel Hill: Univ. of North Carolina Press, 1936.

Reynolds, Helen Wilkinson. *Dutch Houses in the Hudson Valley Before 1776.* Introduction by Franklin D. Roosevelt. 1928. Reprint, New York: Dover, 1965.

Rice, Kym S. *Early American Taverns: For the Entertainment of Friends and Strangers.* Chicago: Regnery Gateway, 1983.

Rightmyer, Nelson. *Maryland's Established Church.* Baltimore: Church Historical Society, 1956.

Russo, Jean B. "A Model Planter: Edward Lloyd IV of Maryland, 1770–1796." *William and Mary Quarterly,* 3d ser., 49 (1992): 62–88.

Sanders, Don, and Susan Sanders. *The American Drive-in Movie Theater.* Osceola, Wisc.: Motorbooks International Publishers, 1997.

Schuyler, David. *The New Urban Landscape: The Redefinition of City Form in Nineteenth-Century America.* Baltimore: Johns Hopkins Univ. Press, 1986.

Seagrave, Kerry. *Drive-in Theaters: A History from Their Inception in 1933.* Jefferson, N.C.: McFarland, 1992.

Severens, Kenneth. *Charleston: Antebellum Architecture and Civic Destiny.* Knoxville: Univ. of Tennessee Press, 1988.

Smith, Daniel Blake. *Inside the Great House: Planter Family Life in Eighteenth-Century Chesapeake Society.* Ithaca: Cornell Univ. Press, 1980.

Stone, Gary Wheeler. "Society, Housing, and Architecture in Early Maryland: John Lewger's St. John's." Ph.D. diss., Univ. of Pennsylvania, 1982.

Strasser, Susan. *Satisfaction Guaranteed: The Making of the American Mass Market.* New York: Pantheon Books, 1989.

Terrill, Tom E., and Jerrold Hirsch, eds. *Such as Us: Southern Voices of the Thirties.* Chapel Hill: Univ. of North Carolina Press, 1978.

Thompson, Peter. *Rum Punch and Revolution: Taverngoing and Public Life in Eighteenth-Century Philadelphia.* Philadelphia: Univ. of Pennsylvania Press, 1999.

Tickner, Lisa. *The Spectacle of Women: Imagery of the Suffrage Campaign, 1907–1914.* Chicago: Univ. of Chicago Press, 1988.

Tunnard, Christopher, and Boris Pushkarev. *Man-made America; Chaos or Control?* New Haven: Yale Univ. Press, 1963.

Upton, Dell. *Holy Things and Profane: Anglican Parish Churches in Colonial Virginia.* Cambridge, Mass.: MIT Press, 1986.

———. "Seen, Unseen, and the Scene." In *Understanding Ordinary Landscapes,* edited by Paul Groth and Todd W. Bressi, 174–79. New Haven: Yale Univ. Press, 1997.

———. "Traditional Timber Framing." In *Material Culture of the Wooden Age,* edited by Brooke Hindle, 35–61. Tarrytown, N.Y.: Sleepy Hollow Press, 1981.

———. "White and Black Landscapes in Eighteenth-Century Virginia." *Places: A Quarterly Journal of Environmental Design* 2 (1985): 59–72.

Valentine, Maggie. *The Show Starts at the Sidewalk.* New Haven: Yale Univ. Press, 1994.

Ware, Donna M. *Anne Arundel's Legacy: The Historic Properties of Anne Arundel County.* Annapolis, Md.: Anne Arundel County Office of Planning and Zoning, 1990.

Weissbach, Lee Shai. *The Synagogues of Kentucky: Architecture and History.* Lexington: Univ. of Kentucky Press, 1995.

Wells, Camille. "The Planter's Prospect: Houses, Outbuildings, and Rural Landscapes in Eighteenth-Century Virginia." *Winterthur Portfolio* 28 (1993): 1–31.

Williams, Michael Ann. *Homeplace: The Social Use and Meaning of the Folk Dwelling in Southwestern North Carolina.* Athens: Univ. of Georgia Press, 1991.

Wingerd, Mary Letherd. "Rethinking Paternalism: Power and Parochialism in a Southern Mill Village." *Journal of American History* 83, no. 3 (Dec. 1996): 872–902.

Wischnitzer, Rachel. *Synagogue Architecture in the United States: History and Interpretation.* Philadelphia: Jewish Publication Society of America, 1955.

Yates, Nigel. *Buildings, Faith, and Worship: The Liturgical Arrangements of Anglican Churches, 1600–1840.* Oxford: Clarendon Press, 1991.

CONTRIBUTORS

SHANNON BELL is a historian with the National Register of Historic Places. She has a B.A. in American history from the University of Southern California and an M.A. in American studies/historic preservation from George Washington University. "From Ticket Booth to Screen Tower" is an excerpt from her master's thesis.

ROBERT W. BLYTHE received his M.A. in the history of architecture from the University of Illinois, Chicago, in 1992. He is currently chief, Research and Inventory, in the National Park Service's Southeast Regional Office. He is coauthor of several historic resource studies for National Park units and has taught architecture history at Goucher College.

KENNETH BREISCH is an adjunct associate professor in the School of Architecture at the University of Southern California, where he directs the Historic Preservation Program. He has taught at the University of Delaware and the Southern California Institute of Architecture in Los Angeles and served on the Board of Directors of the Vernacular Architecture Forum. Breisch is the author of *Henry Hobson Richardson and the Small Public Library in America: A Study in Typology,* which was published by MIT Press in 1997.

TIMOTHY DAVIS is a historian for the National Park Service's Historic American Engineering Record. He received his Ph.D. from the American Civilization Program at the University of Texas at Austin and has written on a wide variety of cultural landscape topics, from parks and parkways to strip malls and satellite dishes. He is currently working on a two-volume history of America's park roads and parkways.

STEPHANIE DYER received her Ph.D. in American history from the University of Pennsylvania in 2000. She is currently a lecturer in the History Department at the University of California, Davis.

WILLIE GRAHAM is the curator of architecture at the Colonial Williamsburg Foundation. He is responsible for overseeing restoration, renovation, and conservation within the historic area of the town. He consults on restoration projects around the country and in the Caribbean.

ALISON K. HOAGLAND is an associate professor of history and historic preservation at Michigan Technological University. Previously, she was the senior historian at the Historic American Buildings Survey, National Park Service. She has written *Buildings of Alaska* (Oxford, 1993) and is currently studying U.S. Army forts in Wyoming and company housing in the copper district of Michigan.

KATHLEEN LAFRANK has an M.A. in architecture and design criticism from Parsons School of Design. She is a historian with the New York State Historic Preservation Office with expertise in rural cultural landscapes, state parks, and parkways. She is the coauthor of the National Register nomination for the Palisades Interstate Parkway, author of the determination of National Register eligibility for the Taconic State Parkway, and coauthor of the historic overview for the Historic American Engineering Record documentation report for the Taconic State Parkway. She has made numerous presentations on New York State's parks and parkways and is involved in an ongoing research project on the history of the New York State Park and Parkway System.

WILLIAM LITTMANN is the editor of *Design Book Review* magazine. He is also an instructor at the California College of Arts and Crafts and a doctoral candidate at the University of California, Berkeley. He earned an M.A. at the Columbia University Graduate School of Journalism. His dissertation examines how labor-management relations shapes the American turn-of-the-century industrial landscape. His interests include labor history, industrial archeology, and business history. He also writes about the history of architectural education in the twentieth century. At the time of the publication of this book, he serves as a Vernacular Architecture Forum board member.

CARL LOUNSBURY is an architectural historian in the Architectural Research Department at the Colonial Williamsburg Foundation. He is a past president of the Vernacular Architecture Forum and teaches periodically at various universities in Virginia. Lounsbury's publications include *Architects and Builders in North Carolina: A History of the Practice of Building* (with three others); *An Illustrated Glossary of Early Southern Architecture and Landscape; From Statehouse to Courthouse: An Architectural History of South Carolina's Colonial Capitol and Charleston County Courthouse;* and *The Early Courthouses of Virginia: An Architectural History of Public Building in the Colonial and Early National Periods.*

Al LUCKENBACH is the Anne Arundel County (Maryland) Archaeologist, a position he has held since 1988. He is founder and director of Anne Arundel's Lost Towns Project. Luckenbach received his undergraduate degree from the University of Virginia and has a doctoral degree in anthropology from the University of Kentucky.

SHERRI MARSH is an architectural historian affiliated with the Lost Towns Project and the Anne Arundel County Office of Planning and Zoning. She earned her B.S. degree at the University of Maryland and carried out her master's work in historic preservation at the University of Delaware. Marsh also instructs in the Historic Preservation Program at Goucher College.

MAURIE D. MCINNIS has a B.A. in art history from the University of Virginia and a Ph.D. in the history of art from Yale University. She is currently assistant professor of art history at the University of Virginia, where she teaches classes in American art and material culture. Her publications include the edited exhibition catalogue *In Pursuit of Refinement: Charlestonians Abroad, 1740–1860.* She is the recent recipient of a National Endowment for the Humanities Fellowship and is completing a manuscript on architecture and material culture in antebellum Charleston.

STEVEN H. MOFFSON is an architectural historian at the Georgia Department of Natural Resources, Historic Preservation Division, and teaches architectural history in the Heritage Preservation Program at Georgia State University in Atlanta. He has also worked at the National Park Service and the Delaware State Historic Preservation Office.

JASON D. MOSER is the Archaeological Field Director for the Anne Arundel County, Maryland, Lost Towns Project. He has an M.A. in history from the University of Maryland Baltimore County and has worked in the mid-Atlantic region as an archaeologist since 1992. His professional interests include earthfast architecture, industrial archaeology, and maritime history.

JENNIFER NARDONE is currently a graduate student in the Department of History at the University of North Carolina, Chapel Hill. Her chapter developed from her thesis research for the master's degree in architectural history at the University of California, Berkeley.

MARTIN C. PERDUE is a doctoral candidate in architectural history at the University of Virginia, where he is completing a dissertation entitled "Building with Bark, Logs, and Twigs: Rustic Wooden Architecture in the United States, 1830–1916." He is currently serving as the bibliographer for the Vernacular Architecture Forum.

MARK REINBERGER teaches the history of architecture and landscape architecture and historic preservation in the School of Environmental Design at the University of Georgia. He attended the University of Virginia and Cornell University and works primarily on early American architecture.

A. K. SANDOVAL-STRAUSZ is assistant professor of history at the University of New Mexico. He received his B.A. in history from Columbia University and his Ph.D. from the University of Chicago. He is currently at work on a social and cultural history of the American hotel to be entitled "For the Accommodation of Strangers."

JESSICA ELLEN SEWELL is an assistant professor and faculty fellow in the John W. Draper Interdisciplinary Masters Program in the Humanities and Social Sciences at New York University, where she teaches courses about the city. She received her Ph.D. in architecture at the University of California, Berkeley. She is presently working on a book on women and public space in turn-of-the-century San Francisco.

DONNA WARE is the historic sites planner for Anne Arundel County's Office of Planning and Zoning, a position she has held since 1983. She has an M.A. in American studies/historic preservation from the George Washington University and is the author of *Anne Arundel's Legacy: The Historic Properties of Anne Arundel County* (1990) and *Green Glades and Sooty Gob Piles: The Maryland Coal Region's Architectural and Industrial Past* (1991). Ware serves on the Vernacular Architecture Forum Board of Directors.

CAMILLE WELLS is founder of the Perspectives in Vernacular Architecture series and editor of its first two volumes. She has an M.A. in architectural history from the University of Virginia and a Ph.D. in early American history from the College of William and Mary. She is now a lecturer in architectural history at the University of Virginia.

INDEX

Page number notations in boldface refer to illustrations in the text.